Contents

All translations, except as otherwise indicated in the text, are by Salvator Attanasio

Illustrations

(FOLLOWING PAGE 228)

I "The Four Elements," a painting which hung over the mantel-
    piece in Hitler's house in Munich

II The ideal Aryan family as represented on a calendar
    [From *Kalender des rassenpolitischen Amtes der NSDAP*, 1938.]

III An example of the kind of poster art that played an important
     role in Nazi propaganda
     [From *Anschläge, deutsche Plakate als Dokumente der Zeit* (Mu-
     nich, 1963), n.p.]

IV The Honor Cross of the German Mother
    [From *Das Jahr IV* (Berlin, 1939), p. 99.]
    Adolf Ziegler's "The Judgment of Paris," illustrating ideal
    Aryan types
    [From *Die Kunst im dritten Reich* (1939), p. 252.]

V "Awakening" by Richard Klein, which was shown at the 1937
   Exhibition of German Art
   [From *Grosse deutsche Kunstausstellung 1937*, p. 23.]
   A painting of the ideal German girl
   [From *N. S. Frauenwarte*, Heft I, Jahrg. 8 (July 1939), p. 69.]
   A film advertisement, 1936
   [From *Schlesische Tageszeitung*, November 16, 1936 (Wiener Li-
   brary Clipping Collection).]

VI Arno Brecker's sculpture representing an idealized Germanic
    hero
    [From *Grosse deutsche Kunstausstellung 1942*, p. 53.]

Introduction

THE THIRD REICH has made a deep impression upon our civilization, and its impact has not diminished with the passing years. How this regime could have come to power in a civilized nation and what was the nature of life under the Nazis are questions that are still asked—especially among those too young to remember what National Socialism meant and those who never lived under the regime. This book seeks to illuminate the nature of the Third Reich through original documents of the period; in this way the flavor and purpose of the regime can best be recaptured. The central question which we seek to answer is a fairly simple one: What was life like under Hitler? Or: How did National Socialism impinge upon the consciousness of those who lived under it?

For this reason documents on foreign policy and on internal administration have been omitted, in favor of those on cultural life and social life. Moreover, in order to give a truer picture of the regime, the book concentrates on the years between 1933 and 1939. The impact of the war heightened many aspects of the ideas and actions which appear in these pages, but it seemed better to look at National Socialism in power before the extreme situation of a war. In any case, not much new was added after 1939 in cultural and social life, as the Nazis wished it to be understood. It is their view of the "good society" which this book seeks to illustrate.

This society would not allow for the differentiation between politics and daily life which many of us naturally make. Today, in most of the non-Communist Western world, politics is regarded as merely one compartment of life; it does not have to penetrate our very thought and being. But Hitler's aim was to construct an organic society in which every aspect of life would be integrated with its basic purpose. And in the terms in which this purpose was promulgated by the National Socialist party, no one could be allowed to stand aside. Politics was not just one side of life, or one among many other sciences; it was instead the concrete expression of the Nazi world view. This world view was held to be the very crux of what it meant to be a German, and therefore politics was the consciousness of race, blood, and soil, the essence of the Nazi definition of human nature.

This is what Hitler meant when he talked about the "nationalization of the masses"; will and power were the keys to winning the hearts of the masses, for they could lead the people back to the consciousness of their race.[1] Such a total view of politics meant—as it was called after January 1933—*Gleichschaltung*, "equalizing the gears" of the nation. All individuals and all organizations in Germany had to be "nationalized," in the sense of making them subject to party control; for the party was the guardian of the Germanic world view and through the will and power of its chief, the Führer, the good society would be brought into being. Thus trade unions were abolished and in their place the "German Workers' Front," which was under party control, was created. Educational institutions were integrated, as the party exercised control over students and teachers. A whole network of party organizations controlled professional and workers' groups, membership in which was compulsory. In addition, individuals were organized in other groups which sought mastery over their private lives, outside their professions—from the Hitler Youth to the organization for "German mothers." The boundaries between public and private activities were abolished, just as the dividing line between politics and the totality of life had ceased to exist.

This was the totalitarian state, and the Nazi party, like the spider in its web, controlled all the lifelines of the nation. For us such a society means that all aspects of life are subordinated to the demands of politics. But the Nazis did not see their society in these terms. Polit-

[1] Adolf Hitler, *Mein Kampf* (Munich, 1934), p. 373.

ical parties and other independent national groupings had to be abolished, for they were a part of that liberal politics which had torn the nation asunder, had set man against man and class against class. In contrast, under the Nazis the individual German had found a sense of belonging, based upon his membership in a community which through its world view reflected his own inner strivings. A party publication, one year after Hitler's seizure of power, sums this up: "The concept of 'political man' typifies a bourgeois mentality. Being 'political' means to act consistently according to a set standard of behavior. Political behavior is not one attitude among others; it must form the basic attitude toward life." [2] In an age of industrialization and class conflict man was to be integrated into his Volk; his true self would be activated and his feeling of alienation transformed into one of belonging.

Such was Nazi theory, even if in practice many people did manage to stand aside from this integration. The phrase "inner emigration" assumed some importance during the period of Nazi rule, for this seemed the only privacy left. There were no groups with an identity separate from party and state which one could join, no kind of group identification which was not in some way related to the "new Germany." To be sure, several important institutions managed to preserve their identity (at least on the surface): the churches, the bureaucracy, some economic organizations, and the military. But these were eventually brought under control by various indirect methods of persuasion. Against the churches a more sustained battle had to be fought, as some of our documents show. Yet this was never waged against a united front of all churches; indeed many important Catholic and Lutheran prelates collaborated enthusiastically from the very beginning of the Third Reich. Moreover, churches were under great pressure from their own members to "equalize their gears." The sad truth is that there was little opposition anywhere in 1933, and even when this developed later it was ineffective in breaking through the cultural conformity of National Socialist Germany.

Censorship was imposed upon foreign books, periodicals, and newspapers, and all domestic literary and artistic output was rigidly controlled. A wall was built around the nation, none the less effective for lacking stone and mortar. Within this wall Nazi culture had a free hand to determine, if it could, every man's attitude toward life.

The Nazis started on their course immediately after Hitler was appointed Chancellor of the Reich. A constant barrage of propaganda

[2] *Kampf: Lebensdokumente deutscher Jugend* (Leipzig, 1934), p. 307.

and exhortations and frequent mass meetings whipped up enthusiasm. This was accompanied by book burnings in every town, the Gleich-schaltung of all cultural and social endeavors—the insistence of a show of conformity to the revolution which had won the day. To be sure, by the summer of 1933 people did start to weary of the speeches, the constant mass meetings and parades which took up all free time.[3] At this point the Nazis applied increased pressures to counter the indifference, much of which came from sheer exhaustion. But by that time the battle for cultural conformity was won; nor did many (especially among the youth) slacken in their original enthusiasm.

The kind of culture that the Nazis, in their barrage, unloosed upon the population and then enforced is illustrated in this book. Within this culture there is no progression, no development, for "truth" was accepted as "given," laid down forever by the race—as eternal as the Aryan himself. We must not, however, think of it as something merely imposed upon the majority by a ruling minority. The soil had been prepared for many decades, during which the German Right, in its opposition to modernity, had developed the identical kind of art, literature, and racial thought. Moreover, Nazi culture appealed to an unchanging popular taste, a fact to which we shall return. Nazi opposition to artistic and literary innovation had solid backing from people everywhere. Thus there was a static quality to this culture, and it would serve no purpose to divide our subject matter by dates or to attempt to show any cultural development, for it did not exist. What developed between 1933 and 1939 was the level of effective enforcement, not the kind of culture which was to be enforced.

Our presentation of Nazi cultural documents provides a further explanation of why so many people accepted and indeed helped to strengthen the Nazi rule. For we are dealing with an emotionally charged and unified ideology which was translated into fact by 1934. This ideology not only stands at the very core of this book but is also the crux of what the "good society" was all about. Adolf Hitler always stressed the ideological factor, the world view, which was of overriding importance to him. The new Germany was to be built upon the foundations of the "new man," and this man in turn was the product of the correct world view. The world view, or ideology (and the terms can be used interchangeably), was all-inclusive: a true instru-

[3] For a good description of this process, see William Sheridan Allen, *The Nazi Seizure of Power: The Experience of a Single German Town, 1930-1935* (Chicago, 1965), Chapter 17.

ment of reform. Originating in the wellsprings of man's nature, it pushed outward into all aspects of human life. Because this world view arose from the depths of the human soul, its expression must be cultural and not material. As a leading Rumanian fascist put it: "History is an aspect of the majestic life of the spirit." [4]

That is why Hitler himself put such a high valuation upon artistic endeavors, and his own artistic ambitions must have played a part in this emphasis. The speech he delivered at the House of German Art in 1937 illustrates this stress upon the primacy of culture as truly expressive of the eternally creative essence of the race. The "new man" must be a culturally centered, creative person who through his creative drives activates his "Germanism." This idea had always been in the mainstream of German nationalism, and it aptly reflected, in its emphasis upon creativity, the frustration of the individual in an ever more impersonal society.

Throughout these documents we shall see the attempt to form this "new man," a process which began with early childhood and pervaded the whole tenor of adult life. Hitler really believed in the world view of race, Volk, and soil, and he had well-developed notions on how to transmit it to the people themselves. This above all else he considered essential.

"Every world view, be it correct and useful a thousand times over, will be without importance for the life of a Volk unless its basic tenets are written upon the banners of a fighting movement." [5] Such a movement must be highly organized in order to capture power in the nation, but this organization must, in turn, be securely rooted in the world view. Propaganda was therefore of the highest importance, though the word "propaganda" itself can be misleading. Hitler never thought you could sell National Socialism as one sells toothpaste or cigarettes; a much more sophisticated theory was involved.

Georges Sorel, to whom fascism is so much indebted, wrote at the beginning of our century that all great movements are compelled by "myths." A myth is the strongest belief held by a group, and its adherents feel themselves to be an army of truth fighting an army of evil. Some years earlier, in 1895, the French psychologist Gustav Le Bon had written of the "conservatism of crowds" which cling tenaciously to traditional ideas. Hitler took the basic nationalism of the German tradition and the longing for the stable personal relationships of olden

[4] Horia Sima, *Destinée du nationalisme* (Paris, n.d.), p. 19.
[5] *Mein Kampf*, p. 418.

times, and built upon them as the strongest belief of the group. In the diffusion of the "myth" Hitler fulfilled what Le Bon had forecast: that "magical powers" were needed to control the crowd. The Führer himself wrote of the "magic influence" of mass suggestion and the liturgical aspects of his movement, and its success as a mass religion bore out the truth of this view.[6]

It is not necessary to ask whether Hitler had read either Sorel or Le Bon. The point is that all of them were expressing the problems of the mass society which the Industrial Revolution had produced and the doubts about the rationality of human nature which came with what Le Bon called the "era of crowds." The basic problem is illustrated by a quotation from Le Bon which Hitler, years later, acted upon with fatal decisiveness: "We see, then, that the disappearance of the conscious personality, the predominance of the unconscious personality, the turning, by means of suggestion and contagion, of the feelings and ideas in an identical direction, the tendency to immediately transform the suggested ideas into acts; these, we see, are the principal characteristics of the individuals that form a crowd." [7]

The irrational behavior characteristic of a mass society had been clearly formulated by the end of the nineteenth century, and the actual behavior of the crowds during the Dreyfusard struggles in France and during the first big anti-Semitic wave in Germany bore out the theories. In the world that industrialism had produced, the individual was alienated not only from his society but also from his rational nature. This was the all-encompassing problem, and Sorel as well as Le Bon envisioned the specter of a wild irrationality, which had to be directed by a leader into positive, constructive channels.

Industrialism seemed to such men to have destroyed the traditional relationships among men and to have exposed the basic irrationality of human nature. There were others, like Karl Marx and Friedrich Engels, who were also concerned with the "alienation" of man from his society, but they continued to hold to a belief in man's basic rationality. Hitler, needless to say, was not the heir of this tradition. He placed himself instead in the camp of Sorel and Le Bon. Hitler's understanding of this approach enabled him to take the road to power in a nation ravaged by crises and defeat. The use of basically irrational prejudices and predilections helped to bring about the acceptance of

---

[6] *Ibid.*, pp. 116 ff.
[7] Gustave Le Bon, *The Crowd* (London, 1922), pp. 35-36.

the Germanic world view which was Hitler's solution for ending the modern alienation of man.

For example, Hitler believed the mass meeting necessary because it enabled man to step "out of his workshop," in which he feels small, and to become part of a body of "thousands and thousands of people with a like conviction." [8] Thus he succumbs to mass suggestion. Alienation was to be exorcised, but the irrationality of human nature was basic to Hitler's own view of the world. These meetings were liturgical rites, staged with close attention to detail and purpose. We have reproduced accounts of two such festivals—one that was frequently held in the schools, the other a summer-solstice festival. The individual, Hitler held, was obsessed by anxiety, and in the mass meeting he received courage and strength through a feeling of belonging to a greater emotional community.

The mass meeting became one of the most important techniques of the Nazi movement, especially in the years of its rise to power, when there were almost daily meetings of this sort in various regions of the Reich. But by themselves such meetings could not accomplish very much; mass suggestion had to pervade every area of culture: literature, painting and sculpture, the theater, films, and education. As a "total culture" it would animate the basic nationalist prejudices of the people, overcome their feeling of isolation, and direct their creative drives into the proper channels of race and soil. This is why there is an astonishing coherence among the documents of Nazi culture, for they all served the same basic purpose.

A part of this pattern is the "dynamic," the urge to fight against evil. We are dealing here with a revolution and therefore the book begins with documents that serve to clarify what sort of a revolution this was supposed to be. There was violence: the battles of the SA, for example. "The masses do not understand handshakes," as Hitler himself put it.[9] But equal emphasis was put upon the "traditional links" of man: the Volk, his family, the proper morality. When the revolutionary impetus clashed with that of the traditional bonds, the latter won out. Hanns Anderlahn's account of a debate in the SA is especially revealing in this regard. The whole Nazi position on women and family is amazingly conservative, even if the Nazis tried to justify it on racial grounds.

[8] *Mein Kampf*, p. 536.
[9] *Ibid.*, pp. 371-372.

The reason for this is clear: the ideology of the Nazi revolution was based upon what were presumed to be Germanic traditions; while the revolution looked to the future, it tried to recapture a mythical past and with it the old traditions which to many people provided the only hope of overcoming the chaos of the present. The omnipresent nationalism was combined with an attempt to recapture a morality attributed to the Volk's past. But that morality was not the one which the ancient Germans had practiced in their forests, or which the peasant, close to the soil, was supposed to exemplify in modern times. Yet this is a belief which the Nazi ideology encouraged and which novels like that of Josefa Berens-Totenohl proclaimed. In reality the morality which National Socialism offered as typically Germanic was the bourgeois morality of the nineteenth century: the sanctity of the family, of marriage, and of the unostentatious, dedicated life. Dedicated to the Volk, not to the making of money: the modern bourgeoisie was condemned because it had become "Judaicized." Nothing could be more typical of such attitudes than the speech given by Hans Naumann, a professor of literature at the University of Berlin, on the occasion of the burning of books in 1933.[10] He begins by stressing the urge to action: it is time to act against the un-German spirit, and if too many rather than too few books are given to the flames, what matter? He ends by stating that such activism is necessary to "make holy" once again the "pious bonds" of family, native land, and blood. The interplay between "heroic" activism and traditionalism dominates the movement.

Hitler called this the "greatest racial revolution in world history," a "revolution of the spirit." [11] It was a cultural revolution, and was not directed at instituting economic changes. He could thus appeal to old prejudices without threatening the existing economic system. This appealed, above all, to white-collar workers and the small entrepreneurs, as some of the statistics presented in this book will demonstrate. It was their kind of revolution: the ideology would give them a new status, free them from isolation in industrial society, and give them a purpose in life. But it would not threaten any of their vested interests; indeed it would reinforce their bourgeois predilections toward family and Gemütlichkeit, and restore the "good old values" which had been

[10] Reprinted in Hildegard Brenner, Die Kunstpolitik des Nationalsozialismus (Hamburg, 1963), p. 188.

[11] Quoted in the Frankfurter Neue Presse, Jan. 28, 1958; and in Ernst Deuerlein, "Hitlers Eintritt in die Politik und die Reichswehr," Vierteljahrschrift für Zeitgeschichte, 7 Jahrg., Heft 2 (April 1959), p. 219.

so sadly dismantled by modernity. This attitude should not be un-familiar, for it pervades Gaullism in France and much of conservatism in the United States.

But the Nazi revolution was connected to a definite world view in which Hitler deeply believed and which is Central European rather than Western. Racism provided the foundations, as shown in our se-lections from the writings of three leading theoreticians, Hans F. K. Günther, Ludwig Ferdinand Clauss, and Alfred Rosenberg. Both Günther and Clauss were university teachers. Their ideas were highly abstract, yet they were made concrete: the outward racial form was linked to the "race soul." From these ideas "stereotypes" emerged—of the Aryan and the enemy, the Jew. Stereotyping was essential to the transformation of the ideology into a "fighting movement," for it made the abstract concrete for the purposes of mass suggestion. The other extracts in the section on the racial foundations point up exten-sions and practical applications of the theory, from the new biology (so important a foundation of racial thought!) to a guide for high-school students on how to recognize the racial soul of a person.

A race needs its heroes, and no revolution has ever succeeded with-out heroic examples. The hero the Nazis presented to their people was rooted in Hitler's world view and was equipped with great power of will. The proper use of the will was what made a man into a hero; it provided the impetus for transforming aspiration into reality. Here the Germans' interpretation of the philosophy of Nietzsche lay ready to hand, ideas which had influenced German intellectuals since the be-ginning of the century. Nietzsche's "will to power" became the will to actualize Hitler's good society. Alfred Baeumler, perhaps the most im-portant academic philosopher of the Third Reich, shows the conse-quences of this use of Nietzsche. Emphasis upon the power of the in-dividual will could be combined with memories of the war, where this power seemed to have been put to use. Ernst Röhm's exaltation of the soldier is typical in this connection. The SA leader himself had fought in the war and afterward with the Free Corps. Röhm illustrates the role which nostalgic memories of the war experience played in the Nazi movement. Adolf Hitler himself glorified the army, in which he had served, as the educator in decision making, courage, and responsi-bility. It represented, so he held, the antipode to the stock exchange.[12]

Activism was important. After all, the Nazis conceived of their party as a "movement." This and the irrational foundations of their world

[12] *Mein Kampf*, p. 306.

view represented strong opposition to intellectualism. Hitler summarized his own viewpoint in 1938: "What we suffer from today is an excess of education. Nothing is appreciated except knowledge. The wiseacres, however, are the enemies of action. What we require is instinct and will." [13] "Instinct" meant the love of Volk and race which came from a realm beyond empirical knowledge, from the soul. "Will" further emphasized the drive to transform this love into reality. The hero is no academic, no man of knowledge, but one who has developed his power of will to the fullest in order to activate his "healthy" instinct for what is right.

Joseph Goebbels' fictional hero, Michael, rejects university studies in order to join the Volk at work and help to save it. Michael reflects the greater social emphasis of the future propaganda minister, the socialism of National Socialism, which meant integration of the individual into the organic whole of the Volk. To the contemporary heroes, of whom Fritz Todt, the builder of the Autobahnen, may stand as example, were joined the heroes of the past. Frederick the Great of Prussia was transformed from the flute-playing friend of Voltaire into a militant activist. The revered Prussian monarch had to be dissociated from the Enlightenment, which stood for hated rationalism.

Albert Leo Schlageter occupies a place of his own in the Nazi gallery of heroes. An early Nazi, he fell in battle fighting against the French in 1923, and the afterword to an edition of his letters is a good example of the homage paid to him. Schlageter, like all Nazi heroes, symbolizes the "new man." The conversation between his friend August and August's father shows quite clearly the exaltation of this "new man"—the young generation. Hanns Johst, the most famous of the playwrights who wrote for the Third Reich, had dramatic power, and his play Schlageter was often performed, especially in the early days of the regime.

Other components of the myth have already been mentioned. The flag-raising ceremony for school children shows how the myth was implanted: the set pieces, the constant repetitions—in fact, the whole liturgical form. The description of the summer-solstice festival gives us some idea of the effect such ceremonies (and the real-life heroes) must have had upon susceptible youth. This was not as formal as the flag-raising ceremony, but its content was more fluid, more directly emotional.

The task of culture was laid down, and it held a central place in the

[13] Quoted in the Danziger Vorposten, May 2, 1938.

Nazi scheme, as we have already made clear: the spreading and root-
ing of the world view for whose sake the revolution had been made. It
built upon the inclinations of the audience. Throughout the extracts
in this book there run not only the themes of race and Volk but also
the drive for rootedness in the Volk. Intellectualism was decried, for
the Volk is one and culture must not separate itself from these roots.
This is what Hitler meant when he said that "to be German means to
have clarity"; thus his pride in having boiled down the Nazi ideology
to a mere twenty-five points in the party platform.[14]

But the purpose that culture served must never be lost from view:
it clarified the world view, it spread it and evoked an enthusiastic reception for it. Once again it was built upon popular taste and prejudices. The masses of people (and not just in Germany) do not like
"problem art," do not care for the distorted pictures of expressionists:
they do not understand the searchings of such art. The same can be
said about literature, indeed all cultural endeavor. People like their
pictures simple and easily understandable and their novels should have
gripping plots and large amounts of sentiment. The lowest common
denominator of popular taste has a sameness about it which does not
vary from the nineteenth to the twentieth century, or indeed from
country to country—whether we think of the "shilling shocker" in
England or the novels of a Courths-Mahler in Germany (without varying her sentimentality or simplicity of style, Courths-Mahler, between
1864 and 1950, wrote more than two hundred nearly identical novels,
which had a combined sale of 27 million copies). But in Germany the
popular taste was skillfully used as a vital part of a whole world view
in the name of creating an "organic" Volk. Goebbels' "cleansing of
art" catered to this taste, which was said to represent the "healthy instinct of the Volk." That instinct, then, was conservative (as it is today) and was used for the purposes of the Nazi ideology.

In this effort the historical connections with the past were exploited
(to Sorel a vital ingredient of the myth), and the virtues of pre-indus-
trial society were stressed. How typical that in the great Exhibition of
German Art in 1937, rural and family motifs overwhelmingly predomi-
nated. In contrast to the uprooted worker, filled with the anxiety of
his alienation, the peasant, rooted in the soil, became the prototype of
the "new man." The novel was the great popularizer of this image.
Josefa Berens-Totenohl sold over a quarter of a million copies of *Der*

[14] *Mein Kampf*, pp. 423-424; *The Speeches of Adolf Hitler*, trans. by Norman
Baynes (London, 1942), Vol. I, p. 587.

Femhof during the Third Reich, from which we offer an excerpt designed to show the idealized peasant and what he stood for. Berens-Totenohl's work is typical of a host of sentimental novels popular during the Third Reich. Their essential crudeness was tempered by a viable plot and, at times, passable writing. Tüdel Weller's *Rabauken!* on the other hand can serve to show the Nazi novel at its most racially crude and blatant.

The theater, radio, and films entered the fray. The typical playbill, the description of what happened to the theater at the beginning of the regime, the list of film titles given in this section will serve to show how the Nazis made use of these media. Radio plays a part of particular importance, for Hitler had great respect for the effectiveness of the spoken word. Speeches played a central role in the Nazi liturgy, whether at mass meetings or festivals. Radio carried the word to the masses. Not only were cheap radio sets put on the market, but loudspeakers were hung in the streets.

Yet, the pace of this cultural drive was always difficult to sustain. The very sentimentality which made it appealing to the public worked against the standards of morality for which Nazism stood. They stressed the bonds of the family, moderation in sexual and social behavior in consideration of the duties owed to the Volk. But the romanticism involved in the ideology could lead to a celebration of love for its own sake as well as abandonment to the pleasures of the flesh, and such attitudes also became part of the social reality. Popular sentimentality easily slips into forbidden regions, and a ruling class is apt to become detached from its own moral strictures—though Hitler himself, in spite of his unpublicized attachment to Eva Braun, never really did so.

This irrationalism seems to clash with what is popularly regarded as the essence of the natural sciences. However, as science had become ever more specialized during the nineteenth century it had withdrawn from a concern with the world as a whole. The age of Newton was long past and the modern scientist could view his specialty according to one set of criteria and the world as a whole according to another. Rationalism in the laboratory could be combined with irrationalism in the scientists' world view. Nazi science went a step beyond this. Here the ideology was so strong, so dominant, that it penetrated into the laboratory. The gap between science and the world was overcome, not in favor of a scientific method but of an irrational ideology. Both Johannes Stark and Philip Lenard were famous Nobel Prize-winning scientists. How they attempted to introduce Nazi ideology into their science, the documents themselves explain. The idea behind such attempts was always to strive for an organic unity between science and the Nazi world view, just as the Volk itself should be an organic whole. Alienation must be ended here as well as in all other fields of endeavor.

It is therefore not surprising that the astronomer Bruno Thüring goes back to an older tradition, that of Newton and Kepler, who had stressed the peaceful harmony of the world, in order to demonstrate the supposed unsoundness of Einstein's theory of relativity. Once more ideological considerations are overriding: Thüring uses racial rather than scientific proof to discredit Einstein's work. The consequences of this "Nazi science" came back to haunt the party. In 1944 Gauleiter Josef Wagner denounced Thüring, among others, for having discredited the "new physics" to such an extent that they were damaging the war effort. Wagner recognized, without mentioning Einstein, that the theoretical physics necessary for wartime scientific development had been stifled by the party in favor of merely one-directional research.[15]

Medicine followed the pattern of the other sciences. Objective research was rejected for the organic, for the treatment of the whole patient, including his soul—and the ideological was again the decisive element. As Hans Schemm, the first Nazi Minister of Culture in Bavaria, put it: "We are not objective, we are German." [16] This becomes obvious in the speech of Kurt Gauger and in the extract from the pen of the medical director of the University Hospital at Kiel. Gauger's references to Jung must be seen in the context of the role this eminent psychiatrist played in Nazi Germany. Jung had accepted the presidency of the German Society for Psychotherapy after Hitler's rise to power, and identified himself with the "expanding form" and "formative seed" of the Aryan as opposed to the Jewish unconscious.

National Socialism was a religion; the depth of the ideology, the liturgy, the element of hope, all helped to give the movement the character of a new faith. It has been shown that Goebbels quite consciously used a religious terminology in many of his speeches. Moreover, Nazism was a total world view which by its very nature excluded all others. From this it followed that traditional Christianity was a

[15] "Gegenwärtige Lage in der Physik," Aktenvermerk für den Reichsleiter (Alfred Rosenberg) von J. Wagner, reprinted in Léon Poliakov and Josef Wulf, Das dritte Reich und seine Denker (Berlin, 1959), pp. 101-103.
[16] Benedikt Lochmüller, Hans Schemm (Bayreuth, 1935), Vol. I, p. 40.

rival, not a friend. But here Hitler at first went very slowly indeed, for he needed (and got) the support of the majority of the Christian churches. Since he was appealing to the bourgeois, as we have seen, it was difficult to uphold the bonds of family and the traditional morality and at the same time exclude traditional Christianity. Yet such was Hitler's purpose and he hoped that the penetration of his world view would work first to weaken and then to shut out Christianity altogether from the German mind. Completely heathen prayers, like the one reproduced in the section on religion, were the exception, though there was an attempt from the first to substitute a Nazi ceremony for Protestant Confirmation. The main effort was centered on combining Christ and the Volk by stripping Christianity of its historical element. Like science, Christianity should be absorbed into the ideology. The so-called "German Christians" noisily devoted themselves to this task. Though they were held down in favor of the established churches, which were supported by the majority of the population, the Nazi future would have lain with the Evangelical Christians had the war been won.

Other selections in this section show how the Nazi effort against traditional Christianity worked in practice and affected the lives of the people. It was covert and cautious in comparison with Nazi activities in other cultural areas. Much has been written about the reaction of the churches, which was slow and only partial at best. But Cardinal Faulhaber of Munich preached a series of Advent sermons which created a sensation at the time for their bravery. This in itself tells a great deal about the atmosphere under the Third Reich as early as 1933. For Faulhaber merely defended the Old Testament and not only was silent about the persecution of Jews that had already begun but also made a clear distinction between the Jews in the time of Christ and those who came after. Theologically well-founded as this may be, it can hardly be called resistance, except when viewed in the context of the ever greater momentum of the Nazi drive for a total culture. Thus he illustrates not only the reluctance of the churches to take a clear stand against the Nazis but also the direction and depth of the Germanic awakening, in which these sermons could be regarded as a trumpet call against the regime.

Faulhaber, like most church leaders, was an old-line conservative, not a Nazi. The Nazis believed that such older men could never really accept their Weltanschauung, even if they were not confessed Christians. The movement made much of the difference between generations. The young were set off against the old, and the same distinction that was made between the old and young nations was operative within the Volk itself. When Hitler damned the bourgeoisie, he was inveighing against the older generation, brought up under the Empire. Hanns Johst expresses this condemnation in his play *Schlageter*. The son, August, is fire and flame for the Nazi hero and his adventurous fight for the Fatherland. Schneider, the father, counsels caution. Moreover, typically enough, the father thinks in terms of social classes and making money (the two go together in the Nazi ideology), while the son wants "not to earn but to serve." The older man ridicules this attitude as "adolescent romanticism," but this romanticism symbolizes in reality the son's urge to "belong" to his Volk.

This emphasis on youth is common to most revolutions, and was employed by the National Socialists from the very beginning. To be vigorous meant to be youthful, the "new man" of heroic will had to be a figure of youth: killed in action against the enemy like Schlageter, dying while vigorously engaged in a great and strenuous effort like the constructor of the *Autobahnen*, Fritz Todt. The Nazi leadership itself was young; Hitler was only forty-four years old when he came to power. Moreover, the Nazis realized that if youth could be captured by their world view, the future was assured. Once again we find an attitude typical of all modern revolutions. Fascism in all countries made a fetish of youthfulness. What a contrast this offered to the elderly politicians haggling in parliaments or to the fossilized bureaucracies which ran the nations (and the political parties) of Europe. The Nazis capitalized on the discontent of youth, its spirit of rebellion against parents and school. Ever since the end of the last century a large and vocal section of bourgeois youth had wanted to detach itself from the "respectable" society into which it had been born. Hitler offered them a way, and many young people (not just the unemployed) streamed into the party ranks, lured by the activism of the Nazis, their stress on the heroic will, and their well-defined goals. They could criticize the "bourgeoisie"—meaning their elders—and still retain their deeply inbred bourgeois prejudices. For many young people, the ideal of action, adventure, and movement may initially have concealed the rights and wrongs of the Nazi goals themselves. The extract from Inge Scholl's memoirs is especially telling here. For her brother passed from enthusiasm to disillusionment and (unlike the majority of youth) to organizing an anti-Nazi resistance which ended in his death.

Evidence that Nazism appealed to youth comes to us from all sides, and the Nazis themselves saw in the young people the key to the future of the movement. That is why we have devoted one of the longest sections in the book to youth. Education is crucial here, for if an ideology can be institutionalized through the educational establishment it has won a major battle. The Nazis realized this only too well, and youth in its turn seemed ready for the message. The account of Paul Oestreich, an anti-Nazi progressive educator, provides additional testimony.

The initial enthusiasm of youth was carefully directed and exploited, as the subsequent extracts demonstrate. They are taken from elementary-school readers, books for young boys, as well as readings for the upper classes of high schools. Some of the themes are constantly repeated. For example, Otto Dietrich's story about the "daring flight" is taken from a primer for the upper grades, but the theme recurs throughout other textbooks as well. In linking the daring flight in stormy weather to Hitler's dominance over the elements, the Nazi party press chief made a point which did not need elaboration. Even the young could understand the analogy with Germany's perilous state in the world. The symbols of sun and fire, so prevalent in the Nazi ideology, are also used in profusion. Baldur von Schirach's "victory" makes use of the myth of the sun and makes it understandable to the students. It is of a piece with the exaltation of the sun and fire at the summer solstice, described in a previous section. The tone which prevailed in the schools is indicated by the list of the subjects which students were required to write on at the end of each school year, or by the way in which an alumni address list handles the Jewish alumni of an earlier day. They are simply grouped together as numbers, not as persons with individuality.

Some readings on education have been used earlier in the book, for they document so well the application of the Nazi theory. Thus the description of the teaching of the new biology could have been placed in this section, or the guide for students on how to read the racial soul. Race was central to the world view, and education was the most important instrument for its diffusion. Educational examples were therefore necessary in discussing the foundations of the ideology

Education was not merely the concern of the schools. Hitler's emphasis upon organization has already been mentioned, and this included the purposeful organization of leisure time. Membership in the Hitler Youth was all but compulsory. The principles upon which it was run are best seen through the eyes of its leader, Baldur von

Schirach. What if this extracurricular activity came into conflict with
the family and the school? It is clear from the readings that Schirach
wanted to avoid such a clash, but in the last resort the ideology triumphed over other considerations, and the Hitler Youth was the organization directly concerned with strengthening the Nazi world view
among the young. It is not difficult to say which would prevail if family and school did not fit themselves into the organic Volk.

The university continued the indoctrination toward a total culture,
and not only by offering courses on race and the Volk. Both student
and professor were integrated into the Nazi conception of the German people. At the university level too the students were required to
take part in an extracurricular activity—the compulsory Labor Service (Arbeitsdienst). Like Goebbels' Michael, they should not stand
apart, but should learn to share the physical labor of the people. The
criteria for admission to the University of Berlin, which applied to all
universities, indicate what kind of students were desired. The student
organization within the university was a branch of the party. Its leader,
Gerhard Krüger, uses the word "socialism" to denote the total service
to the Volk which was demanded of students. This was designed to
keep the students from viewing themselves as an elite within the nation. The party leadership brooked no rival elites.

National unity was also a prime consideration in the role of the
professors, not only unity with the Volk but also an organic unity between the world view and the various academic disciplines. This is the
essence of the talk given by the leader of the Association of University
Professors, in which he defines academic freedom as the fulfillment of
this task of unity. We have already seen a similar spirit guiding attempts to create a new kind of natural science. The organic ideal
always stands in the forefront. The intellectual was to give up his illusions of superior status, just as the worker was to renounce the concept of class struggle. These were divisive forces and therefore evil.

The Volk encompassed all of life, and life gained its fulfillment
within it. There could exist no "eternal" criteria outside this final
good; hence the law too had to be adjusted to this "fact." The concept of law as reflecting a system of values transcending the Nazi
world view was condemned as liberal, serving merely to fragment the
nation. Carl Schmitt, the most celebrated jurist of the Third Reich,
explains this in constitutional terms. A new state has been created in
which all power, and therefore all law, springs from the needs of the
Volk as directed by the leader.

The leadership structure was central to the government of the state, and the organizational principle of the Nazi party was applied to the whole nation: the leader and followers were the poles around which the public life of Germany was to be organized—and as there was to be no division between public and private life, this took in all aspects of human endeavor. The Third Reich sought to create a new hierarchy, once more a part of the urge to substitute fixed personal relationships for the fluidities in human life which industrialization had brought about.

But this hierarchy was not the traditional one of nobility, bourgeois, and working class. The Nazis hated the old nobility and thought that the bourgeoisie had failed. Leadership was to be based on that personality, regardless of background, which had the will and power to actualize the *Volksstaat* (the state of the Volk). In Hitler's view, man's progress had not derived from the activities of the majority, but was the product of the individual personality, its genius and will to action.[17] The "new men" were the leaders, and as they had led the party to victory so they must now lead the state. Hitler envisaged the government of the Reich as a hierarchy of leadership: from the local leaders up to himself as the Führer of all the people. In reality the Third Reich was a network of rival leaders, each with his own followers and his own patronage. Hitler kept them competing against one another and in this way was able to control the whole leadership structure.

The rejection of majority rule meant that all leaders were appointed by those who were above them in the hierarchy and, in the last resort, by the highest leader of them all, the Führer himself. A government of this type has the appearance of being imposed upon the people: they had no say in its making and no control over its activities. Schmitt's stress upon the *Artgleichheit* (equality in kind) between leader and Volk is meant to answer this criticism. For the Nazi system was not to be a mere dictatorship from above, but was supposed to be based upon a truly democratic principle of government.

The world view is basic once again to an understanding of the Nazi meaning of democracy. Führer and Volk were equal in kind because they shared the same race and blood; the human nature of each individual German and that of his leaders was thought to be identical. Therefore their aims must be identical as well, as both wanted to

[17] *Mein Kampf*, p. 379.

fulfill themselves by bringing about the true Germanic state. Leader and led were a part of the same organic Volk. What distinguished the leader from the masses was his ability to make them conscious of their peoplehood and to lead them toward its fulfillment. He had all the attributes of those heroes whom we mentioned earlier.

No independent groupings could exist outside this structure, and no one should think himself superior to his fellow men. Indeed, even the leaders must never have a superior attitude; rather they should be devoted to service and responsibility. This explains Hitler's special concern that intellectuals would feel superior to others because of their knowledge and thus form a separate group within the Volk which would be difficult to control. In the section on education we have shown the attempts to keep students and professors from thinking of themselves as distinct from the "people at work." In the new Germany there could be only appointed leaders and the masses, both tied together by a common race and peoplehood, serving a shared goal which expressed everyone's inner convictions.

Wilhelm Stuckart and Hans Globke, in their official commentary on the Nazi citizenship law, clarify further the implications of the Nazi concept of government. They repeat the contention that the individual can only be thought of as a member of a community—and the German community is one of blood and race. Citizenship in the Reich therefore is based no longer upon mere territorial considerations, but upon the Aryan race. Roland Freisler, later to become the notorious judge of the People's Court, draws the logical conclusions from this view of law and citizenship when he calls for the abolition of an "impartial" officialdom. He holds out the hope that both bureaucratic formalism and legalism (especially rampant in Germany) would be eliminated and a new spirit prevail. If an official is imbued with the principles of National Socialism he will be a flexible new man—having his eye not on the legal paragraph but upon the final goal.

In the documents presented so far both theory and practice mix with one another. The theory was put into practice and made itself felt in the lives of the people. But how did the "little man" actually fare? The workers had never given heavy support to the Nazis in their rise to power, but the Nazis nevertheless had an idealized picture of the worker ready at hand. He works diligently and aims at quality, in the tradition of the medieval artisan. In addition, he seeks ideological strength by attending evening courses offered by the party. If he has been a Marxist, like Müller, he soon finds out how he has been duped: for his Aryan honesty and strength will rebel against Marxist tactics (from which, however, Hitler admitted in Mein Kampf that he had learned a great deal). Like Müller, the German worker was, after all, a Volksgenosse—a member of the Volk. The ugly reality of course was quite different: it was necessary to forbid strikes, and one reading shows how the cause of the Volk could be used to terrorize workers into being content with their present position and wages.

If the workers had never given the Nazis their wholehearted support, the petit bourgeois had. Their position in the Third Reich is shown by a schedule of tax distribution and living costs, as well as by an account of the attempt to reduce the number of independent retail enterprises. In contrast to the peasant, the "trader" had, it must be remembered, always been in bad repute, as a symbol of hated modernity: the ideology supported economic policy. But if the petit bourgeois were disappointed, they failed to show it, except in isolated instances. They seemed to play no part in such small resistance groups as existed. The ideology may well have kept its hold over them to the last.

The assumption of power in the spring of 1933 and how it affected the people has been left to the end. For this will be more meaningful if the whole Nazi revolution has first been understood. From the documents given here it is plain that the revolution arrived not with a rush but covertly and, at times, even comically. There were no battles to fight, no bastilles to storm. Men and women fell into the arms of the new Reich like ripe fruit from a tree. The remarkable account of the Nazi seizure of the City Council of Cologne shows the relative ease with which the change of government was accomplished—here, in the Catholic Rhineland, in a city which had been ruled the previous sixteen years by its mayor Konrad Adenauer. Carl Schmitt could boast with some justice that the Nazi revolution was orderly and disciplined. But the reason lies not so much within the Nazis themselves as in the lack of an effective opposition. For millions the Nazi ideology did assuage their anxiety, did end their alienation, and did give hope for a better future. Other millions watched passively, not deeply committed to resistance. "Let them have a chance" was a typical attitude. Hitler took the chance and made the most of it.

This book begins with an analysis of the nature of the Nazi revolution and ends with the actual assumption of power. In between we have attempted to show what Hitler's call to activate the world view actually meant and how it affected the lives of the whole population. One important aspect of the Third Reich would seem to have been neglected: the increasing terror which accompanied the drive for a total culture. Though many of the readings presented in this book reflect the pressures brought to bear on the people to conform (especially in the section on Christianity), we have not specifically documented the terror itself. The true nature of the terror has to be experienced and cannot be captured in the printed word. How can one convey through documents the hasty glance over the shoulder, the sudden silence in front of a stranger?

No section has been devoted to the real victims of the regime, to those against whom the "spiritual" revolution was in the end directed: the Jews. It would have been artificial to separate the "Jewish question" from the rest of the ideology and from the cultural drive of which it was an inseparable part. Every section of this book is filled with the Nazis' anti-Jewish obsession. They are the liberals who have to be liquidated, the Marxists who must be destroyed—in short, the all-pervasive enemy of the race. The bourgeois emphases upon family, morality, and traditional bonds did not apply to them: their families could be torn asunder, their property could be looted and confiscated, their roots in Germany torn up. As the Nazi revolution focused upon the Jewish stereotype, it entered into every facet of Nazi thought.

The Jewish problem was carried to the people as an integral part of the whole "renaissance of the Volk." It had its impact on mass consciousness as such, and was not something isolated or detached. The Jew was but a protruding peak of the ideological iceberg, and we have tried to convey an impression of the iceberg as a whole, for this is what the Nazis themselves wanted to convey to the people. If for Hitler the Jew was a "principle," [18] for the average German he must have been similarly abstract. Perhaps he witnessed the arrests of Jews and felt sympathy, or saw the burning of the synagogues on November 10, 1938—but his personal involvement would have been small. There were those who tried to help, but this was asking for martyrdom, self-sacrifice; it required a heroism that has always been rare in history. Aiding the "enemy" of the race called for a true heroism, quite different from that which the Nazis advocated. For their heroes were part of a group, the Volk, which gave them strength but also sheltered them. Helping Jews against the "fury of the people" had to be a lonely, individual action. It should not surprise us that so few

[18] Hermann Rauschning, *Gespräche mit Hitler* (New York, 1940), p. 220.

took this course; it is surprising that there were so many thousands who did. In a book devoted to how the Third Reich affected Germans it would be misleading to give a separate treatment to the Jewish question.

This book does not pretend to give a complete picture. Rather it aims to offer a taste of what National Socialism wanted to create, how it met the crisis of the post-World War I world, and how it affected the German population. But these documents also convey an idea of how "mass consciousness" can be created and manipulated in a nation. Hitler and his fellow leaders genuinely believed in their world view, but they also sought quite consciously to induce the population to share this belief. It is no coincidence that the Ministry of Propaganda and Enlightenment became so important, or that Hitler was personally closest to Joseph Goebbels, the expert manipulator of mass opinion.

Yet it would all have come to naught if the world view itself had not reflected already existing prejudices among the people. The bourgeois ideas which had become rooted in the German mind during the nineteenth century were combined with an omnipresent nationalism, and both were built into the ideology of race, blood, and soil. For those millions who yearned for a restoration of morality and family life, and for those who wanted Germany to take its rightful place among the nations, Hitler offered hope—even if they rejected most of his racial ideas. How many said: "He will become respectable in office," and repudiated his racism, which "no sensible person could believe"! But the racism and all that it meant proved to be not excesses but an integral part of the ideology, and those who hoped differently were doomed to disappointment. They became the "old generation" whom Hitler called the "bourgeoisie which is finished" [19] —though he had skillfully used their moral values and their nationalism on his road to power. By "used" we do not mean to imply that these ideas were not part of a world view genuinely held by Hitler. We have mentioned before the constant interplay between theory and application, but to this must be added the equally close interplay between genuinely held belief and its manipulation for the purpose of making it the sole national religion.

There is one late development in Nazism which falls outside the scope of this book: that of the SS. It came to be of truly great importance only after 1939. Here, among those who considered themselves

[19] *Ibid.*, p. 44.

the racial elite, both the bourgeois values and the nationalism tended eventually to drop away. During the war the SS was made up of not only Germans from the Reich but Aryans from other countries as well. Moreover, the bourgeois morality, the traditional family bonds, had little standing in the eyes of men who regarded themselves as a new order (*Orden*) of knights. To them only race and power counted. But this was a late development and did not affect the population as a whole—though it would have done so if the war had been won.

Hitler's world has gone forever. But many of the basic attitudes and prejudices which went into his world view are still with us, waiting to be actualized, to be directed into a new mass consciousness. The documents which follow may seem to the reader, thirty years later, to be so outrageous as to verge on the comical. Yet we must remember that at one point in history a regime did take these ideas seriously and so did millions who lived under it. Nazism was overthrown by a foreign war, not by internal revolution, and a larger resistance to Nazism grew up only as the war was being lost. This is partly explained by Hitler's successes: both in foreign policy and internally. During the years when these documents were written and their ideas put into practice, unemployment had vanished (there were over 6 million unemployed in 1933), the boundaries of Germany were being extended, and the humiliating Treaty of Versailles was being liquidated. The world view was spread against the background of considerable success.

Yet the world view for which Hitler stood is in itself a part of this success. That some of its basic attitudes are still with us should give pause for thought. Perhaps far from being farfetched and almost comical, this ideology appeals to a basic need for an organic community, for historical continuity, and for the shelter of a firm and established morality. A revolution of the spirit is for many men more tempting than one which brings about social or economic changes and which might lead to chaos instead of cementing order. Nazism exemplifies the dangers which can lurk behind this façade of conservatism, a modern conservatism which is vulnerable to extreme views even if it rejects them. It is unfashionable to speak of the lessons of history, but perhaps there is a lesson for the present hidden among these documents of the past.

Nazi Culture

1

Hitler Sets the Tone

WHAT DID ADOLF HITLER himself have to say about Nazi culture? His ideas are written large in all the documents in this book, for he dominated the Third Reich in every phase of its activities. It is therefore only fitting that we should hear from him before we start our inquiry. Hitler wrote and talked continually, and what he had to say about cultural activity would fill many volumes. The purpose of our small selection is merely to reflect in his own words the direction of thought contained in the material which follows.

The first group of selections is taken from *Mein Kampf*. There are two reasons for quoting from Hitler's only published book. *Mein Kampf* was required reading in the schools of the Third Reich (see page 278) as well as in many other organizations. Secondly, even if the book was not read, the speeches made by the Nazis and a host of other books and articles reflect the contents of *Mein Kampf* with great faithfulness. Hitler never changed the world view he had laid down when he started on the road to power, and Nazi culture reflected his all-encompassing ideology. *Mein Kampf* in fact would have been a successful book even if it had never been read: its contents were spread throughout the nation by the whole Nazi cultural drive.

Hitler dictated the book to his deputy, Rudolf Hess, from July to December 1924, when they were in easy confinement in the Bavarian

Landsberg fortress as a result of the unsuccessful Nazi putsch of November 8-9, 1923. At first Hitler wanted to write his autobiography, but he decided instead to combine the story of his life with an account of the National Socialist world view and party organization. There was good reason for Hitler's change of mind: by fusing his own personality with the Nazi party the book would help him regain undisputed party leadership when he left prison. The cry, so often heard in the Third Reich, that "Hitler is Germany, and Germany Hitler" had to be preceded by the cry that "Hitler is the party." Though it took several years after he left Landsberg to re-establish his ascendancy, there can be little doubt that *Mein Kampf* helped him in this process. However, the book had more than a political purpose; it also represented his most profound beliefs.

These beliefs were based upon the primacy of the world view in determining man's fate. The power of an ideal was all-important, and in one passage Hitler links this to the war experience. Idealism is contrasted with materialism, symbolized by what he calls the teachings of Marxism which have also infected the bourgeoisie. His own world view is Volkish: based upon the racial principles which are fundamental to all of life. Thus race is the foundation of all culture. The state is only a means to the end of preserving the race, and we will find this concept of the state made law ten years later in his Third Reich (see page 327). Racial ideas are combined with a belief in an aristocracy which rises from the mass of the population. Hitler stressed the "great personality" who made history—but always on the foundation of a common racism: personal ethics must be related to this basic factor of life. All culture is the product of the Aryan: only he can produce true personalities.

As culture is the expression of an ideal, materialism can never produce culture. Materialism has taken hold of the bourgeoisie through the influence of Marxism, an invention of the Jews. They are the true adversary of the Germanic world view and must be dealt with ruthlessly. Jews cannot produce culture, but they do serve a function: symbolizing all that is evil, they spur the Aryan on to struggle against them and thus to become ever more conscious of his own race. Therefore Hitler, adopting a phrase of Goethe, calls Jews a power which wants evil but produces good.

The "revolution in world view" can succeed only if it becomes part of a mass movement. Propaganda is designed to accomplish this but it must be backed up by an effective party organization. It is worth re-

membering that Hitler devotes half of *Mein Kampf* to problems of
political organization.

Because of his belief that an ideology is unimportant unless it is
embodied in a mass movement, Hitler's concept of the masses is of
the greatest importance. He recognizes the imperative of giving status
to the people, but this is secondary to the techniques necessary to "un-
lock their souls." The masses are swayed by emotion and feeling:
they are a part of primeval nature itself, which reflects not the rational
handiwork of God but instead an irrational view of man and the
world. Hitler builds upon the romantic tradition. Throughout Nazi
culture the parallel between man and nature will be drawn in this
manner. The masses of Aryans are as "genuine" in their basic emotions as Nature herself. The task of the leader is to awaken these emotions, to bring to the surface the belief in race and blood which provide the foundations. From these presuppositions it follows that, as
the people are a part of nature, their feelings are simple, direct, and
partisan. Simple and direct because Nature herself is held to be such,
in contrast with the artificiality of a materialist civilization; partisan
because, in the last resort, the voice of the race will be heard.

This view of the masses is allied with the culture necessary to activate them in the struggle. Propaganda, as Hitler used the word and as
the Nazis put it into practice, is the infusion of cultural attitudes into
the mass of Germans. The anti-intellectualism which resulted will run
like a theme throughout this book. Hitler's own view of the nature of
education will provide the foundation for the attempt to capture
youth. He calls for general rather than specialized education, meaning
that the teaching of the Nazi world view must take precedence.

When he was at the height of his power Hitler gave a succinct
summary of his concept of culture—at the opening of the first "Exhibition of German Art" (July 18, 1937), for this was more than just
another art exhibit. The exhibition, in a new building specially constructed for it, was to exemplify the entire direction of Nazi culture
through the instrumentality of visual art. Representations of nature
played a leading role (40 per cent of the pictures), but peasant and
family motifs also abounded. Art must have clarity, as Hitler stated,
and the idyllic pictures symbolize well the traditionalism of the
framework within which National Socialism did its work. The exhibition was a success; the sales figures reached extraordinary heights.

The Aryan needed an adversary in his struggle. We have seen how
the Jews fulfilled this function and on this occasion too an enemy was

represented. The "Exhibition of Degenerate Art" was held nearby, providing an object lesson for a people who, as Hitler put it, did not "understand handshakes." The moderns were hung under the appropriate slogans: "German peasants through Jewish eyes," "Blaspheming the German heroes of the world war," and "Making fun of German womanhood." What a contrast with the ideal types of peasants, heroes and women who graced the "Exhibition of German Art." We shall meet these ideal types throughout our documents.

This, then, is the setting in which Hitler defined culture, a definition which had already been put into practice throughout the Third Reich. When Hitler spoke in Munich, the "revolution of the world view" was already four and a half years old.

G.L.M.

FROM CULTURE AS THE FAITH IN AN IDEAL REICH TO ITS DIFFUSION AMONG THE MASSES

The Power of Ideals

One should beware of evaluating the force of an ideal too little. Those who today become faint-hearted in this regard, I would like to remind, in case they once were soldiers, of a time the heroism of which was the most overwhelming profession of the force of ideal motives. For, what made people die at that time was not care of their daily bread, but the love of their country, the confidence in its greatness, the general feeling for the honor of the nation. And only after the German people turned its back on these ideals in order to follow the material promises of the Revolution, and after it exchanged the gun for the knapsack, it came, instead of into an earthly heaven, into the purgatory of general disdain and, not less, of general distress.

Therefore it is all the more necessary to oppose the calculating masters of the erstwhile *material Republic* with the faith in an *ideal Reich*.

The Aryan as Custodian of Culture

The Marxist doctrine is the brief spiritual extract of the view of life that is generally valid today. Merely for this reason every fight by our so-called bourgeois world against it is impossible, even ridiculous, as this bourgeois world also is essentially interspersed with all these poison elements, and worships a view of life which in general is distinguished from the Marxian view only by degrees or persons. The bourgeois world is Marxist, but it believes in the possibility of a domination of certain human groups (bourgeoisie), while Marxism itself plans to transmit the world systematically into the hands of Jewry.

In opposition to this, the Volkish view recognizes the importance of mankind in its racially innate elements. In principle, it sees in the

5

state only a means to an end, and as its end it considers the preservation of the racial existence of men. Thus it by no means believes in an equality of the races, but with their differences it also recognizes their superior and inferior values, and by this recognition it feels the obligation in accordance with the Eternal Will that dominates this universe to promote the victory of the better and stronger, and to demand the submission of the worse and the weaker. Thus in principle it favors also the fundamental aristocratic thought of nature and believes in the validity of this law down to the last individual. It sees not only the different values of the races, but also the different values of individual man. In its opinion, out of the masses emerges the importance of the person, but by this it has an organizing effect, as contrasted with disorganizing Marxism. It believes in the necessity of idealizing mankind, as, in turn, it sees in this the only presumption for the existence of mankind. But it cannot grant the right of existence to an ethical idea, if this idea represents a danger for the racial life of the bearers of higher ethics; for in a hybridized and negrified world all conceptions of the humanly beautiful and sublime, as well as all conceptions of an idealized future of our mankind, would be lost forever.

In this world human culture and civilization are inseparably bound up with the existence of the Aryan. His dying off or his decline would again lower upon this earth the dark veils of a time without culture.

The undermining of the existence of human culture by destroying its supporters appears, in a Volkish view of life, as the most execrable crime. He who dares to lay hand upon the highest image of the Lord sins against the benevolent Creator of this miracle and helps in the expulsion from Paradise.

The State Is Not an End But a Means

The basic realization is that the state represents not an end but a means. It is indeed the presumption for the formation of a higher human culture, but not its cause. On the contrary, the latter lies exclusively in the existence of a race capable of culture. Hundreds of exemplary states may exist on this globe, but in case of a dying off of the Aryan culture supporter, no culture would exist which would correspond to the spiritual level of the highest peoples of today. One can even go further and say that the fact of human state formation would not in the least exclude the possibility of the destruction of the human race, insofar as the superior intellectual ability and elasticity, in consequence of the lack of its racial supporters, would be lost.

The Jew Has No Culture

The Jewish people, with all its apparent intellectual qualities, is nevertheless without any true culture, especially without a culture of its own. For the sham culture which the Jew possesses today is the property of other peoples, and is mostly spoiled in his hands.

When judging Jewry in its attitude toward the question of human culture, one has to keep before one's eye as an essential characteristic that there never has been and consequently that today also there is no Jewish art; that above all the two queens of all arts, architecture and music, owe nothing original to Jewry. What he achieves in the field of art is either bowdlerization or intellectual theft. With this, the Jew lacks those qualities which distinguish creatively and, with it, culturally blessed races.

The Necessity of Propaganda

The most striking success of the revolution of a view of life will always be won whenever the new view of life is, if possible, taught to all people, and, if necessary, is later forced upon them, while the organization of the idea—that is, the movement—has to embrace only so many people as absolutely necessary for the occupation of the nerve centers of the state involved.

That means, in other words:

In every really great revolutionary movement propaganda will first have to spread the idea of this movement. Thus, it will untiringly try to make clear to the others the new train of thought, to draw them over to its own ground, or at least to make them doubtful of their own previous conviction. Since the propagation of a doctrine—that is, this propaganda—has to have a backbone, the doctrine will have to give itself a solid organization. The organization receives its members from the followers in general won by propaganda. The latter will grow the more quickly, the more intensively propaganda is carried out, and the latter in turn is able to work the better, the stronger and the more vigorous the organization is that stands behind it.

How Hitler Viewed the Masses

The national education of the great masses can only take place through the detour of a social uplift, since exclusively by this all those general economic presuppositions are created which permit the individual to take part in the cultural goods of the nation.

The nationalization of the great masses can never take place by way of half measures, by a weak emphasis upon a so-called objective viewpoint, but by a ruthless and fanatically one-sided orientation as to the goal to be aimed at. That means, therefore, one cannot make a people "national" in the meaning of our present "bourgeoisie," that is, with so and so many restrictions, but only nationalistic with the entire vehemence which is harbored in the extreme. Poison is only checked by antidote, and only the insipidity of a bourgeois mind can conceive the middle line as the way to heaven.

The great mass of a people consists neither of professors nor of diplomats. The small abstract knowledge it possesses directs its sentiments rather to the world of feeling. In this is rooted either its negative or positive attitude. It is open only to the expression of force in one of these directions, and never to a half measure swaying between them. Their sentimental attitude, however, is caused by their exceeding stability. It is more difficult to undermine faith than knowledge, love succumbs to change less than to respect, hatred is more durable than aversion, and at all times the driving force of the most important changes in this world has been found less in a scientific knowledge animating the masses, but rather in a fanaticism dominating them and in a hysteria which drove them forward.

He who would win the great masses must know the key which opens the door to their hearts. Its name is not objectivity—that is, weakness—but will power and strength.

One can only succeed in winning the soul of a people if, apart from a positive fighting of one's own for one's own aims, one also destroys at the same time the supporter of the contrary.

In the ruthless attack upon an adversary the people sees at all times a proof of its own right, and it perceives the renunciation of his destruction as an uncertainty as regards its own right, if not as a sign of its own wrong.

The great masses are only a part of nature, and this feeling does not understand the mutual handshake of people who assert that they want various things. What they want is the victory of the stronger and the annihilation or the unconditional surrender of the weaker.

The nationalization of our masses will only be successful if, along with all positive fighting for the soul of our people, its international poisoners are extirpated.

All great questions of the times are questions of the moment, and they represent only consequences of certain causes. Only one of them is of causal importance, that is, the question of the racial preservation of the nationality. In the blood alone there rests the strength as well as the weakness of man. As long as the people do not recognize and pay attention to the importance of their racial foundation, they resemble people who would like to teach the greyhound's qualities to poodles, without realizing that the greyhound's speed and the poodle's docility are qualities which are not taught, but are peculiar to the race. Peoples who renounce the preservation of their racial purity renounce also the unity of their soul in all its expressions. The torn condition of their nature is the natural, necessary consequence of the torn condition of their blood, and the change in their spiritual and creative force is only the effect of the change in their racial foundations.

He who wants to redeem the German people from the qualities and the vices which are alien to its original nature will have to redeem it first from the alien originators of these expressions.

Without the clearest recognition of the race problem and, with it, of the Jewish question, there will be no rise of the German nation.

The race question not only furnishes the key to world history, but also to human culture as a whole.

Education Must Be Based on Ideals

It is a characteristic of our present materialized time that our scientific education turns more and more toward the subjects of natural science only, namely, mathematics, physics, chemistry, etc. No matter how necessary this is for a time in which techniques and chemistry dominate in daily life and represent its symptoms, at least as far as outwardly recognizable, it is just as dangerous if the general education of a nation is always directed exclusively at this. On the contrary, this education has always to be an ideal one. It has to correspond more to the classic subjects and should only offer the foundations of a later training in a special field. Otherwise, one renounces forces which are still more important for the preservation of the nation than any technical or other ability. Especially in history instruction one should not let oneself be deterred from studying antiquity. Roman history, rightly conceived in very broad outlines, is and remains the best teacher not only for today but probably for all times. The Hellenic ideal of culture, too, should be preserved for us in its exemplary beauty. One must not allow the differences of the individual races to tear up the greater racial community. The struggle that rages today involves very great aims: a culture fights for its existence, which combines millenniums and embraces Hellenism and Germanity together.

A sharp difference should be made between general education and specialized knowledge. Since the latter, today more than ever, threatens to sink into the service of pure mammon, general education, at least in its more ideal orientation, has to be preserved as a counterbalance. Here, too, one has continuously to inculcate the principle *that industry and techniques, trade and professions are able to flourish only as long as an idealistically disposed national community offers the necessary presuppositions. But the latter do not lie in material egoism, but in a joyous readiness to renounce and to sacrifice.*

Education, Instinct, and Will

A change in education is a further necessity: today we suffer from over-education. Only knowledge is prized. The know-it-alls are the enemies of action. What is needed is instinct and will.

All but one of the preceding extracts are from Adolf Hitler, *Mein Kampf* (1926), translation by Helmut Ripperger (New York: Reynal & Hitchcock, 1939), pp. 651, 579-581, 592, 416-417, 852, 466-470, 631-632. The extract entitled "Education, Instinct, and Will" is from a speech

by Adolf Hitler, Munich, April 27, 1923, published in Werner Siebarth, *Hitlers Wollen* (Munich: Frz. Eher Verlag,
1936), p. 132.

HITLER DEFINES CULTURE IN DEFINING ART

The Cultural Renascence

On July 18, 1937, Hitler delivered a speech at the opening of the
House of German Art in Munich, which was to take the place of the
former "Glass Palace." In the collapse of Germany after the war, he
said, the economic decline had been generally felt, the political decline had been denied by many, the cultural decline had not even
been observed by the majority of the people. It was an age of phrases
and catchwords: in the economic sphere the hard facts of misery and
unemployment deprived these phrases of their force: in the political
sphere such phrases as "international solidarity" had more success and
veiled from the German people the extent of the political collapse.
But in the long run the failure of the parliamentary-democratic form
of government, copied from the West—a West which regardless of
this democratic form still continued to extort from Germany whatever there remained to extort—defeated the phrase-mongers. Far
more lasting was the effect of these phrases in the cultural field, where
they resulted in a complete confusion concerning the essential character of culture. Here the influence of the Jews was paramount and
through their control of the press they were able to intimidate those
who desired to champion "the normal sound intelligence and instinct
of men." Art was said to be "an international experience," and thus
all comprehension of its intimate association with a people was
stifled: it was said that there was no such thing as the art of a people
or, better, of a race: there was only the art of a certain period. Thus it
was not Greeks who created the art of Greece, Romans the art of
Rome, etc.—a particular period had found in each art its expression.
Art is a "time-conditioned phenomenon." So today there is not a
German or a French art, but a "modern art." This is to reduce art to
the level of fashions in dress, with the motto "Every year something
fresh"—Impressionism, Futurism, Cubism, perhaps also Dadaism.

These newly created art phrases would be comic, if they were not tragic.

The result was uncertainty in judgments passed on art and the silencing of those who might otherwise have protested against this *Kulturbolschewismus*, while the press continued to poison our sound appreciation of art. And just as in fashions one must wear "modern" clothes whether they are beautiful or not, so the great masters of the past were decried. But true art is and remains eternal, it does not follow the law of the season's fashions: its effect is that of a revelation arising from the depths of the essential character of a people which successive generations can inherit. But those who do not create for eternity do not readily talk of eternities: they seek to dim the radiance of these giants who reach out of the past into the future in order that contemporaries may discover their own tiny flames. These facile daubers in art are but the products of a day: yesterday, nonexistent: today, modern: tomorrow, out of date. The Jewish discovery that art was just the affair of a period was for them a godsend: theirs could be the art of the present time. Theirs was a small art—small in form and substance—and at the same time intolerant of the masters of the past and the rivals of the present. There was a conspiracy of incapacity and mediocrity against better work of any age. The new rich, having no judgment of their own in art matters, accepted these artists at their own valuation. It was only an attraction that these works of art were difficult to understand and on that account very costly: no one wished to admit lack of comprehension or insufficient means! And if one does not oneself understand, probably one's neighbor will not either, and he will admire one's comprehension of obscurity.

For this "modern art" National Socialism desires to substitute a "German" art and an eternal art. This House of German Art is designed for the art of the German people—not for an international art. "The people in the flux of phenomena is the one constant point. It is that which is abiding and permanent, and therefore art as the expression of the essential character of the abiding people must be an eternal monument, itself abiding and permanent; there can be therefore no standard of yesterday and today, of modern or unmodern: there can be only the standard of 'valueless' or 'valuable,' of 'eternal' or 'transitory.'" "And therefore in speaking of German art I shall see the standard for that art in the German people, in its character and life, in its feeling, its emotions, and its development."

From the history of the development of our people we know that it is composed of a number of more or less distinct races which in the course of millennia through the formative influence of a certain outstanding racial kernel produced that mixture which we see before us in our people today. This force which formed the people in time past and which still today continues that formative activity lies in the same Aryan branch of mankind which we recognize not only as the support of our own civilization but of the earlier civilizations of the ancient world.

The way in which our people was composed has produced the many-sidedness of our own cultural development, but as we look upon the final result of this process we cannot but wish for an art which may correspond to the increasing homogeneity of our racial composition, and thus present in itself the characteristics of unity and homogeneity. Many attempts have been made through the centuries to define what "to be German" really means. I would not seek to give an explanation in the first instance. I would rather state a law—a law previously expressed by a great German: "To be German is to be clear," and that means that to be German is to be logical and true. It is this spirit which has always lived in our people, which has inspired painters, sculptors, architects, thinkers, poets, and above all our musicians. When on June 6, 1931, the Glass Palace was burned down there perished with it an immortal treasure of German art. The artists were called Romantics, and yet they were but the finest representatives of that German search for the real and true character of our people, for an honest and decent expression of this law of life divined by our people. For it was not only their choice of subject which was decisive but the clear and simple mode of rendering these sentiments. Many of their original works are lost, we possess only copies or reproductions, but the works of these masters are removed by a great gulf from the pitiable products of our modern so-called "creative artists." These masters felt themselves to be Germans, and consequently they created works which should be valued as long as there should be a German people to appreciate them. But these modern works we would also preserve as documents illustrating the depths of that decline into which the people had fallen. The "Exhibition of Degenerate Art" is intended as a useful lesson.

During the long years in which I planned the formation of a new Reich I gave much thought to the tasks which would await us in the cultural cleansing of the people's life: there was to be a cultural renascence as well as a political and economic reform. I was convinced that peoples which have been trodden underfoot by the whole world of their day have all the greater duty consciously to assert their own value before their oppressors, and there is no prouder proof of the highest rights of a people to its own life than immortal cultural achievements. I was therefore always determined that if fate should one day give us power I would discuss these matters with no one but would form my own decisions, for it is not given to all to have an understanding for tasks as great as these. Among the plans which floated before me in my mind both during the war and after the collapse was the idea of building a great new exhibition palace in Munich; and many years ago I thought of the place where the building now stands. In 1931 I feared that I should be anticipated and that the "men of November" would erect an exhibition building. Plans indeed were produced for an edifice which might well have served for a railway station or a swimming bath. But when we came to power in 1933 the plan had not been executed: the erection of the building was left to the Third Reich. And the building is so unique, so individual, that it cannot be compared with anything else: it is a true monument for this city and more than that—for German art. . . . It represents a turning point, the first of the new buildings which will take their place among the immortal achievements of German artistic life.

But the House is not enough: it must house an Exhibition, and if now I venture to speak of art I can claim a title to do so from the contribution which I myself have made to the restoration of German art. For our modern German state that I with my associates have created has alone brought into existence the conditions for a new, vigorous flowering of art. It is not Bolshevist art collectors or their henchmen who have laid the foundations: we have provided vast sums for the encouragement of art, we have set before art itself great, new tasks. As in politics, so in German art-life: we are determined to make a clean sweep of phrases. Ability is the necessary qualification if an artist wishes his work to be exhibited here. People have attempted to recommend modern art by saying that it is the expression of a new age: but art does not create a new age, it is the general life of peoples which fashions itself anew and therefore often seeks after a new expression. A new epoch is not created by littérateurs but by the fighters, those who really fashion and lead peoples, who thus make history. It is either impudent effrontery or stark stupidity to exhibit to the people of today works which perhaps ten or twenty thousand years ago might have been made by a man of the Stone Age.

They talk of primitive art, but they forget that it is not the function of art to retreat backward from the stage of development which a people has already reached: its sole function must be to symbolize that development.

The new age of today is at work on a new human type. Men and women are to be more healthy, stronger: there is a new feeling of life, a new joy in life. Never was humanity in its external appearance and in its frame of mind nearer to the ancient world than it is today. *Hitler spoke of the Olympic Games, of sport, of the radiant, proud bodily vigor of youth.* This, my good prehistoric art-stutterers, is the type of the new age. And what do you manufacture? Misformed cripples and cretins, women who inspire only disgust, men who are more like wild beasts, children who, were they alive, must be regarded as cursed of God. And let no one say to me that that is how these artists see things. From the pictures sent in for exhibition it is clear that the eye of some men shows them things otherwise than as they are—that there really are men who on principle feel meadows to be blue, the heaven green, clouds sulphur-yellow—or as they perhaps prefer to say "experience" them thus. I need not ask whether they really do see or feel things in this way, but in the name of the German people I have only to prevent these pitiable unfortunates who clearly suffer from defects of vision from attempting with violence to persuade contemporaries by their chatter that these faults of observation are indeed realities or from presenting them as "Art." Here only two possibilities are open: either these "artists" do really see things in this way and believe in that which they represent—then one has but to ask how the defect in vision arose, and if it is hereditary the Minister of the Interior will have to see to it that so ghastly a defect of vision shall not be allowed to perpetuate itself—or if they do not believe in the reality of such impressions but seek on other grounds to impose upon the nation by this humbug, then it is a matter for a criminal court. There is no place for such works in this building. The industry of architects and workmen was not spent to house canvases which were daubed over in five hours, the painters being assured that the boldness of the pricing could not fail to produce its effect, that the canvas would be hailed as the most brilliant lightning-birth of a genius. No, they can be left to cackle over each other's eggs!

The artist does not create for the artist: he creates for the people and we will see to it that henceforth the people will be called in to judge its art. No one must say that the people has no understanding for a really valuable enrichment of its cultural life. Before the critics did justice to the genius of a Richard Wagner he had the people on his side, while the people has had nothing to do with so-called "modern art." The people regarded this art as the outcome of an impudent and unashamed arrogance or of a simply shocking lack of skill; it felt that this art-stammer—these achievements which might have been produced by untalented children of from eight to ten years old—could never be valued as an expression of our own times or of the German future. When we know today that the development of millions of years repeats itself in every individual compressed into a few decades, then this art, we realize, is not "modern"; it is on the contrary in the highest degree "archaic," far older probably than the Stone Age. The people when it passes through these galleries will recognize in me its own spokesman and counselor: it will draw a sigh of relief and express its glad agreement with this purification of art. And that is decisive: an art which cannot count on the readiest and most intimate agreement of the great mass of the people, an art which must rely upon the support of small cliques, is intolerable. Such an art does but endeavor to confuse, instead of gladly reinforcing, the sure and healthy instinct of a people. The artist cannot stand aloof from his people. This exhibition is but a beginning, yet the end of the artistic stultification of Germany has begun. Now is the opportunity for youth to start its industrious apprenticeship, and when a sacred conscientiousness at last comes into its own, then I doubt not that the Almighty, from the mass of these decent creators of art, will once more raise up individuals to the eternal starry heaven of the imperishable God-favored artists of the great periods. We believe that especially today, when in so many spheres the highest individual achievements are being manifested, so also in art the highest value of personality will once again assert itself.

From *The Speeches of Adolf Hitler, April 1922-August 1939*, translated and edited by Norman H. Baynes (New York: Oxford University Press, 1942), Vol. I, pp. 584-592. (Reprinted by permission.)

2

What Sort of a Revolution?

THE NATIONAL SOCIALIST REVOLUTION stressed both the dynamic of the movement and the "taming" of that dynamic through an appeal to tradition and sentiment. The following documents illustrate this double aspect of the movement. The SA came to symbolize the violence and the fighting spirit of the Nazis before their accession to power. Founded in 1921 for the purpose of providing protection at Nazi meetings, they soon found themselves embroiled in pitched battles (*Saalschlachten*) at these meetings against left-wing elements or those loyal to the Republic. It was not long before the SA themselves began to provoke "the enemy," seeking them out in order to do battle or marching through the streets singing songs of triumph and hate. The SA men were young, drawn largely from the ranks of the unemployed, and less interested in long-range goals than in immediate and . violent change. By 1933 nearly 300,000 men had joined the organization. Most of their leaders were former soldiers who had been unable to demobilize and in their brown uniforms carried on the "war experience" which they could not forget.

Ernst Röhm, who became SA chief of staff in 1930, was such a man. He glorified his war experiences (see page 101) and gave little thought to the long-range purposes and goals which Hitler had in mind. Small wonder that the SA proved a constant challenge to party discipline. The Nazi seizure of power eliminated the enemy who had to be fought in meeting halls and on the streets. The SA was no longer necessary—the struggle for power was a thing of the past—and on June 30, 1934, Hitler acted to bring this restless organization under control. Ernst Röhm and other SA leaders were shot in the "night of the long knives." Not only was the power of the SA destroyed, but Nazi leaders took the opportunity to eliminate other personal enemies as well. From that point on the SA played a minor role in the Third Reich: politically its time was past, but its battles during the Nazi rise to power were idealized in memory. The hard fight in which the Nazis had triumphed was thought to provide a necessary myth for the existence of the Third Reich, but, for all that, it was true that such battles had actually taken place.

Friedrich Joachim Klaehn describes one SA unit's successful attempt to conduct a meeting against the opposition of the regular and auxiliary police as well as that of the Reichsbanner, an organization of volunteers formed to demonstrate for and to protect the Republic. The incident took place in September 1932 after the brief and abortive attempt by the Reich government to ban the SA (April 13-June 14). Instead, a new wave of SA terrorism spread throughout Germany. The restrictions described in this extract are therefore local measures directed against the intimidation of the population by Hitler's Storm Troops. Such restrictions were doubly desirable because of the approach of a November election, which spurred the SA to redouble their efforts. Hitler lost votes in that Reichstag election, and the result only added to the SA's impatience with the Führer's attempt to find a legal road to power, a disillusionment with legal methods which had set in much earlier among the SA. Friedrich Klaehn was well fitted to idealize this incident. He was a propagandist for the SA and, perhaps, a leader of a troop (*Sturm*) himself.

The radical spirit within the SA is further illustrated by Kurt Massmann's account of a meeting-hall brawl. Massmann acted as the leader for South Hanover and Brunswick of the Strength Through Joy movement of the Labor Front (see page 341). The SA leader, the "bear" whom he describes, represents the ideal type of SA man, uncouth and thus a simple man of the people, honest and strong. This idealization of the "days of struggle" was published in a volume which intended to show German youth in action against the Republic. The Minister of the Interior, Wilhelm Frick, wrote the preface.

Both Klaehn's and Massmann's stories were meant to glorify the past struggles of the National Socialists on behalf of the "German spirit" —but they do illustrate the radicalism prevalent among the Storm Troops.

The taming of this radicalism proved no easy task, and Hanns Anderlahn, a prolific writer of books about the SA, warns against the expanding revolutionary spirit. The rejection of all family ties, advocated by some SA men in this meeting, focuses the problem. The rejection of such traditional ties meant a clear and present danger to the Nazi world view. This was anchored in an idealization of the past which included an emphasis upon bourgeois morality. The taming of the activism through an "*embourgeoisement*" of the SA was accomplished by stressing the importance of founding a family—the wife must be regarded as a "comrade." This extract shows clearly how the activism was supposedly combined with harmless relaxation in which the wife could participate. From marching and doing battle the SA passed to drama societies, from cracking skulls to comfortable "togetherness."

The family was the true cell of the state. Not merely was the ardor of the SA tamed through this emphasis, but it was an intrinsic part of the racial world view. Ludwig Leonhardt, an expert on racial theory, clearly states that the family is part of the whole biological inheritance of the individual, and such inheritance is crucial in the formation of a race. Genealogical research must be undertaken in order to discover the importance of one's racial origins. Beyond this, such research is essential in order to make the right kind of marriage, and Leonhardt's book *Heirat und Rassenpflege* (*Marriage and Racial Hygiene*) was designed for marriage counseling.

How far such counseling should go, another expert on racial hygiene, the physician Hermann Paull, takes pains to describe. If one acquires a wealthy husband or wife, one also marries into a high-grade biological and racial inheritance, for such wealth could not have been amassed without native ability typical of the superior race. The bourgeois cast of National Socialism could hardly find a better illustration, and what Paull has to say on the benefits of marriage itself further underlines this. Free love is dangerous to racial health. The puritanical element in the Nazi world view is pushed to the forefront.

This emphasis upon family and marriage brings home the fact that violence, such as that of the SA, was good only if directed against the

enemy, those who opposed the Nazi revolution. Within the movement, and within a racially pure Germany, the "holy bonds" of tradition, including the family, had to be preserved.

The ideal of womanhood is a good illustration of the traditionalism, indeed the conservatism, which pervaded National Socialism and
added so much to its attractiveness for the middle classes. Hitler's
views on the place of women in society are essentially those of the
mid-nineteenth century, and he was followed in this by the other National Socialists whose words are reproduced here. Man was the master—about that there must be no doubt—and it was he who determined the course of politics, of the law, indeed of all public affairs.
The woman's sphere was the family, it was her duty to safeguard this
cell from which the race has its being. The Nazis attacked the ideal
of equal rights for women and rejected the woman's emancipation
movement. This movement had been connected with that socialism
and liberalism which the Nazis hated so much, but the vision of an
idealized past also played its role. Alfred Rosenberg, in his Der Mythos
des XX. Jahrhunderts (The Mythos of the Twentieth Century) (1930),
typically enough inveighs against the emancipation movement as an
affront to the true role of woman, who is an integral part of his historic Volk. Living up to this ideal could mean going back to work at
the spinning wheel and the weaving loom, as suggested by the Völkischer Beobachter.

Joseph Goebbels, in his novel Michael (1929), presents this ideal
of womanhood in so-called poetic form (for more from this novel, see
page 104), while Rudolf Hess, the Führer's deputy, discusses "women
we can love." The stereotype of the ideal woman is always the same:
guardian of the family, mother of her children, and obedient help-
mate to her husband. Throughout the Third Reich, Magda Goebbels
was put forward as the ideal German woman. While his enemies
called her husband a "shrunken Teuton gone dark" (nachgedunkelter
Schrumpfgermane), Magda Goebbels was blond, tall, and the mother
of numerous children. Blond hair and blue eyes were essential elements in the stereotype of the Aryan woman as it had grown up in
racial thought. Small wonder that in 1937 an SS leader could con-
demn the "blond craze," the more so as some girls seem to have
thought that by itself blond hair would serve as proof of their Aryan
descent—a proof necessary for marriage to an SS man. But here racial
thought had only itself to blame, for outward appearance was always
stressed as a sign of the correct racial soul (see page 64).

Simplicity was an integral part of Aryan beauty. In an earlier extract the ideal SA leader was glowingly described as uncouth—that is, simple and straightforward. This kind of primitive simplicity was transferred to the comportment of the female sex. The Nazis condemned lipstick, powder, and other make-up as relics of an age which had substituted artificiality for the naturalness that was intrinsic to the "genuine" Germanic race. The whole opposition of the Nazi world view to "artificial" modernity was involved here. For racial thought, living close to nature was regarded as proof that Germans had not lost touch with the roots of their race. The Labor Service which every German youth had to undergo helped to inculcate this idea. Working with the spade on the land meant a return to the foundations of national life. But such puritanism could go too far, even for Goebbels' paper, Der Angriff—the female bird must pretty itself, as Goebbels put it in his novel. A shiny nose did not serve the Volk. But this article does show what had become the practice in the girls' branch of the Labor Service.

The BDM project "Faith and Beauty" seems closer to the ideal of the Labor Service than to that of Der Angriff. The BDM (Bund Deutscher Mädel) was the party youth organization to which every girl, up to the age of eighteen, should belong—it was the female counterpart to the Hitler Youth. "Faith" is acquired through ideological indoctrination in various subjects, such as foreign affairs and folklore. "Beauty" means gymnastics, hygiene, etc., but not "beauty culture" as we understand it—learning to make up one's face, to dye one's hair, or to obtain the right figure. The Nazi ideal of female comportment is illustrated once more in an official order concerning women charged with forging a close connection between shop or plant and the National Socialist movement. The NSBO (National Sozialistischer Betriebs Obman) was a part of the official labor organization, the Labor Front (see page 341). This office, purely honorary, was now opened to women—but not to those who were painted and powdered or who smoked in public.

In describing the Aryan woman's duties to the Volk, the Nazis often employed a distinctly military vocabulary. The Honor Cross of the German Mother was established (1938) in order to recognize the most important service a woman could render: the bearing of children. Long before this, families with many children had obtained special tax benefits (see page 358). Typically enough, the German mother was likened to the soldier in the front-line trenches. But these trenches were different from those occupied by men. Women students from the universities might proclaim their usefulness to the Volk, and stress their National Socialism, but to little or no avail—though the *Völkischer Beobachter* might occasionally print one of their statements in order to restore a balance in the Nazi view of women. More typical, however, is the pronouncement of the official Nazi publication which strongly rejects the existence of "political women" within the party and demands their return to the sphere of family and motherhood.

The Nazi ideal of womanhood illustrates well the traditionalism of their revolution. They believed they were pursuing the ideal of the Germanic race of ancient times, but in reality they had embraced merely the bourgeois ideal of the nineteenth century: the simple but devoted housewife and mother who lives solely for her family and behaves dutifully toward her husband. The modern concept of beauty is rejected together with the contemporary emancipation of women. Every revolution is puritanical, for men's thoughts should be on "higher" matters than those of the flesh. Did not Robespierre during the French Revolution assert that "virtue must be woman's only ornament." But here this female ideal illustrates the *embourgeoisement* of the Nazi movement, the taming of the activism typified by the SA.

The social reality had to be adjusted to these ideals. The condemnation of the afternoon "tea and dancing" is significant in this regard. "Tea and dancing" was a regular part of the social life of the upper classes in Germany as well as throughout the rest of Europe. The Nazis' condemnation of this custom illuminates some deep preconceptions of their ideology. "Tea and dancing" is international and therefore not properly German; at a time when Hitler stressed the rootedness of the arts such music and dancing represented a cosmopolitan vagabondage. Moreover, puritanism comes to the fore once more: the kind of conversation encouraged here is superficial, not concerned with those essentials upon which the German mind should focus. National Socialism regarded modern dancing as harmful to its ideal of womanhood for its rhythms were thought to be an open incitement to sexual promiscuity. Such dancing amounted to an Asiatic orgy—typified by the "Negro music" of jazz (though the Soviet Union under Stalin, Marxist and Asiatic in Nazi eyes, shared an identical attitude toward jazz and modern dancing).

"Tea and dancing" was a symptom of modernity, of a piece with the degeneracy of modern music and modern art. Such modern art could be seen in the same year that this article was published (1937), in the Munich "Exhibition of Degenerate Art" (see page 11). "Tea and dancing," like everything else, was seen in terms of the Nazi ideology: it is no coincidence that this article was published in the newspaper of the SA, who prided themselves on being the "simple" and unsophisticated representatives of the Nazi movement.

Reality in some cases tended to escape the clutches of ideology, especially when the Nazi elite gave a party. The "love gods" who danced on Peacock Island (near Berlin) and the use of the best dance bands are difficult to reconcile with the criticisms of "tea and dancing" made a year later. Joseph Goebbels gave this party in July 1936, and it was attended by some three thousand guests. To be sure, it was meant to impress the many foreigners who were present, for the Minister of Propaganda was playing host to the participants in the Olympic Games and their guests. However, the entertainment could have been more subdued, folk-dancing exhibitions could have taken the place of dancing to the international tunes of excellent jazz orchestras. The love gods, it must be added, were clad, however lightly. Goebbels did make an effort to see that as little of the festivities as possible got to the press. At his luxurious estate at Schwanenwerder he gave many other parties of this sort; he did not need an international congress to justify a gay time.

Nor did puritan simplicity extend to festive occasions, such as the annual ball for the press. Gambling too was not affected, even in wartime. The advertisement for croupier candidates was published in the official paper of the Karlsruhe NSDAP. This hardly sounds like a fit occupation for the ideal Aryan as represented by the "bear" of an SA leader.

For all this, the leadership as a whole, and especially Adolf Hitler, tended to be frugal and generally lived up to the desired morality. This bourgeois morality served to tame the activism, to channel it against the enemies of the Reich. The Nazi world view, and the culture which sprang from it, made a puritanical, moral ideal its own concern. Thus the Nazi revolution could appeal to traditionalism, to the good old times, and yet provide an outlet for the activism so vital for the dynamic of the movement.

G.L.M.

THE GOOD FIGHT

Here Marched the New Germany
FRIEDRICH JOACHIM KLAEHN

September 1932! The old system still triumphed, the bigwigs in office clung to their titular dignities, the police still wielded their clubs viciously. But we didn't let anyone get the best of us. We wanted to prove to these people that their positions were crumbling beneath them and to show with what holy faith we await the future Reich of Adolf Hitler.

The SA unit had to be defended. For this reason we were called together one evening in the meeting hall of the capital city of the province.

It was forbidden for the assault troops to march in closed ranks. If here and there four or five men started out toward the meeting hall together, a patrol wagon would suddenly appear and the police would begin to swing their rubber truncheons without warning.

Singing was forbidden.

Carrying banners was forbidden.

Transportation by trucks, private automobiles, bicycles, and other means was forbidden.

It was forbidden for the SA units to stand outside the meeting hall. The rabble gathered on the streets. But on this day they did not dare to make themselves conspicuous by shouting or spitting, for then they could be beaten up.

These comrades of the darkness waited for individual SA men in dark doorways and on lonely streets. The patrol wagons of the defense police whizzed over the cobbled streets, and played searchlights over the crowd streaming toward the meeting hall, in order to see whether any formations of SA men were being assembled.

Police patrols streamed through the dark training area behind the hall, not to protect us against the Communists who were lurking about, but lustily looking for Brown-shirt victims for their clubs.

The meeting hall, which could hold 7,000 persons, was gaily deco-

24

rated—at least to the extent that the police had allowed, for the display of posters with inciting inscriptions was thought to endanger the Republic.

A giant rectangle had been kept clear in the middle of the hall. The seats to the right and left of it had been occupied long before the beginning of the celebration by civilians, by the relatives of SA men, by their women and children, and by people for whom the SA had become what it should be: the last hope for and the last faith in the Fatherland.

By way of exception, the police allowed the assault troops to form outside the hall. But on this night, to be sure, the same thing occurred as always: the commanding lieutenant (Krauth was the scoundrel's name) of the police unit professed ignorance of this permission on the part of the police authorities and many telephone calls had to be made before the matter was cleared up in our favor.

But now the friction had begun. The SA formed itself into one block, forty men abreast in forty ranks, banners waving in the first ranks.

This block now was to march through the doors of the meeting hall to the tune of "The Badenweiler March" in a broad front and occupy the space in the hall that had been left vacant.

The SA-unit band had already begun to strike up the tune, but the SA did not come, because First Lieutenant Krauth would not permit the side doors to be opened.

The standard-bearer argued with the First Lieutenant and the Reichsbanner[1] leader, while the SA stood at parade rest.

Hard words were exchanged. At the very moment when the First Lieutenant began to shout in a shrill voice and he was about to call out to his unit to arrest the standard-bearer, the latter's command resounded loudly: "Clear the way!"

The block marched and the police stepped back in the face of the rhythmically raised SA boots and legs. Slowly the block of the SA, flawlessly lined up on the point man and the rear man, moved into the meeting hall. The music boomed out and the civilians stood up and raised their hands in salute. Brightly lit eyes greeted us! Many eyes filled with tears. Here marched the new Germany. Here ancient Germany was reawakening. They are the men who will save us, who are our future.

[1] The Reichsbanner was a voluntary defense organization composed of men loyal to the Republic.

Then joy broke out and all the annoyance over the chicanery of the police disappeared. What was it to us that these men were still there, confused, with woebegone faces, trying to preserve their rotten system? Soon these men would be forgotten, swept away, liquidated! Germany would awake!

Commands resound. The SA stands!

The standard-bearer ascended the broad podium. His gaze swept over his unit, over the glorious banners, and over the people awaiting the future men of the Third Reich. At a celebration like this, there was no point in excoriating the existing system. But the leader could not refrain from dealing it a sudden blow with a trenchant observation to the overzealous police who were present. He said that we National Socialists could not imagine that those who were there today in green uniforms, allegedly in order to preserve order and peace, and who today were called police but who in actuality extended protection only to their like-minded comrades, that these men someday would exercise the same function in our Reich. When soon the swastika waves from all public buildings, this green phantom and terror will vanish.

Before the police had fully understood these words and before the thunderous applause, the standard-bearer returned to his theme and said: "You are SA men not just for these years of struggle or during the service that you are now performing; you are SA men for your whole life. All the spiritual and physical energy that you possess, all your time and means, belongs to the people and to the Fatherland and to the Führer, even life itself. Now the oath! Attention!"

The civilians rose from their seats. The oath of loyalty and commitment was pronounced, word by word, loudly and clearly, by the SA men. Then the standard-bearer paced off and every SA man stepped forward from the ranks, and placing his hand on the banner, declared: "I pledge it to my Führer!"

The "Horst Wessel" song and the "Deutschland Lied" ended this unforgettable celebration.

During the night the patrol wagons roared through the streets. The police were in a state of heightened preparedness.

The SA men went back to their homes one by one. There were many bloody heads that night, but it wasn't only among us, for now one couldn't attack SA men with impunity.

At this celebration the unit leader took leave of his troop. But he did not tell anybody, since here the individual is nothing, the idea everything.

From Friedrich Joachim Klaehn, *Sturm 138: Ernstes und viel Heiteres aus dem SA-Leben* (Leipzig: Verlag H. Schaufuss, 1934), pp. 202-207.

A Meeting-Hall Brawl
KURT MASSMANN

Once we held a meeting in a workers' suburb. The meeting had been called by us National Socialist students.

It was a very small meeting hall. One SA troop sufficed to guard the gathering. Around nine-thirty another SA troop was expected to show up at the close of the meeting in order to protect the participants from possible attack. . . .

At eight o'clock the giant Schirmer, who was to speak that night, rolled up his shirt sleeves and with a friendly smile spat into his hands, which were as big as an average-sized trunk. He had been in Russia for three years and was familiar with the whole swindle there. Upon his return to Germany he became a National Socialist with all heart and soul, one of those who cause shivers to go through the hearts of the timid bourgeois, anxious over the dangerous "Socialism" rampant among the National Socialists! A splendid fellow! A man to whom one could entrust all one's money and who would sooner kick the bucket from hunger before he would take a penny of it.

It is said that one day he was introduced to the Führer. The tall, uncouth lad, who otherwise was never at a loss for words, just stood there, swallowed hard, wiped his eyes with his fore-paw, and finally stammered: "Well, Adolf Hitler . . ." and exuberantly shook his hand. Then he came to his senses, blushed fiery red—oh, holy miracle!—pulled himself to his full height, saluted, and marched off with a smart about-face.

The SA man pushed himself through the roaring crowd, which had been staging a noisy reception for fifteen minutes, and took his place in a very narrow space in front of the podium.

It was a remarkable situation! There was a terrible ruckus lasting a half hour, nothing but a deafening din. There was no act of violence. Schirmer, the bear, stood on the podium, his mighty arms crossed, and smiled at the goings-on in the hall with a relaxed, unconcerned air. . . .

Gradually this smile produced its effect. The din slowly died down and gave way to an air of tense expectancy.

Around eight-thirty Schirmer grabbed the water carafe, placed it to his lips, took a hearty swallow, and then poured the water into a glass that had been placed alongside the carafe. He took this glass and directed the water most skillfully over the heads of the SA and right into the neck of a man in the first row who had been yelling and egging on the crowd in the hall the whole time. Then Schirmer, abruptly and with a powerful voice, roared: "Quiet! Now I'll do the talking!" And indeed quiet descended on the hall in an instant.

Then he let loose. He spoke in simple, plain words, in the everyday speech of these workers. They listened to him.

In the middle of the hall, which had been the source of the din the whole evening, a little Jew with horn-rimmed spectacles set on a thick nose climbed on a chair and began to give an opposing speech in an unpleasant and high-pitched voice like that of a eunuch.

Schirmer made a contemptuous motion with his hand and continued speaking in a voice that was so powerful that the echo reverberated from the walls and completely drowned out the whimpering of the little man on the chair.

But the little man persisted in his aim to break up the meeting and ranted on and on with an unheard-of display of gestures.

When Schirmer, who had just spoken about the community of fate of the Volk, paused for a moment, the little Jew could be heard screaming: "Workers! Proletarians! Your front is the international proletariat! . . . Your . . ." No further words were heard. Schirmer had pushed his way through the thick chain of the SA men and went all by himself through the shouting crowd straight up to the little Jew, the spokesman and leader of the Communists. The Jew cut his speech short in astonishment, and although he was surrounded by three hundred and fifty comrades, he climbed down from the chair with a monkeylike agility and stepped back a few rows. Schirmer shrugged his shoulders, and had a grim expression on his face. Then he roared at the people in the hall: "Workers, look at the toad who brought you here and then look at me! I'm a worker like you are! I produce with my fists like you! Do you belong to him over there or to me? . . ."

The Jew, meanwhile, was screaming: "Comrades, he wants to provoke us!" Schirmer could no longer speak amid the tumult that had
been unleashed. Grimly, he returned to the podium and continued to
speak from there.

But the little Jew had climbed on his chair once more. He certainly
had reason to fear that his people could be influenced by this speaker,
and he gave the signal to break up the meeting. "Let's go!" he
screamed. "Moscow! Let's go!"

In a moment the hall resounded with yells, ear-shattering noises,
blows, and wild screaming.

Schirmer stood on the podium and roared a few times the word
"Germany!" into the hall with such strength that it could be heard
above the din. "Germany!" It sounded like a trumpet call. I did not
know whether this word was actually part of his speech or whether it
was a last exhortation thrown into the meeting-hall brawl. After utter-
ing it he sprang into the fray with a mighty leap.

At that moment the main door of the hall was opened and the
second SA troop stormed in. The little Jew, who a minute ago had still
looked like an unlucky Napoleon, stood on his chair as if paralyzed.
Schirmer, who was knocking down his opponents right and left, had
already gotten close to the Jewish ringleader along with a couple of
SA men. In a really artistic movement, the Jew leaped from his chair,
ran like a weasel through the hall, between the brawlers, and jumped
through the closed window into the courtyard, the shattered glass
panes crashing on the ground with him.

For a moment a current of laughter coursed through the hall.

Most of the Communists, above all the main hecklers, had already
fled through the side door. Only a little band of Reds tenaciously
defended themselves in a corner. I saw that those who resisted were
precisely the best-looking among the Communists, mostly older workers.

Soon even the resistance of these people was broken. They were allowed to leave unmolested, after they had given up.

The hall was a scene of desolation. It was covered with blood, not
a single chair was in one piece, wreckage was strewn everywhere.
Some of the Communists, not those of the last group, had fought
with beer bottles and glasses!

About eight SA men had received head injuries from these rude
and contemptible weapons. The faces of some of them were so en-

crusted with blood that it covered their eyes and they groped around the hall like blind men.

Several Communists remained stretched out on the floor. When the SA medics began to attend to their injuries, an older worker with a good clean-cut face, who had fought to the last and defended himself with real courage, exchanging blow for blow, took his party book from his pocket, tore his party badge from his lapel, and handed both to the giant Schirmer, whom he had demanded to see. He shook his hand and said: "So, now I'm cured!" After he was bandaged he signed an entry blank to join the National Socialist Workers' Party. . . .

The eternal petit bourgeois complained about the "primitivization of politics." They said that things would not improve in Germany by people busting one another's heads in.

They had no idea of what was at stake! The fight for the soul of German man and the new Germany was being fought even in such assemblies and in such brawls at meeting halls!

We National Socialist students did not go into working-class quarters to have our heads broken for nothing! Neither did we do it to win a dozen votes for some election or other, which wouldn't have been worth the effort. We could have held academic discussion evenings, which at least would have been less dangerous.

We fought for the German worker. We wanted to help the worker take his place in the nation!

Often we had to use fists and chair legs in order to reach him and to drive out the racially alien "leaders" and their bodyguards who stood between them and us!

> From *Kampf: Lebensdokumente deutscher Jugend von 1914-1934*, compiled and edited by Bert Roth (Leipzig: Philipp Reclam jun., Verlag, 1934), pp. 228-232.

THE BONDS OF FAMILY

National Socialism Has Restored the Family
HANNS ANDERLAHN

"The family . . ." Wernicke began falteringly, not knowing just what to say. If the others up front would start laughing, he was thinking, then I could get out of it. I have nothing to say on the subject! But they all kept looking at him. The Assault Leader had an ice-cold expression on his face, full of scorn and anger. The minutes became nerve-racking, hammering, overwhelming eternities.

"The family is of no concern to us!" A voice from the audience finally came to his assistance. "We are SA men, we do our duty, we are National Socialists, and nothing else concerns us."

For a moment this seemed to be satisfactory. Indeed, it was very decent of the Assault Leader to come to his aid. So he parroted after him: "Nothing else concerns us!" But this didn't sound quite right. Hadn't the Assault Leader hammered into him a hundred times the phrase: "The service of an SA man never ends"? Wernicke remained silent. He paced up and down, unsure of himself, and then suddenly the pallid, tear-stained face of his wife stood before him: "What am I supposed to fill the children's bellies with?" Perhaps the comrades also saw that face now, and Wernicke felt the hot blood rushing to his brain.

"So you can't say anything on the subject? I thought so. So sit down!" The Assault Leader said nothing else, but every word had felt like a blow, cut him like a lash, and left behind a painful feeling of shame.

SA man Dietrich took great delight in being told to get up and speak. "The family is the most important cell of the state. Whoever disturbs the family acts against the well-being of the state. National Socialism has restored the family to its rightful place. We do not want any petit-bourgeois ideal in the family, with its plush-sofa psychology and walking mannikins, with its contempt for and degradation of the woman and effeminization of the children. We know that the wife has a heavy burden to bear. The National Socialist stands beside her because she lends him a helping hand. The wife is a comrade, a fellow combatant." Everything he said was simple and clear; everybody could understand him, even Wernicke. "What am I supposed to fill the children's bellies with?" How that bored through him and pained him at that moment.

"How was it before?" asked the Assault Leader, his eyes still blazing with anger and contempt.

Otto Dennig had not been asked at all, but he stood up and talked because he had to speak now: "In my assault troop at that time there was one who was married. The young bride knew us all, and if things got tough with someone and he didn't have a place to stay or was hungry, all he had to do was show up at the flat and everything would be all right. Then came a time when her husband would not be at home in the evening for weeks on end. In those days we would travel to the villages on our bikes. We tried to protect each other at our meetings, but when the others lay in ambush for us, there would be bandaged heads.

"The young bride stood at the window every evening until we came back, and sometimes we would not return until dawn. We always saw the light burning from afar; it was like a symbol to us. Before going to our own homes we usually sat around together in the tiny kitchen awhile, unwinding and telling jokes.

"One evening they threw garbage at us in the street. They outnumbered us and occupied well-defended positions. Here retreat was the best defense. We got on our bikes and started down the steep hill. One of our group fell off his bike at the bottom of the hill. We didn't notice it until after we had gone a little further. We turned back and found him lying unconscious under his bike. He died on the way to the hospital without regaining consciousness. And now we had to break the news to the young bride. It was terrible for all of us to see how she wept softly to herself, because she loved him very, very much. But never once did she ask: 'Why?'

"Later she moved back with her parents, for he had had no one besides her and us. When in 1933 we held a great torchlight parade, she suddenly appeared. She went up to each one of us, and when the order came: 'SA, halt! Forward in equal step . . . march!' we saw her smiling. We passed by her, eyes right, as though he stood there too, and a couple of us had to make odd movements with our faces to control our feelings. That was a young family, and at that time I had sworn to myself: No petit-bourgeois marriage for me, no lazy lounging around on a plush sofa and in indifferent luxury. The girl that I marry must be like that young bride. Yes, that's how it's going to be with me. And I am getting married next month."

All this had little or nothing to do with ideology and education. Or did it?

The Assault Leader bowed to Otto Dennig. "Thanks!" Was he referring to the story or to the announcement of the marriage? Actually, he wanted to break off the discussion here. For Wernicke it was enough for the time being, but now the discussion was in full swing. "That's the way it was before, but now it's easier. Life and health are no longer at stake, only comfort. What still remains is the inner sense of commitment and he who does not possess it is not with us. Some have already been weakened by the chatter of their relatives, the plush sofa, the creature comforts. Or the wife bends their ears, nagging them because she gets anxious at night or because she finds it too boring to be alone, she has perhaps no mission, and then the men get upset, become lax and listless, and stay away. . . .

"In the evening each one of us gladly stretches out his legs and sits back and rests, with the thought: 'At last, I'm at home!' But this sitting around and relaxing must not become a purpose in itself and a world view. The purpose of rest is to release energies for a new struggle and for the further march forward. . . ."

Couldn't someone think up an activity in which wives and young women could also participate, so that everyone could get acquainted with each other? Then maybe some would have a different view. Three, four voices expressed this wish. All the others nodded their heads in agreement, and one man immediately developed a program: charades, for example, the dying warrior, and then perhaps a play— Homecoming in the Dawn—and, in between, battle songs. . . .

"Waving banners, patriotic speeches, and then three cheers," Otto Hallmann said, grinning. "It's not so easy to bury this idea of a dramatic group, my boys. Your proposal sounds like something that would be better left to lackluster bowling leagues. If we're going to do anything, let's do it with sense and understanding. In the afternoon, athletics, in conjunction with other branches of the party. In the evening, a big cultural gathering, and SA man Dietrich will be responsible for carrying it out. Then we can also see whether we understood what the Führer has prescribed for us in the way of intellectual orientation."

"Yes, sir, Assault Leader. I'll lay the program before you the evening of the day after tomorrow."

From Hanns Anderlahn, Gegner erkannt! Kampferlebnisse der SA. (Munich: Zentralverlag der NSDAP, Frz. Eher Nachf., 1937), pp. 60-63.

The German Volk Is an Interlacing of Families
LUDWIG LEONHARDT

Deeply perceiving the source of the renewal of the Volk, National Socialism considers the family to be the foundation of the state. In order to grasp the importance of this statement and to evaluate it properly, we must look more closely at the concept of "family." By family we must not understand only parents and children. To a family, in our sense of the word, belong not only those who bear the name or who possess a piece of land or some other property. Neither do legal relationships alone encompass the concept. Rather, the family embraces everything that existed spiritually and psychically as a living patrimony in a definite circle of persons. What we are, what we accomplish, is not due to our own merit; in the last analysis we owe it to our parents and grandparents, our whole line of ancestors, whose heritage we carry within ourselves. In short, we owe it to the spiritual values which have been transmitted to us and which we are to pass on to our children and the children of our children. All this belongs to the family, whose importance in the life of the nation the new state is ready to acknowledge in the fullest sense. And we must always keep in mind that we are not the last configuration of these multiple endowments, that we are destined to pass them on pure and unspoiled in order to continue what we call the family, and to push our heritage ever forward, so that a German Volk may emerge out of an ever-repeated interlacing of families.

In this goal, however, it is clear that each of us bears an enormous responsibility. Just as we cannot let such a precious heritage go to ruin, just as we cannot allow ourselves to be guilty of harming it, so must we strive to extirpate, to overcome, or to destroy the bad and the inferior. How can the individual get a clear idea of just how he represents this responsibility toward the Volk? Can he do this without a precise knowledge of his whole hereditary and physical picture, hence without an exact knowledge of his own being and of the being of his ancestors? No! He who loves only for the day, who is indifferent to the roots from which he sprang, who does not realize the importance of the words "forefathers" and "posterity" in their deepest sense, cannot be regarded as a responsibility-conscious member of the Volk community.

Therefore let us begin by studying our own family picture! It will require a good deal of work in the case of those families where no records of any kind have been made or kept, but it must be done. If we wish to be honest, we must confess that in only the fewest instances is our information adequate for providing even a moderately clear picture. Unfortunately, many people hardly know the color of the eyes of their parents and of their brothers and sisters, much less their grandparents, not to speak of the more important characteristics of mind and disposition. Thus each one of us has the duty to inform himself in the greatest possible detail on this, to find out from which stock he springs. . . .

From Ludwig Leonhardt, *Heirat und Rassenpflege: Ein Berater für Eheanwärter* (Munich: J. F. Lehmanns Verlag, 1934), pp. 7-8.

Marriage, Morality, and Property
HERMANN PAULL

I come back to genealogy. This is possible only where monogamy has led to the formation of the family and thus to clearly perceptible biological hereditary stocks. With free love, which aims to offer man many possibilities of change in the exercise of sexual intercourse and in human breeding, a wholly unsurveyable ancestral series comes into being whose biological investigation is much too complicated and therefore wholly impossible. In free love, in which the mutual impulse to union is contained exclusively in erotic feelings, the confluence of the germ-plasma endowments of both parents is left exclusively to chance, whereas monogamy, through the elaboration of perceptible biological hereditary stocks, enables human reason to bring together high-grade hereditary stocks for human breeding and to exterminate herditary stocks of inferior grade.

In this context free love means the admission of inferior biological ancestry to human breeding and the necessary squandering of high-grade germ endowments, whereas monogamy at least offers the opportunity for biological selection and preservation of the high-grade germ plasma.

Thus biological investigation has uncovered a series of families in which, as a result of the entry of individuals or even only one person of low-grade quality, the whole subsequent generation was ruined. The Kallikak family in America and the Zeros in Switzerland are now universally recognized as prototypes for the degeneration of whole families through the infiltration of inferior individuals.

On the other hand, we are acquainted with a sufficient number of families in which the preservation of a family tradition which took account of soundness and excellence has engendered a great number of high-grade persons. Here I shall mention the clan of Johann Sebastian Bach of Thüringen, which has been thoroughly investigated biologically, and which rightly can serve as a textbook example of the preservation and higher development of a good biological heritage.

Thus the family is the most important instrument of eugenics. It will become even more clear later that the eugenic concept of "family" in its deepest essence is synonymous with the Christian concept of a "religious-moral family," which rests upon the twin pillars of "premarital chastity" and "conjugal fidelity."

The free-thinker: Where in any part of the world have people based their marriage choices on such biological principles? It can be proved that men have indeed never known about the doctrine of the germ plasma and of the law of heredity. And prostitution in all times has found room for itself between the pillars of "premarital chastity" and "conjugal fidelity." Hence mankind should have gone to ruin a long time ago because of the squandering of germ plasma.

Eros is too much of a roguish lad for him ever to bother about the law of heredity, or ever to give it a thought.

The doctor: This objection is not correct in this sharp form, for it can easily be shown that the bonds of a religious, ethical, and economic kind, under which the men living in the times before industrialization, which with some justice can be called the "good, old times," made their marriage choice, to a great measure have had the effect of specializing and breeding germ plasma. Naturally the biological power of these bonds was not always known to man, but this did not limit their effectiveness.

Let us for a moment return to the roots of human culture.

The introduction of monogamy—that is, the overcoming of promiscuity, of the general mixing, of the belonging to all in sexual intercourse—was the first germ-plasma specializing bond. Further, it signifies the fettering, the bridling of the naturally polygamous instinct of the male sex, as opposed to the female sex.

This fettering raised the male Eros out of the depths of the purely animal instincts to the heights of a moral happiness. It freed woman from the immoral and undignified position of being the object of man's lust, and placed her alongside him as an equal marriage partner.

Woman's honor, woman's dignity and material happiness, owe their existence to this fettering of the male Eros through monogamy.

Hence monogamy also stands at the beginning of our culture. It led to a further bond through which germ-plasma breeding was enormously fostered, generally accepted "morals." Morals and morality strive to attain something lofty, to overcome bad conditions. Morality strives for health and beauty. "Good morality" demanded a far-reaching purity in sexual life and it also prevented prostitution in Germany from assuming dimensions that would have been immensely harmful to the people's welfare, at least in the times under discussion here.

It was good morals for a woman to have several children. A childless married woman was regarded as inferior, as was a woman who had many miscarriages, or who brought deformed, sick, or sickly children into the world.

In former times, the doubtlessly greater concern of the parents not only with the moral but especially with the material welfare of their children, the greater feeling of responsibility for the future generation, is closely connected with this. A man who was not yet in a position to feed a wife and a troop of children either had to renounce marriage temporarily or had to rely on his wife's dowry.

In other words, one married frequently, or mostly, on the basis of property. But in those days, since there was no shareholder's right and no mammon-like capital formations, property was linked to the ability of the men concerned. Capital did not yet work independently of the ability of an individual proprietor. Whoever had possessed a fortune either had acquired it through his own ability or had inherited it through his parents, who had acquired it through their ability. The increase and preservation of property could take place only through the ability of the individual proprietor. Property-possessing families therefore were also proficient families. Whoever married property also married a high-grade biological heritage.

The history professor: The guild system also surely worked favorably in a biological sense. Membership in a guild presupposed an extensive proficiency. This was in the nature of the guild. One preferably married within one's own guild or took his life comrade from another guild. This provided a certain guarantee for happiness in life. For in this way high-grade biological heritage was brought together for human breeding.

It is certainly no accident that the musical endowments of the Bach family, cultivated over two centuries in a wholly special way through guild marriages, vanished from the biological heritage of the Bachs with the cessation of the guild system.

The doctor: To be dependent upon others ran counter to the general bourgeois concept of honor. Upon entering a marriage the bourgeois so arranged his affairs that he could live independently as a free man. He strove to acquire esteem among his fellow burghers for himself and his wife. Therefore he looked for a wife in esteemed, proficient families and in consequence of such considerations also married a high-grade biological heritage.

The situation has become wholly different as a result of the extensive industrialization and especially the Marxist spirit of the postwar age.

Thanks to public welfare, broad strata of the people no longer need to concern themselves with the material upbringing of their children. When money for the vital necessities cannot be procured by the parents, the welfare agency takes over this task. This happens especially in the case of children whose progenitors have no reason to be proud of their biological heritage and who therefore, in a biological sense, are unsuitable for producing children. It is well known that the greatest lack of scruples with regard to producing children prevails among inferior-grade families.

Thus, according to the findings of an inquiry made in 1928, the children in the Welfare School in Stuttgart came from families who had an average of 4.6 children. On the other hand, the average number of children possessed by the totality of fruitful married couples of the middle class in Stuttgart is 2.3, and that of the whole population 2.32.

These few figures express the serious life crisis in which the German people finds itself at this time.

From Hermann Paull, *Deutsche Rassenhygiene: Ein gemein-verständliches Gespräch über Vererbungslehre, Eugenik,*

Familie, Sippe, Rasse und Volkstum, Part II: *Erbgesundheitspflege (Eugenik), Rassenpflege* (Görlitz: Verlag für Sippenforschung und Wappenkunde, C. A. Starke, 1934), pp. 17-21.

THE IDEAL OF WOMANHOOD

The Tasks of Women
ADOLF HITLER

. . . So long as we possess a healthy manly race—and we National Socialists will attend to that—we will form no female mortar battalions and no female sharpshooter corps. For that is not equality of rights, but a diminution of the rights of woman. . . .

An unlimited range of work opportunities exists for women. For us the woman has always been man's most loyal comrade in work and in life. I am often told: You want to drive women out of the professions. Not at all. I wish only to create the broadest measure of possibility for her to co-found her own family and to be able to have children, because by so doing she most benefits our Volk! . . .

If today a female jurist accomplishes ever so much and next door there lives a mother with five, six, seven children, who are all healthy and well-brought-up, then I would like to say: From the standpoint of the eternal value of our people the woman who has given birth to children and raised them and who thereby has given back our people life for the future has accomplished *more* and does *more!*

From a speech to the National Socialist women's organization (Die Frauenschaft), published in the *Völkischer Beobachter,* Sept. 13, 1936. (Wiener Library Clipping Collection.)

The so-called granting of equal rights to women, which Marxism demands, in reality does not grant equal rights but constitutes a deprivation of rights, since it draws the woman into an area in which she will necessarily be inferior. It places the woman in situations that cannot strengthen her position—vis-à-vis both man and society—but only weaken it. . . .

I would be ashamed to be a German man if in the event of a war even only one woman had to go to the front. The woman has her own battlefield. With every child that she brings into the world, she fights her battle for the nation. The man stands up for the Volk, exactly as the woman stands up for the family.

> From a speech to the National Socialist Women's Congress, published in the Völkischer Beobachter, Sept. 15, 1935. (Wiener Library Clipping Collection.)

Emancipation from the Emancipation Movement
ALFRED ROSENBERG

Emancipation of woman from the women's emancipation movement is the first demand of a generation of women which would like to save the Volk and the race, the Eternal-Unconscious, the foundation of all culture, from decline and fall.

The age of Victorianism and the "dreamy romantic girl's life" are naturally finished once and for all. The woman belongs deeply to the total life of the people. All educational opportunities must remain open to her. Through rhythmics, gymnastics, and sport the same care must be given to her physical training as is the case with men. Nor should any difficulties be created for her in the vocational world under present-day social conditions (whereby the Law for the Protection of Mothers should be more strongly implemented). Doubtless, however, the efforts of those who would renew our Volkdom, after breaking up the Volk-alien democratic-Marxist system, must prepare the way for a social order which no longer forces young women (as is today the case) to stream in droves to the labor markets of life which use up the most important feminine energies. Hence all possibilities for the development of a woman's energies should remain open to her. But there must be clarity on one point: only man must be and remain a judge, soldier, and ruler of the state.

> From Alfred Rosenberg, Der Mythos des XX. Jahrhunderts (Munich: Hoheneichen-Verlag, 1930), p. 512. (This extract has been taken from the 1938 edition.)

Domestic Diligence from Blood and Soil

It might seem amazing that women and girls should return to work at spinning wheels and weaving looms. But this is wholly natural. It was something that could have been foreseen. This work must be taken up again by the women and girls of the Third Reich.

> From the *Völkischer Beobachter*, Feb. 2, 1936. (Wiener Library Clipping Collection.)

The Female Bird
JOSEPH GOEBBELS

The mission of woman is to be beautiful and to bring children into the world. This is not at all as rude and unmodern as it sounds. The female bird pretties herself for her mate and hatches the eggs for him. In exchange, the mate takes care of gathering the food, and stands guard and wards off the enemy.

> From Joseph Goebbels, *Michael: Ein deutsches Schicksal in Tagebuchblättern* (Munich: Zentralverlag der NSDAP, Frz. Eher Nachf., 1929), p. 41. (Wiener Library Clipping Collection.) (This extract has been taken from the 1934 edition.)

Women That We Can Love

After a performance by an *a cappella* choir, the Führer's deputy, Reich Minister Hess, took the floor and was jubilantly greeted by those present.

The Führer's deputy began his speech with the remark that in Germany the honorable place held by woman as mother, as comrade of her husband, and as an equal member of the Volk community is taken as a matter of course. Then he briefly contested the views of

German women that have been spread abroad, and compared the foreign concepts of woman with the type of woman which the new Germany aims to produce: "We want women in whose life and work the characteristically feminine is preserved—women that we can love!

"We grant the rest of the world the ideal type of woman that it wishes for itself, but the rest of the world should kindly grant us the woman which is most suitable to us. Not that 'Gretchen type' which foreigners imagine as being a somewhat limited, indeed unintellectual creature, but a woman who is capable of intellectually standing at her husband's side in his interests, in his struggle for existence, who makes the world more beautiful and richer in content for him. This is the ideal woman of the German man of today. She is a woman who, above all, is also able to be a mother.

"And it is one of the greatest achievements of National Socialism," continued the Führer's deputy, "that it made it possible for more women in Germany today to become mothers than ever before. They become mothers not merely because the state wants it so or because their husbands want it so. Rather, they become mothers because they themselves are proud to bring healthy children into the world, to bring them up for the nation, and in this way to do their part in the preservation of the life of their Volk."

> From an account of a mass meeting of the Berlin National Socialist women's organization (Die Frauenschaft) and the Frauenwerk (Women's Social Welfare) in the Deutschland-Hall, published in the *Völkischer Beobachter*, May 27, 1936. (Wiener Library Clipping Collection.)

Frau Goebbels on German Women

A woman reporter of the London *Daily Mail* came to Heiligendamm to visit Frau Magda Goebbels, whom she had called "the ideal woman of Germany." She wanted to learn more details about the new status of women in Germany. Frau Goebbels told her visitor that the accounts printed in England about the expulsion of women from their jobs are highly exaggerated. The German woman has been excluded from only three professions: the military (as is the case all over the world), government, and the practice of law.

If the German girl is faced with a choice of marriage or a career, she will always be encouraged to marry, since this undoubtedly is best for a woman. According to the report of the English woman journalist, Frau Goebbels said: "I am trying to make the German woman more beautiful."

> From the *Vossische Zeitung*, July 6, 1933. (Wiener Library Clipping Collection.)

The Blond Craze

Brunswick, May 31.—SS Chief Group Leader Jeckeln attacked the "blond craze" at a meeting of the NSDAP. Blond hair and blue eyes by themselves, he said, were not convincing proof that one belongs to the Nordic race. A girl who wants to marry an SS man today must be above reproach in every respect. Therefore she is required to possess the Reich sports medal. Many people, perhaps even today, could not understand the reason for this requirement. Germany does not need women who can dance beautifully at five o'clock teas, but women who have given proof of their health through accomplishments in the field of sport. "The javelin and the springboard are more useful than lipstick in promoting health."

> From the *Frankfurter Zeitung*, June 1, 1937. (Wiener Library Clipping Collection.)

A Shiny Nose and the German Nation

Recently we read the following in an article on girls' Labor Service camps. It set us to thinking:

> The physical facilities of the camp must never go beyond a certain simplicity, for the girl must be trained along Spartan lines in the Labor Service—by habituation to the pallet of straw, to early risings in the morning-cold, to the simplest washing facilities, to the renunciation of all beauty aids and treatments, to the simplest clothing, which is to be as uniform as possible.

But what is too much, is too much. Even we consider early rising one of the virtues of woman. But to habituate "to early risings in the morning-cold"? Wouldn't it be all right also without the morning-cold? And as far as the "simplest washing facilities" are concerned, this can mean either magic or a country water pump. We don't know whether the author is married or not. In the last analysis this is his private affair. But anyone who writes for life must not sit at his writing desk and dream of a "tough" race and of the old Spartans, who, as is known, knew how to distinguish between the education of men and women on the basis of well-considered reasons. We want German women and not tough-eggs as our comrades along life's path. There is no woman who renounces "all beauty aids and treatments," which we must not confuse with the fabrication of masks in the style of the Kurfürstendamm.[1]

We would still like to meet an acceptable woman who for hygienic reasons will give up, say, powder when her little nose shines . . . and anyone who demands this categorically must, to be consistent, say with Orpheus the Second:

> Only when your countenance shines like bacon,
> Do you fulfill the purpose of the German nation!

Why must we always have such gross exaggerations anyway?

From *Der Angriff*, Jan. 16, 1936. (Wiener Library Clipping Collection.)

Faith and Beauty

Jutta Rüdiger, the Reich reporter of the Bund Deutscher Mädel, has on several occasions discussed the tasks of the BDM project "Faith and Beauty," such as at a convention of Hitler Youth leaders in Hammersbach on February 9 and in the Reich Youth Press Service.

According to her reports, the BDM program "Faith and Beauty" is not a radical departure for the BDM, but marks a logical step forward

[1] The Kurfürstendamm was a main street of Berlin where the most fashionable shops and restaurants were located. To the Nazis it was synonymous with decadent "Jewish" culture, and before 1933 they staged many disturbances there.

in the development of this girls' organization. Hence the usual uniform of the BDM will be maintained and participants in the program will be distinguished only by a special badge. It is planned to set up work communities for gymnastics, handicrafts, folklore, foreign affairs, games and music, health service, and the like. The groups meet weekly, and once a month the meetings take the form of evenings-at-home which are devoted to discussions of cultural life and the structuring and guidance of one's personal life.

> From Das Archiv: Nachschlagewerk für Politik, Wirtschaft, Kultur, No. 47, Feb. 1938 (Berlin: Verlagsanstalt D. Stollberg, 1938), p. 1393.

Right Conduct

The district plant department of the NSBO [1] in Unterfranken published a regulation in which it is stated that lately a great number of women had been accepted. This is a privilege of which women can be proud, and therefore it is also their duty to conduct themselves in a true National Socialist manner. It was therefore announced that painted and powdered women will be forbidden entry to all NSBO gatherings. Women who smoke in public—in hotels, in cafés, on the street, and so forth—will be expelled from the NSBO. Local officials are instructed to adopt similar rules.

> From the Frankfurter Zeitung, Aug. 11, 1933. (Wiener Library Clipping Collection.)

The Honor Cross of the German Mother

"The prolific German mother is to be accorded the same place of honor in the German Volk community as the combat soldier, since she risks her body and her life for the people and the Fatherland as much as the combat soldier does in the roar and thunder of battle." With these words, Reich Physician Leader Dr. Wagner, head of the

[1] National Sozialistischer Betriebs Obman (see page 21).

People's Health Section in the Reich leadership of the party, at the behest of the Führer, announced the creation of a Medal of Honor for prolific German mothers at the Party Day of Labor.

Three million German mothers, on the German Mother's Day in 1939, for the first time will be solemnly awarded the new badge of honor by the leaders of the party. These celebrations are to be held every year on Mother's Day and on the Awarding of Medals Day for prolific mothers.

The youth above all must be brought up with a reverence for the mothers of the people. Thus the honoring of German mothers with many children is not to be limited only to Mother's Day and to the Awarding of Medals Day. In the future the prolific mother will occupy the place that is due her in public life. *The young National Socialist will show his respect for her through the obligatory salute of all members of the youth formations of the party.* In addition, the wearers of the Honor Cross of the German Mother will henceforth enjoy all those privileges which are already possessed as a matter of course by meritorious racial comrades, disabled war veterans, and the martyrs of the National Socialist revolution—such privileges as honorary seats at party and government-sponsored gatherings, special treatment in government offices, and preferred seats assigned by conductors in rail coaches and trolley cars. Further, they are to be provided with old-age care and be given priority for acceptance in homes for the aged or in special sections of such homes already in existence.

For this honoring of the prolific mother and especially of the German aged mother by the Führer is not only an expression of thanks, but at the same time expresses the trust that the Führer, and with him the whole German people, has in all German mothers, that they will continue to help to pave the way for our people, and that they will make us a gift of that youth which, after perilous times, will crown the rise of our Volk. . . .

> From the *Völkischer Beobachter*, Dec. 25, 1938. (Wiener Library Clipping Collection.)

The Woman Student

"Woman student, what do you want in the Third Reich?" "After all, your place is at the cooking pot!" "The Führer does not want you to study." "Intellectual work is harmful to women!" After the seizure of power, we National Socialist women students repeatedly heard such statements. In fact, we still hear them once in a while.

How can it be, we asked ourselves, that anyone would want a National Socialist university without German women?

The National Socialist woman student places her whole life and achievement in the service of the German people. The tasks that are hers to fulfill clearly grow out of this attitude.

> From the Völkischer Beobachter, Dec. 11, 1935. (Wiener Library Clipping Collection.)

Against the Political Woman
ENGELBERT HUBER

There is no place for the political woman in the ideological world of National Socialism. . . .

The intellectual attitude of the movement on this score is opposed to the political woman. It refers the woman back to her nature-given sphere of the family and to her tasks as wife and mother. The postwar phenomenon of the political woman, who rarely cuts a good figure in parliamentary debates, signifies robbing woman of her dignity.

The German resurrection is a male event.

> From Engelbert Huber, Das ist Nationalsozialismus (Stuttgart: Union Deutsche Verlagsgesellschaft, 1933), pp. 121-122.

THE SOCIAL REALITY

Does the Five O'Clock Tea Suit Our Time?

The German people and all cultural-minded people in other countries are still feeling the impact of the Führer's speech at the Munich art festival. This speech is undoubtedly the most important cultural-political document of modern times.[1] And it did not take long to

---

[1] For this speech, see p. 11.

make itself felt in a practical way. The custodians of all government and private museums and art collections are busy removing the most hideous creations of a degenerate humanity and of a pathological generation of "artists" and in this way are helping to bring recognition to a true art imbued with a German spirit. This cleaning out of all works that bear this same Western Asiatic stamp has been set in motion in the field of literature as well, having begun with the symbolic burning of the most evil products of Jewish scribblers shortly after the seizure of power. On the other hand, the fact that a racially alien spirit, in conjunction with artistic impotence here and there, still produces swamp weeds in one of the most important fields of artistic creation, namely music, that even today it still asserts itself in the pages of a gutter journal of a disreputable tradition which doesn't seem to understand what coordination in music means, that it still disseminates an artistic interpretation and gives expression to the glorifiers of Negro music, is betrayed by a feuilleton[2] (this word alone is a fitting designation of this mental attitude) of a Berlin afternoon newspaper of August 19 of this year under the heading "Tea and Dancing." Either the author of this effusion has been living on the moon these past four years, or the dog days are responsible for this remarkable product of his Dada brain.

Tea and dancing: this is not only an excellent alliteration[3] but also an amalgamation of two concepts which, in content and in consonance with each other, are intimately and naturally connected, like the terms of such other alliterations as house and home,[4] bag and baggage.[5] Therefore, we must deal with them together, as a unit, in order to recognize and overcome the inner hollowness and the danger to the Volk posed by these forms of international civilized life.

One may think what one pleases about the custom of afternoon tea. No one can prescribe what beverages are most suitable for drinking, although the good old German coffee hour for family and goodfellowship has a tradition at least as glorious as the custom of the tea hour taken over from northern countries. After all, this is a question of taste, perhaps even of temperament. Fundamentally, however, we should reject the custom of the five o'clock tea which came to us from

[2] Referring to the cultural section of the press. Ever since this had developed in the nineteenth century, its style was highly subjective, introverted, and critical of all aspects of life. The Nazis put an end to it.
[3] In German: *Tee und Tanz.*
[4] *Haus und Hof.*
[5] *Kind und Kegel.*

England, where it is already a degenerate social form. We Germans have never known a five o'clock tea. First it was the modern way of life, shaped by the Jewish spirit, which, through the adoption of alien customs, has in all fields tried to hide the fact that it has no values and cultural forms of its own. Properly understood, it is not a question of the kind of beverage, much less the time of day which one devotes to this pleasure, since the author of the above-mentioned article recommends that in Berlin the tea hour be changed from five to four o'clock and, indeed, that one should not drink tea at all but "preferably coffee." Rather it is much more a question of a wholly distinct form of social life bearing the mark of an alien spirit.

By five o'clock tea, if it takes place in a private circle, one understands a chattering, sandwich-eating, tea-drinking, cigarette-puffing group of people circulating about a rubber-wheeled tea wagon which sets down the expensive cups now here and now there, wherever one pauses momentarily in one's wandering, only to pick them up again immediately thereafter. Five o'clock tea: that is to say, a social gathering in which one cultivates not conversation but gossip. In particular, it is thought that through this abominable American custom (namely, eating and drinking standing up) an especially agreeable and spontaneous conversation can develop, whereas actually only chatter is achieved, not conversation, if one walks up and down in a room with his hat, gloves and cookies in his hand, so that a clumsy waiter can knock over the full cup held with two fingers into the hat which floats from the third finger. One is not supposed to rest in this society, not even in his chair. This, however, is not the German "custom of the house," but Jewish vagabondage which has been transplanted to the salon. These are not community-conscious, sociable German men, but "stray international gypsies on a parquet floor."

Five o'clock tea: according to the writer of the article in the 12-Uhr-Blatt,[6] this is the domain of the young man in his busy "public life." Here he takes his new suit for a stroll. Here he practices the difficult art of "conquering the fair sex." And the conversation! Let no one faint at these flashes of wit: "Do you often come here, my dear?"; "The orchestra plays very nicely indeed, but did I hear one in St. Moritz! . . ."; "At the moment I'm still working in the office, but in six months at the latest I'm going into films"; and such other platitudes as are further wrenched from these lame brains.

[6] A Berlin daily newspaper which featured articles on sports and the theater, light and amusingly written.

Five o'clock tea: this means above all, however, the "third" and most important "prerequisite": "There's dancing!" And what kind of dancing! One dances swing—one hears all the latest hits and learns to recognize all the famous dance orchestras. Actually all this would be no more than a harmless waste of time for the "nice young man" if, a few lines further down, this choppy, noisy, meaningless squeaking were not described as "good music." We most decisively reject the possibility that, in the Third Reich, a newspaper can still exist and serve as the advocate of the Jewish impulse which has been done with once and for all, that a spirit against which the Führer, and with him the whole healthy-minded German people, has declared a war to the death, can again be allowed to worm its way into the field of music.

Let it be clearly understood that we have nothing against light music. Indeed we demand such music and are convinced that composers will find rewarding tasks in this field. We consider it one of the most deplorable losses in the field of music that a specializing, intellectual consideration of art has led German artists to regard light music as commonplace, stale, and second-rate, as an accommodation of the lowest tastes of the people, and that the artist must offer not something simple but something extreme and lofty, in a complicated form with a great display of elaborate technique.

This elaborate technique is in keeping with an intensified experience, whereas simple structure and an ordinary experience supposedly have lesser artistic value. It is not the ordinary general human sensibility, but the effect, the rarefied feeling, that sets the work of art in motion. With respect to his conception we see in light (but nevertheless content-rich) music a conceivably lofty artistic task which our greatest composers have willingly undertaken. It suffices to recall Bruckner, who, unaffected by the international trends in art, dedicated himself to simple, unpretentious musical composition. This was not a concession to a fashion in popular taste, or a mirroring in musical form of a current tasteless literature, or a display of clever contrivances and technique. Rather, his compositions attested to the bond of a creative artist to his Volk, which in the monumentality of their form inevitably drew closer to the simplicity of Volkish song and dance types.

Thus we, too, believe that light music is neither a primitive art expression nor cheap sentimentality, but an interplay of folk-song and folk-dance rhythmics. Behind them stands neither the thinker, nor the world-denying ascetic, nor the dubious genius, but an original, joyously sensual, world-asserting musician who lets the energies of life with its multiple forms flow into his art, smoothly and simply into a structure of meaning and beauty. This music is not a borrowing from alien sources, but an ideal which the artist shapes into significant form.

His relation to light music is not limited to taking over national and Volkish melody types; it also includes finding and developing new forms and melodies in the genre of the folk song and the folk dance. The German people urgently need this light music. One cannot listen to Beethoven, Bach, or Handel every hour of the day. For that one goes to the concert hall, not to the coffeehouse. After all, there is an enormous difference between digestible light music and a din of drums, washboards, guitars, cowbells, rattlers, and other noise-makers, the same difference as exists, say, between the intoxicating spirit of the German waltz and the rhumba or swing, or between a good newspaper supplement and the feuilleton-scribbling of the *12-Uhr-Blatt*.

We gladly leave Kestenberger, Schönberg, and Stravinsky to the civilized and pretentious art circles abroad. We, the young German generation, are in any case aware of the fact that the legacy of a great past in the field of music places a special obligation on us. We, the people of Beethoven, Bach, Mozart, Haydn, and Handel, cannot and will not any longer allow one of the noblest blooms of cultural life to fall increasingly victim to degeneration and to ultimate degradation to satisfy the demands of big-city night clubs and international bordellos.

For this it is necessary that we destroy once and for all the deeper ideological roots of this monstrous degeneration. The issue here is wholly different from the struggle for a new musical style, for the "ideal" of a new formal linear structure independent of harmonics, for the burgeoning powers of a new tonal sensibility, or however the philosophical ornaments of these confusions may be called. Rather, this music quite simply represents the outbreak of the nihilism of the postwar period, and accordingly is no longer expression, revelation, but a shriek, an unbridled discharge of its raw material. "Contemporary music" quite clearly presents both types of every phenomenon of decay.

One of these works almost entirely on the intellect, the other on the nerves. The former can be called paper music, the latter nerve music. Here too the usual dichotomy between soul and body emerges, which is the mark of the Western Asiatic racial and cultural expression. Both types are out of contact with the emotional life and try to make a virtue out of this shortcoming: in the place of intuitively grasped ideas they set rationally constructed work.

The first type comes from mechanistically ill-structured brains. A noisy, meaningless music is its means of expression. The second type is the product of jaded, diseased nerves. The effect achieved constitutes its principal means of expression: complicated cacophony resembling noise and choppy rhythm. It loves to simulate temperament, but in reality it is nothing but impulse. Both types are one-sided, and as a result their effect is weakened. What is more obvious now than the attempt to amalgamate both tendencies, which bear in themselves the germ of quick decay, in order to prolong their short life! But in vain! An amalgamation proved itself to be impossible.

The result was a combination of over-stimulated intellect and pathological impulse. Technique was the only element that held them together. But even technique can only couple; it cannot unite, for it is nothing but an external emergency measure. Besides, "contemporary music" itself leads to absurdity. It has gone beyond itself; it is no longer the expression of feeling but corresponds to the pleasure which the intellect takes in forming combinations and to the craving of the nerves for sensations. No doubt this music is difficult to master, but one can recognize it. It is no longer a rare novelty; it has lost its uniqueness. But it wanted above all to be unique, and rarefied! Thus the level of this music gradually sank lower and lower. It became a kind of night plant living under electric lights in an atmosphere of bad air, cheap perfume, and sticky tobacco smoke, even if it was produced in a setting of "high" society.

Alongside this ideological and general human degeneration there emerged the doctrine of the so-called international character of art and its independence from the Volk spirit and temporal events. The organic relationship between the creative artist and the people was denied. Denied also was the fact that Volk and race constitute the roots of every artistic creation, that, above all, music also is subject to the conditions and uniformities of biological data, that the energies of the people contribute to creativity, just as in a tree the sap rises from the root to the blossom. In this way the artist became incapable of shaping the elements of art, and thus the primordial symbol of his people, into significant form. He borrowed the art forms of alien peoples and races. . . .

> From *Der SA-Mann*, Sept. 18, 1937. (Wiener Library Clipping Collection.)

Fairytale Scenes on Peacock Island

On the eve of the festival days, when the great Olympic Games came to an end, the Reich Minister for the People's Enlightenment and Propaganda, in the name of the German Reich Government, invited the honored guests of the contests to a summer festival on romantic Peacock Island.

Under the command of Major Henke, army engineers on Saturday night dismantled the pontoon bridges leading to the platforms that had been built on the water at Grünau and then put them up again between the shore of Nikolskoe and the island. The flags of many nations fluttered in the breeze from the masts which were fastened to the pontoons. The lights of hundreds of sailboats and canoes were reflected in the dark waters of the Havel, and when the guests arrived at the scene they were encircled by a picture of magical beauty. A chain of pages dressed in white led the way to the great meadow. Numerous lanterns cast a resplendent, hundredfold light; melodies played by the state orchestra of the [NSDAP] district of Berlin, under the direction of conductors Spiess and Wicke, rang out on the air. Loudspeakers carried the music to the remotest corners of the island. A magic light radiated from hedges and bushes, filtering through the lush green of the leaves. Giant night moths glowed in the centuries-old linden and oak trees. The special setting of the festival was created under the general direction of chief government councillor Gutterer and of Reich stage designer Benno von Arent, who was responsible for the decorative scheme and who masterfully transformed the beauties of the romantic island in the Havel into a fairyland. The evening sky of a mild summer night stood over the scene of joy and splendor.

The summer festival of the German Reich Government was especially enhanced by the artistic presentations. Famous soloists and the entire ensemble of the German Opera House of Berlin, under the direction of ballet master Rudolf Kölling, were part of the colorful program, which began with a dance of the Olympic Games to the tunes of the old maestro Johann Strauss.

Love gods from the eighteenth century, with various robes and colorful wings, which had been modeled after figurines from the age of Frederick the Great, fluttered like porcelain figures on the tables as gifts for the ladies. The enormous dancing area, set amid the majestic groves of trees, filled up with couples who danced to the music of bandleader Oskar Joost of the "Femina," Eugen Wolff of the "Eden," and Emanuel Rambourn of the "Kaiserhof."

Late at night a splendid fireworks display won the special applause and admiration of the many guests.

> From *Der Angriff*, Aug. 18, 1936. (Wiener Library Clipping Collection.)

Beautiful Gowns at the Annual Press Ball

One of the most beautiful gowns consisted of pale-blue, delicately threaded mat crepe set off by a short, saddlelike ruffle in the front and a very deep one in the back made of pearl-studded circular figures of the same color. . . . A similar effect was created by a snow-white tulle gown which was not so theatrically insubstantial that it threatened to fly off in a draft of air. . . . No doubt the tulle ruffles, despite their unreal delicacy, had surprisingly great body thanks to an invisible stiffening of their base with horsehair tulle strips. . . . One saw heavily embroidered silver edges combined with blue velvet which formed a contrast to fine-meshed, very thinly woven edges. . . . Half of a heavily ruffled, strongly shaped side was made of strawberry-colored satin silk and the other half of black velvet as a seam end for a freely swinging frock. . . . Wine-red and blue-gray scintillating taffeta with the front part delicately tucked in. . . . Smoothness and dignity were also the leitmotifs of the dancing gowns.

> From *Die Neue Weltbühne*, Vol. I, No. 7 (1934), p. 215. (Wiener Library Clipping Collection.)

Wanted: Croupiers

Several croupier candidates, 25 to 35 years of age, wanted for a training course. Knowledge of languages and skill in dealing with figures required as well as no previous criminal record. Written applications only, to be sent to the management of the Casino, Personnel Division, Baden-Baden.

> From *Der Führer*, May 4, 1940. (Wiener Library Clipping Collection.)

3

The Foundations: Racism

THE FOLLOWING DOCUMENTS, written by the most important racial theoreticians of the Nazi movement, present the racist ideas that were fundamental to the National Socialist culture. Hans F. K. Günther (b. 1891) became a professor at the University of Jena in 1930, before Hitler's accession to power, and held the newly established chair of "racial science." Hitler himself had been deeply interested in Günther's appointment and the then National Socialist government of Thuringia had brought it about. While Günther's personal relationships with the party were stormy at times, his racial ideas were accepted, and his books, such as *Kleine Rassenkunde des deutschen Volkes* (*Short Ethnology of the German People*) (1929), were sold and distributed in many editions throughout the Third Reich. The *Short Ethnology* sold 272,000 copies between 1929 and 1943. The extract we have chosen is especially important, for it demonstrates a crucial point about "racial science." At first glance it reads like a reasonable discussion of anthropology with emphasis on the absence of pure races. But Günther soon introduces the notion that while a race may not be pure, its members share certain dominant characteristics, thus paving the way for stereotyping. For there is a racial "ideal type," as the final part of the extract makes clear. Though not all Aryans are Nordic, they all to some extent share in the "ideal

57

type." In contrast, the Jews are a mere mixture of races. Moreover, physical appearance is important, for Günther uses anthropological measurements of skulls, etc., as well as descriptions of a race's outward appearance.

Günther thus has his cake and eats it too. Obviously not all Nordics are blond or tall, but all have a predominance of such characteristics. Thus a race can be stereotyped. Hitler, after all, had dark hair but was supposedly of the Nordic race.

We have selected a longer extract from Ludwig Ferdinand Clauss's *Die nordische Seele (The Nordic Soul)* (1932). Clauss (b. 1892), a lecturer at the University of Berlin, was another contributor to "racial science"; his book sold 30,000 copies in the first five years of publication. Eventually it went through eight editions. But this extract illustrates more than Clauss's own point of view; it is typical of the general view of Nordic superiority. The qualities of a race are linked to its "genuine" environment, the landscape in which it had grown up for centuries. The picture of the ideal Nordic which is painted here will become common coin, for it combines a longing for power with an equally strong nostalgia for rootedness in the soil. The opposition to the city, which symbolizes modernity, is combined with domination over natural resources and over other races. As with Günther, physical appearance is involved, for the body is the showplace of the soul. But the soul is primary: it is formed by an interplay with nature—the wide spaces and energies which characterize the Nordic.

Clauss's passages about the Nordic's longing to surpass himself, his involvement with higher powers of nature, find echoes in Alfred Rosenberg. The Jews have none of this capacity; they are the very opposite of all that makes man great. Rosenberg continues Clauss's basic argument and applies it to the Jews: he does not borrow directly, for such ideas were general in all of racial thought. Rosenberg (1893-1946), well known for his *Der Mythos des XX. Jahrhunderts (Mythos of the Twentieth Century)*, was one of Hitler's close associates from early party days, and from 1934 on was charged by the Führer with watching over the ideological education of the party itself. He wrote the introduction to the memorial volume dedicated to Dietrich Eckart (1928). Eckart had a great influence on Hitler and probably did more than any other man to put him on the road to political success. He befriended the future Führer from 1919 to his early death in 1923. It was Eckart who deepened Hitler's anti-Semitism: he had made his mark as a minor writer and the editor of a violently anti-Jewish paper called *Auf Gut Deutsch* (*In Plain German*). Hitler was always grateful to him, and he ended *Mein Kampf* with a dedication to his former mentor. Rosenberg had equal reason to be grateful: not only did Eckart introduce him to Hitler, but he became Eckart's successor as editor of the party paper, the *Völkischer Beobachter*. Small wonder that Rosenberg, in the 1934 edition of the book, added triumphantly: "Today Eckart is with us again and a part of our Reich."

Jakob Graf, a teacher, in these selections from his textbooks on the family and racial biology, begins by giving an account of the dominance of the Aryan race throughout history. His approach adds a historical dimension to Clauss's ideas of racial superiority. He proceeds to assign various exercises which will enable schoolboys to identify a person's race at a glance. In this simplified form, racism filtered down to the rest of the population.

Instruction in race became compulsory in the Prussian schools after September 1933 and eventually in all German schools. Secondary schools were required to teach heredity, racial science, and family as well as population policies. The essentials of these subjects were to be a part of the instruction in biology. A biologist, Paul Brohmer, shows how this should be done, and how from out of this subject matter the teacher can construct a proper view of man for the student. Darwinism is rejected as mechanistic; rather, nature and man must be viewed as living interrelated entities, conforming to one eternally fixed organic plan. But they are such entities only within their own landscape and their own race. Once more, this follows up the theme raised by Ludwig Ferdinand Clauss. Brohmer also stresses the importance of the family, and we have seen in the previous section how this was part of the emphasis on tradition which National Socialism used for its ideological purposes. Brohmer integrates into his version of biological science all the fundamentals of the world view: life rooted in nature and Volk, the importance of German living space, and the demand for purity of race.

These "racial insights" were put into practice in the Nuremberg Laws and the Citizenship Laws which expelled the Jews from the Volk (see page 335). But they were also applied soon after the seizure of power in the Hereditary Health Law (*Gesetz zur Verhütung des erbkranken Nachwuches*), which was supposed to make sure that the "less valuable" members of the Volk did not contaminate the community with sick offspring. Similar legislation had been discussed as a matter of hygiene, not race, during the Republic, but the possibilities of abuse had kept the proposals from becoming law. Hitler decreed such a law on July 14, 1933. In justifying the measure, the ideas of men like Günther were brought forward as expert testimony—the race had to be kept strong. Moreover, where Republican drafts of the law had required the consent of the person to be sterilized, Hitler's law did not do so. A director of a clinic or a prison (for habitual criminals were also involved) as well as the person's legal guardian could initiate the process. The final decision on whether or not the person was to be kept from having children was up to the health courts, with a possible appeal to a "superior health court." The members of these courts (two doctors and a judge) were official appointees, and the family doctor was excluded from taking part in the proceedings. The extract from the law presented here derives from the official commentary upon the law itself.

For the sake of racial purity a fundamental change could be made in an individual's biological makeup if the "possibility" existed that his offspring would be physically or mentally sick. The official commentary on Nazi legislation[1] contrasts this attitude toward man quite rightly with the humanitarianism derived from the French Revolution which was now at an end. This law begins the process that led to euthanasia, finally decreed by Hitler in 1939. Euthanasia, or mercy killing, provided a laboratory for the eventual mass murder of Jews.

Racial thought and its consequences are fundamental to the whole cultural drive of the Third Reich. Once this has been understood, everything else will follow.

G.L.M.

[1] Hans Frank, *Nationalsozialistisches Handbuch für Recht und Gesetzgebung* (Munich, 1934), pp. 812-827.

The Nordic Race as "Ideal Type"

HANS F. K. GÜNTHER

Much has already been written on man, on the individual races of man—or what were regarded as such—on the "race problem" and the racial composition of nations. This literature gave rise to a long-drawn-out controversy because it dealt with the question of man's race. The reason for such a protracted and relatively unfruitful dispute over the "race question" lay in the fact that both sides did not clearly understand the concept of "race." In most cases the controversy was not even concerned with races, but with tribes, nations of mixed racial stock, or groups of peoples belonging to the same linguistic family. The dispute raged over the recognition or importance of a "Germanic race" as opposed to a "Latin race" or a "Slavic race"; the concept of a "Jewish race" or a "Semitic race" was put forward. In the process these writers must have completely forgotten that we may designate a human group as a race only when all of their representatives show the identical physical and spiritual features in the most important points. How could anyone speak of a "Jewish race," seeing that there are tall and short, slim and stocky, light and dark Jews with thin and broad faces, Jews with "Jewish noses" and those without them, not to mention the differences in the mental configurations and attitudes of individual Jews?

The idea of a "Germanic race" was put forward, and the race was described as tall, blond, and blue-eyed, and occasionally as long- or oval-headed and thin-faced. Its psychic essence was also more or less defined. Now, the fact that frequently very "un-Germanic" people, in both a physical and a mental sense, could be found among the peoples of Germanic language—as, for example, among the English, the Dutch, the Germans, and the Danes—should have served as a warning against presenting a concept of a "Germanic race"; so, too, the fact that people of typical "Germanic" appearance and comportment were often present among the peoples of the Slavic and Romance languages, and even among Caucasian tribes and Kurds. Further, in view of the large variety of human types among the peoples of the Semitic languages, how could one speak of a "Semitic race"?

61

In short, a proper distinction was not made between the concepts of "race" and "people" or "group of people." Membership in a language group was confused with membership in a racial group, and there was a desire to see racial borders where they were really only language and Volkdom borders. It was only when the concept of "race" was strictly defined and when it found currency among at least a few educated people that a valid and fruitful discussion of the "race problem" or of various "race problems" became possible. Anyone who continued to speak of a "German race" or an "English race," of a "Latin race" or a "Jewish race," betrayed an ignorance of the basic concepts of the subject he wanted to discuss.

"Race" is a concept of anthropology, which has been established in the same way as the sciences of zoology and botany (fauna and flora) and which, like them, discusses families, genera, species, and varieties. Eugen Fischer,[1] director of the Kaiser Wilhelm Institute for the Study of Anthropology, Human Heredity and Eugenics in Berlin-Dahlem, has called the following assertion by Grosse the best definition of the concept of "race."

"By race, anthropology understands a large group of people who are related to one another through the common possession of a certain inherited complex of physical and spiritual characteristics which also distinguishes them from other similar groups."

Consequently, a race must necessarily show, in all its representatives, a uniformity of physical and spiritual features, and must continue to reproduce from within itself people with the same physical and spiritual characteristics. Where there exist in a group of people essential differences in physical and spiritual endowment, where children essentially differ from their parents, or from one of them, there can be no question of a race or of parents with the same inherited set of features. I regard the following definition of the concept of "race" as useful:

A race is made up of a group of people which is distinguished from all other groups of people by a combination of endowed physical features and spiritual characteristics and which repeatedly reproduces only its own kind.

Hence a race is a group of people possessing an identical hereditary

[1] Here one so-called "respectable" racist cites another. Eugen Fischer (b. 1874) was a world-famous anthropologist who became an advocate of the "eternal race" and was much respected and cited by the Nazis.

endowment. Whoever tries in this way to visualize the nature of a race must immediately admit that it is hardly possible to find a race anywhere in the world as a self-enclosed human group. The human groups in this world that are linked by the same language, the same customs, or the same faith and thereby constitute a nation are, with hardly a single exception, a mixture of races, not races. All Western nations are mixtures of races which include, in certain percentages, pure and mixed, all the races of Europe, or in which, at least, several European races are represented.

What is different from nation to nation—from the ethnological viewpoint—is not, for instance, the race as such, but the proportion in which the races are mixed. In the mixture of one nation one or more races may be more strongly represented than in the race mixture of another nation. Anyone who would try to gather together the peoples of Europe who are related by race—or, rather, the people who appear to be related by race (since the inherited and the apparent image do not necessarily correspond)—in order to form uniform groups of people who appear to possess identical hereditary endowments, would have to collect these people from among all the nations of Europe. At the same time he would discover that these uniform groups of people are small minorities, in comparison with the great mass of Europe's population, since the majority of the people of the West, as well as of the whole world, consist of a blend of two or more races.

From the standpoint of the definitions given above, the Jews cannot be viewed as a race. Rather, they constitute a nation of mixed races. If popular usage is reluctant to give up the term "race" in the case of the Jews, the reason lies in the fact that in the racial mixture of the Jewish people physical and spiritual hereditary endowments of non-European peoples are predominant and these are quite noticeable when seen among the differently composed racial mixtures of the European population and especially that of northwestern Europe. The average European in Europe is not regarded as the bearer of racial features, but this is certainly the case with the average Jew. Therefore, popular usage will continue for a long time to speak of a "Jewish race," even though educated persons will long have recognized that the Jews, like other peoples, represent a mixture of races.

For the research of the races of mankind according to their physical appearance, for the identification of different human races in a certain geographical area where various race mixtures are found (tribes, nations, national groups), anthropology avails itself of specific procedures of the measurement and description of physical features which cannot be indicated here in detail. . . .

The Nordic race is tall, long-legged, slim, with an average height, among males, of above 1.74 meters.[2] The limbs, the neck, the shape of the hands and feet are vigorous and slender in appearance. The Nordic race is long-legged and narrow-faced, with a cephalic index of around 75 and a facial index above 90. As in all races, at least in the medium- and long-headed ones, the female head, in comparison with that of the male, appears to have a higher cephalic index and a lower facial index. The back of the Nordic head characteristically projects far beyond the nape of the neck. The projecting part of the back of the head, however, is comparatively low, so that in Nordic people the head springs backward, as it were, over the part of the neck visible above the collar. The face is narrow, with a rather narrow forehead, a narrow, high-built nose, and a narrow lower jaw and prominent chin.

The cut of the face of the Nordic race—at least in the male—creates the effect of a unique boldness through three striking traits in the lines of the profile: first in the flat, backward-tilting forehead, then in the straight or outwardly curved nose springing from high nasal roots, finally in the prominent chin. The smooth parts of the face support the expression of clean-cut physiognomy. In the female the chin is mostly arched rather than tilted backward; the nose is less sharply delineated, and the chin less prominent.

The skin of the Nordic race is roseate-bright and the blood shines through, so that it looks especially enlivened, and at the same time mostly somewhat cool or fresh. The facial complexion, at least among the youth and among the females, often looks like "milk and blood" even in middle age. The hair is smooth-straight or wavy; in childhood also curly. The individual hairs are soft and thin. The hair color is blond; among most of the existing types it can extend from a pink undertone of light blond to golden blond up to dark blond. Nordic children are often white-blond. People who were light blond during their youth will later become dark blond, dark-haired, a phenomenon which is called "darkening" and which is viewed as a sign of Nordic (or also Phalian or East Baltic) strain also among non-Nordic peoples. . . .

If an illustrator, painter, or sculptor wants to represent the image of a bold, goal-determined, resolute person, or of a noble, superior, and

[2] Approximately 5 feet 8½ inches.

heroic human being, man or woman, he will in most cases create an image which more or less approximates the image of the Nordic race. He will also create a man who will be regarded as a typical representative of the upper social strata. For example, the artists for the humorous journals will endow their creations with the features of the Nordic race rather than the features of the non-Nordic races of Europe.

Actually, one could conceivably designate will power, a definite faculty of judgment rooted in a coolly deliberating sense of reality, the impulse to truthfulness, an inclination to knightly justice, as the repeatedly striking psychical features of Nordic men. Such features can be intensified in individuals within the Nordic race to a pronouncedly heroic disposition, to a transcendent leadership in statesmanship or creativity in technology, science, and art. The relatively great number of Nordic people among the famous and outstanding men and women of all Western countries is striking, as also is the relatively low number of famous men and women without noticeable Nordic strain.

> From Hans F. K. Günther, *Kleine Rassenkunde des deutschen Volkes* (Munich, 1929), pp. 9-13, 21-25, 59. (This extract has been taken from the 1933 edition.)

Racial Soul, Landscape, and World Domination
LUDWIG FERDINAND CLAUSS

The manner in which the soul reaches out into its world fashions the geographical area of this world into a "landscape." A landscape is not something that the soul alights upon, as it were, something ready-made. Rather, it is something that it fashions by virtue of its species-determined way of viewing its environment. It cannot, of course, arbitrarily fashion any landscape out of any kind of geographical area. The area is the matter, so to speak, into which the soul projects its style and thus transforms it into a landscape. But not every matter lends itself to the same formative activity of the soul. The area offers the soul possibilities for shaping it in accordance with the soul's unique manner of perceiving it. But not every area offers the same possibilities. An area that is "proper" to the man who reaches out into the world, the accomplishment-oriented man, and can become expressive of his style, must be differently constituted than an area that other races find suitable for the formation of landscapes. The area that contains regions suitable for landscape formation in the accomplishment-oriented style is the "Nordic" geographical area. It provides the proper background for his style. Hence we call the style peculiar to him the Nordic style and we call him Nordic man.

We shall now contrast the Nordic landscape of Nordic man with a landscape of another style which constitutes the background, the living area suited to the style of another race, the Mediterranean-land race, so-called because of its landscape, namely, the landscape of the Mediterranean region suited to its style. The designation of the landscape of a particular race is at the same time an interpretation of the style of this race. According to its style, the Mediterranean race is clearly to be distinguished from the Nordic as well as the Eastern race.

Anyone who has sailed in the heavy seas around Cape Skagen has experienced how, at that point, two seas rush into each other with a deafening roar, each one having a different color and a different groundswell in terms of rhythm and pace: the gray-green North Sea has long-drawn-out, mile-long, high waves, whereas the bluer Kattegat thunders with waves of a shorter length. Here everything seems to become closer and narrower, everywhere we see the shores or sense their existence, and even beyond the Öresund and the "open" Baltic Sea we never again fully get that feeling of limitless expanse, infinite distance, we never again get that compelling feeling of power which the landscape of the North Sea gives. Nevertheless, the landscape styles of the two seas seem similar to the person who compares them with the landscape of the Mediterranean. Indeed, the Adriatic Sea is, seemingly, somewhat like the Baltic Sea. But anyone who travels southward through the narrow strait between the Albanian mainland and the Greek "Kerkyra" (Corfu) experiences clearly how the sea here differs from the other. . . . When the northern sea storms and rages with a terrific uproar, with a wind that rushes from one distant point to another, then the sea around Greece moves in moderately high but always even waves—strong but powerfully restrained in the entirety of its motion.

If one knows the northern sea and is familiar with its style, or, even more, if one feels its wave rhythm in his own soul, it would seem to him that the Greek sea was no sea at all and that we must find another word to describe it. . . . The south, the Mediterranean and its shores invite the beholder to a permanent stay: here everything is nearness, presence.

We have grasped the landscape of the north as the land of the North Sea and the landscape of the south as the Mediterranean land; thus we look upon these lands as the shores of the seas which determine their style. The land of the North Sea is characterized by distance and movement; over broad stretches it is integrated into the depths of space. . . .

The will for space awakens in the soul that is born in this landscape and truly lives in it. The Nordic space drags one along into the distance. It wants to be overcome. The overcoming of space means speed, the will for space urges and impels one to race through space. The Nordic landscape cries out to be traversed by rails over which express trains can speed. It is a characteristic of all Nordic vehicles to increase their speed. Ever-increasing velocity is a built-in characteristic of the rails themselves, the rails by which, in the Nordic experience of the world, the whole world is penetrated. Rails that are already in existence and those that must constantly be constructed for ever newer, ever faster vehicles on which men who experience the world Nordically may strive toward ever new goals. The Nordic soul experiences its world as a structure made up of countless thoroughfares—those already at hand and those still to be created—on land, on water, in the air, and in the stratosphere. It races like a fever through all segments of the Nordic community, a fever of speed which, infectiously, reaches out far beyond the world of the north and attacks souls who are not Nordic and for whom, at bottom, such action is contrary to their style and senseless.

In the Nordic landscape everything points to places beyond and tempts the soul, born of it, to cross the borders of this landscape. The Nordic soul has an innate urge to push on into the distance, and this means mostly southward. Anyone who has crossed the southern barrier of the northern geographical area—past the St. Gotthard range, for example—knows what is happening there. The northern region is perhaps enveloped in a thick fog, so that from the train we can see only the trunks of the mountains; then we plunge into the night of the tunnel and, suddenly, a radiantly blue day lights up our darkened eyes. And all the travelers, as with one voice, utter a cry of joy. The light of the south is like a benediction to the Nordic soul, blissful and at the same time fatal, like the light of the candle for the moth. First we feel as if we were wonderfully liberated from the call of distance, the urgent forward movement of the north, for here everything is simply present, magnificently beautiful and consummately finished. But then the eternal nearness of this landscape envelops the soul and stifles it to the point of suffocation. We may not really say that this landscape is "narrow"; it is not exactly without a certain distance from the soul. Such words do not do justice to its character. And in our language we probably cannot find the right word to express its charac- ter because all our words are fashioned out of the Nordic way of per- ceiving our world. We can say only what this landscape, in terms of ours, is *not*: it is without distance, without a deep movement; it is magnificent surface with nothing behind it—it is devoid of enigma, bereft of mystery. What it is, according to its nature, might perhaps best be expressed by a foreign word—it is *imposant*.

Wherever the human eye wanders—and it cannot really wander much here—it comes smack up against mountains which ring the re- gion, high and beautifully curved, all of them seeming to know and assert how beautiful they are. It is as though they point to themselves with an imposing gesture and demand: "Look at me!" When the land does open into a broader vista, it is only in a prescribed circle— one's gaze looks downward, then upward, around and along the crests of the mountains, and finally back to its starting point. Nowhere, not even on the sea, can one truly look out into the great beyond. Every- thing goes back and forth in a circle. Even the clouds seem to follow no path or direction, but stroll, so to speak, in a circle. Here reigns Zeus, the "gatherer of clouds," not Wodan, the wild hunter who roars with his armies high above—no one knows whence and whither. . . .

The mountains of the south are bare. Above them the glaring sun paints everything with a dazzling color and lights up every crevice. The light forces itself upon, intrudes upon everything, wherever we may look. Several times I caught myself saying: "This shameless sun!" Here there is no darkening mountain forest hiding a fairy tale, no night with flowing fog formations, with "a thousand monsters," no castle enveloped by a whispering legend. Here everything is clear, there is nothing but utter clarity. The Acropolis towers magnificently over the countryside, a miracle in white on blue. It tells us gripping tales from a time that no longer reaches into the present; it tells us very much, but it does not whisper to us. Even the wind knows of no mystery, it caresses. Even the storm wind still caresses although it tugs at your hair.

We said that the Mediterranean invites one to stay forever. But we must ask further: Whom does it invite? The person who was born in this landscape and who perceives in its style the style of his own soul —namely, the person who has it in himself as his *inner landscape*. Such a person is able to "tarry" in the authentic sense of the word. When, however, persons whose inner landscape is the north succumb to the enticement of the south and stay there and settle·down (as some Nordic tribes did in ancient times), the first generations will live in opposition, albeit unconscious, to the landscape which is alien to their kind. Gradually, then, the style of the souls undergoes a change. They do not change their race, they will not become Mediterranean people—in the strict meaning of the word as used here—but their Nordic style will undergo a transformation which ultimately will make them into a southern variety of Nordic man. In their eyes the southern landscape will not be the same as that seen with the eyes of those who are the children of this landscape. Through their Nordic way of seeing, the landscape will acquire a new, northern type of configuration. The landscape forms the soul, but the soul also forms the landscape. And when both, the Mediterranean man and the Nordic man who has settled in the south, look into the same geographical setting, each sees a different landscape—until, finally, miscegenation tears down the barriers and victory (that is, duration) is on the side of those who come from this soil.

This was the fate of the early Greeks, of the Romans, and of all peoples of Nordic origin who settled in the south. . . .

Among non-Nordics the Nordic man is frequently considered to be cold and without passion. The combination of concepts—"cold and without passion"—completely misunderstands the very roots of the Nordic soul. Indeed it is precisely this feature that is characteristically Nordic: to combine an outer coldness with the deepest passion, or, at least, to be able to effect this combination. All the "coldness" of Nordic man stems from the distance which separates him from his environment and which he cannot violate without violating his style, the law of his breed. To describe the Nordic soul's mode of experiencing the world is equivalent, first of all, to showing the possibilities of experience arising from this distance. A description of the Nordic soul must begin with its characteristic reaching out within the frame of distance.

We shall begin with examples from everyday life. When Nordic people enter a train they will with great thoroughness look for the coach that is least occupied, and then, if possible, will sit down in a seat where there are no neighbors. If, however, they get into a confining situation in which they are closely surrounded by fellow passengers, they will not establish any psychological contact with them except for the superficial courtesies—"Do you mind if I open the window?"—which can exhaust a conversation for hours. Perhaps they may even feel a compulsion to strike up a conversation; perhaps they find the person near them very attractive. But between each individual and his neighbor lies an unbridgeable distance and therefore they are not able to find the level of true conversation. Nordic man can overcome almost everything in the world save the distance separating man from man. In general, he is never really able to surmount it: the distance remains to the last, even in the most intimate community.

When a Nordic enters an inn, he looks for the last vacant table. If he cannot find one, it can happen that, despite his hunger, he will leave the inn to look for another, which he hopes will be empty. If he is distinguished, he is sensitive at table: the "good" society of Nordic style has developed special laws of etiquette, a strict set of table manners excluding all "letting oneself go," thereby protecting each individual from untoward familiarities. A violation of such table discipline has the effect of a violation of the distance—the discipline guarantees distance. The use of the toothpick in company first began in the German south and east, becoming generally more widespread and flourishing in countries where other needs are publicly satisfied, needs which the Nordic satisfies in privacy.

The Nordic endeavors to live alone—alone with his kin group, far away from neighbors. Even when he is at a summer resort, he keeps away from others as much as possible. For a time I lived in an old castle, on what for the time being is Italian territory, which now, like so many others, is operated as a resort hotel. In this old structure the rooms were widely spaced out and there were several small towers in the immediate vicinity. A new section had been added in which the rooms were close together. The towers and the rooms that were spaced out were occupied by Germans and Americans, the new section by Italians. The Nordic man never feels comfortable in apartment houses where the tenants live piled in layers upon one another and where the most intimate sounds penetrate everywhere. He is least comfortable in one of those large blocks of flats where sometimes ten people are crowded into one room. Under these circumstances, the Nordic people are the first to languish, to die, first spiritually and then physically: they succumb because of the loss of physical distance and perish because of the lack of social distance. The Nordic man can no more live without external and internal distance than fish can live without water. Nordic men cannot thrive between the stone walls of long lines of streets which deprive them of all distance—in other words, in the large city. If they cannot afford to take up residence beyond the city, then they succumb to emotional and psychological atrophy. Perhaps they are unaware of it, but they are forced to overcome an unconscious opposition; nevertheless, the Nordic soul is slowly stifled. The sins that parents have committed against their own soul-style is avenged in their children. Nobody who lives contrary to the law of his species goes unpunished.

The style of distance determines that Nordic man cannot live unpunished in regions which are narrow in terms of his law of style. The big city is not the only example of this; there is also the valley in the high mountains, and the sea inlet surrounded by high walls. In the Black Forest, for example, the wide valleys as well as the grassy lands and plateaus were settled by the Alemanni—that is, Germanic peoples—whereas the narrow valleys here and there remained predominantly in the hands of the original Eastern population. The difference between these two types of people in this area is so strikingly obvious that even as a boy, before I ever knew anything about races, I was sometimes surprised to hear these people, too, speak the Alemannic dialect. They seemed so strange to me then that I expected to hear them talk an entirely foreign language.

Now it can happen, however, that Nordic people nevertheless live in narrow regions. This habitation has a special meaning. We are thinking of the inhabitants of the deep-set fjords of the Norwegian coast. There the mountain wall, on both sides, grows precipitously out of the sea, solidly with no break, so that the sun never penetrates to the narrowest points. Settlements are spread out few and far between, only in the wholly low-lying areas where the fjord widens or where the mountainside clings to a ridge. The people there feel hemmed in, confined, and yearn to get to the top of the Fjell and beyond it where there is no limiting barrier. Their sons, to the extent they are still authentic racial types, go to sea or emigrate and, often, even the young girls cannot be held back. . . .

There is another kind of narrowness, however, for the Nordic soul, another lack of distance in space. It is not felt as distinctly as the narrowness of close walls but it has an effect on the soul at a deeper level. This is found in the area of the southern landscape alien to the north, namely, the "closeness" we mentioned above; that sun-drenched closeness which at first delights the person accustomed to northern climes and then, increasingly—perhaps imperceptibly—cuts off his breath and makes him homesick for infinite expanses. This is why the Germanic people who migrated southward did not find in the Mediterranean land what it can give—only to its own children!—the bliss of a sojourn in the sun. They were driven on and on, this way and that, in every direction. It was from the southern lands that the whole earth for the first time was circled by Nordic people. We are thinking of Marco Polo, the Venetian, and of Columbus, the Geno-ese: both men had a Nordic countenance and a Nordic style of soul. And once the example was set, it was as if a storm went through the sons of the aristocracy of northern origin, so that they set out—from Portugal, from Spain—one after the other, in order to bring the most distant parts of the world within Europe's ken and to open them up to its trading centers for their peoples. They were the grandchildren of those elements of the Germanic people who had traveled farthest, the grandchildren of the Suevi and Goths who, centuries before, had subjugated the Iberian Peninsula. Although the blood of the ances-tors might no longer be pure in the grandchildren, and not without an admixture of southern blood, obviously the northern style of life-experience was stronger in them than in many others whose ancestors had never left the north.[1] They were the descendants of those among the Germanic people who most enjoyed plying the seas, those who reached out furthest into the world, the grandchildren of the most Nordic among the Nordic peoples. There is a variation in the extent to which a soul is perfected in terms of its type. Applied to the Nordic type, this means that the power and capacity to reach outward is vari-able. The highest peak of a species-style is not necessarily broken or weakened in the first instances of blood-mixing. Indeed, the Nordic style of reaching out may become more rugged in the miscegenated soul because it is continuously forced to fight against what is alien to its soul, and as a result it becomes more conscious of itself and feels a compulsion over and over again to confirm its existence to itself. What the pure-blooded father did under the lash of obscure urges, the sons and grandsons do in response to a more conscious urge, and

[1] There is not the slightest evidence that the ancestors of men like Marco Polo or Columbus had ever lived in the north. This is a typical line of reasoning, using racial presuppositions to establish a fact.

they nurture and intensify this urge in order to remain worthy of the fathers. Of course, the more that foreign blood is injected into the veins and souls of those who are born later, the more the example of the fathers is suspended in mid-air, as it were, and also more and more is there a decrease of tension between the Nordic style of the soul and the style of the landscape alien to the north—the very tension which drove those who had gone south out into the open spaces with an intensified power, thrust, and impetus. Nevertheless, the Nordic blood has not completely run dry in the nations of the south, and there is still an urge in these late descendants which drives them out to sea. Still today we can find among Italian sailors, for example, many types who really belong on northland coasts.

The Nordic style of reaching out, in its ultimate and boldest intensification, obliges us to broaden the concept of the Nordic landscape in a unique sense: in a sense which, for example, is not viable with respect to the concept of the Mediterranean landscape. In this expanded sense, the whole earth, finally even the whole universe, becomes a Nordic landscape to the Nordic soul, for, in its reaching out it aims to penetrate simply everything, and, accordingly, to integrate it into its style and subject it to its law. Everything that has not yet been grasped and stamped by it, stretches out before it as a new land—its new land—which must be discovered, explored, put under cultivation, and hence conquered. In the last analysis it will recognize only the limits of the possible as its own limits. It may even happen that at this point it will fall ill and will try to ignore all limitations—a characteristically Nordic illness.

After the surface of the globe had been traversed so far and wide that there were now only a few small unknown spots left on the map —when there was no longer any new land left to discover—the Nordic craving for the faraway found other outlets. If there was no new region to be found, the Nordic now took the whole global space more firmly into his grasp. The enveloping of the earth took the place of discovery. Here the craving for speed, which we mentioned earlier, finds its real meaning; it is the urge to grasp the entire world with one grip. All the same, the spiritual homeland, in accordance with the style of Nordic man, will always be—and can only be—the north. Nordic man carries it around with him as his inner landscape wherever he might roam or settle. If in his inner self he becomes unfaithful to it, he loses himself, becoming rudderless and anchorless: from a man of enterprise he becomes a calculating predator, transformed

from hero to monster. But for a long time now the northern region of
the earth no longer provides him with sufficient space to develop his
physical existence in accordance with his style. Every bit of ground is
occupied and distributed, the smallest piece of land is recorded in a
land register. The Nordic soul, needful of space, had no choice but to
recast the whole world in accordance with its image and inner landscape. If today trains race through the desert on rails, airplanes build a
quick bridge from one part of the globe to the other, and the radio in
a few minutes flashes news of an event in Peking to London, this
means that the will to space of Nordic man has reached out beyond
the natural border of his landscape and has placed the stamp of his
style on the entire globe. The others, the non-Nordic inhabitants of
the world, the Mediterraneans, the Eastern peoples, and, further, the
East Asians and even the Negroes—all are forced to cooperate, they
now must traverse their own regions in the Nordic way, and this
means that they have to give up their own space and exchange it for
the space, the global space, which has now become a Nordic-tilled
field. They must give up their space, yet they cannot do it without
giving themselves up, for every authentic racial stock is bound up with
its space. A Chinese racing through the countryside in an automobile
is an absurdity, like the pheasant that would imitate the flight and
grip of an eagle. Nevertheless it is a reality. The world increasingly
assumes a Germanic exterior appearance and with it destroys the
stamp of the unique character of its non-Nordic racial stocks. Almost
everybody today wears a Germanic costume. (By this I do not mean
only clothing, although the victory of the Germanic style of clothing
—even in the time of the Romans long pants was the characteristic
Germanic mode of dress—has a much greater importance than the
superficial observer may believe. The mode of dress is expression, and
it determines the appearance of the body, which, after all, is the first
and most important showplace of the soul; it makes a difference
whether someone moves around in a dinner jacket or a caftan.) It lies
in the essence of the Nordic soul to resolve that it must penetrate the
whole world with its style and Nordicize and hence falsify what lies
beyond the natural border of the Nordic style. No Nordic enthusiasm
should deceive us on this score, namely, that the Nordic encircling of
the world, albeit necessary as a result of the Nordic law of species, is a
falsification and a destruction from the point of view of the law of the
other racial stocks. Whatever Nordic man may bring, for the others it
is bound to be a garment which is not cut for their particular figure

and which disfigures them. They will have to change their gait and bearing in order to wear it. Some are able to copy the northern gait most accurately, but this does not make them into Nordic people. To assert that the world becomes Nordic means that countless hidden values are being opened up and made useful and productive—mines of iron ore, oil wells, water power, as well as animal and man power; they are made useful in the Nordic sense, they become material to be formed by Nordic hands. But it is through this very action that this man power loses its own specific value; as a racial stock the Nordic stamp devalues its inner essence. Nordic man goes out as a bearer of culture and believes he is bringing gifts to the world, and he has often celebrated himself in this role, especially in recent times. He has been praised as a savior who sacrifices himself for the world.

> From Ludwig Ferdinand Clauss, *Die nordische Seele: Eine Einführung in die Rassenseelenkunde* (Munich, 1932), pp. 19-32. (This extract has been taken from the fifth edition, 1936.)

The Earth-Centered Jew Lacks a Soul
ALFRED ROSENBERG

Let us repeat once more, and again and again, the most important point that has been made up to now: the Jewish religion completely lacks the belief in a supra-sensible Beyond. Indeed, one even gets an almost positive impression that, in the course of time, everything that in the least could foster a belief in an incorporeal life after death was intentionally eliminated. The Jews, with their religion oriented to purely earthly affairs, stand alone in the world! This should not be forgotten for a single moment; it is highly significant. For it is this exceptional situation which explains why a "shady nation" such as that of the Jews has survived the greatest and most glorious nations, and will continue to survive, until the end of all time, until the hour of salvation strikes for all mankind. The Jewish nation will not perish before this hour strikes. The world is preserved, as we shall see, only by a positive yea-saying to the world. Among the Jewish people this world-affirmation is totally pure, without any admixture of world-denial. All other nations that have ever existed, and exist today, had, or have, such an admixture, characterized by the idea of a Hereafter,

even if only a trace of it. This mere trace would have sufficed, or
would suffice, to provide the necessary counterweight to the unadulterated yea-saying to the world, as embodied in the Jewish people. For
the inner light—and belief in immortality is the inner light—does not
need always to shine with the brightest glow in order to produce an
effect; it must simply be there, it must not be allowed to be snuffed
out, or otherwise mankind would be lost forever to the terrestrial
world. Everything takes its own time, however, a fact which is all too
often overlooked. The denial of the world needs a still longer time in
order to grow so that it will acquire a lasting predominance over affir-
mation of the world. At this time it seems again to have sunk to a zero
point; its opposite, symbolized by the Jewish people, is triumphant as
never before. It seems as if the inner light has completely vanished
from this earth. But, to anticipate, it merely seems that way. Denial of
the world cannot perish because it is part of the soul of mankind and
the soul is immortal. Where the idea of the immortal dwells, the
longing for the eternal or the withdrawal from temporality must always emerge again; hence a denial of the world will always reappear.
And this is the meaning of the non-Jewish peoples: they are the custodians of world-negation, of the idea of the Hereafter, even if they
maintain it in the poorest way. Hence, one or another of them can
quietly go under, but what really matters lives on in their descendants. If, however, the Jewish people were to perish, no nation would
be left which would hold world-affirmation in high esteem—the end
of all time would be here.

This would also be the case if the Zionist idea were to become a
reality, namely, if the entire Jewish people would unite to become a
national entity in Palestine or somewhere else. Such a unification of
Jews has never existed before: this must be stressed not twice but
three times, inasmuch as it is little known. Long before the destruction of the Temple in Jerusalem a large part of the Jews lived in the
diaspora, that is, dispersed among the "heathen" people. And, as
every schoolboy knows, at the beginning of their history they were
"guests" among the Egyptians. What arose afterward in Palestine was
anything but a state structure. At best it was an attempt to build one,
when it was not a preparatory school for the exploitation or the destruction of foreign peoples. To the Jew Weininger[1] his own nation is

[1] Otto Weininger (1880-1903) wrote *Geschlecht und Charakter* (*Sex and Character*) (1903), which became a classic not only of Jewish self-hate but also of
racist literature.

like an invisible cohesive web of slime fungus (*plasmodium*), existing since time immemorial and spread over the entire earth; and this expansionism, as he correctly observes (without, of course, proving it), is an essential component of the idea, of the nature of Judaism. This immediately becomes clear if we again regard the Jewish people as the embodiment of world-affirmation. Without it, nothing of a terrestrial character, and thus no nation, is conceivable. Hence, the Jew, the only consistent and consequently the only viable yea-sayer to the world, must be found wherever other men bear in themselves—if only in the tiniest degree—a compulsion to overcome the world. The Jew represents the still necessary counterweight to them; otherwise that urgent craving would be fulfilled immediately and thereby would not usher in the salvation of the world (since the Jewish people would still remain in existence), but would destroy it in a different way through the elimination of the spiritual power without which it cannot exist either. I will discuss this idea more fully later on; here I wish merely to demonstrate that the world could not exist if the Jews were living by themselves. This is why an old prophecy proclaims that the end of the world will arrive on the day when the Jews will have established the state of Palestine . . .

From all this it follows that Judaism is part of the organism of mankind just as, let us say, certain bacteria are part of man's body, and indeed the Jews are as necessary as bacteria. The body contains, as we know, a host of tiny organisms without which it would perish, even though they feed on it. Similarly, mankind needs the Jewish strain in order to preserve its vitality until its earthly mission is fulfilled. In other words, the world-affirmation exemplified by Judaism in its purest form, though disastrous in itself, is a condition of man's earthly being—as long as men exist—and we cannot even imagine its nonexistence. It will collapse only when all mankind is redeemed.

Thus, we are obliged to accept the Jews among us as a necessary evil, for who knows how many thousands of years to come. But just as the body would become stunted if the bacteria increased beyond a salutary number, our nation too—to describe a more limited circle—would gradually succumb to a spiritual malady if the Jew were to become too much for it. Were he to leave us entirely (this is the aim of Zionism, or at least what it pretends to be) it would be just as disastrous as if he were to dominate us. The mission of the German nation will come to an end—and this is my firm conviction—with the last hour of mankind. But we could never reach it if we lost world-affirmation, the Jew among us, because no life is possible without world-affirmation. On the other hand, if the Jew were continually to stifle us, we would never be able to fulfill our mission, which is the salvation of the world, but would, to be frank, succumb to insanity, for pure world-affirmation, the unrestrained will for a vain existence, leads to no other goal. It would literally lead to a void, to the destruction not only of the illusory earthly world but also of the truly existent, the spiritual. Considered in himself the Jew represents nothing else but this blind will for destruction, the insanity of mankind. It is known that Jewish people are especially prone to mental disease. "Dominated by delusions," said Schopenhauer about the Jew. . . . To strip the world of its soul, that and nothing else is what Judaism wants. This, however, would be tantamount to the world's destruction.

Even now, while the Jews still live among us, all their undertakings reveal this aim, and necessarily so. Their aim is to strip mankind of its soul. This is why they endeavor to break any form behind which the living soul is operative. For as arch-materialists it is their insane opinion that it is precisely the spiritual, which they sense only obscurely, that is connected with the form as a matter of life and death and must perish with it. Hence they are also, all and sundry, anarchists, consciously or unconsciously. In fact, they cannot be anything else but opponents of order and law, because order and law, in a unique way, bear the radiant imprint of a purer world. Schiller calls order "the daughter of heaven," and for the divine origin of law we find much evidence in Schiller and still more in Goethe.

Without order and law no conception of state can be actualized, since they are the indispensable foundation for it. For this very reason, the Jew, the mortal enemy of order and law, can never create a viable state in Palestine. The result would again be chaos. For this word, correctly translated, means an infinite void, nothingness.

From *Dietrich Eckart: Ein Vermächtnis*, edited by Alfred Rosenberg (Munich: Verlag Frz. Eher Nachf., 1928), pp. 214-219.

Heredity and Racial Biology for Students
JAKOB GRAF

The Aryan: The Creative Force in Human History

In the second millennium B.C. the Aryans (the Nordic race) invaded India and established Aryan culture there. A branch related to the Aryans created the foundations for the power and the flowering of the Persian empire. Ancient Hellenic culture likewise is traceable to the blood of Nordic immigrants. Paintings that have come down to us, as well as descriptions dating from that period, attest to the fact that the Hellenes, as long as they kept their race pure, were tall, light-skinned, light-eyed, blond people. The Roman Empire was founded by the Italics, who were related to the Celts. With the vanishing of the Nordic component—that is, with the disappearance of Nordic blood—the fate of these proud empires was sealed. The Goths, Franks, Vandals, and Normans, too, were peoples of Nordic blood. A renaissance took place only in the Western Roman Empire, not in its eastern counterpart, because in the west Nordic blood developed its creative power in the form of the Longobards. Remnants of the western Goths created a Spanish empire. The spread of Christianity in northern and eastern Europe was in the main supported by Nordic people, and the Nordic longing for freedom of the spirit found powerful expression in the Reformation. It was Nordic energy and boldness that were responsible for the power and prestige enjoyed by small nations such as the Netherlands and Sweden. The successors of the northern Franks, Goths, and Germanic peoples created the might and greatness of France in the past centuries, and even the Russian empire was founded by Normans. The opening up of North America, South Africa, and Australia was carried out with unequaled success by the Anglo-Saxons, the descendants of the Saxons and Normans. Everywhere Nordic creative power has built mighty empires with high-minded ideas, and to this very day Aryan languages and cultural values are spread over a large part of the world, though the creative Nordic blood has long since vanished in many places. Ethnological historical research has proved that the Nordic race has produced a great many more highly talented people than any other race.

Nordic boldness not only is a precondition for the martial exploits

of nations of Nordic origin, but it is also a prerequisite for the courageous profession of new, great ideas.

How We Can Learn to Recognize a Person's Race

ASSIGNMENTS

1. Summarize the spiritual characteristics of the individual races.

2. Collect from stories, essays, and poems examples of ethnological
illustrations. Underline those terms which describe the type and
mode of the expression of the soul.

3. What are the expressions, gestures, and movements which allow
us to make conclusions as to the attitude of the racial soul?

4. Determine also the physical features which go hand in hand
with the specific racial soul characteristics of the individual figures.

5. Try to discover the intrinsic nature of the racial soul through
the characters in stories and poetical works in terms of their inner
attitude. Apply this mode of observation to persons in your own environment.

6. Collect propaganda posters and caricatures for your race book
and arrange them according to a racial scheme. What image of beauty
is emphasized by the artist (a) in posters publicizing sports and
travel? (b) in publicity for cosmetics? How are hunters, mountain
climbers, and shepherds drawn?

7. Collect from illustrated magazines, newspapers, etc., pictures of
great scholars, statesmen, artists, and others who distinguished themselves by their special accomplishments (for example, in economic
life, politics, sports). Determine the preponderant race and admixture, according to physical characteristics. Repeat this exercise with
the pictures of great men of all nations and times.

8. When viewing monuments, busts, etc., be sure to pay attention
to the race of the person portrayed with respect to figure, bearing, and
physical characteristics. Try to harmonize these determinations with
the features of the racial soul.

9. Observe people whose special racial features have drawn your
attention, also with respect to their bearing when moving or when
speaking. Observe their expressions and gestures.

10. Observe the Jew: his way of walking, his bearing, gestures, and
movements when talking.

11. What strikes you about the way a Jew talks and sings?

12. What are the occupations engaged in by the Jews of your ac-
quaintance?

13. What are the occupations in which Jews are not to be found? Explain this phenomenon on the basis of the character of the Jew's soul.

14. In what stories, descriptions, and poems do you find the psychical character of the Jew pertinently portrayed. ("The Jew in the Prickle" from Grimm's Fairy Tales; *Debit and Credit* by Gustav Freytag; *Ut mine Stromtid* by Fritz Reuter; *The Hunger Pastor* by Wilhelm Raabe; *The Merchant of Venice* by Shakespeare.[1]) Give more examples.

From Jakob Graf, *Familienkunde und Rassenbiologie für Schüler* (2nd ed.; Munich, 1935), pp. 107, 114-115.

The New Biology: Training in Racial Citizenship
PAUL BROHMER

How did it come about that Darwin's doctrine aroused his contemporaries to such a pitch of violence, that passionate quarrels broke out for and against the new theory? His fellow biologists soon espoused one or the other shadings of the Law of Descent. . . . The success of this doctrine derived from the fact that all events in nature were reduced to a single formula by which everything was explained. . . . In addition, there was also the strong desire for a mechanistic explanation of events, as this also found expression in the philosophy of positivism. Darwin's theory, however, is purely mechanistic. . . .

From our pedagogical standpoint, which considers the task of the school to be the inculcation of Volkish thinking and volition, in opposition to the carrying-over of Darwinian ideas to the teaching of biology in schools, it can be objected that teaching these ideas will hardly serve this pedagogical aim. These teachings are, so to speak, international, since they examine all the countries of the world for the phenomena which the laws of the theory of descent supposedly predict. Thus, we find that textbooks deal with almost more foreign animals and plants than native ones; the selection is made on the basis of localities where the phenomena under consideration—mimesis, pro-

---

[1] All these works were widely read, and in all of them the Jewish stereotype appears, even if not yet dressed up in racial garb. With the exception of Shakespeare, the authors lived in the nineteenth century.

tective coloration, adaptation—can best be recognized. Thus the student learns all about the Indian meal moth, the walking-stick insect, the walking leaf, but not about the parasites which destroy the harvest in our own orchards or cause enormous losses in the fields of German agriculture. The student might be familiar with the Australian monotremes and marsupials, but know hardly anything about the animals and plants that are most frequently come upon in the fields and forests of the homeland.

Such knowledge may well be of use to the researcher, but not to the German who is not an expert in the field of biology. It is no exaggeration to assert that much of the subject matter of biology teaching is alien to life, the homeland, and the Volk. The reason for this aberrant development in the teaching of biology lies mainly in the fact that, owing to the tendencies of the time, the Darwinian ideas became the principal content of instruction in the schools. . . .

The inclusion of physiological viewpoints in the teaching of biology leads to a specific technical procedure, to an elaboration of biology as subject matter for the school based on instructive work-experience. In this sense there has already been a great improvement in the past few years. But this is not the essential problem. It is not just a question of improving the teaching procedure, but rather of transforming the content of our subject, of guiding the student to a new conception of nature! To accomplish this, teachings taken from physiology must be introduced. Consequently, this purpose is not served if a number of physiological experiments are carried out and interpreted as postscripts or appendices, so to speak. Here, too, from the very beginning the student must be guided to an over-all, total view, and not, say, to one that is encyclopedic. He should perceive and feel that behind the individual achievement there is a meaningful plan, that behind it stands the whole organism. Let us take, for example, an experiment showing the action of saliva in changing starch into sugar. This is not just a random interesting fact, but a real accomplishment, a process in the service of the preservation of the whole organism. Or, let us consider the process of seeing: the eye by itself is not able to produce any visual images but requires the cooperation of a number of organs. Thus, the act of seeing is also an accomplishment achieved by the entire organism.

These examples show us two ways in which physiology considers the whole: first, in that the accomplishment is in the service of the whole; second, in that it is achieved by the whole. Hence these two methods of observing an event from the standpoint of the whole organism are intimately connected: the conception that every occurrence is planned, as a part of the total accomplishment, and the conception of the organism as a totality, in which everything that occurs is conditioned and regulated by a meaningful plan. If we guide the student to this conception of nature as a unified totality by way of repeated concrete examples, we shall have helped to provide him, at least in this branch of biology, with a modern method of observation and he will have acquired the basis for an organic Volkish-based thinking. Naturally, this must also be done in the other branches of our subject. . . .

The importance of emphasizing physiological ideas in the teaching of botany and zoology is also to be found in the fact that the way for it is prepared by the new teaching of anthropology. The physiological processes in plants and animals with which the student becomes acquainted create a basis for an understanding of the corresponding processes in man. In the actual teaching of anthropology, however, a strong emphasis on physiology is necessary because it prepares the way for teaching hygiene, and it certainly is a task of this branch of instruction in biology to provide a guide for a rational way of life. Individual hygiene, again, is a prerequisite for racial hygiene, which is so important. Thus the study of physiology is likewise connected with this problem. It can be successfully utilized, however, only on the basis of a total view, which must be introduced into all branches of the teaching of biology.

The concept of the total view will come to the fore in the study of living plant or animal communities more than it will in any other branch of biology teaching. . . . Unfortunately this idea has been understood by many methodologists in a purely external way as a principle of the organization of matter. It is more than that. Behind it stands a repudiation of an outmoded tendency in research; the aim should be to present a view of the whole, to apply methods of instruction relevant to the subject matter, to arrive at a national formulation of biology teaching and the discovery of internal interconnections in the occurrences of life. The metabolic changes in a closed biotic community reveal a meaningful plan in the greater occurrences of nature, and when we come to understand that the whole world is a living space for one biotic community, we can then discover ultimate interconnections, and finally arrive at a concept of nature that does not conflict with religious experience, whereas this was necessarily the case with the former purely mechanistic attitude.

Introducing the student to this mode of observation is in the spirit of a Volkish education. On the basis of the elaboration of the laws of biology we turn to the emotional life of the student: he must come to see Germany as his "living space" and himself as a link in the German biotic community and the German destiny; and he must regard all Germans as his blood relations, his brothers. If we reach this goal, then all party and class divisions sink into nothingness, and more is accomplished for education in citizenship than is done by studying governmental and administrative structures.

For the very reason that the theory of the biotic community is so important for the development of biological knowledge and for education in organic Volkish thinking, it would be expedient to base the school curriculum on this idea. When we go into the free, open spaces we always come upon animals and plants in their specific living space in which they form biotic communities. It is not a mechanical system which orders the natural arrangement of organisms, but the living space. This living space not only presents an external frame of community but links its inhabitants to each other with indissoluble bonds. Whoever, in teaching the concept of the biotic community, utilizes it only as a principle of the organization of matter has not grasped the deeper meaning of bionomics. He stands, as it were, in front of a deep well of precious water and draws nothing from it although his companions are dying of thirst. Thus it is a question of opening up Volkish values to the students.

At the same time this produces effects which, from a didactic point of view, are not to be scorned. For one thing, instruction along the lines of the concept of the living community compels the teacher to take his students on frequent trips outside the classroom and to collect observations for later evaluation. Thus a true teaching of life is striven for, not just an accumulation of knowledge acquired by studying "animal skeletons and dead bones." There is little justification for a "museum" biology in the instruction which we are striving to establish. Even the illustrative specimens, which in many school lessons still must serve as a substitute for nature, can be dispensed with in most cases. They may still serve as a supplement to what has been seen in a living context, but they can no longer be the source for the formation of views.

It is not enough to make one visit to a biotic community, such as a beech wood. Rather, it must be visited at least once every season. How different is the effect which a beech wood, for example, makes on us in early spring, when the ground is covered with a carpet of anemones, from that which it makes on us in midsummer, when a mysterious penumbra prevails, when it looks to us like a cathedral with high, slender columns! Anyone who absorbs the atmosphere of the landscape, its soul, begins to love his homeland, and it is precisely love of the homeland which we want to arouse and can arouse with the help of the concept of the biotic community. It is almost self-evident that educational hikes to the biotic communities in his regional environment provide the student with a knowledge that is not limited to the field of biology but includes knowledge about the homeland.

It is necessary to take several such hikes through a biotic community in order to be able to grasp fully the metabolic changes which take place within it. The seasonal changes in the world of the organisms play an important part in this metabolism. From this results a methodological conclusion of great significance. For most schools it is not feasible to deal with only one kind of biotic community in the course of a school year. Even though this would involve a very thorough investigation of one living space and its inhabitants, it is opposed by the requirements of life, which demand a certain versatility. According to my experience, it is easily possible in one school year to deal with three or four biotic communities, putting more stress on one than on the others. If it is desired to visit each one of these biotic communities at least once every season, then it is impossible to treat the individual biotic communities as self-contained teaching units— for example, by dealing with one in the first semester, the second in the following semester, etc. Rather, the treatment of the three or four biotic communities prescribed by the school curriculum for one year would parallel each other. In this way the summer can be used mainly for gathering observations and the winter can serve more as a period of evaluation. . . .

Another change we must make in the teaching of biology if its cultural value is to be increased concerns the position of man in our discipline. In the usual textbooks, anthropology is treated as a supplement to biology; man is dealt with in somewhat more detail than any other mammal, but according to the same points of view. The only difference is that, on the basis of the knowledge of the structure and functioning of the organs, some rules on health may be offered, and it has been said that the teaching of anthropology should offer the student a guide to intelligent living. No doubt, anthropology should fulfill this task too. But all it does is promote knowledge as such; it does not add to the growth of the student's intellectual or religious culture. . . . Furthermore, knowledge as an individual accomplishment must be supplemented by a knowledge of a supraindividual character, because German man must not think only of himself, but should be cognizant of his duty to place himself in the service of the people.

Our aim is not merely that man be made the object of the study of nature, but that he should also be placed as subject in the biological consideration of nature. To be sure, everybody must have a certain fund of knowledge about the structure and function of his "body tools," and everybody should also know how to keep healthy. Hence we should welcome the methodological demand that the road to the teaching of anthropology should always be prepared by the teaching of biology. Consequently, it is possible in zoology to elaborate, for example, on the nature of digestion, breathing, etc., and then refer back to it in anthropology. The study of botany, too, offers many opportunities for preparing the way for anthropological knowledge. . . .

Beyond and above this, the place of man vis-à-vis nature must constantly be discussed in the teaching of biology. This is made easy precisely by arranging the subject matter, and the insights deriving from it, in terms of a biotic-community approach. We would start with— since our concept of biotic community is a broad one—the domain of "house and home." In it man is the master; he has taken into his household the animals and plants which he keeps either for his use or for his pleasure. He gives them shelter, food, and care; he has changed them through breeding and he holds their lives in his hands. Without him most of the organisms he keeps as domestic animals or indoor plants would perish. At this point we can discuss in an elementary way the attitude of man toward nature. In this biotic community we meet first and foremost the will to rule over nature, the viewpoint of utilitarianism, which is, however, accompanied by the joy in the beauty of the things of nature and love of nature itself. Similar discussions will come up in the study of biotic communities in the garden, field, and meadow.

It might be thought that with the "anthropological idea," as I should like to designate the emphasis on anthropology in biology teaching, our aim is to return to the anthropocentric point of view which has been justifiably attacked; or that we wish to foster a utilitarian pedagogy by discussing more thoroughly than was done in the past domestic animals, useful plants and their parasites, and eugenics from the viewpoint of the individual and the race. It is anthropocentric if it is assumed that nature has been created only for man. We decisively reject this attitude. According to our conception of nature, man is a link in the chain of living nature just as any other organism. On the other hand, it is a fact that man has made himself master of nature, and that he will increasingly aim to widen this mastery. The teaching of natural history must contribute to this. Thus its task is not merely to transmit theoretical knowledge, to foster joy in nature, to arouse love of one's homeland and one's country; it has, in addition, practical aims. One may call this utilitarian pedagogy if one so pleases. But in our view instruction in biology that does not take the problems of agriculture, forestry, gardening, and fishing into consideration is a failure; it is a form of teaching that is alien to the practical life of our people. School is not a research laboratory, but an institution which aims to educate Germans, and these should stand at their posts in the life of the German Volk. We are as far removed from a one-sided utilitarian viewpoint as we are from pedagogy that is alien to life. . . .

Still more important, it seems to me, is the fact that the task of biology teaching, briefly referred to above, can be fulfilled by an orientation toward the concept of the biotic community. It must be grasped here once more on the basis of another idea. We have said that the student must be led to the conception that Germany is his living space to which he is linked by the bond of blood. We have explained in detail that the bionomic approach teaches that the organisms within a living space are dependent on each other as well as dependent upon the whole, and that each link must perform an indispensable function in the total accomplishment. When this insight is applied to the human biotic community, when the future German racial-comrade feels himself to be a link in the German biotic community, and when he is imbued with the idea of the blood relationship of all Germans, then class differences and class hatred cannot take acute forms, as was often the case in the past due to a misunderstanding of the actual bond that unites all estates together. Once every German regards Germany as his living space and feels himself to be a link in the German biotic community, he will be fully conscious of the fact that every individual within the metabolism of the biotic community into which he was born must fulfill his own important task. Thus a supra-individualistic attitude is created which constitutes the best possible foundation for training in citizenship. Indeed, it can be said that it has achieved its deepest fulfillment once this attitude is transformed into action.

Racial eugenics works in the same direction, namely, the education of the student in a national sense. Although it constitutes the finishing touch of biology teaching, its concepts should from the very beginning permeate all biological instruction in all types of schools, and not be left for discussion in anthropology, which concludes the study of biology. It should be repeatedly emphasized that the biological laws operative in animals and plants apply also to man; for example, that the knowledge acquired from studying the genetics of these organisms can, in a general way, be applied to man. Thus, the teaching of animal breeding and plant cultivation can effectively prepare the way for conceptions of racial biology. Naturally, a more systematic discussion of these questions will first take place in the teaching of anthropology.

It is not so much a matter of making the student knowledgeable on all questions of eugenics, but of creating motives for his action. Racial eugenics is particularly valuable for school because of its educational significance. If the emphasis on the ideology of the biotic community creates a feeling of belonging to our people and state, then racial eugenics creates the will to struggle, body and soul, for the growth and health of this biotic community.

This is also the place for discussing, from a biological viewpoint, the family as a value, and the improvement of the sense of family which has been sorely neglected by many modern pedagogues. The family, after all, is the smallest biotic community since it forms the germ cell of the state. If we take up these questions, the fields of individual hygiene and racial eugenics, of genetics and sex education, combine to form a meaningful unit, just as, generally, the teaching of biology, which in the past was fragmented into many unrelated individual fields, will be fused into a unified whole once our efforts achieve fruition. In these discussions on the family we are less concerned with the student's enlarging his knowledge and more with the aim that he be imbued with a sense of responsibility, that he begin to sense that the deepest meaning of human life is to grow beyond himself in his children, and that nothing he could leave to them would be more valuable than the German heritage which he has received from his ancestors, and that, through race mixing, he could taint and impair his progeny in a most unfavorable way.

Such ideas lead to an ethnology of the German people, which we mentioned earlier by way of a few pedagogical observations. All that remains to be discussed is at what stage it should be introduced. As we have explained, the way to it is already prepared in zoology and botany and it is concluded in the teaching of anthropology. Now a short remark on the goal of ethnology: the knowledge of physical and spiritual features of the individual races has little value if it does not lead to the firm will to fight against the racial deterioration of the German nation and if it does not imbue the student with the conviction that the fact of belonging to a race imposes a responsibility. . . .

The actual method of teaching racial eugenics of necessity will vary with the individual types of schools. Even the simplest village school may not pass over these problems. It can build upon the children's own radius of experience in the fields of animal breeding and plant cultivation. From this, simple rules of heredity can be deduced; these, however, do not need to involve cellular research and the theory of chromosomes. Children are familiar with symptoms of degeneration in animals and plants, and not much initiative is required to find such signs of degeneration and decline in man too. Thus a point of departure is created for introducing racial eugenics during instruction in zoology and botany. At suitable opportunities—this can also be done in the teaching of geography and history—such ideas will be elaborated further until they are most fully treated in the teaching of anthropology. Not one elementary-school pupil should leave school without having internalized the iron command that he is to bear part of the responsibility for the fate of his fatherland, without the awareness that he is only a link in the chain of his ancestors and descendants and the carrier of the future generation. The higher schools can devote more time to racial eugenics: the students in the later classes are more mature than those in the elementary and intermediate schools. Here, too, the way will be prepared in zoology and botany. Further, the teaching of history can be made very meaningful through racial eugenics, since we know that modern historians consider the cause of the collapse of the ancient world to lie in non-eugenic racial mixtures. . . .

When teaching the theory of family and race, as well as eugenics, it is methodologically important to stimulate independent activity on the part of the student to the greatest possible degree. It can be suggested that the student draw up a genealogical chart of his family as far back as he can go. In addition, he can be asked questions about the physical characteristics of his parents and other forebears as far as they can be determined (size, figure, shape of head and face, color of hair and eyes, form of nose, etc.), about their intellectual and characterological qualities, their special achievements (for example, rescues during the war, scientific or literary publications, compositions), their life span and cause of death. In given cases, deformities and hereditary diseases should also be reported. The number of children produced by the student's ancestors should be determined. This is the kind of material in which the student will be directly interested. But when explaining hereditary diseases the teacher must take care not to arouse feelings of inferiority or fear of such diseases in students who come from families with handicaps of a hereditary character. It also goes without saying that he is duty-bound to keep certain information confidential as far as the other students are concerned. In every class, then, there will be sufficient usable material which can serve as a basis for teaching in the afore-mentioned fields.

> From Paul Brohmer, *Biologieunterricht und völkische Erziehung* (Frankfurt: Verlag Moritz Diesterweg, 1933), pp. 8-10, 68-72, 74-80.

To Preserve the Strength of the Race: Compulsory Sterilization
ERICH RISTOW

There is complete unanimity on the decision which stipulates that a recommendation of sterilization is not to be postponed for the reason that the person subject to this measure is pregnant. Consequently, the measure has to be carried out and the order thereto is to be issued by the Hereditary Health Law Court (*Erbgesundheits-Gericht*).[1]

The decision of the Hereditary Health Law Courts will be carried out in such a way that the ovaries of the woman are removed or unbound. Care must be taken to make it as difficult as possible, if not in fact impossible, for surgery to undo this measure, so as to avoid the

[1] These courts were composed of two doctors and one judge.

rejoining of the parts that have been separated. . . . Persons who have been sterilized must be prevented from traveling abroad in order to have physicians there counter the effect of the surgery.

When a Hereditary Health Law Court has legally decreed the sterilization of a woman who is pregnant at the time this measure is to be carried out, the pregnancy can be interrupted with the permission of the pregnant woman, except when the fetus is already in a stage of viability or if the interruption of pregnancy would seriously endanger the woman's life or health.

> From Erich Ristow, *Erbgesundheitsrecht* (Stuttgart and Berlin: Verlag W. Kohlhammer, 1935), pp. 127, 159, 226, 256.

4

Building Myths and Heroes

MYTHS AND HEROES were all-important in what Hitler called the "magic influence" of mass suggestion. A myth is an image which can inspire men. It must have some element of truth in it, but it is twisted into a vision that conforms to the desired ideal. Nietzsche did live, and his name was familiar to most Germans, but Alfred Baeumler (b. 1887) transformed Nietzsche's thought into a myth which put the famous philosopher at the service of the Nazi world view. Baeumler stresses Nietzsche's heroism, his emphasis upon the power of the will, and his advocacy of an aristocratic community. Such ideas can be found in Nietzsche, who was a singularly unsystematic philosopher, and there can be little doubt about Nietzsche's opposition to Christianity and democracy. However, Baeumler does not mention the philosopher's hatred of nationalism and his contempt for Germans. The philosopher of the "heroic" became a part of the Nazi world view. Baeumler himself was one of the leading academic philosophers of the Third Reich. As professor at the University of Berlin, he became the chief liaison man between the German universities and Alfred Rosenberg's office, which was charged with the ideological education of the Nazi party.

Baeumler connects Nietzsche's activism to Nordic and soldierly virtues. Indeed, the war experience produced an important renewal of supposedly heroic virtues. Ernst Röhm (1887-1934) catalogues them for us: plain talk, defiance, passion, and hate—a soldier is rough and direct. These virtues are identical with those "genuine" qualities of the Volk which the Nazis praised so much: they are natural as opposed to artificial (see page 27). Röhm himself had fought in the First World War, and afterward against the left-wing uprisings in northern and southern Germany. Soldiering was his whole life, and he continued it when he became the leader of the SA. Röhm's autobiography is called *Die Geschichte eines Hochverräters* (*The Story of a Traitor*), and it was as a traitor that Hitler regarded him when he was murdered in 1934. In reality, he was done away with because the independence, power, and revolutionary fervor of the SA had to be brought under the Führer's control.

The idealized war experience was made to serve the Nazi ideology just as Baeumler had transformed Nietzsche into a prophet for the Third Reich. Joseph Goebbels' *Michael* is the hero who sacrifices himself for his people. Goebbels always had literary ambitions, but *Michael* (1929) was his only novel, though by 1942 it had gone through seventeen editions. Michael gives up his studies to go down to the people at work, to "a war without cannons." The experience of the trenches becomes a court of appeal: there all Germans had been united, regardless of class, through their work for the Fatherland, and now they must recapture this unity once again. The anti-bourgeois prejudice of Goebbels comes through in this novel. Soldiers, students, and workers will build the new Reich. But for Goebbels, as for Hitler, "bourgeois" is not a class term, but rather a label for the older generation still imprisoned in liberalism and held enthralled by the lure of Mammon.

Michael does not succeed. At the end of the novel he is killed in a mining accident. But a heroic death in a just cause is an important factor in the building of heroes. Albert Leo Schlageter (1894-1923) became one of the most celebrated heroes of the Third Reich. He had fought against the French when they occupied the Ruhr Valley in order to obtain reparations for war damages. The French captured Schlageter, probably while he was performing an act of sabotage. He was condemned to death by a military tribunal and shot. Like Michael, he was in search of his people and, like Michael too, he died in their cause. But he was also a soldier (he had fought in the Free Corps after the war), and the slim memorial volume of his letters stresses his simplicity as well as his activism—a note very similar to that of Röhm's autobiography and Baeumler's essay on Nietzsche.

Hanns Johst's play *Schlageter* had its première in Hitler's presence and on Hitler's birthday (April 20, 1933). It was performed throughout the Reich by a series of theatrical touring companies. Johst (b. 1890) was the only distinguished playwright to put himself wholly at the service of the Nazi cause, becoming president of the *Reichsschriftstumskammer* (see page 135). The excerpt from the play illustrates the stress put upon the differences between generations. The son wants to join his hero, Schlageter, while the father holds back. The "young generation" were the "new men" who confront the old bourgeois generation, which (so the Nazis hoped) was "finished."

Fritz Todt (1891-1942) died in the glory of his great accomplishment: the building of the *Autobahnen*. He was burned alive in a plane crash while returning from a visit with Hitler, whom he was then serving as Minister of Munitions. Here was a contemporary hero for whom the superhighway was symbolic of speed and activism in the service of his leader. Moreover, his work is linked to a lively sense of history and an appreciation of the genuineness of nature. But what about heroes of the past? The cult of Frederick the Great goes back to the party's years of struggle and was expanded during the war. Goebbels was the high priest of this cult.[1] Wilhelm Ihde puts forward the Nazi version of the Prussian King. His strength of will stands in the foreground, while his artistic interests and his philosophical predilections are relegated to unimportance. Such had to be the case, for Frederick was, after all, a man of the hated Enlightenment. Ihde himself was a former journalist who rose to high rank in the SS (*Obersturmführer*) and became the director of the *Reichsschriftstumskammer*.

The creation of heroes and the creation of myths are closely interrelated. No doubt, for the young SA bride Hermann Göring was a living hero, surrounded as he was by the acted-out mythology of the summer solstice celebration. The marching, the torches, the fire—this was the "magic" that produced enthusiasm among many a youth (see page 271). This account of a Nazi experience was written four years before Hitler came to power, at a time when Nazi strength had not yet made an impact upon the voting behavior of the boys' and girls' parents.

The myth was institutionalized; it became a part of the official rhythm of the Third Reich. As the instructions for festivities in the

[1] Ernest K. Bramsted, *Goebbels and National Socialist Propaganda, 1925-1945* (East Lansing, Mich., 1965), pp. 444-445.

school state, the teacher battles for the human soul on the cultural-political front. Here celebrations are important, because they help root the mythology of the movement in that soul; they are indeed "confessions of faith." Like all Nazi festivities, these are set up in the form of recitations, responses, and choruses: the Christian liturgical framework is adapted to the content of the Nazi world view.

Building myths and heroes was an integral part of the Nazi cultural drive. The theme, specifically illustrated here, runs throughout this book. Racial thought produced strong myths and the peasant provided the constant culture hero of National Socialism. The flight from reason became a search for myths and heroes to believe in, and National Socialism was only too glad to provide both in full measure.

G.L.M.

Nietzsche and National Socialism
ALFRED BAEUMLER

Nietzsche and National Socialism stand on the other side of the traditions of the German bourgeoisie. What does that mean? The spiritual forces which have formed the German bourgeoisie in the last several centuries have been Pietism, the Enlightenment, and Romanticism. Pietism was the last truly revolutionary religious movement on Lutheran soil. It led men from a hopeless political reality back into their own selves and gathered them together in small private circles. It was a religious individualism which strengthened the inclination toward concern with self, toward psychological analysis and biographical examination. Every apolitical state-alien tendency necessarily had to find support and nourishment in Pietistic Germany. The wholly different individualism of the Enlightenment also worked in this direction. This individualism was not of a religious-sentimental character. It believed in reason, it was rational, but it was "political" only in that it denied the feudal system; it was unable to erect an enduring political system of its own and was capable only of breaking the path for the economic system of capitalism. Man was viewed as a wholly individual entity, cut off from all original orders and relations, a fictitious person responsible only to himself. In contrast, Romanticism saw man again in the light of his natural and historical ties. Romanticism opened our eyes to the night, the past, our ancestors, to the mythos and the Volk. The movement that led from Herder to Görres, to the brothers Grimm, Eichendorff, Arnim, and Savigny,[1] is the only spiritual movement that is still fully alive. It is the only movement with which Nietzsche had to wrestle. . . .

When we call National Socialism a world view we mean that not only the bourgeois parties but also their ideologies have been annihilated. Only ill-willed persons could maintain that everything that has been created by the past must now be negated. Rather, we mean that we have entered into a new relationship with our past, that our view has

---

[1] These are all Romantic writers of the late eighteenth to the middle of the nineteenth century.

been cleared for what was truly forceful in this past but which had been clouded by bourgeois ideology. In a word, we have discovered new possibilities for understanding the essence of German existence. Precisely in this Nietzsche has preceded us. We hold a view of Romanticism that is different from his. But his most personal and lonely possession, the negation of bourgeois ideology as a whole, has today become the property of a generation. . . .

The foundations of Christian morality—religious individualism, a guilty conscience, meekness, concern for the eternal salvation of the soul—all are absolutely foreign to Nietzsche. He revolts against the concept of repentance: "I do not like this kind of cowardice about one's own action; one should not leave one's own self in the lurch before the assault of unexpected disgrace and vexation. Rather, an extreme pride is in order here. For, finally, what is the use! No deed can be undone by repentance." What he means here is not a reduction of responsibility, but rather its intensification. Here speaks the man who knows how much courage, how much pride, is necessary to maintain himself in the face of Fate. Out of his *amor fati* Nietzsche spoke contemptuously about Christianity with its "perspective of salvation." As a Nordic man he never understood for what purpose he should be "redeemed." The Mediterranean religion of salvation is alien to and far removed from his Nordic attitude. He can understand man only as a warrior against Fate. A mode of thought which sees struggle and work only as a penance appears incomprehensible to him. "Our real life is a false, apostatic, and sinful existence, a penalty existence." Sorrow, battle, work, death, are merely taken as objections to life. "Man as innocent, idle, immortal, happy—this concept of 'highest desirability' especially must be criticized." Nietzsche turns passionately upon the monastic *vita contemplativa*, against Augustine's "Sabbath of all Sabbaths." He praises Luther for having made an end of the *vita contemplativa*. The Nordic melody of strife and labor sounds strong and clear here. The accent with which we pronounce these words today we heard from Nietzsche for the first time.

We call Nietzsche the philosopher of heroism. But that is only a half-truth if we do not regard him at the same time as the philosopher of activism. He considered himself the world-historical counterpart to Plato. "Works" result not from the desire for display, not from the acknowledgment of "extramundane" values, but from practice, from the ever repeated deed. Nietzsche employs a famous antithesis to make this clear: "First and above all there is the work. And that means training, training, training! The accompanying faith will come by itself—of that you can be certain." Nietzsche opposes the Christian proscription of the political sphere, of the sphere of action altogether, with the thesis that also overcame the contrast between Catholicism and Protestantism (work and faith): "One has to train oneself not in the strengthening of value feelings, but in action; one has to know how to do something." In this way he re-established the purity of the sphere of action, of the political sphere.

Nietzsche's "values" have nothing to do with the Beyond, and therefore cannot be petrified into dogma. In ourselves, through us, they rise struggling to the surface; they exist only as long as we make ourselves responsible for them. When Nietzsche warns, "Be true to the Earth!" he reminds us of the idea that is rooted in our strength but does not hope for "realization" in a distant Beyond. It is not enough to point out the "this-worldly" character of Nietzsche's values if one at the same time does not want to refute the notion that values are "realized" by action. Something inferior is always attached to the "realization" of given values whether these values are of a mundane or extramundane character. . . .

Nietzsche's Nordic and soldierly valuation opposes that of the Mediterranean world and that of the priests. His critique of religion is a criticism of the priest, and arises from the point of view of the warrior, since Nietzsche demonstrates that even the origin of religion lies in the realm of power. This explains the fateful contradiction in a morality based on the Christian religion. "To secure the rule of moral values, all kinds of unmoral forces and passions have to be enlisted. The development of moral values is the work of unmoral passions and considerations." Morality, therefore, is the creation of unmorality. "How to bring virtue to rule: This treatise deals with the great politics of virtue." It teaches for the first time "that one cannot bring about the reign of virtue by the same means used to establish any kind of rule, least of all through virtue." "One has to be very unmoral to make morality through deeds." Nietzsche replaces the bourgeois moral philosophy with the philosophy of the will to power—in other words with the philosophy of politics. If in doing so he becomes the apologist for the "unconscious," this "unconscious" is not to be understood in terms of depth pyschology. Here the concern is not with the instinctive and unconscious drives of an individual. Rather, "unconscious" here means "perfect" and "able." And beyond that, "unconscious" also means life as such, the organism, the "great reason" of the body.

Consciousness is only a tool, a detail in the totality of life. In opposition to the philosophy of the conscious, Nietzsche asserts the aristocracy of nature. But for thousands of years a life-weary morality has opposed the aristocracy of the strong and healthy. Like National Socialism, Nietzsche sees in the state, in society, the "great mandatary of life," responsible for each life's failure to life itself. "The species requires the extinction of the misfits, weaklings, and degenerates: but Christianity as a conserving force appeals especially to them." Here we encounter the basic contradiction: whether one proceeds from a natural life context or from an equality of individual souls before God. Ultimately the ideal of democratic equality rests upon the latter assumption. The former contains the foundations of a new policy. It takes unexcelled boldness to base a state upon the race. A new order of things is the natural consequence. It is this order which Nietzsche undertook to establish in opposition to the existing one.

In the face of the overpowering strength of the race, what happens to the individual? He returns—as a single member in a community. The herd instinct is basically altogether different from the instinct of an "aristocratic society," composed of strong, natural men who do not permit their basic instincts to languish in favor of a mediocre average —men who know how to curb and control their passions instead of weakening or negating them. This again must not be understood from an individualistic point of view. For a long time emotions will have to be kept under "tyrannical" control. This can be done only by one community, one race, one people. . . .

If there ever was a truly German expression, it is this: One must have the need to be strong, otherwise one never will be. We Germans know what it means to maintain ourselves against all opposition. We understand the "will to power"—even if in an altogether different manner than our enemies assume. Even in this connection, Nietzsche has supplied the deepest meaning: "We Germans demand something from ourselves that nobody expected from us—we want more."

If today we see German youth on the march under the banner of the swastika, we are reminded of Nietzsche's "untimely meditations" in which this youth was appealed to for the first time. It is our greatest hope that the state today is wide open to our youth. And if today we shout "Heil Hitler!" to this youth, at the same time we are also hailing Nietzsche.

From Alfred Baeumler, *Studien zur deutschen Geistesge-schichte* (Berlin: Junker und Dünnhaupt Verlag, 1937), pp. 283-285, 288-294.

A Soldier Believes in Plain Talk
ERNST RÖHM

I have opened here the book of my life to the understanding friend as well as to the nagging philistine.

The narrow-minded petit bourgeois may find my attitude injudicious, but that does not bother me.

Many books have been written, but few with such reckless frankness.

Even my political friends may have found some of my opinions objectionable; my soldier's sensibility compelled me, in spite of the prevalent onesidedness of thought and feeling, to recognize the merits of the enemy no less than the shortcomings of the friend.

I am a believer in plain talk and have not hid my heart like a skeleton in the closet.

I must write without fear, with defiance—just as it comes from my soul.

And yet nothing was further from my intention than to offend or to injure anyone. Soldiers' talk is rough and direct, but we soldiers all speak the same language and understand each other.

The "soldiers' emperor," Napoleon, is reported to have said on one occasion during his exile: "Soldiers will never be able to hate me, even if they have faced me on the battlefield."

The wife of a soldier in my company, whose political convictions were far removed from mine, said to me on one occasion: "In the heart of my husband, his captain takes the first place; there is nobody to outrank him. Only then come his mother and I."

And another of my soldiers, a Communist, during the period of the soldiers' councils, jumped up in a meeting at which the officers were being denounced, and shouted: "I don't know whether what you are saying about the officers is true, but I know that as far as my captain is concerned, it's not true."

This is the way in which the hand of a soldier reaches out beyond all differences of class, rank, and political philosophy. Soldierly comradeship, cemented with blood, can perhaps temporarily relax, but it can never be torn out of the heart, it cannot be exterminated.

Still, all of Germany has not been awakened yet—despite National Socialism. My words shall be a trumpet call to those who are still asleep.

I am not appealing to the hustling and sneaky trader who has made accursed gold his God, but to the warrior who is struggling in the battle of life, who wants to win freedom and with it the kingdom of heaven.

I approve of whatever serves the purpose of German freedom. I oppose whatever runs counter to it. Europe, aye, the whole world, may go down in flames—what concern is it of ours? Germany must live and be free.

One may call me a bigoted fool—I can't help that. I am opposed to sport in its present form and to its effects. Moreover, I consider it a definite national danger. We cannot rebuild the Fatherland with champions and artificially nurtured "big guns of sport." Only the most careful development which provides physical strength and capability, with spiritual elasticity and ethical backbone, can be of use to the Volk community. Indeed, it is in keeping with these times of pretense and advertising: rubbish, confusion of the senses and sensation, have no enduring essence. I leave the sport mania to Ullstein and Mosse.[1] I remain with Jahn.[2]

The Germans have forgotten how to hate.

Virile hate has been replaced by feminine lamentation. But he who is unable to hate cannot love either. Fanatical love and hate—their fires kindle flames of freedom.

Passionlessness, matter-of-factness, objectivity, are impersonality, are sophistry.

Only passion gives knowledge, creates wisdom.

"Peace and order" is the battle cry of people living on pensions. In

[1] The two leading publishing houses of Germany.
[2] Friedrich Ludwig Jahn (1778-1852) combined patriotism, defined as allegiance to the Volkdom, with preparedness through physical fitness. He founded the gymnastic associations and the modern fraternity movement.

the last analysis you cannot govern a state on the basis of the needs of pensioners.

"One is being circumspect," wrote the *Münchner Zeitung* in 1927 on the occasion of French attacks in the occupied zone,[3] "if one peacefully takes a punch in the ears."

Translated into German it means "peace and order," hence simply shaking at the knees.

Once more to hell with this peace and prudence, with the half-hearted, the middlings, the cowards!

"Non-circumspect" persons fought four and a half years at the front! The "circumspect" ones remained at home!

"Immature" persons fought in Upper Silesia for the preservation of the Reich. The "mature" persons locked themselves behind their doors.

"Irresponsible dreamers" for years and years have called upon the people to rise up against enslavement and oppression. The "responsible politicians" of the new Germany in these same years have sold Germany lock, stock, and barrel.

Our people and Fatherland are slowly but surely going under because of "circumspection" and "maturity."

From time immemorial Germany was not suited to "diplomacy" and "politics." The sword has always determined the greatness of its history.

"I most respectfully beg of the diplomats not to lose again what the soldier has gained with his blood." This is what Blücher had to write his king, Frederick William II, after the Battle of "Belle-Alliance."[4]

Only the soldier could lead his people and Fatherland out of wretchedness and shame to freedom and honor.

From Ernst Röhm, *Die Geschichte eines Hochverräters* (Munich: Verlag Frz. Eher Nachf., 1928), pp. 365-367. (This extract has been taken from the seventh edition, 1934.)

[3] That is, the French occupation of the Ruhr Valley.
[4] A battle in the wars of liberation against Napoleon.

Michael: A German Fate
JOSEPH GOEBBELS

June 3

Intellectualism is becoming a big bore to me. I feel nauseous at every printed word. I don't find anything in it that could redeem me.

Richard wants to help me in small ways.

I cannot very well speak uncivilly to him.

Sometimes I sit for hours in listless indecisiveness, do nothing, and think nothing. Then again I am pursued by a thousand demons and forge plan after plan.

But I don't begin to carry any of them out. Every evening I read the Sermon on the Mount. I find no consolation in it, only despair and shame. Something is wrong about it.

In Germany's higher schools much work is done, but little of it for the future. It is all only day laborer's work.

The wisdom of university chairs will never be able to redeem us!

June 7

If Christ were to be restored as he was, perhaps that would be our redemption.

June 10

Before me rises a new fatherland.

I am learning to love this fatherland again. And the more disgraceful its shame, the more ardent becomes my love for it.

When I see the new man, I seek first for the German man.

I will root myself in the soil of this fatherland. It is the mother of my thoughts and longings.

We will not be blind to its failures and shortcomings. But we shall love these too, because they are our failures and shortcomings.

The new nationalism desires Germany's future, not the restoration of a broken past.

What does nationalism mean? We stand by Germany because we are Germans and because Germany is our fatherland, the German soul is our soul, because each of us is a piece of Germany's soul.

I hate the tongue-warriors who always carry the words "fatherland" and "patriotism" in their mouths.

Fatherland: that must again become something that is self-evident to us.

All of German history is nothing but a continuous chain of the battles of the German soul against its enemies.

The German soul is Faustian! In it lies the instinctive bent toward work and its possibilities and the longing for redemption from the mind.

There is a German idea, just as there is a Russian idea. They both will have to take each other's measure in the future. . . .

June 15

The battle that is raging through Europe today is a battle between newly emerging aristocratic classes.

Every history-making epoch has been created by aristocrats. Aristocracy = the rule of the best.

Never do the people rule themselves. This madness has been invented by liberalism. Behind its concept of the sovereignty of the people hide the most corrupt rogues, who do not want to be recognized.

It is easy to see that it is all a cheap swindle, which can deceive only a fool whose head is stuffed with straw.

The mass is victorious: what madness! Just as if I were to say: marble makes the statue. No work of art without its creator. No people without a statesman. No world without God!

History is a sequence of many virile decisions. Armies are not victorious, but men within armies.

Europe will be reconstructed by peoples who will be the first to overcome the mass madness and find their way back to the principle of personality.

However, the new aristocracy is being created on the basis of new law. Tradition is being replaced by ability. The Best One! This title is not inherited, it has to be earned.

Geniuses are only the highest forms of expression of the national will. They represent, so to speak, the incarnation of the creative Volkdom.

No oak tree grows without soil, root, and strength. No man comes out of the unsubstantial. The people are his soil, history his root, blood his strength.

Great ideas are always championed by minorities. In the end, however, they create a condition which enables whole nations to exist.

Works of art, inventions, ideas, battles, laws, and states—at the beginning of all of them stands always the man.

Race is the matrix of all creative forces. Humanity—that is a mere supposition. Reality is only the Volk. Humanity is nothing but a multitude of peoples. A people is an organic entity. Humanity has only the chance to become organic.

To be organic means to possess within oneself the capability of creating organic life.

The forest is only a multiplicity of trees.

I cannot destroy nations and keep humanity alive, just as I could not uproot the trees and keep the forest.

Trees—that is, in their totality a forest.

Peoples—that is, in their totality humanity.

The stronger the oak grows, the more will it beautify the forest.

The more thoroughly a people is people, the greater its service to humanity . . .

Everything else is invented, not organically grown. For that reason it cannot stand up to history.

A minority, if it includes the best, will turn the German fate.

We must, therefore, be more courageous, more clever, more radical, and have more character than the majority; then we will automatically be victorious.

That other peoples are ruled by their social scum should give us no headaches. The better the prospect of our success.

If the most courageous hold the helm, they shall openly pronounce: We practice dictatorship! We assume responsibility before history—who will cast the first stone at us?

But if the cowards have the helm in their hand, they say: The people rule. They avoid responsibility and stone all those who unite to turn against this hypocrisy.

Rule will always be an affair of a minority. The people have only the choice to live under the open dictatorship of the courageous, or to die under the hypocritical democracy of cowards.

This is an account that is as simple as it is logical. . . .

July 2

"I will have to go to work, Agnes Stahl. It is my only salvation."

"You always worked."

"No, I was a dreamer, an aesthete, a fine talker.

"I wanted to redeem the world with phrases.

"I had a high regard for myself.

"But now I would like to take my place in the middle of things. Nobody can remain neutral when two enemies, armed to the teeth, battle each other for the future."

"Two enemies? Where and when?"

"Yes, you don't see it, you don't want to see it. But it's so just the same. Money has made slaves of us, but work shall make us free. With the political bourgeoisie we staggered on the edge of an abyss; but with the political working class we will achieve a resurrection."

"But you are opposed to the class struggle, and now you preach the rule of a class?"

"Labor is no class. Class derived from the economic sphere. But labor has its roots in politics. It is a historical social estate. Nations have importance only if their ruling social estate has reality. The political bourgeoisie is nothing and does not want to be anything. It wants only to live, to live wholly primitively. For that reason it is doomed to destruction.

"We can maintain life only if we are ready to die for it!

"But the working class, on the other hand, has to fulfill a mission, above all in Germany. It must free the German people internally and externally. This is a world mission. If Germany goes under, the light of the world will be extinguished."

"You are not very modest."

"Only scoundrels are modest. The less I ask for myself, the more passionately I fight for the rights of my Volk. And since I see this sold out and betrayed by the bourgeoisie, I write off the past and begin with my work from the bottom up."

"You may make revolutions, as many as you want. Fat will always swim on the surface."

"Correct, the fat ones will always say the big words; they will own country villas and will deliver the speeches on national holidays. Mass man rules today and the morrow as well. But we will engrave our name on history. We alone!

"The others live only for today. That is why they will be dead in the future. But those who are willing to renounce life today will be alive tomorrow."

"Why renunciation? Who will thank you for it?"

"Thank? I don't know the word. I want no thanks. What difference does this bit of life make?"

"But you yourself come from the bourgeoisie."

"That is why I learned to hate it so devoutly. One has to experience a thing in order to learn either to love or hate it thoroughly.

"I hate the bourgeois because he is a coward and no longer wants to fight. He is only a zoological organism, nothing else.

"Soldiers, students, and workers will build the new Reich. I was a soldier, I am a student, I want to be a worker. I have to go through all three steps to show the way. I was not granted the word, so I must begin to act. Each one to his post."

"You love to sacrifice?"

"Yes, sacrifice is necessary. I don't like it, but I must do it. I must descend to the deepest abyss. We have to begin from below.

"Up to now we were inheritors. We have accepted what was transmitted to us with thanks.

"But we must start from the beginning.

"I shall be most ruthless and completely commit myself."

"You have always been totally committed. You were always all ardor and sacrifice."

"But in connection with wrong things. The new German man will be born in the workshops, not in books.

"We have written, twaddled, and romanticized enough. Now we must work."

"You will ruin yourself in the attempt."

"No, I shall live. I want to make a beginning."

"Work will reduce you to serfdom."

"No, I shall ennoble my work. Work is not a thing in itself, it is only a step."

"You put us all to shame."

"I can take no credit for it; I have to be and act the way I am."

Both of us are silent for a long while; it is getting late and the day is dying. . . .

September 15

I feel good only if it crashes and thunders down there. When the pit props crash and the stone breaks. When the noise of work roars so that you can't hear your own voice.

Symphony of work!
Satiated, full life!
Creation! Work! To use one's hands!
To be master! Conqueror! King of life!
And then I yearn again for the divine loneliness of the mountains and the virgin white snow.

September 18

It is not the spirit that sets us free, nor is it work. Both are only forms of a higher power.

Struggle stands at the beginning and at the end. I have undertaken the struggle with myself. We must first overcome the scoundrel in ourselves. The rest is child's play.

Out of spirit, work, and struggle we create the motor which will set our age into motion.

It will be an age of the newly formed aristocracy of achievement.

September 20

Money is the curse of mankind. It smothers the seed of everything great and good. Every penny is sticky with sweat and blood.

I hate Mammon.

It breeds sloth and satiated rest. It poisons our own values and subjects us to the service of low and base instincts.

To me the worst day of the week is payday. They throw the money at us like bones to a dog.

This world is hard and cruel. As hard as money in the thin hands of a miser.

Thrift is a sticky virtue.

Let them collect treasures and gold—I shall be spendthrift with the surplus of my soul.

Money is the yardstick for the values of liberalism. So insubstantial is this concept that it can elevate mere appearance to reality. That is what will eventually lead to its ruin. Money is the curse of labor.

One cannot set money above life. Where that is done, all noble forces must run dry.

Money is a means to an end, not an end in itself. If it becomes a purpose unto itself, then it must of necessity devaluate all labor until it becomes the means to an end.

A Volk which evaluates everything in terms of money already

stands before its own dark end. It will slowly be eaten up by the disintegrating forces of gold, which since time immemorial have led peoples and cultures to ruin.

While the soldiers in the Great War offered their bodies for the protection of their homes and two million of them bled to death, the speculators coined gold out of their red and noble blood. And they later used this gold to cheat the returning soldiers out of house and home.

The war was won by money and lost by labor. The peoples are not the victors or the vanquished. They performed only day labor in the service of money, or defended work against this slave labor.

Germany battled for work. France fought for money. Labor lost the battle. Money won it.

Money rules the world! If true, this is a horrible statement. But today we die because it is a reality. Money and Jew—they belong together.

Money is without roots. It stands above the races. Slowly it eats its way into the sound bodies of nations and little by little poisons their creative force.

We must deliver ourselves from money through struggle and work. We must destroy this delusion in ourselves. Then the Golden Calf will come crashing down.

In its deepest sense, liberalism is the philosophy of money.

Liberalism means: I believe in Mammon.

Socialism means: I believe in work. . . .

September 28

I'm beginning to gain recognition among my fellow workers.

Here and there one of them says a word to me. Some of them even initiate me into their sorrows and hardships.

Slowly their distrust vanishes.

Even my landlords become friendlier.

This afternoon I found a few modest flowers on my table.

How they filled me with joy!

The children now call me by name when they see me and hang on to to my hands.

October 3

"You're wearing yourself out, Michael. You can't keep it up. You will ruin yourself."

"A man can endure more than we think. One can't take care of oneself. One has to assume great burdens in life.

"During the war we wrested even more from our bodies and our defiance and we didn't go to ruin."

"But we suffered grievously in body and soul."

"True, Matthias, it was not easy to overcome it all. But see here, we did it together, worker and master.

"We lay together in the trenches, he who came from a palace and he who hailed from a miner's cottage.

"We clung together, became friends, and for the first time knew each other.

"But when the war was over, the unholy cleavage opened up again.

"Work is a war without cannons. Here too we must hold together, brawn and brain. We must for once understand each other, the sooner the better.

"Life is difficult. We don't have time enough to be each other's enemy. We must raise bread for the millions already born and for the millions yet to come. Otherwise, sooner or later we go to ruin."

"Yes, but none of them up there thinks as you do: only money and power count with them."

"These creatures have to be forced. There are people who are impressed only by the fist under their nose. There can be no special considerations. We young people have the greater right before history.

"The old ones don't even want to understand that we young people even exist. They defend their power to the last.

"But one day they will be defeated after all. Youth finally must be victorious.

"We young ones, we shall attack. The attacker is always stronger than the defender.

"If we free ourselves, we can also liberate the whole working class. And the liberated working class will release the Fatherland from its chains."

"What you said about labor and war is absolutely right. And the most beautiful part of it is that you yourself make these words come true.

"You do not merely mouth phrases like the others. You act.

"As soon as you arrived here, when I saw you for the first time, I knew that you were a pioneer of the idea of labor.

"Alas, we see many university students here. They are all eager and do their duty below in the pit.

"But most of them fail to understand us miners. They climb down to us. Moreover, they condescend to come down to our level. There always remains an open space between them and us. That is the reason for the brooding hatred between us and the 'white hands.'

"You will find here much animosity against the students. But I know that you want to improve things. You don't want to come down to us, you want to help us to come up to you.

"You understand how to grasp this correctly, because you see the comrade in us. Therefore you easily find the right word that opens our hearts."

I kneel beside Matthias Grützer deep down in the pit during our breakfast break. We can only talk after long intervals and must shout in order to understand each other.

From Joseph Goebbels, *Michael: Ein deutsches Schicksal in Tagebuchblättern* (Munich: Zentralverlag der NSDAP, Frz. Eher Nachf., 1929), pp. 112-115, 118-120, 137-142.

Germany Must Live
FRIEDRICH BUBENDEN

ALBERT LEO SCHLAGETER'S WAR SONG

Though at first we are but few,
You perhaps, we, a couple of others still,
The road is broad—the aim is clear;
Forward, step by step!
Courage, come along!
Though at first we are but few,
We shall carry it off, nonetheless!

The November day of the year 1918 when Germany fell to pieces was dying, oddly worn out, languid, yellow intermingled with the bitter-sweet fragrance of falling autumn leaves.

Suddenly the stillness of death over a sea of battlefields, the stillness of death over millions of dead bodies.

At the crossroads, on the empty fields, on the cloud-enveloped mountainsides, on the wet shore, on which the waves beat sluggishly, astonished, startled faces of soldiers still hot with battle, there is a catching of breath, the restless shrugging of shoulders, a leaderless forlornness, a deeply alarmed questioning:

"Over?"

"Yes—over!"

A war comes to an end. A world war ends with a final bang. A smirking skeleton squats and giggles inaudibly over victor and vanquished.

Who is the victor?

In this brief moment, in which the very earth stands still, nobody knows. Even afterward nobody knows.

The primordial, eternal laws governing our planet are again set in motion, and the earth rotates once more. The petrification dissolves. One draws a breath, another draws a breath. Hands, forlornly, rub foreheads. The earth rotates faster and faster, already it spins at the usual speed; by now the clever have understood. The blood again pulsates through their veins.

The smokeless chimneys of the Wendel mines on the Lorraine frontiers point like steel fingers in the air, and a lieutenant, with fluttering red ribbons in his buttonhole, stands smiling in the door of his quarters.

Discarded rifles pile up in the Cologne railroad station. On them, also discarded, lies an inconvenient dagger, and train after train rolls, rolls, rolls eastward along the bare rails. And now men are flowing into the heart of the homeland from all sections of the front.

A small cluster of heroes remains behind in the forgotten war lands, still deeply rooted, still uncomprehending. They do not yet know that the earth is once more rotating.

Among them stands Albert Leo Schlageter.

The cowardly Soldiers' Council stepped back from their flashing, angry eyes, and even more from their clenched fists, and let them pass.

But in the homeland the Reds are victorious! Frenzy, ardor, greed for life, have replaced paralyzed shock. Liquor glasses clink. And as warehouses and granaries slowly and gradually fill up, it is forgotten that the earth's crust is cracking. Ho! Good times are here again! Business as usual! A spirit that goes arm in arm with everything that promises and pledges peace and quiet.

But one person sits restlessly there. Among students at their books.

He is always on the lookout for leadership. It never comes. Shall Germany live or who? Under colorful caps in Freiburg one man moans: it is Albert Leo Schlageter.

Suddenly he disappears. Riga, German Riga calls! The battery sprays flaming lightning on narrow bridges. Riga is delivered.[1] Among those who breathe freely, the happy ones, the rejoicing ones, is Albert Leo Schlageter, the leader of that battery. Schlageter the mercenary. The mercenary?

The waves rise higher in the homeland. Greedy hands reach out for gold, which flutters away in paper form. That's nothing! Just don't listen. Enjoy life. It's peace after all! The peace of Versailles!

Only one listens: Albert Leo Schlageter! He hears the subterranean rumbling of the mountains of the Ruhr. The goaded, wild, misled Red mob rises up! The petit bourgeois only shudders. He doesn't even see the insolent, yellow Muscovite mask. Albert Leo Schlageter again, impetuously firing off his battery, scatters the Red rabble.

The easily adjusting bourgeois smiles: it wasn't so bad after all.

Where is the leadership?

Here! calls Albert Leo Schlageter! Free Corps officer in Silesia!

The Annaberg looks down on German heroes. The Pole grates his teeth, pulls back. German land is saved. But how much German land was lost altogether?

The merchants and usurers call: Away with the Free Corps that has saved us! The war is over! Now let's have some peace and quiet. Become civilians!

In the background the Marxists smile, the Communists smile, the Jews smile, a Reich government smiles contentedly.

But one man does not smile! Doesn't he take a rest then? Does Germany still call? She calls! But only to those who listen! And those who listen must withdraw. They must always be on the move. They must keep hidden. From the police and the burghers. Restlessly they move here and there. Among them again stands—he! There he hears him call, the unnamed, unknown soldier, whom only a few know at first. He, without being called to leadership, also shouted his "Here!" Under the earth, near the Reich's capital, but nevertheless under the earth, Albert Leo Schlageter dedicated himself to the flag of this man.

But the fate of the German earth calls Albert Leo Schlageter to another task. Between the Rhine and the Ruhr the fires are burning

[1] Delivered from the Bolshevists' advance. In 1920 they were forced to recognize the independence of Latvia, with Riga as its capital.

again! According to the "Treaty and Agreement," the cowardly enemy[2] may invade and seize, jail, and assault Germany's sons and daughters; he may steal and rob. Silent war in the Ruhr territory.

Albert Leo Schlageter sets out when Germany calls again. He does not know that it is the last time in his life that Germany will call him. The war becomes increasingly more hidden, increasingly more secret. From an open fight in an open battlefield, it turns into a dark, secret, almost powerless defense. But he grits his teeth, and his fiery spirit, dampened into what only seems like powerlessness, fights on.

Muffled explosions and crashes. Railway tracks and iron bars split open! Bridges fly up in the air. Fear sits day and night in the shaking knees of the "victor."

But suddenly base treachery stands alongside unfettered heroism.

Incomprehensible, this going under of the holy light in the murkiness of hell! Again and again someone must experience this on this earth, and end with death. Lord, forgive them, for they know not what they do!

The cross of Golgotha is raised anew in the lonely pile in the sandpit in Golzheim. A Great One must again—how often in world history—sink lifeless to his knees because all the petty ones hate him, must hate him.

A salvo flashes, roars in the pale gray dawn of May 26, 1920.

Albert Leo Schlageter is dead!

Is he dead? Odd! Where he is dead everything now springs to life around him and his heroism.

He had fought on in the battalions of German heroes after the war. Alongside him, with him, before him, behind him, his comrades fought for the same prize: for Germany. . . .

This Albert Leo Schlageter who was restless in life, because he sought Germany, now dead, spread restlessness among ever more and new thousands.

Who was Albert Leo Schlageter?

Anyone who reads these simple letters and thinks about them knows. Certainly no one could have written more simply! Was he a creator of illusions? A gifted talker? A singer of freedom? A herald of the word, a lord of speech? A poet?

This slender little volume of letters says: no!

However, this Albert Leo Schlageter, wasn't he, and isn't he, much, much more? He was nothing else, wanted and could be nothing else

[2] France and Belgium.

but a true son of his Volk and of his homeland, nothing else but a living deed!

He did not preach the deed, he was the deed itself!

But because he was a man of action and not of words, because he accepted the bitter chalice for the sake of his faith in Germany and drank it to its last dregs, standing upright, he was and is—the German conscience!

This German conscience was threatened by struggle as long as he lived. Today the silent, despairing struggle of the unenlightened among us still goes on against this German conscience!

Again, again, and again will there be this struggle between God and the Devil, between light and darkness. It will come to an end only with the final redemption of the world.

Until then, we who call ourselves German and who feel in our blood that we are Germans must persevere in this struggle, even if it costs us our lives! We must do it, as did Albert Leo Schlageter, for the sake of Germany.

If, however, courage and strength forsake us and if we are in danger of sinking into a non-militant contemplation—then the testament of these plain letters that have been bequeathed to us shall once more open the path to heroism. Then the German conscience in these pages shall smite us.

> From the afterword to *Deutschland muss leben: Gesammelte Briefe von Albert Leo Schlageter*, edited by Friedrich Bubenden (Berlin: Paul Steegemann Verlag, 1934), pp. 70-75, 77-78.

The Difference Between Generations
HANNS JOHST

AUGUST: You won't believe it, Papa, but that's the way it is. The young people don't pay much attention to these old slogans any more . . . they're dying out . . . the class struggle is dying out.

SCHNEIDER: So . . . and what do you live on then?

AUGUST: The Volk community!

SCHNEIDER: And that's a slogan . . . ?

AUGUST: No, it's an experience!

SCHNEIDER: My God! . . . Our class struggle, our strikes, they weren't an experience, eh . . . ? Socialism, the International, were they fantasies maybe . . . ?

AUGUST: They were necessary, but they were . . . they have been . . . with respect to the future, that is, they are historical experiences.

SCHNEIDER: So . . . and the future therefore will have your Volk community. Tell me, how do you actually envision it? Poor, rich, healthy, upper, lower, all this ceases with you, eh? A social land of Cockaine, eh . . . ?

AUGUST: Look, Papa . . . upper, lower, poor, rich, that always exists. It is only the importance one places on this question that is decisive.

To us life is not chopped up into working hours and furnished with price charts. Rather, we believe in human existence as a whole. None of us regards making money as the most important thing; we want to serve. The individual is a corpuscle in the bloodstream of his people.

SCHNEIDER: That is the romanticism of adolescence! Redemption of the people through minors. Rub your nose in reality first!

World views aside for now. . . . Let's talk about something concrete: What is the attitude of your corps and your "Volk community" toward passive resistance?

AUGUST: We want to turn it into a putsch, into a national uprising.

SCHNEIDER: Turn it into a putsch . . . ?

AUGUST: You, as an old revolutionary, I must say, stress the word "putsch" rather oddly. The government either will march with us or it will vanish!

SCHNEIDER: You are talking to a regional president and he tells you: the government will raise hell with putschists!

AUGUST: I'm talking quite cheerfully and agreeably with my old father.

SCHNEIDER: Your old father is an official of the state, which considers passive resistance right and proper!

AUGUST: And your son is a revolutionary!

SCHNEIDER: My son is a lout who is going to get a box on the ears. . . . Now obey!

AUGUST [moves back, laughing gaily]: As a regional president you still manage things like an old work master. That's all right for teaching children good manners. But . . .

SCHNEIDER: But . . . but. . . . We oldsters are not as stupid as you
   youngsters imagine. To you, Schlageter and his cronies are national heroes . . . to us here, they are just an event.

   Schlageter is a dead man if he doesn't obey orders. The governments of Europe are agreed that the last adventurers and fa-
   natics and firebrands and bandits of the world war must be exterminated with fire and sword!

   We want peace! That's what I tell you, young man, and I
   stood four years under fire for Germany, as it is today and as it
   will remain, so long as I draw breath!

AUGUST: No!!

   And I say this to you, that I have no idea of what a battle is in
   which equipment is decisive, or of barrages, flame-throwers, and
   tanks.

   We young people, who stand by Schlageter, do not stand by
   him because he is the last soldier of the world war, but because
   he is the first soldier of the Third Reich!!!

CURTAIN

From Hanns Johst, Schlageter (Munich, 1934), pp. 82-85.

Fritz Todt: Contemporary Hero
EDUARD SCHÖNLEBEN

At the very beginning of his work, on the occasion of the opening
of the short *Autobahn* built to bypass the town of Opladen, on
September 27, 1933, he said: "The new road of Adolf Hitler, the
Autobahn, is in keeping with the essence of our National Socialism.
We wish to fix our goal far ahead of us, we want to achieve our aims
directly and in a straight line. We build bridges over crossroads; unnecessary connections are alien to us. We do not need switch tracks;
we create for ourselves a road that leads only forward, since we need a
road which permits us to maintain a speed that suits us.

"Thus do we build our roads in the Third Reich, thus do we educate our people, thus do we erect the whole National Socialist Reich."

The second secret of Dr. Todt's ability to accomplish great things
was an unremitting hardness against his own self, which never permitted him to demand from others what he was unwilling to do himself.

"He who is privileged to live in the times of Adolf Hitler must subordinate all desire for personal comfort to the sacred obligation of accomplishing any task the Führer assigns to him."

A few sentences, typical of Dr. Todt's artistic views, must be repeated here:

"The master builder who builds in the stone-ocean of a great city must envision his creation amidst the forms and modes of human expression of earlier times. He must express the greatness of our time in relationship to the accomplishments of earlier periods. But the attitude of the master builder who is called upon to create in the wide-open space of the all-German landscape must be altogether different. His building site is the wide room of nature. The attempt to be even more monumental, even greater than nature, will seem arrogant and presumptuous."

From Eduard Schönleben, *Fritz Todt: Der Mensch, der Ingenieur, der Nationalsozialist* (Oldenburg: Verlag Gerhard Stalling, 1943), pp. 13, 72.

Frederick the Great: Prussian Hero

WILHELM IHDE

Anyone who understands what the ancient Greeks, in their wordly wisdom, were trying to represent by the classic figure of Prometheus may also speculate whether Frederick does not occupy in history the position of the Prometheus of the Prussian state. Obviously, in his physical stature Frederick could not compare with the muscular demi-god chained to the rock. But, then, it is not always the physically heroic figures who are chosen by Fate to awaken, through their own will, the determination of a Volk. When the exulting rhythm of the Hohenfriedberger March sounded—when flags waved proudly in the crimson dawn of the Prussian-German morning—when the people of Berlin bared their heads in silent reverence—when all of Europe paid more than due respect—when the Mediterranean corsairs freed Prussian ships—when in faraway China there was awestruck whispering at the sight of the ensigns of Prussian ships—when even a sophisticated posterity must admit its unconditional admiration—when all this happens, it is not alone due to the King of Prussia, but much more to the man Frederick, whose Prussian will overcame the weaknesses of his body and who in the forty-six years of his reign always did more than just his duty.

What is there to say of this Prussian will of Frederick's, this inflexible will to live? Fortunate is he whose will finds open doors and favorable circumstances among men and things; he may unfold the fullness of his being undisturbed. But flaming sparks are ignited only then, when the genius of a great man is engaged in desperate battle with unyielding Fate, when the harmoniously peaceful purpose of his planning is transformed into the stormy, roaring hurricane of his will. Then the human will shines as a sublime heavenly flame which illuminates true human greatness beyond all time and earthliness. Only when a man's iron will wrestles breast to breast with Fate, when, gnashing his teeth and panting, he tears the disguise from the awesome power and punishes it with the club of his will—only then does the human spirit tear itself away from all matter and soar to the heights, leaving earth behind and boldly demanding entry into the realm of the Godhead. Only then does the reality of daily drudgery disappear before our eyes and in a flash of sudden awe we understand how man's struggling will can hurl thunderbolts which tear the rainbow-bridged path between earth and the universe and force the Godhead to extend its benediction. His will pushes the Gods from their "golden seats" and forces them to give justice to the human race.

Frederick never experienced good will and luck. From his youth he was forced to stand question and answer, to receive blows and to repay them with even harder blows. From year to year his spirit grew in this never-ending dialogue. Fate raised her own enemy. He was not concerned with the petty joys of life, he hardened his heart early and eventually grew far beyond the everyday world to greatness during the hardest battles of the Seven Years' War.

Four and a half million Prussian subjects defended themselves against a European coalition of 96 million. But Frederick could muster only 150,000 soldiers against many hundred thousands. He marched back and forth across the land, joined battle wherever the enemy could be found, and through cleverly conceived maneuvering kept the multitudinous pack of his enemies before the edge of his sword. His will made up for the lack of troops, his mind for the lack of allies. . . .

Perhaps, then, the great King of Prussia was a philosopher? Many who understood that Frederick could not be explained either as a coldly calculating general, as an unfeeling diplomat, or as a personally ambitious statesman thought it possible to attribute these qualities to him by calling him a philosopher in whom the lives and sufferings of his subjects and the wishes of the surrounding world aroused no sympathy. Nothing could be more wrong than such fabrications! Of course, he was called the Philosopher of Sanssouci,[1] but this philosopher was a human being who was involved in reality with all the fibers of his feelings. He had been forced to look into the weakness and the baseness of the human character. And he had to take them into consideration every day, had no leisure to search for hypotheses alien to reality. There was hardly a man of his time, filled as it was with so-called philosophical speculation, who expressed his scorn and derision for them as strongly as did Frederick. True, in some situations he seemed to be a fatalist, but on the whole he had his feet solidly on the ground and he avoided philosophical speculations which seldom can awaken the interest of active people. In fact, he hated them in his innermost soul. He himself confessed: "A little rest, a little sleep, a little bit of good health—these constitute my whole philosophy." His whole so-called "philosopher's conceit" was nothing but a splendid humaneness, tempered by suffering and woe, by victory and glory, a heart that was not alien to anything human.

This then is the golden key to Frederick II, King of Prussia: he was nothing but a human being!

He had no less need than others for human joys and happiness; indeed, because of his artistic sensibility he could even have laid a greater claim to them. Who would deny that the bitter disappointments of his youth and his forced marriage made him worthy of a share of some compensating human happiness? A man of Frederick's capacities would have known well what loveliness, what enrapturing felicities and artistic enjoyments, life holds for the connoisseur, and his own capacity for life was equally ready to give and take. The temptations that beset this gracious prince were not small. At the small price of national dignity, the whole of Europe would have been willing to let him lead a life that would have provided the greatest opportunities for his personal inclinations. And in view of the real power relations, posterity would have found little cause to criticize him for it. This Frederick was not forced to be a hero. If he had succumbed to the blandishments of life, it would certainly have been an expression of the will to live on the part of the most charming and

[1] Frederick's palace at Potsdam.

intellectual prince in Europe, but we would have searched in vain for the Prussian will to live.

This man Frederick, gifted and blessed for the pursuit of human happiness, made the decision himself. On the day that he, alone in the world and before God, was charged with the future of his people, it was as if a glowing stream of fire went through his heart; he tore himself loose from his personal fate and made this avowal: "It is not necessary for me to live, but that I do my duty." From then on he was Frederick of Prussia, the first servant of his people, and nothing else. Far behind now lay the idyl of Rheinsberg, lost were friends and joys, and before him rose the terror of the battlefield, and for all the future, until the hour of his death, the unfailing clockwork of service. Now, as Fate had declared war on him, he became a hero. In the face of sorrows and hardships he knew nothing of a hero's glory, but when he raised his eyes to his generals—when his glance swept over his grena-diers—when from his desk he inspired his ministers—when he in-structed the ambassadors of foreign powers—when he looked like a father upon the least of his Prussians—then appeared before all of them the hero Frederick.

When finally he fell asleep in the arms of his valet in Sanssouci and wrote finis to seventy-four troublesome years, he left no more personal property than a single threadbare uniform coat of his own guards regi-ment, an old and tired whippet hound, the old gray charger Condé, and a few snuffboxes. Every general and minister possessed more.

But the great king left behind a Prussia which he had put into the world with will and might, so that it could look forward to its German destiny.

From *Kämpfer, Künder, Tatzeugen: Gestalter deutscher Grösse*, Vol. I: *Kämpfer*, edited by Ernst Adolf Dreyer and Heinz W. Siska (Munich, Vienna, Leipzig: Zinnen-Verlag, 1942), pp. 182-184, 203-205.

The Diary of an SA Man's Bride
GUDRUN STREITER

Although I am very tired, I just cannot sleep. The events of the last days have filled me with such a great enthusiasm that despite the late hour I take up my beloved diary in order to write in it what has so deeply stirred me. It was cloudy and overcast when I set out for the Rhine yesterday with my Hitler comrades, men and women. Nevertheless, we paid no attention to the unfavorable weather. Our hearts flamed with a glowing enthusiasm and a great joy. The lutes played and our song-happy lips never rested. Men and women party comrades boarded the train at almost every station and brought even more cheer to the frolicsome group. Time flew by so quickly with all the singing and jingling and jangling and before we were aware of it Germania was already greeting us from the Niederwald. Upon arriving in Bingen, we were still undecided whether we should go by ferry in order to travel up the other side of the Rhine by train or whether we should proceed to our destination by steamboat on the German Rhine. The weather decided for us. An opaque black mass of clouds had formed in the skies. The clouds were riveted together like iron chains. While we were looking up at the skies pondering alternatives, a violent storm began to rage and pound the waves of the Rhine with terrible force. Then we were all seized by a yearning for wild waves, stormy wind and rain. We boarded the steamer and clambered to the upper deck, to let the storm wind blow through us and to lift our heads to the elements. How loudly our hearts pounded and how proudly waved our swastika flags and pennants in the storm wind. Legend-woven castles greeted us boldly and stubbornly from both banks. And our enthusiasm and ecstasy grew even more. The beautiful trip was concluded much too quickly and soon we could spot the little Rhenish town, our destination, greeting us. A great stir of life could be seen on the shores of the Rhine. Unnumbered bands of Brownshirts marched with their blood-red flags to assembly on the banks of the Rhine. Roaring shouts of "Heil!" greeted us, echoing back and forth. We were met by a wonderful panorama when we entered the town. The streets were a regular forest of flags. From every house waved the glorious German banners. Garlands and a profusion of flowers decorated the streets. There was liveliness everywhere. SA men hurried past us, carrying out the orders of their leaders. From every side we could hear stirring tunes of Prussian military marches. And then I saw something I had never seen before: women and girls in the brown Hitler uniform. They sold us badges for the solstice celebration. This touched me in a wondrous way, and a desire began to burgeon and to burn within me, to be permitted to help, like these women and girls, in the great work of our leader Adolf

Hitler. A torch had been thrown into my heart and continued to flame and blaze. There was no place for any other thought within me.

Almost in a trance, I followed my girl comrades to our quarters. I no longer heard or saw what was happening around me; I just sat on my cot and wondered how I could become a helper in the reconstruction of the Fatherland. I was still lost in thought when one of my girl comrades found me and took me to the open-air concert of the SA. Deep inside I was annoyed that I had been disturbed in my thoughts. But outwardly, of course, I gave no indication and acted as though I were in high spirits. But in spite of the eager talk of the other girls, I was soon lost in my thoughts again, not at all aware of the fact that I was already beginning my work for the Hitler movement. As we approached the square, we heard the last few bars of the Petersburg March, and then there was a pause in the music program. I soon lost my comrades in the press of people. I went along a stretch of the Rhine promenade and suddenly found myself before the statue of our great Blücher. I stood on the spot where, on New Year's night in 1814, the Prussian army led by Blücher had crossed the Rhine. My thoughts rushed back to that memorable night and, fully occupied with meditation on this great deed of the courageous Prussians, I just stood there. I was torn out of my thoughts when I heard a man's voice beside me and I saw an SA man standing in front of me. He said to me: "Pardon me, are you a party comrade?" "Yes, of course," I answered. "Heil and greetings." I looked up and saw before me a weather-browned manly face with a pair of strikingly large and sunny eyes. He looked at me questioningly. "Wouldn't you like to help the movement a bit by selling some cards?" "With pleasure," I responded, and received a stack of cards from his hands. With joy I rushed toward the mass of people that surrounded the band. In only a quarter of an hour I had sold all the relief cards and joyfully delivered the money to the SA man for the movement. He was overjoyed and thanked me by shaking my hand. He told me his name, Wolfgang Jensen. I told him my name in return. We exchanged a few more words and then I hastened to rejoin my comrades to tell them about my card selling.

In the evening, at ten o'clock, there was a great assembly before the Blücher monument. We had bought torches from the SA men and now we took our place in the ranks of the Hitler legions. Countless people stood in formation. SS and SA men, Hitler Youth, National Socialist women and girls' groups, Stahlhelmer, Pfadfinder, Wander-

vögel, and thousands of others formed the endless ranks of the participants in the solstice festival. In the van stood the standard-bearers
with their blood-red swastika flags, and countless pennants waved between the ranks in the evening breeze. We stood like that in rank and
file for more than two hours. At twelve-fifteen finally came the great
moment. The order came to march off and the torches were lighted.
We marched with joyful song, accompanied by lutes, through the
streets of the little town. After a short time we were in top marching
form. As we entered the market square, there was a roar of "Heil!"
There stood Flight Captain Hermann Göring, his hand raised in the
Hitler salute, and he reviewed the long line of marchers, while shouts
of "Heil!" echoed in the square. After we left the town, the road led
us up into the mountains toward the solstice fire. It was a splendid
sight. The road led to the mountain in serpentine twists and turns.
From the top we could look back on the long marching columns. The
brilliant glare of the torches in the night was glorious. It was an overwhelming sight. My words are too poor to portray this experience. For
a long time we let this picture enter our thirsty souls to their utter-
most depths until our eyes were focused on one mighty flaming fire. It
was our solstice celebration. We were received by the tunes of Prussian military marches. Then, with the Dutch Prayer of Thanksgiving,
the inspiring festival began. Heads were bared. With folded hands we
listened devoutly to the solemn melody: "We come to pray before
the righteous God . . ."

Toward the end Hermann Göring rose again to deliver a flaming
address. In his call to battle for Germany's freedom the rustle of the
Rhine sounded like a prayer for redemption from foreign despotism.
In the deep darkness of the night, the iron words of Ernst Moritz
Arndt[1] sounded forceful and thundering on Hermann Göring's
tongue: "The Rhine, Germany's river, but not Germany's border."

After singing the national anthem, we all sat down around the great
fire and sang our songs. Göring stepped into the circle and remained
standing, proud and upright. It was a glorious picture, the great air
hero standing there, surrounded by the light of the solstice fire. But
his face remained somewhat in the dark, since the dying flames did
not reach that far. I had the luck to sit directly behind him. With a
sudden decision I jumped up and held my torch over his shoulder,
and now his face, too, radiated a great glow. Then came a great,
eventful moment for me. He turned and nodded thankfully to me.

[1] Ernst Moritz Arndt (1769-1860), a patriotic Romantic poet.

Who could have been happier than I? Then we sang Löns's[2] song of
the Red hussars. Again, the main speaker addressed us in imperative
and flaming words and stepped out of our midst, accompanied by
roaring shouts of "Heil!" Our eyes followed him for a long time until
he vanished in the dark night. I thought that I would not see him
again for a long time. I had not noticed that meanwhile an SA man
had stepped to my side. I turned around only after I heard myself
addressed by name, and encountered the manly face of SA man Jensen. He shook my hand and asked about my impressions of the solstice celebration. I began to tell him in my stormy and elated state of
excitement. He looked at me with joyful and shining eyes, sharing my
enthusiasm and joy. After I had expressed all my feelings about the
solstice celebration, we both fell silent. I noticed that his facial expression had changed. A deadly seriousness was on his face. He looked at
me silently for a long time and then he asked how long I had been a
follower of Hitler and what had prompted me to become a National
Socialist. He did not turn his eyes from me, but continued to look at
me, steadfast and probing. I shall never forget these hours. His eyes
plumbed the depth of my soul. His gaze was strong and powerful, but
without importunity. I felt his eyes in the deepest corner of my heart
and it would have been impossible for me to make a secret of anything
that he wanted to know of me. I answered his question and explained
clearly and simply when and why I had become a National Socialist.
He was silent for a while, turned his head, and looked thoughtfully
into the flames of the solstice fire. Slowly he turned his face to me,
looked deep into my eyes, and, shaking my hand, said in all seriousness: "You have truly grasped what National Socialism is!" Meanwhile the fire was banking. Some threw their torches into the flames.
Wolfgang Jensen and I followed the example of the others and once
again the flames shot up. We looked silently and seriously into the
fire. Then Wolfgang Jensen said admonishingly, almost solemnly, to
me: "Don't ever forget the solstice fire. Let it flame in your heart and
let its rays reach out to your racial comrades. Then you will truly help
in the great work of Adolf Hitler."

From Gudrun Streiter, *Dem Tod so nah* . . . : *Tagebuch-
blätter einer S.A.-Mann's Braut* (published by the author,
n.d.), pp. 8-11.

2 Hermann Löns (1866-1914), a writer, mostly of peasant and regional novels.

On Festivities in the School
HERMANN KLAUSS

The German school is not an institution devoted only to the transmission of knowledge; it is not a dead organizational form—it is a form of life itself. The teacher is not just an instructor and a transmitter of knowledge. He is more than that. He is a soldier, serving on the cultural-political front of National Socialism. True, the battle on this front is of a different nature and is fought with different weapons, but it is no less important, because the struggle is for the soul of the people. It would make no sense whatsoever to win the political but lose the cultural-political battle.

The task of the German educator is to form human souls. The festive hours in the school are charged with the highest mission of leadership—hours in which the task of forming human souls is most urgent.

Hence the festivity can never be something secondary, something, say, that is off to the side, that merely deflects everyone from their real task.

The daily school work all too easily leads a class to withdraw into its work assignment and to a separation from the school community and the outside world. At a festivity, however, teacher and students stand together, whether the occasion is a simple flag-raising ceremony or a great celebration involving the whole school community.

Nowhere can we discern the spirit that prevails in a community as clearly as in the manner in which its celebrations are conducted. This applies to a ceremony of a single class as well as to a ceremony of the whole school. The old proverb could be changed to read: "Show me how you celebrate, and I will tell you who you are."

Every festive hour is a confession of faith. The school administration has clearly recognized the great importance of school celebrations. This is distinctly shown in the regulations for the curricula of the various types of schools.

The regulations for education and instruction at the grade-school level set forth on page 7:

> In school celebrations, the incorporation of the school into the great Volk community is most strikingly expressed. It is the climax

of the school's community life and must therefore be organized with special love and care.

The corresponding regulations for education and instruction in the intermediate school read:

> The community life of a school finds its loftiest expression in its celebrations. Specific celebrations should be held if they grow organically out of the life of the school and its link with the great Volkish events. Since it is the purpose of these celebrations to serve as climaxes, they should be held only infrequently.

The regulations for education and instruction in the higher schools also explain how the various school subjects can be integrated in the school festivites.

Festivities during the School Year

Individually school celebrations show a great variety, ranging from the simple morning speech and song to the flag raising, the morning celebration, the memorial hour, and the festive drama, to the great celebrations of national holidays in a form suitable for young people.

The great celebrations of the school community should be few; they should represent climaxes in the life of the school. If these celebrations follow each other too frequently, they lose their effectiveness. But celebrations are also held in small groups in order to prepare the youth for the experience of the great national holidays.

School celebrations can be grouped as follows:

Celebrations under the Flag
    Brief flag raising or massing of colors on the first and last day of a
        semester or on special occasions.
    Celebrations under the flag.

The School's "Own" Celebrations
    Upon entering the school—the road into school.
    Upon graduation from school—the road into life.

National Holidays
    The Day of the Reich—January 30.
    The Day of the Führer—April 20.
    The Day of Labor—May 1.
    The Day of the Farmer—Thanksgiving Day.

Heroes' Memorial—The Day of Langemarck[1] and Heroes' Memorial Day.
November 9.

Celebrations during the School Year
The Day of the German Mother.
The Day of German Volkdom.
Pre-Christmas Festive Hour—the Light Celebration.

General Morning Celebrations
The Weekly Festive Hour.

Festive Hours on Special Occasions
Historical memorial days.
Current events.

Concerning the Organization of a Festive Hour

Action, speech, and music are the pillars upon which the great national celebrations rest.

Music serves to prepare the celebrants. Speech opens bridges to their hearts. Action creates meaningful customs. . . .

The Flag Orders Our Day

The law of the flag rules over our lives. It also stands above our school work.

We begin each section of the school year with a general flag-raising ceremony. We close it with a general flag lowering. The first great experience of a new student is the ceremonial flag raising. The school year ends with the flag lowering on the last day of school. On the holidays of the school and the Volk community the school hoists the flags of the Reich and its youth.

Flag raising is honor, elevation, admonition, and avowal of faith. The external expression—assembly, speech, song, greetings, and retreat—is an unfailing indication of the spirit which prevails in the community.

Generally, the flag-raising ceremony is quite brief and is limited to a recitation and song. In some cases it will be enlarged to include an appeal, reflection, and avowal of loyalty in recitation, song, and address. Such would be the case on the occasion of the flag raising

---

[1] A battle in World War I (1914), fought by youthful volunteers, most of whom perished.

at the beginning of a new school year, on the first day in the country boarding school, on national holidays, and on other similar occasions.

The flag song is always a "We" song, a song of the community. A large selection of such songs is readily available in all collections, so that it is not necessary to list them here. . . .

The following suggestions for celebrations—"The Flag Is Our Faith" . . . —are so conceived that they could take place before the flag raising with the song of the nation. It is, of course, also possible to have the flag raising precede these ceremonies. In that case the first song could be dispensed with.

The narrator of the words of the Führer stands before the ranks of the assembled teachers; the narrators of the avowal of faith and loyalty stand in the front rank of the pupils.

"The Flag Is Our Faith

We sing together:
    "Under the Flag We March."

A student speaks:
    The flag is our faith
    In God and Volk and Land.
    Whoever wants to rob us of it
    Must take our life and hand.

A teacher speaks:
    Thus the Führer admonishes us:
    "Everything that we demand of Germany in the future, that, boys and girls, we also demand of you.

"This must you practice and this must you then pass on to the future, because whatever we create today and whatever we do, we will have to pass on. But in you Germany will live on, and when there is nothing left of us, it will be up to you to hold in your fists the flag which we once raised out of nothingness.

"Therefore you must stand solidly on the ground of your soil, and you must be hard so that this flag does not slip from you, then may you be followed by generation after generation from whom you can make the same demand that they be as you were. And then Germany will look upon you with pride."

Or a brief address:
    Main idea: The flag is a symbol and an obligation.

A student recites:

> We boys carry the flag for the assault of youth.
> It shall stand and rise and glow like fire in the skies!
> We are sworn to the flag
> For always and ever.
> Forever cursed be he
> Who besmirches the flag.
> The flag is our faith
> In God and Volk and Land.
> Whoever wants to rob us of it
> Must take our life and hand.
> For our flag we will care
> As we do for our own mother,
> For the flag is our tomorrow
> And our honor and courage!

We sing together:

> "We Youngsters Carry the Flag."

From Hermann Klauss, *Feierstunden der deutschen Schule* (Stuttgart: Franck'sche Verlagshandlung, 1941), pp. 7 ff.

5

Toward a Total Culture

In the Third Reich the central task of culture was the dissemination of the Nazi world view. What was the place of the intellect in this culture? The National Socialist world view was based upon the rejection of rationalism, and any emphasis upon man's reason was thought to be "divisive," destructive of the unity of the emotionally centered ideology which the whole Volk could understand. Man's "creativity" was put into the foreground of his striving, which was defined through art and literature as well as politics. The very totality of the world view embraced all of these as one interrelated cultural whole.

Those who are involved in cultural creativity must always turn the energies of the German people toward their German mode of being— as Hermann Burte puts it in his speech to the assembled poets of the Greater German Reich in 1940. The emotional basis of this commitment is made quite clear: Hitler is the poet turned statesman—a poet because he has a vision of the inmost German being, a statesman because from out of that vision he has created a new people. The differences between poetry and statesmanship vanish in such an analysis. All of fascism has this element in common; the Belgian fascist leader Léon Degrelle called Hitler and Mussolini "poets of revolution."

Hermann Burte had made his mark early in the century with a novel which portrayed a hero in search of his Volk (*Wiltfeber, der ewige Deutsche*, 1912). He became a supporter of the Führer and felt that the new leader was superior even to the great Goethe because of his grasp of the organic nature of the German people. The intellectuals belong to the people, he said, and by this he asserted the primacy of the primordial German image, of German being, over human reason. The Wilna newspaper describes the intellectual as one who believes that everything can be arrived at through reason. Labor Service, performed on the soil, is a good corrective to such an attitude. The very word "intellectual" is twisted into an anti-intellectual meaning: Julius Streicher is offended because those who have fled the Reich do not regard his racist vituperations as part of the "intellectual" struggle between themselves and the Nazi dictatorship. In a nation which bestowed great prestige on academics, it was impossible for many to admit to the anti-intellectualism that was one of the hallmarks of the Nazi ideology.

Even the Heidelberg students no longer wanted to educate the mind but merely to build character—that is, the right ideological attitude and way of life. It is, perhaps, significant that three years later a military newspaper protests against such opinions. A balance between character and mind must be maintained—but now it is wartime and the army needs good minds and cannot win battles equipped only with the proper world view.

The anti-intellectualism rests upon an organic view of the German people. The Reich Peasant Leader and Minister of Agriculture, R. Walther Darré (1895-1953), illustrates this well in his speech on the anniversary of a Medieval peasant uprising. The German peasant is symbolic of the Volk, he is the driving force and purifier of all German history. Here is the substance of Germanism, evolving independently of political boundaries, princes, or bishops. German racial stock, German uniqueness, indeed German history—all of these are in his custody. This might be considered a piece of special pleading by the Reich Peasant Leader, if the same theme did not run throughout Nazi culture: we will meet it often in this chapter and have met it earlier. The peasant was the culture hero of the movement, though other, more recent party heroes existed side by side with him.

The relationship of organization to the Nazi concept of artistic freedom is defined by Joseph Goebbels, whose business it was to enforce this definition. Goebbels' speech of 1937 was addressed to the

Reich Chamber of Culture (Reichskulturkammer). This organization was founded by a law of September 22, 1933, and was given the ambitious task of encouraging "all forms of artistic creation or activity which are made public." The Reich Chamber became an instrument of cultural control closely linked to the Ministry of Propaganda and Enlightenment. Goebbels himself assumed its presidency.

The Reich Chamber of Culture was divided into seven subordinate Chambers, concerned with literature, music, films, radio, the theater, fine arts, and the press. Each of these had its own president and administrative apparatus, always linked to the relevant department in Goebbels' ministry. This corporate structure was supposed to give the appearance of self-government by the artistic professions, but in reality the Chambers were an integral part of the complex apparatus of cultural control, directed from a single source. Membership in a Chamber was compulsory for the exercise of any artistic profession; denial of membership meant, therefore, the effective silencing of any undesired creative voice in the nation.

The Reich Chamber of Literature (Reichsschriftstumskammer) is of special importance for our purposes: it included not only all German writers but publishers and libraries as well. Its first president (1934-1935) was a writer who specialized in Old Germanic stories and legends, Hans Friedrich Blunck (1888-1961). His subject matter was close to that of Josefa Berens-Totenohl, who is represented in this chapter. But he proved too old-fashioned and was replaced by the playwright Hanns Johst (see page 116). The secretary of the Chamber was Wilhelm Ihde, who wrote history with a Nazi slant (see page 119).

Typically enough, this elaborate structure was never without its challengers from within the party itself. Alfred Rosenberg and his office, established to "supervise the entire spiritual and ideological education of the NSDAP," maintained a separate department devoted to supervising German letters. Moreover, Philip Bouhler, on the basis of his "party commission for the protection of NS literature," published lists of approved books on his own. There was bound to be friction between all these agencies, but it was Goebbels' ministry which censored all published books, while the Reich Chamber of Culture printed lists of forbidden books and silenced those authors and artists who refused to conform.

Goebbels' speech laid down the principles which were to govern cultural activity. In putting these into practice, publishing was obviously an important cog within the cultural machinery. The German tradition of publishing was highly personal, and publishing houses were known by their specific orientation. Adolf Spemann, the proprietor of the medium-sized Engelhorn publishing house, had in the past published books by Jewish authors as well as translations of Romain Rolland. Spemann was one of those men who, though politically indifferent up to 1933, were captured by the *élan* of the Third Reich. However, he never became a party member and his only public activity was to direct, for a few years, the "belles-lettres and popular science" section of the professional association of the German book trade.[1] This was a subsection of the Reich Chamber of Literature.

Spemann, however, was a popular speaker, and at a meeting called by Rosenberg's office he defined the new position of the publisher in the Third Reich. This speech also found approval in the eyes of Bouhler, whose list of approved books could only "joyfully underline Spemann's words." [2] Spemann does give reasons why publishing should share responsibility for the National Socialist cultural drive. He writes about ideals which were to become reality. A recent study has shown that by 1937 some 50 to 75 per cent of all book sales were accounted for by approved National Socialist literature. Peasant novels, historical novels, and novels set in the native landscape were the biggest sellers. From 1939 onward their place was taken by novels glorifying the early struggles of the Nazi party, war literature, and books by German writers living on foreign soil, such as Heinrich Zillich (see page 165).[3]

These were, of course, the kind of books publishers put out, but they were bought by the public. Such cultural control meant opposition to all meaningful criticism of literature and art. Goebbels says as much in his speech and he had already carried it through. For on November 27, 1936, he had forbidden the "continuance of art criticism in its past form." The place of the art critic must be taken by the "reporter of art." The public must be the judge. This was indeed safe, for Nazi artistic criteria did correspond to a low common denominator of popular taste. Goebbels sums up this point of view (and gives himself away) when he stresses the unchanging taste of the masses as the only stable element in the process of artistic evolution.

[1] Adolf Spemann, *Menschen und Werke: Erinnerungen eines Verlegers* (Munich, 1959), pp. 250 ff.
[2] *Nationalsozialistische Bibliographie*, Heft II (November 1938), p. xviii.
[3] Dietrich Strothmann, *Nationalsozialistische Literaturpolitik* (Bonn, 1960), pp. 384-385.

For Hitler the visual arts were the most important and effective part of culture. Kurt Karl Eberlein, art historian and literary critic, summarizes the official line. He expounds at greater length the point which Goebbels makes both in his speech and in his order forbidding art criticism. The rural family (and the peasant is the primordial image of the Volk) does not "judge" art, but accepts it and lives it—if this art is of the right Germanic kind. Clarity and simplicity are important here, as well as the idealization of familiar and traditional themes.

But if these factors were important, the ties to the history and tradition of the race were equally vital. Heinrich Zillich (b. 1898) was a writer of novels which were set among the Germans in Rumania. Ever since the twelfth century a large German peasant settlement had existed in the Rumanian Carpathians. Zillich's ancestors had for generations lived in that mountainous territory. Small wonder that he advocates the bursting of narrow political and territorial confines. The people and its mission must stand at the center of the poet's work, and history must inform his consciousness. Zillich echoes the point made by Darré in his speech: not dynasties determine history, but the evolution and ambitions of the people themselves. The poet becomes a historian in the service of the race.

Zillich spoke as a German separated from his homeland, but his ideas were "official." He expressed them in one of the principal speeches at the meeting of Greater German poets at Weimar in 1938. The Nazis furthered these gatherings at the historical shrine of German culture; Burte made his speech at another such meeting in 1940. Nazi culture and the culture of the age of Goethe and Schiller could in this way appear to clasp hands across the centuries.

What results did these definitions of culture produce? We must confine ourselves to a very few examples. Josefa Berens-Totenohl (b. 1891) wrote in an older tradition of the romantic peasant novel. She was one of the most popular and widely read authors during the period of the Third Reich. She produced the kind of escapist literature which could be tolerated, for it praised peasant virtues, strength, and rootedness. Purely sentimental novels like the immensely popular stories of Hedwig Courths-Mahler (1867-1952) were not considered desirable reading. Her more than 200 novels (27 million copies sold up to 1950) were love stories written for the lower classes and without any ideological overtones. The ideology, however, was present in the writing of Berens-Totenohl, if in muted form (she was never a party member and never played any part in the organizations for culture control, though she did receive the literature prize of Westphalia in 1936).

Der Femhof (1935) was her first book and it brought her immediate fame. It had sold 226,000 copies by 1944. It may be regarded as typical of the peasant novel, which idealized its subject and painted the mythology of peasant life, far from the crossroads of the world.

Tüdel Weller's work is included with some regret, but its bad taste and the blatant glorification of brutality directed against the Jewish stereotype do belong to the totality of Nazi culture. Even this book, *Rabauken!* (1938), ran through seven editions by 1943. It is only one example of a whole literary genre. But even the Nazis seemed dissatisfied with such products, and by 1941 there was some official agitation to further the writing of a "good racial and blood novel." [4]

The theater had been one of the glories of the German Republic, and the Nazis attempted to use it as a forum for their own cultural ideas. Eckart von Naso, then a young script editor, describes the effect of the Nazi seizure of power upon the Prussian State Theater in Berlin. Though a powerful director with Göring's support could keep up, for a time, a semblance of standards, in the provinces the decline was rapid and inevitable.

The playbills of the city of Herne in the Ruhr Valley (see also page 375) are informative. Johst is represented and so are classical German writers like Schiller and Goethe. But the vast majority of the repertory is filled with light opera—some by good composers like Franz Lehár and Johann Strauss—but mostly with works by second-rate tunesmiths who are rightly forgotten. There was an attempt to further a Volk theater. Konrad Dreher had founded the Tegernsee Peasant Theater in 1892 in order to revive an art form which had its roots in the Jesuit drama of the sixteenth and seventeenth centuries as well as in the passion plays. But by the time the troupe appeared in Herne it had long been stocked by professional actors and it performed modern plays with peasant themes and in peasant dialect (two such plays appear here, one by Dreher himself and the other by August Hinrichs). Foreigners are sparsely represented, and then through light entertainment. Calderón's comedy falls into that category, and so does Rossini's opera and even Shakespeare's *As You Like It*. The only exception is the realistic war play by the Englishman R. C. Sheriff; *Journey's End* portrays the brutal life in the trenches. The Third Reich

4 *Ibid.*, p. 406.

used the stage for light entertainment (the practical result of Goebbels' assertion that "the people seek joy") or for patriotic propaganda.
Gerhard Menzel's *Scharnhorst* would be in the latter classification,
and so would the Kleist and Grabbe cycles in nearby Bochum. Either
the public was to be amused in a harmless way or it was to be uplifted.

Goebbels was obsessed with the power of the radio, and indeed the
Nazis made wide and thorough use of this medium of communication. They inherited a system of centralized control, for ever since
1928 the Post Office dominated the National Broadcasting Company
(*Reichsrundfunkgesellschaft*) and influenced the provincial broadcasting companies as well. After the seizure of power the Propaganda
Ministry acquired all the shares of the National Broadcasting Company and through the Reich Broadcasting Chamber (*Reichsrund-
funkkammer*) controlled not only the broadcasters themselves but
also the manufacturers of sets. The National Broadcasting Company
lost its importance and became merely the executive organ for day-
to-day operations. Through pressure upon manufacturers cheap radio
sets were produced, so that every German could afford to own one.
These were made in such a way that no foreign broadcasts could be
received. From 1933 to 1934 the number of German homes owning a
radio set increased by over a million, and by 1936 some 30 million
people could be reached over the radio. This figure does not include
those subjected to radio through public loudspeakers on the streets or
in such places as restaurants and factories.

This was a powerful weapon in Goebbels' hands. The radio program for the winter of 1936 gives an idea of how it was used. The
speech by the director of the National Broadcasting Company lays
down the principles under which all broadcasting operated. There was
to be no criticism of the Nazi movement or ideology; "humorous
sketches" were explicitly forbidden.

The Reich Film Chamber (*Reichsfilmkammer*) controlled the
lively German film industry, while a Film Credit Bank (also under
Goebbels' control) centralized the financial aspects of film production. The largest remaining independent German film company,
the UFA, was bought out by the Propaganda Ministry in 1937.
Through the Film Chamber it had been brought under control long
before then. The titles of the films officially submitted to the biannual
international film festival in Venice show the kind of motion pictures
the Nazis thought especially valuable as their international "visiting
card." German film stars were encouraged to represent the Germanic

ideal of genuine womanhood (see page 39) in contrast to the painted and perfumed "degeneracy" of Hollywood. As a matter of fact, Paula Wessely was an outstanding actress who had come to the film from Vienna's famous Burgtheater. But this fact was less important than her conformity to those emotional ideals which a valuable film should portray.

The people are praised for recognizing the worth of such genuineness, just as they were relied upon to have an intuitively proper attitude toward art. Nazi culture sought a popular base and often found it. At any rate, the sales figures of Nazi-sponsored literature and art seem to lead to this conclusion. There is no reason why the millions for whom the Nazi world view made "life worth living again" should not also be attracted by the products of Nazi culture. Moreover, as has been mentioned earlier, the Nazis did cater to popular taste and preconceptions. But no risk was taken: a thorough apparatus of cultural control accompanied such popularity as Nazi culture may have achieved on its own. In any case, no alternatives were available. Modern dictatorships have sought to spread their total culture widely throughout the population, however this has led not to the elevation of popular taste but to the confirmation of its prejudices.

G.L.M.

Intellectuals Must Belong to the People

HERMANN BURTE

Contemporary German poetry need not lower its eyes before the outstanding figures of the past. "No art is created during war and revolution," says Balzac. But in her poets struggling Germany seems to belie this assertion: like larks amid a shower of bullets, her poets sing also in war. In the greatest yearning and passion to find and to grasp its own essence, to give it form, speech and value, spirit and taste, in the face of the difficult task of harmonizing a Volkish experience without parallel, of endowing an extraordinary event with an understandable meaning, of changing the shriek of suffering into the song of joy, and finally of existing and enduring as a people through the spirit—German poetry of the present can boldly take its place alongside every other in the world! Before all things it seeks the heart of its own people, it wants to be one with the feeling of all, and the calling that is most uniquely its own is to create a special breed.

It must turn all the vital energies of the German people toward the discovery, solidification, and perpetuation of the German mode of being. For how would it help German poetry to win the world but to lose the soul?

The German poet is better than his reputation. We shall mention no names. He whom today the shadows of silence envelope, tomorrow can find light and sound. The wonderful poem of Hebbel,[1] that thinker among the poets, is applicable here: "You have sowed pearls, suddenly it begins to snow, And one sees them no more; Hope for the sun, it comes!"

Like Schiller in his time, present-day German poetry emerges hopefully before the people and the world and awaits its judgment. It respects this judgment, but it does not fear it.

The Germans are scolded and rebuked for being original, and they are, for they knowingly and willingly recognize the excellence of others and seek to understand their essence.

Shakespeare belongs as much to us as he does to the English; indeed, we know him and perform his plays better than they do. And

[1] Friedrich Hebbel (1813-1863), a Romantic poet and dramatist.

we boldly assert that as Germans of 1940 we in truth are closer to the spirit of the Elizabethan English and their genius William than the Englishmen of today, behind whose throne lurks and rules that Shylock whom Shakespeare recognized and rejected.

Because Goethe's nature was complete, fully sure of itself, he could unhesitatingly absorb all alien things, create the concept of world literature, and entertain the belief that though the great literatures of the world spring from different roots, their branches rise into the lofty atmosphere which belongs to all, into the realm of space up to the very stars!

At this level the poet has indeed achieved fame. As soon as the magic word "fame" is uttered, it is time to look not only at things but through them!

A man whose fame is spread by foreigners, whom one plays off against his people and fatherland, or whom one esteems because he has denied his people and his fatherland and betrayed them in spirit, is a pathetic ghost, a Herostratus, a deception, not a man with a mission!

The fame of a poet must reflect as much on his people, country, and Reich as on himself. Otherwise he must reject it like a poisoned shirt! A German of our militant age achieves the most honorable fame when he steps forward as an accuser before the world, and lashes it for an outrage, an injustice, a fundamental criminal attitude, when he hurls a lightning-like, flaming thought into the stifling expanse around him, and when through the strength of his reasoning, the tone of truth, the force of the accusation, he compels the adversary to respond, against his will and in the agony of confessing his guilt. . . .

The dying Chamberlain[2] had this feeling: a novum has come into the world, and new too in the way in which it came. A book was written, not poetry in a low common sense, and yet a poem, a view of a new people in a new state! The man who wrote it is called Adolf Hitler! At last the stirring, noble Hölderlin, who wandered through his Germany with the question "Will the books soon come to life?" has received an answer, an unhoped-for answer: Yes, the books live, and not only the books—living men emerge and charge them with life! Here is the primordial and model image of the future German being! The spirit journeys forth before the deed as the morning wind goes before the sun! Before he embarks upon his work, the great

[2] Houston Stewart Chamberlain (1855-1927) (see p. 256) acclaimed Hitler as the future leader as early as 1923.

statesman of the Germans is a kind of poet and thinker, his mind clarifies for itself how things ought to be in the world of things! A prose comes into being with a surging quality uniquely its own, a march-like step, with tensions and projections of that attitude which Nietzsche had in mind when he said: "I love him who hurls forth the great word of his deed, since he wills his fall!" But since the spirit of Hitler lives in Germany, one no longer seeks the tragic, ultimately sweet decline and fall, but the tough, day-bright, enduring upward thrust and drive. Neither the individual nor all are to go under. . . .

Everything is possible in Germany, except the tragedy of the whole! To prevent this tragedy, as the curse of curses, is precisely the meaning of Being and hence of the meaning of poetry. Poetry and this direction of life are as one! The European mission of German poetry is one with the European mission of the German Reich. The Reich of the poets lies in the German world, and its shrine is in Weimar!

A new man has emerged from the depth of the people. He has forged new theses and set forth new Tables and he has created a new people, and raised it up from the same depths out of which the great poems rise—from the mothers, from blood and soil.

In its deepest essence, in the core and star of its being, the European mission of German poetry is one and the same with the European mission of the German people and its Führer. It should be of little concern to us whether this new type and newly won form, created on the Faustian path to the birth-giving energies of the people, from the sources of our blood, to the ruthless homecoming to ourselves, at first appears pleasing or not to others. For just as we saw that the new conception and configuration of the Volk and the state was at first not understood in the world and, at a decisive moment in the war, proved itself to be superior and overwhelming, so we believe and feel too that the psychic and spiritual configuration of poetry also brings forth an equally surprising, and unbelieved, but true and truthful, altogether alive work, since it creates out of the same sources as do the state-creating and military values.

In *Truth and Poetry* Goethe says that the highest life-content in German poetry came into being through Frederick the Great.

Now, dear comrades, how much more great and more powerful is the life-content and the life-power which Adolf Hitler, through his manner and his work, has brought to the German people and thereby to German poetry.

If Frederick the Great, the far-sighted monarch, the friend and pupil of the rationalist Voltaire, could fructify poetry through his deeds, all the more so can Adolf Hitler, the son of the people, risen from its powerful depths, steeled by suffering and privation, familiar with all that is human, a volunteer soldier in the world war, close to death and the eternal night, rescued and preserved, designated by the Norns as elect, and provided with an earnestness and will, an energy for action and knowledge of people, insight and broadness of perspective, great as orator, greater as man of action. Everyone can feel what an enormous content, what a racially suited form he has bequeathed to our people, and first of all to the intellectuals! For the intellectuals belong to the people or they are nothing!

If fate has bequeathed us the great Führer, it will not deny us the great poet!

From the depths of our heart we thank the Führer, from the fullness of our faith we hope for the future great poet!

He will stand to Adolf Hitler as Goethe stood to Frederick the Great. We know very well that the genius does not come when one calls to him, the spirits will not be ordered about! But just as the remarkable poetry of the Elizabethans arose from the victory over the Spanish Armada, so will—we see it in our minds' eye—a new poetry arise from our victory. Fully developed through competition among all segments of the people, everywhere educated and hardened to what is most lofty, true to the mind, devoted to the soul, the great poet will rise like the crystal from the mother-lye!

This future poet will have something which the great of Weimar in their time, in their place, could not possess: the people as a configuration! In place of a social stratum, the multiple I, the people as a whole, emerges as an element.

And we, what should we do during this time? We all serve the future Best One. He will include all that we accomplish in the sum of his accomplishment, without naming names! For he will be a kind of King of the Spirit, to whom belongs all that waves over the summits. To him who has will be given! A serene Siegfried who slays dragons, throws precious stones at ravens, and sings in competition with the birds of the woods, an eternal young German, like Goethe!

With an innate drive to perfection, he will work on himself as did Goethe, and shape and present his essence in peace on a new height. Then the Best in the other peoples will again recognize their Best One in the figure of this German and honor him like the poet of Faust.

Then the European mission of German poetry will again be ful-filled in a new time, in a new space! What must we give and send in this moment before he comes?

"We greet the Führer!" Such is the beautiful, heart-felt expression of the people as they rise in order to thank their savior, to be mindful of him in love, and in order to find and to feel themselves in him!

Following this custom, dear comrades, let us greet the Poet, the unknown one, the future one, who will arise to us—we deliberately repeat ourselves—and who must likewise be nourished to a loftier life-content and a stronger poetical power by the mighty manner and the extraordinary work of Adolf Hitler, as Goethe was by the deeds of Frederick the Great. He will not be a Hamlet who flees from himself, because he will set aright the times that are out of joint!

He will be of use to his time as the joint in the socket. He will not, like Werther, suffer the plague of his time; he will not be a Hyperion among the all too inadequate Germans, nor a Wiltfeber in the court,[3] which went under. For through the deeds of the Führer the Father-land will be so transformed that neither the ruler nor the poet will be tragic figures! They will freely and joyfully fulfill their being, continu-ously fulfill themselves, and show the world their essence!

But until the poet comes who will gather us all and therefore sus-tain us, let us in this hour and in this place greet the Master and the great of Weimar!

> From a speech delivered in 1940 at the meeting of the poets of the Greater German Reich, published in *Sieben Reden von Burte* (Strassburg, 1943), pp. 19-21, 27-32.

The Birth of Intellectuals

The accomplishments of which the mind is capable lead from a true appreciation of its value to an over-estimation, and this tempts one into the delusion that everything in the world is to be arrived at exclusively through the mind. . . . Thus is born the human type we designate as intellectuals. Labor service is an excellent defense against the danger of intellectualism. Manual work makes demands not only on one's physical powers but also on one's character and thus brings

[3] *Wiltfeber, der ewige Deutsche* (1912) was Burte's most famous book.

about a transformation of one's mental attributes and assists in the full development of the mind.

> From the *Wilnaer Zeitung*, Aug. 21, 1942. (Wiener Library Clipping Collection.)

Streicher the Intellectual

The Jews know how to falsify the authentic concept of intellectual struggle. Otherwise, for example, Gauleiter Julius Streicher's remarkable struggle could not have been dismissed as "unintellectual" in the émigré press.

> From Carl Schmitt, "Streichers geistiger Kampf: Das Judentum in der Rechtswissenschaft," in the *Fränkische Tageszeitung*, Oct. 3, 1936. (Wiener Library Clipping Collection.)

A Balance Is Necessary

We read the following in a book review in a 1937 issue of the Heidelberg student newspaper: "Here the mind is discussed, that is, one's intellectual endowment. We merely wish to declare that today we no longer want to educate this mind; we want to educate the character." This statement betrays a serious and—we must say it openly—deplorable misunderstanding of the situation, especially for a student. Mind and character cannot be played off *against* each other. Reason, of course, by itself does not make the whole man, but neither can we get very far or accomplish anything of importance without reason.

> From the *Militär-Wochenblatt* (the independent newspaper of the German Army), Jan. 12, 1940. (Wiener Library Clipping Collection.)

The German Peasant Formed German History
R. WALTHER DARRÉ

At the beginning of today's address in remembrance of the Stedinger struggle for freedom 700 years ago,[1] we first of all wish to establish a fact which is valid for the whole German people: while German historiography is industriously engaged in presenting "German history" as the effect of the interests or conflicting interests of imperial rulers, of ecclesiastical and territorial princes, this same historiography is remarkably silent about what one might call "German peasant history." This is all the more striking because no matter how zealously the historians have portrayed matters concerning lords and princes, the German people has preserved in its subconscious the remembrance of the great peasant catastrophes of its history much more forcefully than the cares and tribulations of its ruling lords.

This is seen to be particularly obvious if one bears in mind, for example, that the slaughter of thousands of Saxon peasants by Charles the Saxon butcher[2] in Berden on the Aller more than a thousand years ago has not only been preserved in the memory of Lower Saxonians for the whole last millennium but preserved even despite the fact that a deliberate historical forgery was perpetrated for the purpose of blotting this deed from the memory of the German people. Let us take another example: Schiller's drama *Wilhelm Tell*, which describes the freedom struggle of the Swiss free peasants against the arrogance of the Habsburgs, contributed much more to turning the German people against its territorial princes in Wallung than any other tendentious play of that time. Incidentally, in learned circles the rumor persists stubbornly that Schiller after the publication of *Wilhelm Tell* received a warning from the Freemason Lodge, which was not pleased by this glorification of the free peasantry. It would be useful for us historians to investigate such a rumor objectively, on the basis of documents, in the interest of the German people, instead of wasting time and energy trying to keep the German

---

[1] Conrad of Marburg, with the support of the Dominican order, accused the Stedinger peasantry of heresy in 1234. In reality he wanted to take away their rights and bring them under his princely control. His "crusade" was successful.
[2] Namely, Charlemagne.

people in a state of unclear or false knowledge concerning the cultural level of its Germanic ancestors.

In reality, however, what we call Volkdom was never brought about by German emperors, German ecclesiastical princes, and German territorial princes. Rather, the precondition for Volkdom was exclusively bound up with the existence of the German peasantry. First there was a German peasantry in Germany before what is today served up as German history could develop from it—and unfortunately often on its back. Neither princes, nor the Church, nor the cities have created the German man as such. Rather, the German man emerged from the German peasantry. To be sure, princes, Church, and cities were able to place their stamp on a special kind of German man. Nevertheless, the German peasant down the centuries has been their raw material and thus the precondition, the foundation, and the determinant of their impact. We National Socialists, who have retrieved the old truth that the blood of the people is the formative element of its culture, see these things with a crystal-clear knowledge. In every period of history the blood of our cities was supplemented by the peasantry and thus the blood of this peasantry repeatedly determined the Germanic content of our city culture.

Traveling through the German countryside today, one still finds among our peasants customs which have survived for a thousand years. In this we have clear proof that it is here that the ground of a Volkdom is to be sought, rather than in the bloodless abstractions of the scholar's desk. And if we then go through the documentary sources, or search for the historical sources, we find to our amazement that these thousand-year-old customs among our peasantry have not developed, for instance, through the kind understanding of the ecclesiastical or territorial princes. Rather the opposite is true—the peasantry defended their customs with bitter tenacity against these very ecclesiastical and territorial princes. In this connection it matters little precisely where one comes upon a confirmation of this assertion, whether in the old peasant territory of Lower Saxony, or in Hesse or Thuringia, or in Upper Bavaria or Franconia. Everywhere one will find primordial peasant customs that reach far back into the past. Everywhere there is evidence that the German peasantry, with an unparalleled tenacity, knew how to preserve its unique character and its customs against every attempt to wipe them out, including the attempts of the Church. And it preferred to go under rather than bend its head to the alien law imposed upon it by the lords.

Although the German-minded among our scholars have for some time now turned away from the above-mentioned methods and have begun to devote themselves to the true significance of the peasantry, some of our scholars still stubbornly assert that the contrary is correct, and they are still attempting to prove to us that the Germans, said to be nomads, were first laboriously given culture through what is called a German history—that is to say, by the fatherly efforts of their imperial, ecclesiastical and territorial princes. Against this sort of scholar I once and for all will coolly and soberly maintain the following: Before there was a German scholarship in Germany, the German peasant was already there and had preserved his essence and his breed. Despite this thousand-year effort to alienate the German peasant from his nature, the common sense and the deep blood-feeling of the German peasant knew how to preserve his German breed, and indeed in the face of a scholarship that with scientific methods aimed to prove the very opposite. If the German peasant during a thousand years possessed enough common sense to be able to survive this form of scholarship, then may the above-mentioned scholars become clearly aware that much of this understanding is still in existence today and will surmount and survive their scribbling. What a thousand years could not destroy, the eager industriousness of certain scholars will not be able to destroy in the next few years.

On the contrary: when today we speak of German racial stocks, of German uniqueness, it is customary to maintain that the unique qualities of these racial stocks are exclusively contained within the frontiers of the territorial principalities that still exist as German regions. This has gone so far that some, for example, consider the frontiers of the South German states so important that they would have the Germany newly awakened under National Socialism believe that the borders of the South German territories are divinely ordained and that to violate them in any way would signify a desire no longer to take into account the racial uniqueness of their population.

The nonsensical character of this assertion can be seen most clearly in the case of Bavaria, Württemberg, and Baden, for the borders of these states are neither racial borders nor borders of any kind of principality or any kind of racial stock. Rather, the borders of these states were arbitrarily drawn by Napoleon I, who never gave a thought to racial stocks and history or traditions of any kind. These particular South German border relations prove that the individual landscapes of these states have preserved their primordial uniqueness independently of the borders that were marked out. The fact that they did this, despite the state borders, means that they did it on the basis of laws which have nothing at all to do with these state borders.

For what preserved the unique character of these individual land-scapes and gave them their peculiar characteristics was the peasantry that had been preserved in them. A city like Munich, for example, did not receive its Bavarian quality from its monuments or its other peculi-arities, for any other German tribe could perhaps have developed these things in its cities. Rather, what we come upon in Munich as typically Bavarian—as was the case a hundred years ago and before—are the Bavarian peasants, who today still live on their farms the way their forefathers lived for centuries and who still send their sons to Munich. And what I say here about the Bavarian peasant also applies to the peasantry of every other German tribe. It was on the old peas-ant landholdings, whose economic structure has in most cases remained unchanged for five hundred years, that German man ac-quired the special quality of his racial stock. Wherever the genera-tion which occupies such old peasant landholdings clung to the cus-toms of their fathers, there grew the individual German racial uniqueness which today still embodies and represents the variety and multifariousness of German Volk life. No German city can make the same claim. For no German city can produce evidence that the peo-ple now living within its walls are authentic blood descendants of those who centuries before gave the city its characteristic stamp. Un-doubtedly, however, on our German peasant landholdings there sit, if not the direct, at least the indirect descendants of those who culti-vated the soil there centuries before. Here is anchored the eternalness of a racial stock of unique character. When a few weeks ago someone in South Germany said that the Hereditary Health Law[3] would do more to guarantee the unique character of the racial stock than any kind of regional particularism could ever have done, he was absolutely correct. One can say that the blood of a people digs its roots deep into the homeland earth through its peasant landholdings, from which it con-tinuously receives that life-endowing strength which constitutes its special character.

From *Rede des Reichsbauernführers und Reichsministers R. Walther Darré* (on the occasion of the 700th anniver-

[3] See page 90.

sary of the Stedinger struggle for freedom, Altenesch, May
27, 1934), pp. 3, 5-7.

Freedom and Organization
JOSEPH GOEBBELS

My Führer! Your excellencies!
My racial comrades!
Organization plays a decisive role in the lives of peoples. It has the
task of forming human groups into units so that they may be brought
purposefully and successfully to a starting point. Thus organization is
a means to an end and is related to the aim to be striven for, a necessary evil so to speak. Just as organization, when correctly established
and formed, can shorten and simplify the way to success (indeed,
sometimes it is the only way to success), it is capable, on the other
hand, of restricting and holding up natural developments, especially
when it forgets its real task and becomes an end in itself.

This possibility, however, which is more or less innate in any organization, must not mislead us into denying the necessity and purpose-
fulness of organization as such. Leadership requires it for the guidance of men and in order to prepare the way for developments in the
various vital spheres of politics, economy, and social functions as well
as culture. Here organization is most difficult to carry through and
thus it is also exposed to the most dangers.

For every organization must demand that its members surrender
certain individual private rights for the benefit of a greater and more
comprehensive law of life, and thereby a goal-directed point of departure for energies which if isolated are powerless, but which if united
have a striking, penetrating effect.

Therefore one should scrupulously see to it that every organization
does not lose its specific aim and that the renunciation of individual
rights is always promoted only to the extent necessary for its success.
One should, therefore, to express it briefly, organize only what must
be organized, not everything that can be organized.

Only in this way will a great and complete effect be achieved by the
total engagement of all energies. Obviously, it is in the nature of the
matter that in the operation of this total engagement of all energies

one is often and easily inclined to overestimate the renunciation of private and individual rights as against the purpose and aim that is to be achieved through the total engagement of energies.

In addition, a host of old habits and prejudices, to which many people had become fondly attached, had to be overcome through the organization of the German creative artists in their Reich Culture Chamber and in their individual Chambers.[1] Despite this, these old habits and prejudices still play a certain role in the ideas of some people who have not found the correct door to the new times and its demands. These critics of course eagerly claim, almost as a matter of course, and without any special expression of thanks, the advantages and success brought about in the main through this organization. On the other hand, they do not want to acknowledge that one conditions the other and that the advantages and success of the whole could be brought into being only by the renunciation of individual demands as against the demands of the time.

Hence it has been our constant effort to carry out the inner regeneration of the German art world not so much through a profusion of laws as through a continuous program of self-help. That which in the first months of 1933 was still considered impossible has become a fact, and it now operates in such a way that it is almost taken for granted. Meanwhile the difficulties of solving the countless individual problems which at that time had fallen due, so to speak, have long been forgotten. The reality is there, and it continuously creates new facts. . . .

Our enemy's cry that it is impossible to expel the Jew from German cultural life, that he cannot be replaced, still rings in our ears. We have done precisely this and things are proceeding better than ever! The demand of National Socialism has been thoroughly carried out in this field and the world has visible proof that the cultural life of a people can also—and indeed meaningfully and purposefully—be administered, led, and represented by its own sons.

How deeply the perverse Jewish spirit had penetrated German cultural life is shown in the frightening and horrifying forms of the "Exhibition of Degenerate Art" in Munich, arranged as an admonitory example. We have been frequently attacked in the so-called world press on account of this exhibit. But up to now no foreign enthusiast has been found who, in reparation for this cultural barbarism, is prepared to buy the "art treasures" on exhibit in Munich and thereby save

[1] See page 135.

them for eternity. They do not like them, but they defend them. And they defend them not on cultural but exclusively on political grounds. It requires barely a contemptuous wave of the hand to dispose of their arguments. It is maintained that one should allow this movement to work itself out, that in this way it would soon come to a standstill. One could have said the same in domestic politics in regard to Marxism or parliamentarianism, in the economic sphere in regard to the class struggle or to class conceit, in foreign policy in regard to the Versailles Treaty or to the theft of German sovereignty rights. A thing of this kind does not come to a dead stop; it must be overcome. The more thoroughly, quickly, and radically this occurs, the better it is!

This has nothing at all to do with the suppression of artistic freedom and modern progress. On the contrary, the botched art works which were exhibited there and their creators are of yesterday and before yesterday. They are the senile representatives, no longer to be taken seriously, of a period that we have intellectually and politically overcome and whose monstrous, degenerate creations still haunt the field of the plastic arts in our time.

How healthy this purging operation was is shown by the reaction of the public and above all of the art buyers to the Greater Germany Art Exhibition in the House of German Art in Munich. Never were so many paintings sold as on this occasion, paintings which were in the main really creative works of art. Never had the general public participated in the questions of the plastic arts in such a lively and intimate way. That the appearance of a new artistic creativeness was combined with the end of a period which had lain on our souls like an oppressive nightmare, was actually greeted as a redemption.

Does this now signify a narrowing of the much-discussed artistic freedom? If so, then only when the artist should have the right to withdraw from his times and its demands and lead an eccentric life outside the community of his people. That, however, cannot and ought not to be. The artist stands in the midst of his nation. Art is not a sphere of life that exists for itself, which must defend itself against the invasion of the people.

Art is a function of the life of the people and the artist its blessed endower of meaning.

And just as the leadership of the state claims for itself the political guidance of other areas of the people's life, likewise does it make the same claim here. This does not mean that politics must interfere in the inner function of art, or that it even desires to do so. It means only that the state regulates and orders its great beginning and total engagement. This right is a sovereign right. It springs from political power and responsibility.

The abolition of art criticism was proclaimed at the congress held last year. This act was directly related to the goal-directed purging and coordinating of our cultural life. The responsibility for the phenomenon of degeneration in art was in large measure laid at the door of art criticism. In the main, art criticism had created the tendencies and the isms. It did not judge artistic development in terms of a healthy instinct linked to the people, but only in terms of the emptiness of its intellectual abstractness. The people had never taken part in it. It had only turned away in horror from an art tendency which could no longer be brought into harmony with its healthy sensibility and could be appraised only as the abortive product of a snobbish decadence. The abolition of art criticism and the introduction of art observation, which has for almost a year now been decried by large sectors of world public opinion as barbaric and impracticable, has in the meanwhile been effected everywhere in our country. Now the public itself functions as critic, and through its participation or non-participation it pronounces a clear judgment upon its poets, painters, composers, and actors.

The purging of the cultural field has been accomplished with the least amount of legislation. The social estate of creative artists took this cleansing into its own hands. Nowhere did any serious obstructions emerge. Today we can assert with joy and satisfaction that the great development is once again set in motion. Everywhere people are painting, building, writing poetry, singing, and acting. The German artist has his feet on a solid, vital ground. Art, taken out of its narrow and isolated circle, again stands in the midst of the people and from there exerts its strong influences on the whole nation.

To be sure, the political leadership has interfered in this, and today it still interferes daily and directly. But this occurs in a way that can only work to the benefit of the German artist: through subsidy, the commission of works, and a patronage of the arts, whose generosity is unique today in the whole world. Theater and film, writing and poetry, painting and architecture, have thereby experienced a fruitfulness which heretofore was wholly unimaginable.

The radio broadcasting system has become a real people's institution. Since the National Socialist revolution the number of listeners has increased from four to nearly nine million. The German press, in a rare demonstration of discipline, daily conducts its educational mission among the German people. The way to the nation has been cleared for all cultural efforts and strivings. We have not only sought for talent but have also found talent. In the new state, opportunities have been offered to talented people as never before. They need only to reach out for them and make themselves master of them.

It is true that in the long run every great art can live only by inducting healthy recruits. Therefore our major concern has been directed to this problem. It cannot be doubted that in a history-making time, so highly tension-ridden, as our own, political life absorbs a host of talents which normally would have been partly at the disposal of cultural life. In addition, there is the fact that the great philosophical ideas which have been set in motion by the National Socialist revolution, for the moment operate so spontaneously and eruptively that they are not yet ripe enough for elaboration in artistic form. The problems are too fresh and too new for them to become artistically, dramatically, or poetically formed. The recruits who one day will have to solve this task are still in the offing. In order to prepare the way for them, we can do nothing else but offer them every opportunity to develop their intellectual and technical aptitudes and skills in the broadest range possible. . . .

What was first achieved for the creative artists of the stage should in no way be an ending. It is the cornerstone on which the old-age security program for all art creators must be established. The necessary preliminary work for the attainment of this goal is already in progress. It is a question of finding an organizational and economic form for every profession in this new field.

Along with this we have also turned our attention, in this year, to the establishment of old-age and recreation homes. Through the magnanimity of the Prussian Minister President not only was a new home for the aged in Weimar bequeathed to German veterans of the stage, but the Marie Seebach Foundation, which has been in existence for many years, was given a secure financial basis. In addition, we created a new old-age and recreation home in Oberwisenthal and two new beautiful recreation homes in Arendsee on the Baltic Sea. They are to be opened next spring and will provide accommodations for seventy to eighty German artists seeking rest and recreation.

The projects which have been successfully carried out here and in other fields of art are cultural acts of the first rank and thus truly worthy of the National Socialist German nation. Nothing similar has even been tried ever or anywhere else in the world. In this field we have not presented any high-sounding program; we have acted. We have courageously tackled these questions, and here also it has been proven that problems can be solved, if one wants to solve them. Germany marches ahead of all other countries not only in art but also in the care which it showers upon artists, and thus sets an illuminating example.

We are all the more obligated in this respect when today German art encompasses the whole nation. The people, participating by the million, have made it their own cause.

One speaks so often in a contemptuous way of mass taste and tries to contrast it to the taste of the propertied classes, the cultured or the upper ten thousand. Nothing, however, is more unjust than that. While the taste of the so-called cultural persons, precisely because they are cultured and have read so much, was exposed to the most manifold ill will and therefore also to fluctuations, the taste of the broad masses has always remained the same. They do not have so many possibilities of comparison in order, in the end, no longer to know whether the good is really good or the inferior really inferior. Nor are they so satiated that out of sheer lack of spiritual hunger they ultimately succumb to the most inane confusions and degenerations of the primitive and thus of clear and pure artistic feeling. Their joy in the healthy and the strong is still naïve, untroubled, and sensuously moved. They still feel with the heart, and this heart does not stand in the shadow of an all-knowing, all-perceiving mind which in the end is also destructive and doubtful of all. Their unchanging taste is the only stable element in the great artistic evolutionary processes.

The people have a healthy feeling for authentic accomplishment, but also for words which indeed speak of accomplishments but behind which there are no accomplishments. Its taste derives from a solid predisposition, but it must be correctly and systematically guided. In its sometimes primitive expressions it is nevertheless always right and unwarped. True culture is not bound up with wealth. On the contrary, wealth often makes one bored and decadent. It is frequently the cause of uncertainty in matters of the mind and of taste. Only in this way can we explain the terrible devastations of the degeneration of German art in the past. Had the representatives of decadence and decline turned their attention to the masses of the people, they would have come up against icy contempt and cold mockery.

For the people have no fear of being scorned as out of step with the times and as reactionary by enraged Jewish literati. Only the wealthy classes have this fear, when it is combined with insecurity in matters of taste. They succumb all too easily to that kind of demi-culture which is coupled with intellectual pride and conceited arrogance. These defects are familiar to us under the label "snobbism." The snob is an empty and hollow culture lackey who eats only the rinds from the fruits and who then cannot digest them. He goes in black tie and tails to the theater in order to breathe the fragrance of poor people. He must see suffering, which he shudderingly and shiveringly enjoys. This is the final degeneration of a rabble-like amusement industry. In the theater the rich want to see how things go with the poor. What a brutalization of the sensibility! But also what a bestialization of taste and of the whole artistic sensibility!

The Volk visits the theater, concerts, museums, and galleries for other reasons. It wants to see and enjoy the beautiful and the lofty. That which life so often and stubbornly withholds from the people, a world of wonder and of gracious appearance, here ought to unfold before their eyes, gleaming with astonishment. The people approach the illusions of art with a naïve and unbroken joyousness and imagine themselves to be in an enchanted world of the Ideal, which life allows us only to guess at but seldom grasp and never obtain. Here lie the origins and the eternally operative driving energies of every great art. Snobbism is sick and worm-eaten. Its taste cannot set the standards and erect the forms for an era. We have had the courage to reject the products of its insolent arrogance. Today they are assembled in the "Exhibition of Degenerate Art," and the people, by the million, walk by this blooming nonsense, shaking their heads angrily, especially because this snobbism, in its insolence and arrogance, presumed to make its appeal precisely to this Volk. In fact, the Führer had acted in the fulfillment of a national duty when he interfered here and again established order and a sure footing in this chaos. The people hardly knew this. Wherever they met it, they punished it with mockery and contempt. This kind of art was right to avoid the bright, clear eye of the people and to withdraw from them into their salons. The primitive and healthy popular taste demands a corresponding spiritual diet. One does not raise strong people with snobbish over-refinements. Let no one here raise the objection that the people desire only to be entertained. The people seek joy. They have a right to it. We have the

duty of giving this joy to them. Most of us have barely an idea of how
joyless in general is the life of the people and therefore of how important it is to provide a remedy.

"Hence bread and circuses!" croak the wiseacres. No: "Strength
Through Joy!" we reply to them.

This is why we have thus named the movement for the organization of optimism. It has led all strata of the people, by the million, to
the beauties of our country, to the treasures of our culture, our art,
and our life. Certainly, entertainment has at the same time found
abundant expression. In most cases it is the preliminary stage to
purely artistic enjoyment. This is where true art almost always origi-
nates. . . .

Foreign circles hostile to Germany often attempt to project an image of the contemporary German artist as an oppressed and beaten
creature who, surrounded by laws and regulations, languishes and
sighs under the tyrannical dictatorship of a cultureless, barbaric regime. What a distortion of the true situation!

The German artist of today feels himself freer and more untram-
meled than ever before. With joy he serves the people and the state,
who have accepted him and his cause in such a warmhearted and
understanding way. National Socialism has wholly won over German
creative artists. They belong to us and we to them.

We have not brought them to our side by means of hollow programs and empty phraseology, but by means of action. Ancient artist-
dreams have been fulfilled by us, others are in the process of being
actualized. How could the German artist not feel sheltered in this
state! Socially secure, economically improved, esteemed by society, he
can now serve his great plans in peace and without the bitterest cares
for his livelihood. He again has a people that awaits his call. He no
longer speaks to empty rooms and before dead walls. A noble competition has begun for the laurel of victory in all fields of our artistic life.
National Socialism has also drawn the German artist under its spell.
It is the foundation of his creativity, the solid basis on which he
stands with all of us. He fulfills the task that a great time has assigned
to him as a true servant of his people.

In this hour, we all look reverently upon you, my Führer, you who
do not regard art as a ceremonial duty but as a sacred mission and a
lofty task, the ultimate and mightiest documentation of human life.

You know and love art and artists. Even as a statesman you come
from their circles. You follow the way of German art in our time with

an ardent heart. You point out its direction and goal as the blessed giver of meaning.

We all thank you for this. May you keep your protecting hand in the future as well over German art and the German race. Accomplishment and deeds will be the answer and the solemn vow of the German artist for this protection.

Our people today, however, are around us and with us. They render their thanks to their artists for the countless hours of joy, recreation, and edification, liberating laughter and excitement. A year of work lies behind us. A year of work lies before us. The success we have achieved summons us to new deeds. By building upon this success, we aim to dedicate ourselves to our tasks with ardent hearts and glowing idealism in the service of art, the great consoler of our life.

> From an address by Dr. Goebbels at the Annual Congress of the Reich Chamber of Culture and the Strength Through Joy organization, Berlin, November 26, 1937, published in *Von der Grossmacht zur Weltmacht, 1937,* edited by Hans Volz (Berlin: Junker und Dünnhaupt Verlag, 1938), pp. 416-426.

On the National Responsibility of Publishers
ADOLF SPEMANN

There have always been publishers—and not the worst ones—who saw it as their function to subordinate themselves, in a purely servile capacity, to the creator of literary works, that the writer himself bore the full responsibility for his work and that the publisher's task was merely to be the most perfect reflection possible of contemporary cultural achievements. In this way the publisher keeps to himself his personal attitude—which, to use that favorite expression, one is always wont to suspend when one does not wish to take a position or has no point of view. Often this was conceived not only in a purely business way but as a kind of flawless idealism, in which the freedom of discussion appeared more important than any definite idea. But this is precisely the form most often taken by liberalism, out of which ultimately a political, moral, and artistic theory of relativity has emerged.

This attitude of the publisher was strongly influenced by the prevailing views in aesthetics and music and literary criticism, which increasingly came to hold that all artistic, musical, and literary monuments must be grasped and understood in terms of their historical premises. Out of this quickly emerged a second principle: to understand all is to forgive all—and in the diligent effort to understand all, even that which was fully race-alien to us, one lost every footing and point of reference. Thus it is a sad but indisputable fact that it was precisely the growing knowledge concerning the process of becoming which began to destroy sound judgment concerning being. This attitude which permeated the whole degenerate conception of art before the accession to power of National Socialism, which was mirrored in countless published writings, naturally could not avoid influencing the publishers of these books and periodicals, and for the very reason that they were unable to oppose this decadence with any clear world view or any clear cultural political aim. And thus the ring closed: these publishers in good faith brought out works which fostered the dissolution of all solid forms. . . .

The great fundamental reversal, however, took place only through the seizure of power by National Socialism. The great master of the education of his people, Adolf Hitler, has in a few years transformed our souls and has also sharpened in the whole book-publishing trade the feeling that it bears a tremendous responsibility. The first decisive act in this direction was the establishment of personal responsibility, since from it also arises complete liability: the publisher, in reproducing and distributing a piece of writing, is just as responsible for its contents as is its author. Hence he is forced to concern himself closely with the contents of his books, as closely as should have been decreed long ago by law. Thus the great distance that separates the present-day conception of the publisher's calling from yesterday's becomes quite clear: instead of an inwardly uninvolved cultural-mirror he is a cultural-politician imbued with his task. The servant of the writer has been changed into a deputy of the state. The self-satisfied noninvolved connoisseur has become a militant fighter in the front ranks. Thus today it is not enough for the publisher to master his craft and to be as cultured as possible; he must be thoroughly imbued with the idea of the state leadership of Adolf Hitler and in this idea he will find the guidelines for his own work. No one will be able to say that he is in no position to do this. The countless great speeches of the Führer, along with his book, afford an exhaustive exposition of the state idea that he has created and espoused, down to the smallest details of personal life. Anyone who fully absorbs, over and over again, the lavish fullness of this brilliant mind which literally runneth over and this example of a truly great life will know what he has to do. . . .

Likewise, however, the publisher will always be conscious of the fact that literature is not to be separated from politics, which in the last analysis is the guidance of man and therefore his education. It all depends on the reply to the question: do books influence or change people or do they not? Now, one of the beliefs of the age of degeneracy that is now behind us was that it was a superstition of anxiety-ridden, power-hungry headmasters that books could warp and destroy the soul. With this cleverly conceived distortion, the literary man created his own license to wash his dirty linen in public and even to get paid for it. Whether one decides that pernicious books are a consequence of decadence or one of its causes is meaningless, and is at bottom a question of taste. The fact is that in daily life cause and effect have entwined themselves into an indissoluble knot. What does one do, however, when one cannot untie a knot? One cuts it in two and masters it. This is what National Socialism has done. In the face of this imperishable accomplishment the fact that it at first believed that it had to destroy many other real values, perhaps unjustly, carries little weight. It is well known that in every great housecleaning some pieces of porcelain are bound to be broken. . . .

The decisive consideration which the publisher today must pose to himself should not, therefore, be the following: "Will this book be a sensation? Will it be a hit? Can I create a need so that I may satisfy it? Can I add new riddles to the ones already in existence? Can I open a discussion which my magazine can feed on for months on end? Can I get hold of this or that famous name for my house? How shall I make a neat turnover at any price?"

No! The publisher must ask himself: "Will this book that I publish now, and in years to come, when I have long departed this earth, fill my children with pride in the accomplishment of their father? Does this book make people stronger, without making them stupid? Will it imbue the soul of the reader with strength and joy, or will it leave a bitter taste and will it steep the heart in lye and jar the nerves? Does it give the individual the strength which aspires to the Whole and forms the community or does it lead him to that deceptive pseudo-consolation of self-sufficient solitude and to flight from this world and the present? Does it broaden the reader's point of view, without alienating him from the roots of his own Volkdom? Does it show him the greatness of the German present and past without obscuring or indeed making contemptible the imperishable cultural accomplishments of other peoples and times, to the extent that these enrich and strengthen us? Will it direct his gaze to greatness in all its associations, without alienating him from loyalty to little things, to details? Will the book be a contribution to the efforts to sharpen the ear of the people, so that it can learn to distinguish the genuine from the false tone, so that it does not imbibe the sparkling brilliance or the intoxicating semi-darkness of stylized language without an inner view and a moral attitude for true poetry, so that it does not confuse handy maxims, cheap sloganeering, or finely spun dialectics with valuable scientific research, so that it does not take foggy haziness for philosophical depth? Does it increase the German cultural patrimony in any way or is it wholly irrelevant to it? In the 2000-year history of our people is it worthy, perhaps, of the unique period which we are experiencing today? Does it serve, if only in a very small way, the great aim of the Führer to create the new German man, that indispensable, irreplaceable building material for the next millennium of German history, whose threshold we have just crossed with wildly throbbing hearts?"

From Adolf Spemann, *Einsamkeit und Gemeinschaft* (Stuttgart: J. Engelhorn Nachf., 1939), pp. 142-147.

Goebbels Forbids Art Criticism

Because this year has not brought an improvement in art criticism, I forbid once and for all the continuance of art criticism in its past form, effective as of today [November 27, 1936]. From now on, the reporting of art will take the place of an art criticism which has set itself up as a judge of art—a complete perversion of the concept of "criticism" which dates from the time of the Jewish domination of art. The critic is to be superseded by the art editor. The reporting of art should not be concerned with values, but should confine itself to description. Such reporting should give the public a chance to make its own judgments, should stimulate it to form an opinion about artistic achievements through its own attitudes and feelings.

From *Der Deutsche Schriftsteller*, Jahrg. I, Heft 12 (1936), pp. 280 ff. Reprinted in Rolf Geissler, *Dekadenz und Heroismus* (Stuttgart: Deutsche Verlagsanstalt, 1964), p. 30, n. 20.

What Is German in German Art?

KURT KARL EBERLEIN

Art is never objective. It is an offense against romanticism to call the naturalism of our debased "sailor painting" romantic. "The spirit, in terms of which we act, is the loftiest." And this art spirit is as loveless as a medical diagnosis, a photograph, or a statistic. The *plein-air* civilization of modern painting which began with French Impressionism does not belong either to the soul or to the language of the soul: it does not contemplate, but looks. Its art is seen, with susceptible time-conditioned nerves, with time-conditioned eyes, newspaper-like, and in the same way, therefore, is this art to be seen, to be enjoyed, but not to be experienced. Art is contemplation. Here the inner eye decides. Artists have the landscape in their hearts, because they contemplated, because their soul becomes landscape, and their landscape becomes soul. German art is homeland and homesickness and therefore always landscape even in the picture, the land of the soul becomes and grows into soul, it is the language of the homeland even in an alien atmosphere, in the alien atmosphere of foreign lands as well as in the alien atmosphere of animals, flowers, things. Either one speaks German and then the soul speaks, or one speaks an alien tongue, a cosmopolitan, fashionable, Esperanto language and then the soul speaks no more. The casing of this homeland is the house that the German loves so much, the room, the mirror image of his being, the thought of home which the German carried with him even amid the sufferings and death of the trenches. Anyone who knows this German room image knows what I mean, this soul becomes a room, the soul of a room that hardly survives today because the fashion in decoration killed the German room the way it has killed

German dress, because the model makes everything equal, alike, and spiritually poor. The new Germany lives in the world on the basis of such rooms, since the magic circle from which all that is called Volkdom unfolds—namely, the family—encloses its law of growth here in the family room, whose holy, state-forming character Pestalozzi described so magnificently. Today the principal task of architects is to create a family living room in which the family spirit can dwell and exert its influence. Here lie the real roots of our strength. All those to whom Germandom was an essential entity saw in the family the health, salvation, and future of the state; around the family table they saw the circle sheltering and protecting the qualities of the soul. . . . The homeland, the landscape, the living space, the language community are embodied in the family which roams and grows beyond the borders. In it lives the child with mores and customs, the dialect of play, of celebration, in it live the song, the fairy tale, the proverb, native costume and furniture and utensils. In it lie the ultimate energies of primordial folk art, the work done in the home, handicraft, tradition, in it lies also that salutary and profound sentimental feeling for family arts which it would be hazardous to underestimate, for it is the bread and joy of the house. Here work music, dancing music, family music, house music, have a last abode and a potent health-giving magic. Here the life rhythm of the year pulsates squarely through house and field, growing close and vitally out of the very soil. How distant is this venerable life-maturity from all that which stirs the big city, the changing fashion of the day, which revolves around the abiding customs like the earth around the sun. How laughable, puppetlike, and cinematic do the art groups of the big city appear here, the art fashions which are best compared with the exotic animals inside the cages of the zoological gardens of the big city. One may object that the family, especially the rural family, was never a connoisseur or judge of art nor could it be. Certainly not! Thank God, for here nothing is being judged, it is not a question of criticism, but of something much more essential, namely, life itself. It is not a question of the blossom, but of the tree. It is an "achievement" and a result of the Renaissance that art is considered only the surface of aesthetic values, of phenomenal and formal values, that it is enjoyed aesthetically as adornment for a wall, as a decor for a room, as a concert or an exhibit.

Our museum, for this reason, is not a museum for the people. It has not yet lost the character of a castle, the decorative style and charm of an aristocratic, uncomfortable, awesome palace of culture. A visit to it brings to mind a world's fair, a panoptikon, a castle. "Art," therefore, for most racial comrades—let's be honest about it for once! —is not the bread of life, not a life value, not a nourishment for the soul. Rather, it still is the priceless unnecessary, the delicate pastry in the store window, the comfortable accouterment of the propertied classes, the speculation stock of the wealthy, the collective ownership of the state. The life of the working people unfolds beyond this art. Bread and work are more important. This is the situation, despite such slogans as "art for everybody," "art for the people," "art without an entrance fee," "art with a sunset glow." This art is still "culture," hence uncomfortable, alien to the people. The fault lies neither with the state nor with the individual, but with that art which is cut off from blood and soil.

From Kurt Karl Eberlein, *Was ist deutsch in der deutschen Kunst?* (Leipzig: Verlag E. A. Seemann, 1933), pp. 56-59.

The Poet Summoned by History
HEINRICH ZILLICH

No, I mean poets who are kindled by history and forced to speak because they are overcome by this kinship with a great event, and who must restlessly revolve around this illuminating point in the crisis of their spiritual existence until, in an act of self-redemption, they endow it with that form through which the people can share in former living spaces and in their past being because their meaning is revealed to them.

It must be a deep kinship that touches, summons, torments, and blesses the poet. He will become conscious of this kinship only when he finds the way to it from its most characteristic blood drenched experience, that representatively anticipates the necessary and same experience of the people and actually brings it about later through the creative work.

The greatest experience that grew in the German, bitterly at first in the last war and in the subsequent years of tribulation, but then radiantly in the time of ascent, was the self-discovery of the body of his own Volk with all its members, the bursting of the close-fitting skin of the state which had been left over and which was ridiculously restricting the Volk-consciousness by virtue of racial cleavage and political narrowness and which first required the collapse of a world in order to be stripped off and to reveal all the Germans created by God. In this way the reality of the Reich and the Volk became alive in a new form, in a natural wedding as never before. For a poet to remove himself from this amplitude means to lose the ground under his feet. His attitude toward history and its evaluation through science today can rest only upon the new consciousness of the nation, whose strength and relevance to the times, whose noble modesty and at the same time crystalline sense of responsibility intertwined with the world, were truly overwhelmingly proved this year when ten million Germans were able to return to the Reich without striking a blow.[1]

On the basis of this consciousness, of this feeling of the common citizenship of Germans, we can now finally approach a historiography whose judgments are made in accordance with Volkish criteria, in accordance, that is to say, with whether events satisfy the whole people and its mission—neither just the one or the other—but both the people and its mission. This does not mean that we must falsify the purposes of our actions and ideas into our ancestors' in order to grasp for ourselves external confirmation from history. History confirms to us—who are rich in history—the wide spaces that are open to us in the future. But it does mean that, despite our full understanding of the substantiality and uniqueness of past ages, we seek the specifically German dimension in its totality everywhere, which up to now was not perceived in the historiography of dynastic power and territorial interests.

Many a deed whose greatness is indisputable, if considered from the viewpoint of the whole people, only now allows us to see the tragic consequences as well as those of a more fruitful character. To cite an example: If we were to consider the wars of Frederick the Great, we must ask whether those long years of German fratricidal struggle were not a cause of the fact that the broad territories of the Southeast, at that time still sparsely populated ever since the Turkish wars and subject to Vienna's control, were only insufficiently settled by Germans. We must ask whether at that time we did not definitely lose a vast living space which Providence had assigned to us as a sphere of dominion and as a prize for saving Europe from the deadly

[1] That is, in the Austrian *Anschluss*.

Islamic threat and which we at a later time had to relinquish completely perhaps only as the ultimate consequence of our fratricidal struggles. Thus must the historical researcher formulate the question to himself, without, of course, attaching any blame to the actors of that time, who in accordance with their value-consciousness could not have foreseen this result.

Thus the poet also is summoned by history to place the amplitude and the unity of the people in the center of his view. At the same time he should try to avoid the error of transferring the spirit of his age into the past. But he should certainly look for the whole people in past ages and give significant form to its fate. For the whole German people also lived at that time. Even at that time—to conjure another example—the axes of the Swabian settlers resounded in the Banat, alone, often forsaken, in order to build a new province, while the rulers of the people quarreled over whether an old province, whose German-ness was not under any threat, should be transferred from one German hand to another. What a subject for a heart-rending epic when one considers that the new province remained unfinished!

The amplitude and unity of the people—this is the kinship which the poet today must perceive in history, and there he will also perceive the relations between the people and the Reich, between the people, the Reich, and Europe, those indissoluble relations of the primordial bond of fate, co-determining the human world order, which redound to the special honor of the Germans.

The Reich often reached out beyond the sphere of the German people, but later it constricted itself until after 1918 it did not encompass more than two thirds of the people. Again a subject to sear the soul! And actually the tragedy of the division of the people in the recent past, within a few years, which we can count on the fingers of our hand, abruptly caused, like a miracle, a number of poets to emerge one after the other with works of a militant, passionate character with the power of created truth born of the most particular experience. They shout forth the song of tribulation of the Germans which touches not only us—we experienced it a few weeks ago in the unparalleled restoration of a part of the suffering! [2]—but also Europe to its vital nerve, since we do belong to the responsible master-builders of this continent whose way of life subjected the world. Therefore the poetry of the fate of Germans beyond the Reich, in its most important works, does not cling to territorial and spiritual narrowness,

[2] This refers to the annexation of Austria by the Third Reich.

which often enjoys dubious praise as homeland poetry. No, with its presentation of the fate of the homeland, it bursts open larger contexts and becomes a meaningful scripture of German and European fate. In it germinates also the poetry of the law of the eastern spaces and of their bond with the mission and tragedy of our people. A poetry, which—if all is not deceiving—in a few years will correctly present the image of the East, up to now distorted by historiography, above all of the Southeast, in terms of its relevance to things German.

From Heinrich Zillich, "Die deutsche Dichtung und die Welt der Geschichte," in *Weimarer Reden des Grossdeutschen Dichtertreffens* (Hamburg: Hanseatische Verlagsanstalt, 1938), pp. 43-45.

Wulfe's Manor: Two Episodes in a Peasant's Life
JOSEFA BERENS-TOTENOHL

I

Several leagues downward where the Lenne doubles back in a northwesterly direction, there lay a free manor called the Wulfe manor. Here dwelt the clan of the Wulfes, lordly, free, secluded. The ancestral father of the clan had founded the manor when the hills were still ruled by savage robber bands. Strong, courageous—wild blood had coursed through the veins of many members of the family. All had increased in number and defended themselves, regardless of the illustrious lords, von Arnsberg, von Mark, and von Köln, whose boundaries were in this region and who attacked each other whenever they had the opportunity. Through all the dangers the Wulfes had kept their holding free and raised it to a power which stood inviolable on the eternally flaming borders between the three princes.

The Lenne River surrounded the lonely manor, towering on a hill, in a thundering bracket which was ominously threatening in times of danger. On the mountainside the water was dammed by a weir. The mill, which stood on the manor, extended to the edge of the weir. Then the Lenne flowed around the whole manor, which, itself almost a mountainous protrusion, pushed out obliquely into the valley.

So that the manor would not be cut off during a flood tide, a solid dam had been built to the weir because the waters of the Lenne become a sea when they rush past the steep precipices of the mountain.

And this occurred every year in November. This affliction was called Catherine's flood.

The manor, built out of the stones of the mountain, covered over by a gray thatched roof, lay in solitude and darkness. At once a refuge and a defense, the walls presented the aspect of a fortress rather than a house. The manor court was narrow. It was enclosed by stables for the livestock, granaries, barns, and workshops. This garland of buildings necessarily lay lower on the hill. A wall also closed this off against the open Lenne. A heavy portal formed the barrier against the outside world.

In these times the Wulfes kept a guard over the manor at night. The peasant collected a body of men, as many as the holding could support, and gathered them for his defense and honor.

Troubles and crises afflicted the countryside. The lords, big and little, wrested power and lands from each other and were heedless of the fact that they were tearing each other apart. The smell of fire pervaded the land. Misery sat on the hearth. People recited the "Our Father" more frequently than they usually did for the one good petition, the one for bread. But everyone who lay on his deathbed and breathed his last did not pray to the end. In such times it was easy to hate, there were many acts of trespass and trespasses in the making, more than acts of forgiveness, God knows! The hostile hordes of mercenaries tore at each other for the booty like the wild predatory animals in the mountains, forgetting that they had sprung at each other for its sake. Only the Wulfe manor defended itself from becoming booty.

The present peasant, a stocky, fifty-year-old man, sat in an armchair, a brown bearskin spread on the floor in front of him. His grandfather had felled this king of the woods. The armchair was elaborately carved. The arms were formed of two sculptured wolves, the heraldic animals of the Wulfes. The back of the chair showed two eagle-owl heads, which a later ancestor of the Wulfes had added to the escutcheon. The old pagan defiance had sprung up once more in this ancestor and he had the image of the female companion of this God, the owl, the knower among the birds, secretly carved in the ornamental strip of the church pew of the Wulfes in Wormbeeke. The priest, a fanatical persecutor of pagan abominations, had opposed this. The ancestor, firmly defiant, unconcerned at the prospect of being burned at the stake and receiving a harsh court sentence, had said: "Count me out without it!"

Thus the eagle-owl remained on the Wulfes' escutcheon in the church and in the house. For the priest did not want to do without Wulfes and their tithe. The eagle-owl heads gazed, unmoved, upon the Wulfes in their thoughts and in their prayers, when they sat between them. The young Wulfes of several generations had cut their teeth on the springing wolves of the arms of the chair, which were barely perceptible, and had almost reduced them to nothingness with cuts and thrusts.

The peasant was the last Wulfe. His wife Margret had given him only a daughter. Then she was afflicted with an incurable paralysis and sat year after year in her chair near the other windows of the enormous room. Her feet rested on a beautiful wildcat skin with which the peasant had honored her on her wedding day, never imagining that her dead feet would burden it for a whole life. The stillness of old age floated for a long time around this armchair and one perforce already saw deeply, if he wanted to perceive this, that even here a life had been lived far, unutterably far, from peasant life and its necessities.

At that moment the daughter Magdlene came in with the warm evening beer for her father.

"It's going to be bad outside tonight," she said.

"No worse than any other time," decided the peasant.

"It could be, nevertheless. I feel it in my bones like never before," warned the peasant's wife. Thereupon the daughter helped her mother to the bedroom. . . .

The peasant sat still for a long time in the enormous room. Magdlene went into the weaving room, sent the maids away, and worked at the looms by herself. Her loom beat time with the blows of the storm outside, which pounded the corners of the walls, picking up new strength after a moment's pause.

Suddenly a lightning bolt struck, followed by the clap of thunder. The Wulfe daughter hurriedly ran over to her father's side.

"A storm now."

The old man remained silent, serious as though he had heard nothing. He was in another world with his thoughts. . . .

And in addition the merchant had to come today! How he hated him! Him, who was only a nothing! He had once placed himself in the hands of this nothing! Of course, it was a long time ago. He had hated him since then. In particular he hated that hour, which he saw as the lowest in his life, and in this hour stood Robbe. Wulfe had never bowed before any prince, yet he had given him, whom he called a dog, he had at one time given him power over him.

It was the only sin that Wulfe recognized in his life. Each time Robbe came, Wulfe thought about this shame, and he certainly would not let him come into the manor if it had not occurred. The peasant always read this triumph in the look of the other, which the shrewd merchant himself never made reference to. But it remained in the abyss, which continuously spewed forth poison.

"Satan!" cursed Wulfe in the direction of the barn.

Wulfe was young, strong, and happy like no other lad in the valley. He had once captured a live wolf and brought him home to his parents. He was the only son and heir of the old manor. In their last progeny the Wulfes were no longer really fruitful! And he was quite aware of his uniqueness.

For years Margret, a rich peasant girl from the Cologne area, had been reserved for him as his future wife. Then fate threw a wild, black-haired gypsy witch into his arms, a girl with smoldering eyes and a fiery passion for rutting, and he forgot all about his blond and quiet Margret and he pulled the alien woman into his riotous nights.

His bedroom, when he was a youth, was located in the wing over the eternally gray weir, the same one which had been swept away by the flood. Hei! How his body flamed when the black witch cowered in the night darkness under the window and cooed up to him. When he flung open the window and she drew close to him! When he grabbed her by her wild lock of hair, and when he heard the wild heartbeat of the woman pound against his equally wild heartbeat, when he hurled his blood into the scorching whirlpool of her flaming desire and lost himself with her in ecstasy! For whole nights, for whole weeks! Then the owls outside screeched their "Huhuhhh!" in vain, the waters roared their warning song to no avail, their song of flood, distress, and disaster.

It was a wild autumn that year, long ago, and it glowed like no other. To this day still, Wulfe's eyes sparkled when on occasion, as on this very night, his thoughts dwelt upon it. He still liked to take delight in this wild exultant time of his life, which otherwise had known only harshness. But then always a stooped, gray shadow crept in, Robbe, and the exultant mood died.

One day, however, the turning point came, the moment in which fate poses the question. For a long time he had secretly tried to flee from her. Many nights it drove him up to the mountains, instead of into her tempting arms, it drove him on the trail of the lynx and the wolf into danger, hardship, and death, instead of to the satiated desire of his senses. A cry for freedom resounded in him, for the proud freedom of his being, which he had betrayed. He wanted to hunt and to fight again for what he had lost on the steep flanks of the cliffs.

Up there in the mountains the old spark sprang up in him, which always drove out the over-drunk sensual frenzy and sated covetousness: hate. The lawful instinct of his peasant blood raised this terrible sword for the revenge of the offenses committed against his being.

Of course, when he came down to the manor again and found the woman waiting for him below, then lust still loudly cried down this spark of salvation. Nevertheless, he returned home hesitatingly, and one wild autumn night he stayed away completely. The mountains resounded with the mighty battle cries of the bucks, the earth trembled under the thud of their hooves. There the woman found him on the owl cliff, from where he had spied upon the raging fury of the battling animals. Thus had he overheard the approach of footsteps.

Even to this day Wulfe shook whenever he thought of this moment, when the shaggy head of the gypsy witch suddenly appeared above the edge of the cliff and was raised higher and higher with a searching, spying look. He had grabbed his javelin, ready to hurl it, for he had thought it was a she-wolf. Then he recognized the eyes.

"You—here?"

"Yes! Me! You made me wait a long time!"

"You shouldn't have followed me. See!" He showed her the spear. "I was just about to throw it!"

But she just stood there, unmoving, flashing her eyes at him, so that he almost gave way to confusion. He mastered the surge of his blood, or his hatred mastered it. He threw the weapon to the ground.

"Go, go back to your people, woman!"

"My people have gone away, peasant, and you know it! I want to come to you, and I want to ask you: When will you make me your peasant wife before all the people?"

"Woman, are you mad?"

"Mad? Didn't you swear to that? A thousand times!"

"What are vows sworn in the night, woman?"

"What are vows, you scoundrel?" she cried, and lunged at him, hanging on his neck, biting and scratching him. "What are vows? Then ask my body, you . . ."

If he had not suddenly thrown her back, she would have bitten through his throat like a she-wolf. As though the heavens joined her anger, a fiery glow played around the blazing woman, who stood with smoldering eyes before him, her fists clenched.

"You traitor! Watch out for my people! They will find you! Revenge is sacred!"

Then he stood alone. Before he could lift up his arm to strike her, she had slid down the rock at breakneck speed. No other person could have come out of such a drop alive. Had she saved her life? She had vanished as though the waters of the Lenne had swallowed her and dragged her along. She had left behind with him only her word of revenge and he had brought it home with him.

Thus she was not out of his life.

"If only I had done it!" he wished a thousand times, and every time he regretted that he had not hurled the spear. For, later, she had produced a black gypsy brat, and because of this worm he had to pay with corn and more corn, money and more money. No one was to know about it, neither his old parents nor his quiet bride.

Robbe played the role of intermediary. The rogue! The dog! To this day the peasant always shook with anger whenever the merchant came. But it was too late to order him off the manor. He must be killed. This had always been the peasant's idea, but he never laid him low.

So even today Robbe was again a guest at the Wulfe manor, and even today he had been seated above the domestic servants at the evening meal. . . .

II

"Is Father really dying?" asked Felix, in order to say something, for the silence was becoming oppressive.

"You must adjust yourselves to that! It happens, of course, a little early. How old is he?"

"Barely fifty."

Wulfe was silent.

"He hasn't been able to do anything for a long time now," said Job. Felix, secretly observing Wulfe, added: "There is not much that can really be done on our place."

Here Wulfe was in his element, in which he could find the proper word.

"Everybody knows that the Öd manor is falling to pieces. It is all the more regrettable because there are young hands on the place who should be able to do something about it."

He again wanted to summon the devil, but then he thought he heard the throat-rattle from the bedchamber through the rafters of the room, and he did not summon him.

"What shall we do? We don't know to what extent Father has already placed the manor in debt to von Arnsberg," Felix said.

"Your father, indeed, has not worked in a long time. He could do no more. I believe that if his sons had supported and administered the manor in a good, meaningful way, it would not have declined to the point where he had to go to the Count looking for help, which is really not help. Where there are young hands, there should be no decline. This is against all peasant laws."

The sons sat down and were silent. Wulfe continued:

"Your father will not revive. When a tree is rotten, it falls and no support helps. But the land remains. It does not decay. It builds new trees. The manor is your land. You are the new trees. You should know that."

They also knew it. At least they acted as though they did. But to Wulfe their words seemed to have little worth.

"When one lets death come over a manor, then one betrays the immortal soul in creation and God avenges it without mercy. It doesn't matter if your Öd manor is run by you or by another. Every manor, however, in the long run requires a strong protector. It rejects the traitor."

The two sons sat before Wulfe as though crushed. They knew his reputation in the whole mountain country and took his words as a judgment and a sentence upon them. Felix was especially depressed. He had nourished a secret hope to marry Wulfe's daughter. Today he realized clearly that he would never be accepted by the people of the Wulfe manor. After his father died, he would find out whether all of them would have to go away from the manor with nothing but a beggar's staff. And such persons would never find mercy at the hand of the peasant Wulfe.

After a while Job arose from his chair. Felix spoke with Wulfe about the work on the manor and in the woods.

"Manual work itself is not even the principal concern of the owner of the manor. Any servant knows how to do that, because otherwise he loses his bread. What counts is the goal of the work. Or its meaning, and this, you say, no longer exists on the Öd manor. I say that it is to be found on a manor that is one's own, never on that of another. Happiness too lies in one's own manor. One must only have courage and want to see and conquer it."

"You may talk that way, peasant Wulfe. You would seek yours in vain on the Öd manor."

Wulfe looked sharply at the young man. Had things already gone so far that nobody understood him any more? Or did death in the room above lie so heavily on all of them that it wrapped everything in gloom? Wulfe felt a bitter taste on his tongue. What did they want from him? If the freedom of the Öd manor was already lost, what was there to do? And his thoughts rose threateningly against the man in the room whom death was now seizing in its grip.

Cecilie's shout interrupted his thoughts: "Hurry, come quickly! He's dying!" She sounded as though she were out of her senses.

In the room, much had changed in one hour. The dying man had acquired a wholly different countenance. The cheeks were completely sunken, the temples showed a deep hollow that gleamed blue and cold. The whole face was waxen, the heart no longer sent a single drop of blood up there. The forehead was beaded with cold sweat. The eyes looked out as though they were already in a distant world. The dying man's breathing was hard and intermittent. They thought that every breath would surely be the last. But his chest rose still once more.

Wulfe remained standing at the door. He saw that Cecilie had also brought in the sisters. They crowded around their mother, fearfully, as though they didn't know what to do with their weeping. The brothers kept in the dark, until Felix came in and supported his father, who wanted to sit up.

The proprietor of the Öd manor must still have had something in mind, for he looked around him with eyes that were already dimmed. His thoughts must have achieved a degree of clarity once more. Then his gaze found Wulfe.

Wulfe went up to him immediately. He took the chilling hands in his strong grip, which once had strangled a wolf. And gently Wulfe bent over the man and tried to read his wishes from his lips, but the man could not speak. His tongue no longer obeyed him. A choking gripped the dying man, yet those around him saw that despite this he made every effort to make himself understandable. It was terrible to watch. After a little while, however, it was all over. He had to depart from life, unabsolved, without being able to express the word and his thoughts.

Wulfe let the dead man sink back on his bed and left the room. He had to leave the relatives alone with him. His breed was not good at comforting others, so he took a walk in the night through the manor. It would soon be time for the new day to dawn. The roof of the house already set itself off slightly from the gray sky. He stood there and watched how the beams pushed outward. They stood steep against the sky. It was a lord who had set them up in this way, mused Wulfe the peasant, and he shook his head at the thought that now the Öd manor was coming to an end.

But while he was standing before the house, thinking his thoughts, he saw that pieces of the beautiful gable were missing and that a deadly air of forlornness hung like a cloud around the protruding rafters. In the garden the snow had been trampled by wild animals and the manor's own livestock. A broken fence had not been repaired. The stables were poorly protected against the cold. Wulfe's anger rose with every step he took. A dog howled behind the stable. Then Wulfe was struck by a shuddering thought. He was familiar with the belief that faithful dogs often quickly follow their masters to the grave. But when he saw this wretched creature, half-starved and forgotten, tethered outdoors in the cold, he could give solemn assurance to the dead man upstairs that he would not have long to wait before the beast would also have gone his way.

Wulfe did not have the heart to go further. The dilapidated condition of the manor affected him so deeply that he decided to take his stallion and ride home. He did not mourn for the dead man in the house; he saw only the death of the manor and to him this was like murder.

He said so to the two sons, whom he soon met, still and speechless, in the room. They did not know how to lend a hand like the women, who everywhere know better how to cope with the things of life. When he spoke about the dog outside behind the stables, the eldest son asked: "Which dog?" Wulfe refused to answer him.

"My daughter said that the Öd manor had lost its honor. She was even more right than I imagined."

His words were heard by the dead peasant's widow, who had just come into the room. She was carrying a piece of linen which was to be the dead man's shroud.

"If only you would speak with von Arnsberg, peasant Wulfe, and tell him that he shouldn't send us a stranger to the—" She could not go on. She was overcome with emotion. The little children gathered around her. Before this poignant scene, Wulfe's bones burned as though he had a fever.

"I'll speak with him," he promised, and rode off.

He sent his daughter to the burial. He could no longer set foot on the desolation of this manor.

It turned out that the deal with the Count had really been concluded. For soon after the burial a proxy of von Arnsberg arrived in order to pick out the best cow and horse for the feudal lord. The members of the Öd manor realized that they had lost their freedom. It had happened even before the wretched, neglected dog followed his master to the grave.

> From Josefa Berens-Totenohl, Der Femhof (Jena, 1935), pp. 14-17, 39-43, 208-213.

A Rowdy as Hero: From an Anti-Jewish Novel
TÜDEL WELLER

"In any case—they must already be shrewder than we are, because one thing is certain: they sit on top today in our dear Fatherland and we squat here below. And we pay twelve per cent interest . . ." This brought him back to reality.

"First of all, for once I'm now going to look into it," he said. "It's bad enough that this is the first time I've heard about it. Maybe we can get a reduction."

"Do you plan to see Löwenstein?" said his mother in astonishment.

"Why not? He won't gobble me up then and there."

"But you won't get anywhere, Peter. When we were in great need we agreed to everything, and we signed everything."

"Will you still be going away now?" his sister broke in.

"Of course—but only after everything is settled. After all"—he held his breath, a little less deep now—"I do want to study, if it goes right. As I've had in mind for a long time."

The old lady's face lit up. "That would be splendid, if you could do it, Peter. But what will you live on? You know how things are with us right now!"

"Well, I'll try to struggle through as a working student like count-

less others. I've heard of young men who night after night work at
their factory shifts and are to be found in the lecture halls by day.
Shouldn't I be able to do something like that?" He looked into the
faces of his family with an air of triumph, now more assured. His
mother, he could see, was already in agreement with him. When is a
mother not in agreement when it involves the well-being and the future of a beloved son?

"And we," she said, indicating the daughter, "we'll live in a smaller
space, and rent some rooms to strangers. That way we can give our
student a little helping hand now and then." But he would not hear
of it. "I'll get by all right, Mother, but first I want to give this twelve
per cent Jew a good dressing down."

More easily said than done. He came to Poststrasse, to a building
constructed like a palace. To the right of the lordly entrance glittered
a marble tablet on which was inscribed in golden letters: "Sigfried
Löwenstein, Real Estate, Mortgages, Purchase and Sale of Landed
Properties, Loans." Nice set-up, the young man said to himself. Nothing so clever about that: after all, should he live in a large block of
flats, or maybe even in a barn, at twelve per cent?

Already anger began to smolder in him, and it was not inconsiderable.

He had never been able to stand the chosen sons of Israel. He
hardly knew why; it must have lain in his blood. Besides, even in the
days of his childhood there had been a guiding experience. He didn't
like to think about it. It was a dirty Jewish story. In any case, Löwenstein lived in a palace—that was certain. And now a young fellow
named Peter Mönkemann stood before his fancy door. And if things
were rightly considered—that is, viewed soberly and clearly—he came
here as an insignificant and modest petitioner. His imperceptibly
smoldering anger was meaningless. It could have sprung up from
nothing but his inner feeling of powerlessness. For he was little fit to
be a petitioner . . .

He was received by the chief clerk, who in the new building lorded
it over a dozen clerks bent deeply over their desks. "How was that now?
Speak with Mr. Löwenstein? Speak with him personally, you mean?
Anybody can say that! What do you want from him, then? A mortgage matter, isn't it?"

"Yes—a mortgage matter."

"Fine. Now what's it about? You can settle matters with me at any
time, my good man. You think the boss has time for such things?"

"First," said Peter Mönkemann, "I am not your good man, understand? Second—I want to see Sigfried Lowenstein personally, understand? And as quickly as possible!" Now there was hardly a doubt that this young man would achieve his goal. But before that something new cropped up.

The chief clerk became officious, straightened his crooked back, and said condescendingly: "Obviously you didn't come here on a matter that concerns you personally. Certainly you have come at the bidding of your parents. So you will first have to bring us a certificate stating that you have authorization to act for them."

"But I dropped in only in connection with a possible reduction of the interest and I am here at my mother's request!" Peter protested.

"Precisely!" replied the chief clerk, bowing his head. "We must have that in writing, because in the last analysis anybody can say anything."

So Peter returned home without result, but he was sure that he would not give in. Not he. And when he reappeared with the required authorization and the police certification of his mother's authorization was demanded, he also obtained that, although now he was seething with rage and he had to make a strong effort to control himself in order not to fly at the graybeard.

At last he stood before Sigfried Löwenstein. This at least could not be prevented.

He was sitting, broad and bulky, in a big chair behind a writing desk overloaded with piles of documents and papers. His bloated face revealed cheek pouches. Lachrymal sacs like stuffed pillows hung under his oval, ink-colored, shining bullet-shaped eyes. There was no perceptible neck; the cranium seemed to sit directly between the shoulders, which were pulled up high on the fat torso.

He did not stir when Peter Mönkemann entered. He hardly raised his head.

Peter said his little piece: Twelve per cent was too much. Would not half that figure be enough? It did not exactly sound subservient.

"What's that, please?" asked the fat man. He seemed not to have understood at all, and perhaps had not listened.

The young man repeated what he had said.

"Who let you in to see me?" the fat man asked, and raised his head.

"Nobody! I have come to see you so that you yourself can decide whether a reduction ought to be made."

"A reduction . . ." came the echo in the deepest astonishment. "Is that correct? Did I hear 'reduction'!"

"Yes, that's correct! After all, you must admit that twelve per cent means . . ." He wanted to say "usury." But he controlled himself. Perhaps by being prudent he could still attain something. "Twelve per cent, in the long run, means an impossibility for us, since my father died a short time ago and at home we simply have no income!" he concluded.

The other again bent over his desk. "Go to my chief clerk," he said.

"But I just came from there," the younger man remonstrated. "He can't make a decision on that matter. I would like to hear from you yourself about what's to happen now. I was detained long enough back there. I'm simply tired of being shunted back and forth, do you understand?"

No—Löwenstein did not understand the tone at all. Not at all. . . . Rather, he raised his head again toward the speaker in disbelief and in utter surprise. He saw the other's gaze focused on him, in which hatred and contempt were clearly expressed. At this very moment the youth was forced to think: His face looks like a pig's snout; indeed, like a pig's snout!

No—Sigfried Löwenstein understood not a word of all that. Who let this fellow push his way into his private office? This in itself was an act of unheard-of insolence. . . . So he at last removed the long-extinguished cigar from his big fish-mouth and then he straightened up slightly in his chair, as much as was possible in view of his extraordinary obesity. And then he said: "Young man, if you speak to me any further in that tone of voice, I'll have my house servant throw you out, do you understand? As for the rest, who are you, and what do you want from me anyway? Do you think I've nothing else to do except listen to your trivialities?"

Peter Mönkemann stood there and stared at him, repressing his anger. Did he not come here as a petitioner? If he now gave in to his inner impulse, if he kicked this fat sack in the belly and landed a punch on his pig's snout, then the whole mess would really get worse. Then the mortgage would be foreclosed—that was for sure. Then too the police might come with rubber truncheons and handcuffs and he could kiss his studies and his future good-by.

So he just stood there, swallowed hard, and quivered a little. . . .

What did the Jewish pig mean just now? Call the house servant, have him thrown out . . . ?

"Be careful, mister," said Peter Mönkemann with difficulty. "It takes two to throw me out, so far as I know. And it will not be wholly undangerous, but . . ." Now he controlled himself, stiff and steel-like in his bearing. "Besides, it's probably completely unnecessary. I'll disappear without further ado as soon as you agree to a reduction."

Sigfried Löwenstein was moved by an inexplicable feeling. The instinct of his race told him that here really a hidden danger was in the offing, and he always got out of the way of physical danger—this also was taught to him by his instinct—like all the members of his race for millennia before him.

So he turned the whole matter into a stupid and bold phraseology, thus toning down the threatening scene. So, smirking broadly and striking his fleshy, ring-studded hand on the table, he said: "May the righteous God strike me dead if I am in the wrong. But I still hear 'reduction.' How can you imagine such a thing? Do you believe, for instance, that it can be done just like that? I didn't find money on the streets either! I don't deal with interest, young man . . . whatever you may think!"

"But after all you live only from trade," the young man almost roared, "and an interest of twelve per cent is profiteering. It's usury and nothing else!"

Now the lad had called things by their right names and now he had certainly lost his chance.

Sigfried Löwenstein withdrew his arm from the flat part of the desk. He stuck the cigar into his big fish-mouth, leaned back, and placed the thumbs of his two hands jauntily behind his vest. Circumspectly, calmly, and quite the master of this situation, Sigfried Löwenstein said:

"Let me tell you something, young man. I could sue you for accusing me of usury. But I won't do it. I'm a businessman, understand? But to teach you a little lesson, the mortgage is foreclosed, understand? And if your mother doesn't bring the whole sum—and she never will—if the money isn't there on the dot, then there will be an auction, understand? Then I'll auction off the place. . . . It's my good and proper right."

Peter Mönkemann took one step forward. He looked threateningly at the fat man, looked squarely into his ugly, fat face.

"You won't do that," he said tonelessly. His fists clenched and un-
clenched convulsively, but he himself was unaware of it. "You won't
do it," he repeated, and stood up against the front of the desk.

Löwenstein's face paled. Suddenly he had a muddy-gray coloration.
He expressed an unutterable fear. His eyes almost rolled out of their
sockets, the pulsing of the spongy veins was perceptible on his temples, and one bead of perspiration after another arranged itself on his
wrinkled forehead, as high as the leather-colored dome of his cranium.
The master of the situation suddenly had lamentably collapsed, and
despite his physical dimensions he now presented only a pathetic
scrap of a man. He rose from his deep chair, drew backward slightly,
while his hand stretched out over the flat surface of the writing desk
and pressed the buzzer. "Take your paws off the buzzer!" ordered his
visitor, and fury glowered behind his forced composure, but the other
kept on pressing the buzzer vigorously and now he suddenly began to
scream: "This is a threat . . . blackmail, yes indeed . . . blackmail . . . !"

His voice tumbled over itself. The word echoed through the room
and the man repeated it, meaninglessly, as if crazed with fear. He was
still screaming it when the door opened and his house servant stood
on the threshold. Peter Mönkemann stepped back. His anger had collapsed like a house of cards at the sight of the frantic fear of this
miserable wretch. Now he was the master of the situation. This ridiculous scene, in no way justified, suddenly brought him back to reason.

The broker pulled himself together, and he regained his bearing
with such swiftness that Peter Mönkemann was filled with astonishment. He pointed to the lad. "Take the man to the door," he said,
but his voice was still not wholly clear. It sounded something like the
rattle of a beast. "It's not necessary," answered Peter Mönkemann,
"I'll find the way back by myself." His look had the effect of prevent-
ing the servant from coming any nearer. "You will certainly think the
matter over," he continued as he was about to leave the room. Nevertheless, when he closed the door he heard the man saying, insolently
and provocatively as during the beginning of the dispute: "I won't
reconsider it at all, it will be foreclosed . . . immediately! And then
—legal execution of the foreclosure!"

The young man hesitated imperceptibly. Should he . . . should he
not? This scoundrel—just minutes ago he was a whimpering bundle
of flesh—was baring his teeth again. Peter Mönkemann still held the
doorknob in his hand, literally uncomprehending. Where does the

fellow get such insolence? But naturally—now he has a witness, his house slave, his protector.

On the steps he said to the servant: "Give your Sigfried a nice greeting from me. Do that immediately and tell him that he will really get to know Peter Mönkemann if he tries to carry out his intention."

But that did not mean too much; he knew that very well. As he sat in the train on his journey homeward, he thought about the case. He had achieved nothing. Of this there was no doubt. On the contrary, it would have been much better if he had remained at home. Now things were worse than before. This Manichean would make short shrift of it; he would push for legal foreclosure, because these carrion vultures have a greater knowledge of conditions in the money market than anybody else. Money indeed is scarce in these bad times. He would not be able to find anyone to refinance the mortgage. Things are in a sad way in the German Fatherland, he said to himself in discouragement. . . . In a word, it makes you vomit! What could be the reason? he brooded. We won the battles in the war, but we lost the war. And it was no different with the Freikorps.[1] We scattered the Red pack, but we didn't triumph at all. On the contrary, afterward, when the work was done, there was the kick in the ass from the top.

Other people triumphed. Just look around you! You see that everywhere. . . . Where do they sit, do you mean? Stupid question! Rather, you should say, where don't they sit? For there is no high position, no government office, no authority, no trade union, no business office, no management, no board of directors, and no government in which they do not make their way. The same whose necks you wanted to break, to be sure only in harmless song, you stupid novices.[2]

Your Freikorps fought against the red terror, against the Communist gang of murderers, from east to west, from the Baltic to the Ruhr, but you forgot the Jew. And today he is breaking your neck, and sometimes it is twelve per cent. Today you sit below, and he sits on top. And who knows? Perhaps it would have been better if you

[1] The Free Corps, army units that refused to disband after World War I and fought first in the Baltic and Silesia and then against the Communist governments in Bavaria and Saxony. They were also active against the French in the Ruhr (see p. 94).

[2] This reference is to the threat against Jews in the Nazis' "Horst Wessel" song.

had let Spartacus[3] in. Doesn't one often expel the Devil with Beelzebub?

"No," murmured the young man. For after all it is one and the same gang—it's chips from the same block. Have you forgotten how the city commandants of March 1920 looked? Oh, it's a cursed world! . . .

[Peter Mönkemann now definitely leaves home for study in Berlin. On his way he passes again through Löwenstein's town.]

The next train would not be leaving for two hours, and for one who was so immersed in himself as this traveler, this was a long time. He did not want to fall once more into brooding. Instead, he wanted to be alert and open to all that was new. He wanted to burn all the ships behind him, strike the tents, the past was to be a dead thing, he would march with a light pack. With an assault pack, so to speak, because otherwise he would not move forward fast enough and this he must do.

What then should he do in these two hours? Naturally—the only right thing. Obviously, to go to Sigfried Löwenstein and tell him: "In order that you may know what's what—the money for the mortgage is ready. It will be paid off and then, praise God, we shall have nothing more to do with each other. Now you can swindle others with your twelve per cent. You usurer. And there won't be a legal execution of the foreclosure either. I've taken care of that, you Jew!"

He could not very well deny himself this triumph. Besides, it is a good thing to do anyway. Without any clear declarations, this fat fellow would probably try new tricks with Peter's womenfolk.

Peter Mönkemann made his way up to his private office. The Jew was terrified no little: "Are you here again already?"

"It's me, Mr. Sigfried Löwenstein. To your regret, I must declare to you that I have the money for the refinancing of the mortgage. It's all over with usurious rates of interest. You have swindled yourself out of business. At least with us, Mr. Sigfried."

He smiled. Fat and spiteful. "So," he said slowly, almost enjoying it, "so you found a stupid person. I was mistaken . . . it can happen . . . so much money—so much money—but whom have you conned? —if it's true!"

He didn't say any more. Peter Mönkemann leaned over the desk, grabbed him by the collar with one hand, shook him from one side to the other, and pushed him back and forth. Then in a sudden, flaming,

[3] The Spartacus revolt was a Communist uprising in Berlin (January 1919).

unbridled rage he hurled a word at him that will remain a word of abuse and insult as long as the world goes round and round: "You Jew!—You Jew!—You dirty Jew!"

Löwenstein made a rattling sound. But he didn't scream. He didn't scream even when the angry bull let him go.

He hunched himself—ashen-pale and in a state of collapse—in the big chair. Then with a tired movement he picked up two shirt buttons that had fallen off and which were lying on the desk. When Peter was about to leave the room, he noticed that the Jew's ring-studded hand was picking up the telephone receiver.

Now's the time, thought the young man.

Sigfried Löwenstein thought it over. What had happened? A chap, a *goyim*, had screamed a word that always strikes out at him more painfully than the lash of a whip. As true as it may be. . . . And this chap had grabbed him by the collar, not exactly very gently, oh not at all, and only because he had used the expression "conned"? That was a bit thick, a bit thick, but to call the police for this reason? Ridiculous! Sigfried Löwenstein had other methods. Methods which gave him a chance to vent his lustful rages and at the same time brought in more money.

> From Tüdel Weller, *Rabauken! Peter Mönkemann haut
> sich durch* (Munich: Zentralverlag der NSDAP, Frz. Eher
> Nachf., 1938), pp. 14-15, 17-23, 29-31.

Events at the Prussian State Theater
ECKART VON NASO

Although mostly already "coordinated" and "Aryanized," the press and public had lost nothing of the spontaneous sureness of their judgment, and when winter returned, with prudent regret they were forced to realize that the *Staatsbühne*, which was much quarreled over and nonetheless interesting, was in danger of becoming a philistine provincial theater. At that time they could still express such criticism; later it was no longer possible.

Specifically, Goebbels invented "art observation" in the place of criticism. One, to be sure, had the right to "observe"—but was forbidden to pronounce a judgment. Thus criticism was stripped of all meaning. The "art creators," which was the name given to actors, composers, painters, sculptors, and writers, no longer saw themselves. There was no mirror. They did not know whether their accomplishments were good or bad. All one learned was that they had accomplished something, though the masters of the journalistic craft could smuggle in the carefully camouflaged truth between the lines. Remarkably enough, one was allowed to praise. Obviously this was not a judgment, but observation. And the whole invention thereupon led to removing the, in part, pathetic propaganda plays in brown uniform from the danger of adverse criticism.

Many funny things happened at that time. Thus at first Charlemagne was prohibited as a dramatic personage because he had proved himself to be a race-alien "Saxon-slaughterer" and had slaughtered with Christian chauvinism. Then upon further consideration one convinced oneself that after all he had certainly accomplished something for German interests: so Carolus Magnus was again a dramatic persona grata. On the other hand, Cromwell was regarded as harmless and was liked by the Führer. Real mushroom cultures of Cromwell sprouted from the earth. Julius Caesar also seemed to be much in demand, although he had come to a questionable end. But one probably thought if one could go as far as he had, the Ides of March no longer played a role. But it was not at all easy to find one's way through this maze of prohibitions and desiderata, because often enough the desiderata, for undiscoverable reasons, were sooner or later placed on the prohibition list.

The tragedy was permeated with farcical events. Among the 2400 manuscripts which were sent in to the script department in 1933, among which were 500 dramas about Arminius and Thesnulda,[1] there was also a bloodthirsty, anti-Jewish play of an undiscussable kind. "Be careful," said Johst,[2] "I know the author." I dictated a polite letter of rejection. Johst signed it—not a pleasant function, which soon enough was to be assigned to me. An angry letter came back which read something like the following: "Esteemed Party Comrade Johst! Do you dare to send back my play? Don't you know that I have a party number in two figures—and what do you have? A party number in six or seven figures! I will file a protest with the Führer. Heil Hitler!" We both had to laugh. "That's how they are," said Johst. "The

---

[1] Arminius was a Germanic hero who defeated the Roman legions at the battle of the Teutoburger Forest (9 A.D.). Thesnulda was his wife.
[2] See page 135.

party number decides all." Yes, these were the farcical events of a tragic time. . . .

Since the director had suddenly given up apprentice, journeyman, and master tests, the producer[3] now needed only to give free play to his motor powers in order to bring the machine to high speed. His secret was that he did not start out from the world of literature but from the world of low comedy. He had and still has a flair for the theater, indeed for the primitivity of the theater, if it is real and kindles a spark. A man named Shakespeare had the same. He did not believe in ghosts; he himself had said so in his great monologue in Hamlet: ". . . from whose world no traveller returns. . . ." Despite this he began the play with a ghost scene, because he understood the theater and knew that a ghost on the stage has a sure-fire effect.

The producer Gründgens wanted a Dionysian, not a literary, theater—certainly not the philosophizing theater of the deep thinking to which he gave a very funny name in which only the syllable "deep" was repeated. He also knew that tragedy once had arisen from the intoxication and bewitchment of the wine god, in order to couple play-instinct and poetry. Therefore he decided to play Scribe's Glass of Water with more determination than his friends could assume at that time, who urgently advised him against such an old, used-up "theatrical" antique.

Gründgens did not let himself be side-tracked from his opinion. The theater first of all needed a public, and the public, weary of "blood and soil," had again deserted our theater. It had to be won back. This, however, could be done only by giving the play program an electrical charge. If the tensions were perceptible, the sparks would fly further. . . . This bold experiment succeeded. Kleist's Hermannsschlacht, otherwise no play for the public, performed three days after Glass of Water, was drawn into the success of the witty Scribean dialectic. With such a two-pronged attack, which forged a connection between the play instinct and poetry, the theater became once again an interesting place. People talked about it; they sensed the vibration. The long line at the box office, which formerly had looked like a blind worm, now finally resembled the legendary Mittgart,[4] which circled

[3] Gustav Gründgens (1899-1963), perhaps Germany's best-known actor, became the producer of the Prussian State Theater in Berlin, over which Göring maintained control.
[4] The serpent which, according to Germanic legend, entwines itself around the globe.

around the Gendarmenmarkt the way its predecessor had encircled the world.

Even the premières were hits. Thus I had the dramaturgist's pleasure to assist at the birth of two playwrights who had stumbled upon the theater from other fields: the epic poet Hans Friedrich Blunck and the lyric poet Hans Schwarz. Of course, Blunck had also written lyrics of great form, as is proved by his *Ballads*. Schwarz was the editor of the collected works of Moeller van den Bruck, whom the Nazi state at first had praised to the skies. . . .[5]

Be it as it may: Blunck's *Country in the Twilight* with the man-and-wife acting team of Kayssler and Helene Fehdmer and *The Rebel in England* by Hans Schwarz with Hermine Körner as Elizabeth and Paul Hartmann as Essex, were impressive visiting cards. The great representative drama had again replaced the peasant play.

> From Eckart von Naso, *Ich liebe das Leben: Erinnerungen aus fünf Jahrzehnten* (Hamburg: Wolfgang Krüger Verlag, 1953), pp. 617-618, 648-649. (Reprinted by permission.)

Playbills of the Herne City Theater, 1936-1940

The 1936-37 program unfolded as follows:

1936	October 29	*Maria Stuart* by Schiller (very well attended)
	December 2	"Franz Kraus" Evening
	December 15-16	Marionette Theater
1937	January 28	*Scharnhorst* by Menzel [1] (well attended)
	February 18	*The Barber of Seville* by Rossini
	March 30	Dance Evening by the Günther Dance Ensemble
	April 22	*Zigeunerbaron* by Strauss
	April 29	*Emilia Galotti* by Lessing

[5] For Blunck, see page 135. Hans Schwarz (b. 1890) refined the technique of the Greek chorus in his plays, a device much used in the Nazi liturgy.

[1] Gerhard Menzel (b. 1894) wrote *Scharnhorst* in 1935. Scharnhorst (1755-1813), a Prussian general, reformed the army by introducing universal military service. It was in 1935 that Hitler reintroduced conscription in Germany.

In July 1937 the chief office of the National Socialist Cultural Community was transferred to the Strength Through Joy organization. The local theater directorate, naturally, announced a new winter program, but it could not carry it out. As a result, the performances were sponsored by the Strength Through Joy organization. This led, as far as such was still possible, to a further superficialization of the program, which in 1937-38 unfolded as follows:

1937	October 27	*Journey's End* by Sheriff [2]
	October 28	*Spitzentuch der Königin* by J. Strauss
1938	January 13	*As You Like It* by Shakespeare
	March 6	*Petermann fährt nach Madeira* by Hinrichs[3]
	March 17	*Der Waffenschmied* by Lortzing
	March 24	*Graf von Luxemburg* by Lehár
	March 26	*Frau ohne Kuss*, operetta by Kessler and Kollo
	April 8	*Dorothee*, operetta by Vetterling

The city now also involved itself in the new theater season and granted subsidies to the Strength Through Joy organization, without thereby improving the quality of the program.

Winter program 1938-39:

1938	October 14	*Thomas Paine* by Hanns Johst
	November 23	*Schneider Wibbelt*, comedy by Müller-Schlösser[4]
	December 20	*Lotte an Bord*, folk play
1939	February 9	*Strassenmusik*, comedy by Schuth
	February 15	*Das sündige Dorf*, Tegernsee Peasant Theater[5]
	April 13	*Land des Lächelns* by Lehár
	April 28	*Afrikanische Hochzeit*
		Der Manöversepp by Konrad Dreher[6]

[2] A realistic war play (1929) by C. R. Sheriff.
[3] August Hinrichs (b. 1879) wrote books and plays in native peasant dialect.
[4] Written in 1913 on a theme by the nineteenth-century author Eduard Mörike.
[5] Konrad Dreher founded this group in 1892.
[6] Konrad Dreher, after World War I, continued with his own "folk theater" ensemble.

Program for 1939-40:

1939	October 15	Dame Kobold by Calderón
	November 29	Scampolo, comedy by Dario Niccodemi[7]
1940	January 7	Das blaurote Strumpfband, Tegernsee Peasant Theater
	January 11	Die Fledermaus by J. Strauss
	February 1	Der Vogelhändler by Zeller[8]
	February 23	The Six from the German Dance Stage
	February 29	Chamber Dance Ensemble of the Berlin State Opera
	March 27	Parkstrasse 13, detective drama

Thus the level had sunk more and more; the program contained almost only propaganda pieces, comedies, operettas. If to this one adds the cabaret-like performances, a cultural nadir was reached below which one could no longer sink. This is astonishing in view of the fact that the National Socialists in other cities promoted an authentic cultural life or at least guaranteed it. Thus during these years the Stadttheater in Bochum, under its director, Saladin Schmitt, attained a new high cultural level with its cycles of Kleist, Grabbe,[9] and others. One must assume that the taste of the people responsible for cultural life in Herne was so shallow and bad that they were not able to offer the people anything of a special character. During the war years an attempt was made at first to carry out a program, but after the proclamation of total war, actors and musicians were integrated into the war economy.

Program for 1940-41:

1940	October 31	Der Zarewitsch, operetta
1941	January 2	Eine Nacht in Venedig by J. Strauss
	April 10	Kabale und Liebe by Schiller

From Herne, 1933-1945: Die Zeit des Nationalsozialismus, edited by Hermann Meyerhoff (Herne, 1963), p. 63.

[7] Dario Niccodemi (1874-1934), a writer of comedies. This, his most famous, was written in 1915.

[8] Karl Zeller (1842-1898), Austrian composer.

[9] Both Kleist and Grabbe were chosen as patriotic nineteenth-century writers. Kleist was acclaimed wholeheartedly by the Nazis as the "conscience of the nation." Christian Dietrich Grabbe (1801-1836) wrote "heroic" historical dramas. The Nazis created a special "Grabbe week" in 1936.

The Winter Program of the German Radio, 1936

Munich, October 28. Reich broadcasting director Hadamovsky,[1] at the order of Reich Minister Dr. Goebbels, in the main broadcasting studio of the German radio broadcasting system of Munich, announced the winter program of the German radio to the directors and co-workers of the radio broadcasting system and representatives of the party and the government. According to the Reich broadcasting director, the main purpose of future programming is to create joy and to solidify the community. Hence the new program is called "Joy and Community." The German Labor Front and the Strength Through Joy organization are to be drawn into the program through a uniform regulation of work breaks, an energetic propaganda campaign among workers, and the shaping of leisure evening hours.

This year, for the first time, a preliminary program containing all the important broadcasts of the winter will be given to the German public and to radio listeners abroad.

The program contains the political broadcasts of the Reich broadcasting directorate and the major radio features and broadcasts of the Reich broadcasting system and the German short-wave broadcasting system. The major political broadcasts of the winter can be found in the section entitled "The Party Has the Floor!" The programs for the work breaks of the German workers are to be broadcast under the motto "Joy in the Plant and at Home." The work-break broadcasts in the Reich railway repair works at Munich-Freimann will begin with a festival under the slogan "Music and Dance in the Plant." The work-break concerts will take place from 6 A.M. to 8 A.M., from 8:30 A.M. to 9:30 A.M., and from 12 A.M. to 1 P.M. Plant managers are urged to cooperate in this program by arranging work breaks in the plants in such a way that they correspond with this schedule.

During the winter the German radio will hold evening leisure hours in which conductors and soloists of the first rank will interpret important musical works. These broadcasts will also be transmitted to factories. Under the title "Peasantry and Landscape," provisions have been made for general broadcasts on the German peasantry along with agricultural news. The Hitler Youth and the National Socialist

[1] Eugen Hadamovsky was the first National Socialist Reich director of radio broadcasting (Reichsendeleiter).

Teachers' Association will jointly sponsor the "Hour of the Young Nation" on Wednesdays and the "Morning Celebrations" on Sundays.

The Reich broadcasting director gave details on the music program of the radio station. According to him, the music program of the radio broadcasting system has been continually broadened since the seizure of power by National Socialism, increasing from 25,000 broadcasts in 1932 to more than 40,000 broadcasts in 1935. In the future, overtures, feature programs, and the great dramatic works of world literature are to replace lectures and readings more frequently than has been the case up to now.

The *Deutschlandsender*[2] is to visit the Reich *Autobahn*, the airports of Lufthansa, the German coal-mining districts and the blast furnaces, porcelain factories and amber-laundries, cloth and linen weavers, herring ships and herring fishery centers, fishing ports and refrigeration plants, the auxiliary Bavarian troop and the motorized troop "Deutschland" of the NSDAP, and in addition provide a series of radio reports on the NSDAP and its organizations. The section "Germany Calls the World!" contains a summary of the important broadcasts of the German short-wave broadcasting system. The German short-wave system broadcasts forty hours daily. Six separate programs are especially designed for the various areas of the world: Southern Asia and Australia, Eastern Asia, Africa, South America, Central America, and North America.

The radio broadcasting system in Germany today includes about 8,000,000 owners of radio sets, and counts on about 30,000,000 listeners. There are about 70,000 broadcasting hours and over 250,000 individual broadcasts. In the last years the number of listeners has increased by about 1,000,000 annually.

From the *Frankfurter Zeitung*, Oct. 29, 1936. (Wiener Library Clipping Collection.)

Fundamental Features of Radio Programming, 1938

Berlin, August 9. Each year the members of the German radio broadcasting industry come together from all the districts of the

2 Main central radio transmission station.

Reich to meet in Berlin during the great Radio Broadcasting Exhibition. This year's gathering, which was held on Tuesday in the meeting room of the Kroll Opera House, received its special slogan from Dr. Goebbels with his declaration that "Germany must become the strongest radio broadcasting country in the world."

Reich Superintendent Glasmeier[1] read his report on the basic features of the programming of the German radio broadcasting system. His main point was that the basic attitude of the radio broadcasting system is National Socialist. Moreover, on the basis of this attitude the radio broadcasting system must strive to include the whole range of public life today, to give it support where necessary, especially the enormous program of the Strength Through Joy organization, the great Winter Aid programs, and the activities of the individual branches of the movement.

In connection with the problem of light dance music versus music of greater artistic value, a question which has been widely discussed among radio listeners, Reich Superintendent Glasmeier declared that the radio broadcasting system has held to a healthy middle course, which it would continue to follow in the future.

Reich Superintendent Glasmeier sharply opposed the reinfiltration, by way of the "humorous" sketch, of the destructive Jewish spirit into the radio broadcasting system. We cannot have a situation in which the leaders of the movement extol the sacredness of marriage and the ethos of the German soldier, who must risk his life and blood for the Fatherland, while in the evening these very values are insulted and ridiculed in "colorful" entertainment sketches with the corroding sarcasm of so-called variety programs. (Loud applause.)

Superintendent Glasmeier addressed an urgent appeal to his musical colleagues not to fall asleep at their desks, filing cabinets, and music cabinets, but to set forth on journeys of discovery in the field of German musical literature, to find unknown precious pearls, which can be transmitted to the German people, works of the past as well as works of contemporary creative artists.

At the conclusion of his discussion, Superintendent Glasmeier distinguished between the tasks of the Reich broadcasting stations and the tasks of the Deutschlandsender.[2] The Reich broadcasting stations, which originated because of the particularism of the individual

---

[1] Heinrich Glasmeier, director-general of the German Broadcasting Company (Reichsrundfunkgesellschaft). Before 1933 he was an archivist in Westphalia.
[2] See page 192.

German states, in the new Reich have a twofold task: on the one hand, they must represent their territory; on the other, they must always be conscious of the fact that they are Reich radio stations, that they are the heralds of the idea of the Reich and that they must contribute their share, that clan and provincial borders are increasingly vanishing, and that in all German districts it is the German man who inhabits the German soil.

The *Deutschlandsender*, however, must present a wholly different face. It is the representative of the German Reich government, of the National Socialist movement, in short a representative of German culture. It must not attend to the needs of the individual territory as such; it must portray the face of the whole German land.

After Dr. Glasmeier's discussion, which received enthusiastic applause, the President of the Reich Radio Chamber, Kriegler, took the floor. In his speech he pointed out that the Radio Broadcasting Exhibition had never before met with such a great response from the public. Obviously, much of this was due to the new "German small receiver 1938," which was a truly socialistic community accomplishment of the radio broadcasting directorate and the radio industry.

Today about 54 per cent of the households in the Reich are linked to the radio network. Of the rest, only a relatively small part has remained outside broadcasting range because of disinterest. The majority of the population, however, for financial reasons has not been in a position to buy the 65-Reichsmark Volk-receiver and in addition to pay the monthly radio fee of 2 Reichsmarks. Our special promotional efforts and concern must be directed at these racial comrades.

From the *National Zeitung* (Essen), Aug. 10, 1938. (Wiener Library Clipping Collection.)

German Films for Venice, 1938

German films will be strongly represented at this year's Biennale exhibition. The following films will be shown:

"Olympia-Film[1] ("Feast of the Peoples," "Feast of Beauty"); *Homeland; The Model Husband; Furlough on Word of Honor; Traveling People; Youth.*

[1] Taken at the 1936 Olympic Games.

Other films to be shown are the documentaries *The Bee State; Feathered Seaside Guests on the Baltic Sea; Riemenschneider, the Master of Würzburg; German Racing Cars in Front; Fliers, Radio Operators, Cannoneers; Black Forest Melody; Splendor of Color at the Bottom of the Sea; Speed Streets; Pilots of the Air; Nature in Technique; Cuttlefish; Moorlands; Youth in Dance.*

From *Der Mittag* (Düsseldorf), July 20, 1938. (Wiener Library Clipping Collection.)

The Film Public Is Not So Stupid

At the Gloria-Palast in Berlin one can witness a remarkable event—a film in which the leading lady is something less than a movie beauty. Whenever this actress, who has none of the charms of Hollywood, appears, the audience is enthusiastic and applauds at the end of each scene. We would advise all film producers to attend one of the ordinary evening performances. They would then see that the usual answer, that the film public demands platinum blondes, girls with mascara around the eyes, and a sexy look even as in toothpaste ads, is a poor answer. The excellent film at the Gloria-Palast is called *Masquerade*, and the lady is Paula Wessely, the most outstanding of the new young actresses of the stage. Here, in her first appearance on the screen, she plays the part of a simple young girl unaffectedly and directly, with an astounding power to portray human beings. A stir of excitement runs through the theater—this is the impact her acting has upon people. Why? This is not the first time that such acting has been seen. But it is a rare event, even in German films, when one can look to the great actress, rather than to the charming starlet for one's enjoyment. This success has proven the Vienna Film Society right: the public is not as stupid as we are led to believe. Sometimes it exhibits perfectly good instinct—for instance, when it laughed during the deadly serious scenes of a certain new film drama that was based on mechanical hodge-podge and banal dialogue. Or when, as here, it applauds the achievement of a real actress and finally leaves the theater visibly moved to its innermost being.

Today in Germany we should ponder this, and instead of sensational effects we should allow real artistic accomplishment to come to the fore. Unfortunately, this seldom happens. But it can be done earnestly and—this is very important for the film—cheerfully. Then we will once more attain the leading place that is due to us even in the eyes of the most demanding people.

From the *Düsseldörfer Allegemeine Zeitung*, Aug. 26, 1934. (Wiener Library Clipping Collection.)

6

Science and
National Socialism

Two Nobel laureates were instrumental in building a bridge between science and the Nazi world view. Philipp Lenard (1862-1947), who received the Nobel Prize in 1905 for his work on cathode rays, occupied the chair of theoretical physics at the University of Heidelberg. Together with his fellow Nobel laureate Johannes Stark, he declared himself a follower of Hitler as early as 1924. Lenard's *Deutsche Physik* (*German Physics*) (1936) was praised by the official party bibliography for making science relevant to the political struggle,[1] and indeed this was the aim of the work. Lenard divided all knowledge into the natural and spiritual sciences. In this scheme all animate matter is brought into the world of the spirit, which, in turn, is determined by the racial origins of the organism itself. But inanimate matter is also included in the "mysteries of nature" by emphasizing the interconnection between all natural phenomena, animate or inanimate.

Stress upon the "organic" and the fundamental unity of all of nature according to a divine plan is basic to National Socialist science, indeed to its view of nature (see also page 81). This theme appears throughout the chapter. With this hypothesis Lenard is able to avoid

[1] *Nationalsozialistische Bibliographie*, Jahrg. I, Heft III (March 1936), p. 4. No. 25a.

"materialism" and can, instead, subordinate scientific investigation to the "greatest mystery," which is one of the spirit. Of itself, matter is merely a mechanism which does not comprehend the spiritual dimension all-important to scientific investigation. We have already seen how the spiritual dimension was linked with race. Lenard thus lays the foundation for the absorption of science into the world view.

Johannes Stark (1874–1951) further elaborates these ideas. After receiving a Nobel Prize for his work on electromagnetism, he had to retire from his chair at the University of Würzburg because of his polemics against Albert Einstein and the Theory of Relativity in 1922. He devoted the rest of his life as a scientist to the cultivation of fruit trees and to forestry. Under the Nazis he became the president of the Deutsche Forschungsgemeinschaft, the state organization concerned with supporting scientific research. Stark makes a direct and simple equation between science and Volk. What remains of science is the emphasis upon exact and disinterested observation of natural phenomena, but this is immediately tied, once again, to the Nordic race. With its emphasis upon race the Nazi world view envelops all scientific activity. Stark stands the truth upon its head: German science, as he defines it, is objective and factual, while Jews are advocates of opinion—and the proof for this is seen in the quite unobjective science of race. Scientific respectability depends on the racial soul.

Lenard mentions Newton as one of the true scientists; indeed National Socialist scientists regarded themselves as descended from scientists of the seventeenth century. For these men did, as a matter of fact, believe in the organic nature of the universe; they were interested in religion as much as in science and their theories sought to encompass the whole universe. Science had changed in the nineteenth century: the "new physics" had denied the organic nature of the Newtonian universe and the Theory of Relativity sounded its death knell.

That is why Bruno Thüring's attack on Einstein is important. Thüring (b. 1905) was a young astronomer and mathematician, active in the Heidelberg Association of Students of Science, a branch of the National Socialist student organization. It was before this body that he gave the talk (September 4, 1936) that was reprinted in the official mathematical journal, Deutsche Mathematik, from which our excerpt is taken. The year after his speech, Bruno Thüring became a lecturer at the University of Munich, working at the university's observatory. Thüring, like the others, emphasizes the so-called spiritual factors in science, but he also presents a good exposition of the National Socialist history of science. His opposition to the course of modern science is obvious, and modernity is, in typical Nazi fashion, linked to the Jew. The materialism of Einstein's space-time concept and the supposed absence of "energy" from his system are contrasted with the Nordic's instinctual understanding of the meaning of energy. The influence of Nietzsche is not to be denied in this passage.

If a certain view of human nature is implicit in Thüring's approach to science, as it is in that of Lenard and Stark, what then of psychoanalysis? Kurt Gauger gives us the official Nazi version of this science. Though he had taken a medical degree, he was not active in that field. He was associated with the government office in charge of educational films and edited its series of pamphlets. Moreover, as a side line he wrote novels about seafaring men. Gauger was a propagandist, and as such helped to lay down the line for a German psychotherapy: the world view must be primary. Small wonder that he appeared at the International Medical Congress for Psychotherapy in 1934 as a political leader rather than as a practicing psychoanalyst. For to that title he could lay no claim—certainly not before an international audience.

Gauger's attacks against Freud are very similar to those of Thüring against Einstein. The materialism of the Freudians is contrasted with the positive values which National Socialism has brought to science. When he comes to discuss the actual nature of mental illness, he moves toward the theories of Carl Gustav Jung, not just by contrasting Jung and Freud but in a more fundamental sense. The emphasis upon the "collective unconscious," which expresses itself in the community linked together by a shared archetype (or soul) derives from Jung, as does the denial that the ego and the id (defined as soul and mind) are opposed to each other. At one point Gauger takes Freud's famous metaphor—that the relation of the ego to the id is like that of a rider to a horse—and changes Freud's wild horse into an animal in complete harmony with its rider. Once again the organic is stressed, the genuine unity of all nature. Jung, it must be remembered, had taken over the presidency of the German Society for Psychotherapy in June 1933. He began to refine his concept of the "collective unconscious" in the pages of the journal of the association—writing about the differences between the Aryan and the Jewish archetype while advocating the necessity of understanding the German soul. Thus another distinguished scientist came to the aid of the Nazi cultural drive.

The physician in the new Reich must be a "biological soldier." Hanns Löhr (b. 1891), the medical director of the University Hospital at the University of Kiel, defines the place of the medical sciences in the National Socialist state. He calls for a basic revision in medical studies toward building character and personality rather than merely transmitting knowledge. This approach to medical education has its parallel in the general educational theories of the Third Reich (see Chapter 8). Empirical knowledge is integrated into the total biological picture and here the basic spiritual fact of Volkish belonging is primary. If Volk and race are the chief reality, then a medical science which is divorced from these is merely mechanical. On the other hand, an emphasis on race is not anti-intellectualism, but rather leads to intuitive insights. Löhr's book *Aberglaube und Medizin* (*Superstition and Medicine*) (1940) stresses the immanent laws of nature which only the Nordic, with his talent for observation, can understand—a point made by Lenard. Superstition is the belief that healing derives not from nature but from supernatural causes, such as those advanced by Christianity.

In these documents the Nazi world view is equated with organic nature: Volk and race are part of an interconnected totality of which nature is one facet—all held together by spiritual principles which were expressed in Nazi culture. The "biological soldier" must be aware of this totality so that he can serve the truth and through it his Volk. For Löhr this also meant encouraging the propagation of the race through healthy child-bearing as well as approval of the sterilization law (see page 90).

Science was absorbed by Nazi culture, and in turn helped to give this culture an air of intellectual respectability. The importance of empirical facts was never denied; instead they were integrated into the world view. There can be little doubt that Nazi science, in departing from the famous tradition of German scientific accomplishment, contributed to the final failure of the Third Reich in the war effort. It was no accident that the Allies, not Germany, developed the atomic bomb, the "miracle weapon" for which Hitler waited in vain.

G.L.M.

The Limits of Science
PHILIPP LENARD

Natural Science and the Spiritual Sciences[1]

Originally, physics meant—and essentially continues to mean even today, especially in our conception—natural science in general. This is one part of human knowledge; the other part consists of the spiritual sciences.

Natural science—physical—deals with the totality of nature, or the world, as far as it is perceptible to us. Its subject is everything that exists that is observable. And this is a great deal, for it reaches to the farthest celestial bodies. Obviously, however, it is not everything, not the entire world. There is, as our innermost being teaches us, a portion of the world that is inaccessible to our senses.

We call the portion of the world that is accessible to our senses the material or substantial world; the other part, of which our inner being gives us information but whose existence is also apprehended by our senses when we observe organisms, we call the spiritual world.

Our subject, therefore, is the material world and everything that happens in it; the spiritual sciences, on the other hand, deal with matters of the spirit. Among these spiritual sciences are history, theology, so-called philosophy, jurisprudence.

The work of the investigator of nature who furthers the natural sciences is very different from that of the man who deals with the spiritual sciences. The investigator of nature relies entirely on his senses; he uses them to gather daily ever more extensive and new information about the material world. Thus he generally focuses his observations on the inanimate part of the material world, since that part has most easily confirmed and still confirms for him the simple uniformities of the processes of the entire material world. The animate part is strikingly different from the inanimate; it is marked by processes of a highly intricate character, and it is this difference, accessible to sensory perception, which indicates to the senses the existence of an extra-material world. Obviously it is the same "spiritual world" of

[1] *Geisteswissenschaften*—that is, the social sciences or the "humanities."

201

whose operations we are informed by our own inner being. The animate part of the material world is influenced by the "spiritual world,"
which is not noticeably the case with the inanimate part. Animate
organisms exhibit phenomena in which the spiritual world and the
material world work together. Life consists precisely in this cooperation; we designate matter which has spirit (soul) as "living."

In the case of the spiritual sciences, the basic data do not come to
the investigator from the outside, through the portal of his senses, but
from within, from his own spirit. The representative of the spiritual
sciences is mainly concerned with animate, inspirited nature, and he
uses his senses essentially only for commerce with other matter-
bound spirits, mostly with other human beings.

The endeavor of the spiritual sciences should produce a new cognition wrested from the spiritual world. Nevertheless, in reality such
new knowledge reaches us only seldom, and it does not come from
the professional representatives of the spiritual sciences. The great
founders of religions, of whom barely one appears every thousand
years on earth, are the bearers of such knowledge. Also true artists,
thinkers, poets in words and music, and true statesmen, of whom perhaps one may be given to us every hundred years. The spiritual scientists at the universities should, at least, administer this knowledge, but
not in such a manner that the knowledge at hand or that which can
be reclaimed from the past is eruditely tossed back and forth, with the
result that the best of this knowledge remains mostly unnoticed.
Rather it should be exchanged in a manner that feeds and nourishes
the spirit of the people and thus truly educates the people. This obviously has been entirely lacking during long periods of history, in consequence of the profound decline of the German spirit. One did not
understand how to provide the German spirit with a nourishment
suitable to it because not even spiritual scientists were sufficiently conscious of the most fundamental differentiations in the spiritual world
—namely, that every organism has its own special spirit (that portion
of the total spirit world which its body is able to hold on to) and that
the greatest differences among spirits are based on groups varying in
physical structure according to their inherited physical constitution.
They did not grasp clearly enough that, just as fleas and elephants
have different spiritual constitutions, so the spirits of different human
races and ethnic groups are totally different from each other. Down
the centuries attempts have been made to nourish the spirit of the
German people with "the spirit of humanity," as though spirits could

be patched together at will, as though fleas could be educated profitably by elephants, or vice versa. Thus the spiritual sciences were incapable of increasing the spirit of the German people, or even of preserving the sterling quality which it had already achieved in the lap of nature, without these sciences. . . .

The Truth-Value of the Investigation of Nature

The conceptions and laws derived from the observation of natural processes, which are adapted to them and constantly tested against them and which are the main results of the investigation of nature, are cognitions of realities, of things and structures which exist independently of us and of our thinking and existed long before us. These findings have a truth-value. The true is that which, in our own spirit, corresponds to the reality which is independent of the arbitrariness of our spirit. The true is not that which is "verified" here or there, but that which must always verify itself because it is derived from a wholly interconnecting reality.

The perception of a total interconnectedness in nature is one of the most distinguished achievements of the investigation of nature. The progress of natural science has shown with increasing clarity and comprehensiveness that all processes of the observable world are closely tied to other processes in that world; every discovered natural law is seen to be linked to a number of other laws in such a way that they mutually support each other and none could be valid without the others. . . .

Hence it can be asserted that the understanding of things that are as yet unintelligible also depends on discovering and on making evident in detail their interconnection with what is already known to us and with everything else in nature. It was precisely the yearning of Nordic man to investigate a hypothetical interconnectedness in nature which was the origin of natural science. His guess was correct, but after following it down paths strewn with unexpected difficulties, reality was in most cases constituted very differently from the way it was first imagined. The marvels of reality were not to be found in our own spirit; they had first to be discovered in the external world before our spirit, surprised at first, could assimilate them, and thereby grow truer and richer in conscious harmony with the totality of nature.

The intuition that all of nature is interconnected—which spurred on the great researches—was also correct when it included our own spirit within this interconnectedness. The simplicity of the results seemed to point in this direction, for what is suitable to our spirit, what is arranged for its comprehension, seems simple to us . . . .

The Limits of Understanding

Some of the laws which transmit to us the understanding of nature have been shown to be valid only within definite limits. This means that their applicability is dependent on the fulfillment of certain conditions. The progress of knowledge, therefore, has frequently shown what is valid outside of these limits and has thereby discovered even more general laws which encompass the narrower concepts. In this way we can also expect further progress.

The complete comprehension of any given natural process must be regarded as impossible. Because of the interconnectedness of nature, such comprehension would involve understanding the totality of the infinite world—from which we, in the true sense of the word, must remain forever infinitely removed, if for no other reason than because of the finiteness of our body to which our cognitive spirit is bound. We know from experience that we are not capable of understanding everything at once, and even the successive comprehension of an infinite number of things of limited extent would take an infinitely long time. This accounts for the fact that beyond every uncovered mystery of nature we find an even greater mystery.

But progress in the investigation of nature has also shown that even in the material world—hence apart from the spiritual world—there exist things more difficult to understand than others. If we consider matter alone, we are dealing with mechanisms of which the spirit can form pictures, or models, which behave according to the laws of mechanics and with which it is relatively easy to work. But even the phenomena of heat pose difficult cases of matter in motion. More difficulties arise when we observe the ether, because of its component light and energy. To be sure, concepts have been formulated which give solid support to our notions of the ether, but we have sought in vain for mechanisms in the ether; every experimental presumption in this direction fails to tally with reality. The ether seems more difficult to grasp than matter; it seems already to indicate the borderline of comprehensibility. It is obvious that these borders have been definitely crossed in the attempt to understand the spiritual world; for no human mind can even comprehend its own spirit. . . .

Materialism: A Delusion

The peculiar tendency to recognize only matter and not spirit must be mentioned here since it is an outgrowth of natural science. The great achievements of natural science in understanding hitherto insufficiently known portions of the totality of the world have led to an arrogant dismissal of what is incomprehensible. The greatest investigators never shared this attitude; they were always aware of the limits of understanding; even if they crossed old borders, they immediately saw new borders ahead before which they had to come to a halt. But the lesser spirits, for whom the great ones had already blazed a trail and made their work easy, adopted an insolent omniscient attitude. Such was the case after Newton and again after Darwin.

In recent times, the successes of technology have produced a special form of arrogant delusion with respect to matter. The actualization of practical possibilities opened up by a greater comprehension of nature gave rise to the notion of the "mastery" of nature. "Man has slowly become the master of nature." Such utterances on the part of spiritually impoverished "grand technicians" acquired a great influence because of the impressive display their new techniques and inventions made possible. And that influence has been even strengthened by the all-corrupting foreign spirit[2] permeating physics and mathematics. In the face of this development, the spiritual sciences—increasingly estranged from the comprehension of nature and not cultivated in a truly German manner—have utterly failed.

> From Philipp Lenard, *Deutsche Physik*. Vol. I: *Einleitung und Mechanik* (Munich: J. F. Lehmanns Verlag, 1936), pp. 1-2, 11-13.

Respect for Facts and Aptitude for Exact Observation Reside in the Nordic Race
JOHANNES STARK

The slogan has been coined, and has been spread particularly by the Jews, that science is international. It refers not so much to science as such as to scientific researchers and demands a special position in the

2 The Jews are meant here.

nation for them. They ought not to be considered from a national point of view, but are to be evaluated strictly on the merits of their scientific activity without regard to their ethnic origin. According to this concept, Jewish scientists ought to be inviolable even in the National Socialist state and should be allowed to continue to exert a standard-setting influence. From the National Socialist side, in opposition to this view, it must be insisted upon with all possible emphasis that in the National Socialist state, even for the scientist, the duty to the nation stands above any and all other obligations. The scientist, too, must consider himself a member and a servant of the nation. He does not exist only for himself or even for his science. Rather, in his work he must serve the nation first and foremost. For these reasons, the leading scientific positions in the National Socialist state are to be occupied not by elements alien to the Volk but only by nationally-conscious German men.

But aside from this fundamental National Socialist demand, the slogan of the international character of science is based on an untruth, insofar as it asserts that the type and the success of scientific activity are independent of membership in a national group. Nobody can seriously assert that art is international. It is similar with science. Insofar as scientific work is not merely imitation but actual creation, like any other creative activity it is conditioned by the spiritual and characterological endowments of its practitioners. Since the individual members of a people have a common endowment, the creative activity of the scientists of a nation, as much as that of its artists and poets, thus assumes the stamp of a distinctive Volkish type. No, science is not international; it is just as national as art. This can be shown by the example of Germans and Jews in the natural sciences.

Science is the knowledge of the uniform interconnection of facts; the purpose of natural science in particular is the investigation of bodies and processes outside of the human mind, through observation and, insofar as possible, through the setting up of planned experiments. The spirit of the German enables him to observe things outside himself exactly as they are, without the interpolation of his own ideas and wishes, and his body does not shrink from the effort which the investigation of nature demands of him. The German's love of nature and his aptitude for natural science are based on this endowment. Thus it is understandable that natural science is overwhelmingly a creation of the Nordic-Germanic blood component of the Aryan peoples. Anyone who, in Lenard's classic work *Grosse Na-*

turforscher (Great Investigators of Nature), compares the faces of the outstanding natural scientists will find this common Nordic-Germanic feature in almost all of them. The ability to observe and respect facts, in complete disregard of the "I," is the most characteristic feature of the scientific activity of Germanic types. In addition, there is the joy and satisfaction the German derives from the acquisition of scientific knowledge, since it is principally this with which he is concerned. It is only under pressure that he decides to make his findings public, and the propaganda for them and their commercial exploitation appear to him as degradations of his scientific work.

The Jewish spirit is wholly different in its orientation: above everything else it is focused upon its own ego, its own conception, and its self-interest—and behind its egocentric conception stands its strong will to win recognition for itself and its interests. In accordance with this natural orientation the Jewish spirit strives to heed facts only to the extent that they do not hamper its opinions and purposes, and to bring them in such a connection with each other as is expedient for effecting its opinions and purposes. The Jew, therefore, is the born advocate who, unencumbered by regard for truth, mixes facts and imputations topsy-turvy in the endeavor to secure the court decision he desires. On the other hand, because of these characteristics, the Jewish spirit has little aptitude for creative activity in the sciences because it takes the individual's thinking and will as the measure of things, whereas science demands observation and respect for the facts.

It is true, however, that the Jewish spirit, thanks to the flexibility of its intellect, is capable, through imitation of Germanic examples, of producing noteworthy accomplishments, but it is not able to rise to authentic creative work, to great discoveries in the natural sciences. In recent times the Jews have frequently invoked the name of Heinrich Hertz as a counter-argument to this thesis. True, Heinrich Hertz made the great discovery of electromagnetic waves, but he was not a full-blooded Jew. He had a German mother, from whose side his spiritual endowment may well have been conditioned. When the Jew in natural science abandons the Germanic example and engages in scientific work according to his own spiritual particularity, he turns to theory. His main object is not the observation of facts and their true-to-reality presentation, but the view which he forms about them and the formal exposition to which he subjects them. In the interest of his theory he will suppress facts that are not in keeping with it and likewise, still in the interest of his theory, he will engage in propaganda on its behalf.

Only his theory is valid for him, and in the face of doubts he demands a faith in his theory as if it were a dogma. The dogmatic zeal and propagandistic drive of the Jewish scientist leads him to report on his achievements not only in scientific journals but also in the daily press and on lecture tours. The phenomenon, for example, of Jews pushing themselves prominently to the foreground at scientific congresses, such as the gatherings of German natural scientists and physicians, can be explained in the same way.

> From Johannes Stark, *Nationalsozialismus und Wissenschaft* (Munich: Zentralverlag der NSDAP, Frz. Eher Nachf., 1934), pp. 10-12.

Nature Presupposes a Spiritual Disposition
BRUNO THÜRING

Einstein's work can be understood only as counterpart and antithesis to the intellectual tendency of a Kepler or a Newton. Whereas, still intoxicated with the tremendous successes of Kepler and Newton, their successors and spiritual heirs already became partly conscious, but increasingly less so, of the fact that the creative power of these two great men did not rest so much on their logical intellect as on their world-embracing outlook on life, with its simultaneous and equal concern for the realm of the material and the realm of the spiritual and non-material—that is, on qualities of soul and disposition. Others of their followers turned deliberately toward what was essentially a purely materialistic conception of spiritual and material nature, in the hope of being able eventually to grasp the whole of nature in one mathematical formula. However, Kepler and Newton made their own anti-materialistic mode of thinking perfectly clear. The instinctive knowledge that nature and creation were not to be divorced from their creator and that the world of our paltry five senses, the world of matter, simply could not be the whole world, was so valuable and essential to their investigations that they expressed this knowledge not only in numerous private letters but also in their justly famous treatises. Their scientific aspirations, their drive to understand, and their inquiry into nature were in the first instance born of a deep religious feeling—the word being used here in its true meaning—and whenever they raised the question of the meaning and purpose of scientific inquiry, they never furnished any answer except their desire to comprehend and explain the existence and operation of God in the investigation of His plan of the world and His works. The ancient magnanimity of soul of the Germanic man, directed away from the world and all external appearance, posed the first world-encompassing question about nature and thus became the mother of natural science. If the generation from which Kepler and Newton sprang had been exclusively devoted to materialism—if indeed it had been incapable of an inner view extending far beyond mere sensory perceptions—Kepler's search for the divine harmony of nature would have been impossible and therefore unsuccessful. At the same time, his success did not come to him easily. Not only for years but for decades, he exerted all his genius for mathematics and creative combinations, which he knew how to subordinate to the primacy of exact observation. No failure, no disappointment could ever shake his rocklike conviction that the world had to be in harmony, for its progenitors were perfection and beauty. "With God's help I shall certainly conclude this undertaking—and indeed in a military manner, by issuing my orders boldly, daringly, and triumphantly today, and worrying about my funeral tomorrow," he wrote in a letter. And in another letter: "My whole being strives to penetrate form and existence, God Himself, the architect of creation—and here is where the greatest joy beckons me." And again: "Here I throw the dice, and write a book either for my contemporaries or for posterity. Maybe it will have to wait centuries for its readers, but then God Himself waited thousands of years for someone to describe His works." Kepler wrote all this in the glowing flame of supra-terrestrial exultation over having finally succeeded in finishing his work. The drive to comprehend what can be perceived by the senses, born of a conviction and faith in what cannot be grasped by our senses, and a modest yet persevering devotion to the exact observation of nature, determined the scientific attitude which made Kepler the prototype and example of the German natural scientist. Therefore, his scientific achievements were, and remain, despite their international reputation, the products of a thoroughly German and nationally conditioned conception of nature. The fairy tale of an international and absolute natural science that is independent of Volk, history, and race is smashed to pieces on Kepler. Conversely, a liberal theory of science could have come into being only in a period which, under the influence of persons of alien blood, increasingly fell

victim to materialism and which was no longer able to see Kepler and
Newton as anything more than great intellectualists and mathemati-
cians.

But how can such a conception do justice to a man like Newton,
who found it necessary in his main work, *Principia Mathematica*, to
delve extensively into the problem of divinity and who, on the basis of
his world-encompassing view of nature, could demand that divinity be
evaluated as a problem of natural science? "Thoroughly similar only
to itself," he describes divinity, "entirely ear, eye, brain, arm, feeling,
insight, activity, and all in a manner not human, even less corporeal,
but in an entirely unknown manner. We see only the structure and
color of a body; we hear its sounds, we feel its exterior surface, we
smell and taste it. But as regards the inner substances of matter, we
can comprehend them neither through our senses nor through our
intelligence. Even less do we have a conception of the substance of
God." And he concluded this part of his contemplations as follows:
"This I had to say about God, whose works it is the task of natural
science to investigate." Is not such thinking and such knowledge of
the threads that bind the realm of matter to the realm of the spirit,
is not this awareness of the fact that with our limited number of
senses we are able to grasp only a restricted part of the whole world,
worlds apart from materialism, worlds apart from that relativistic conception according to which every description of nature may deal only
with relations of matter to matter and according to which even space
and time are only attributes of matter because there is, allegedly,
nothing but matter? The formulation of general relativity as a principle of nature, as is done in Einstein's theory, can be nothing more
than the expression of a thoroughly materialistic attitude of mind and
soul. The feeling for nature and the racially determined concept of
nature possessed by Nordic man, who strives to comprehend nature
not only with his intellect but also with his heart and soul and with
his imagination, are here opposed by a concept of nature which aims
to set up the intellect alone as the cognitive principle in the investigation of nature and which consequently disregards the possibility of
conceptions geared to our spirit in favor of a purely symbolical, mathematical, formalistic, and non-concrete representation of nature. . . .

By starting out from facts alone, even though based on observation and experiment, we cannot arrive at a "decision" with respect
to the "correctness" of either [the Nordic or the Einsteinian conception of nature]. Rather, the complex of facts is identical in both cases.

The difference between the two concepts goes deeper; it lies on another level, namely, where natural science as an activity takes its point of departure. For that reason, the assertion of books popularizing the theory of relativity that it is a conception of nature based on experience is utterly untrue. For the substratum and essence of natural science are not to be found in this or that measurement, in this or that experiment, or in the exact reading of an instrument. All these are merely its exterior forms of expression, its *results*, and as such something which is objective, a datum provided by nature. But what is essential in connection with what concerns us today is to determine what lies at the base of inquiry, what it springs from, what use the investigator makes of it and what it can be utilized for. It is not the What which is the decisive factor, but the How, Whence, and Why. If that were not so, there would be no explanation for the fact that the natural sciences came into existence and blossomed among the valuable peoples and races of Europe, and among these overwhelmingly in the Germanic segments thereof. This fact cannot be ignored; it attests to the communality of an identical basic attitude of mind and spirit which coincides with the communality of racial and Volkish characteristics. Not only Kepler and Newton, but also Galileo, Guericke, Faraday, Gauss, Maxwell, Robert Mayer, and many others attest to this fact.

But a word about the space-time problem. The conceptions of space and time are thought frameworks given to us by nature, into which we order and arrange all physical and chemical phenomena, but also all manifestations of life, mind, and soul. They are forms of thinking of our innermost being, so to speak, our "weapons" for confronting the outside world. Newton, as a true Germanic natural scientist, was fully conscious of that and he regarded space and time not as purely logical concepts, but as concepts strongly anchored in intuition. It is altogether different with the Jew Einstein. The attempt to view space and time as attributes of matter exclusively and the desire to understand them solely as matter, so that on the basis of this mental attitude it had to be claimed that the motion of matter is meaningful only in relation to other matter, are fully in keeping with the thoroughly and onesidedly materialistically oriented spirit of the theory of relativity. For the relativist, this is a self-evident concept and in return he acquiesces in all the violence done to intuition. Intuition and feeling are sacrificed to the worship of matter and pure logic. . . .

Still another closely connected difference between the relativistic-

Jewish and the Nordic-Germanic conception and representation of nature lies in their attitude toward the concept of energy. Power, strength, energy, is something immediately clear and understandable to the Nordic man; not only does he possess it himself, but it has confronted him from the primordial beginnings of his history and from the beginning of his personal life in his work as a craftsman, in the effort of physical activity. He knows from experience that through energy one can set bodies in motion or bring moving bodies to a stop. For Kepler and Newton, as Germanic men, it was immediately obvious, whenever they encountered such changes in motion, to speak of the effects of energy. Kepler was the first to give voice to the idea that the sun was the source of an energy which determines the trajectory of the planets. Newton founded his general mechanics on an exact and measurable definition of energy.

It is no coincidence that the half-Jew Heinrich Hertz[1] and the full-Jew Einstein attempted to create a structure of mechanics from which the concept of energy has wholly vanished. The Jewish philosopher Spinoza likewise was ignorant of the concept of energy. It seems to be entirely alien to the world-feeling of the Jew, and he is therefore at pains to exclude this alien phenomenon from his consideration of nature. Hertz clothed this aspiration in his demand that all anthropomorphisms, such as energy, be excluded from natural science. But in doing so he overlooked the fact that every construction of a scientific concept arises in principle from human experience, that is, from a cognitive process in which the specific nature of the cognizing subject is as essentially involved as the specific nature of the cognized object. Finally, even Hertz's attempt is anthropomorphic if in place of energy he postulates the coupling of mechanical systems, whose motions thereupon lose all freedom.

Einstein's theory of relativity, however, sets aside the concept of energy through the most radical upheaval of all space-time concepts. He postulates, in a purely mathematical, formalistic way, a *curvature of space* in the environment of all matter and necessarily connected with it. In this curved space the planets follow trajectories analogous to the so-called geodetic lines, that is, to the shortest possible lines between two points in curved planes. Thus, through the elimination

---

[1] Heinrich Hertz (1857-1894), physicist, discoverer of the electrical frequencies. Johannes Stark praises him because his Aryan half may have broken through (see page 207). The Nazis had it both ways.

of the concept of energy, dynamics become, with Hertz as well as with Einstein, a kind of cinematics.

We can see by this example what is involved here: Not new cognitions of natural events, not new findings of scientific research, but something relating to human inwardness, something concerning the soul, world-feeling, attitudes, and racial dispositions.

There have been repeated attempts in lectures and books to present the theory of relativity as the grand capstone of centuries of progressive scientific development, which began with Copernicus and Galileo and led, via Kepler and Newton, to Einstein. No! Copernicus, Galileo, Kepler, and Newton are not Einstein's predecessors and pathfinders, but his antipodes. Einstein is not the pupil of these men, but their determined opponent; his theory is not the keystone of a development, but a declaration of total war, waged with the purpose of destroying what lies at the basis of this development, namely, the world view of German man. Therefore, it could be so joyfully saluted and enthusiastically celebrated only by a generation that had grown up on purely materialistic modes of thought. This theory could have blossomed and flourished nowhere else but in the soil of Marxism, whose scientific expression it is, in a manner analogous to that of cubism in the plastic arts and the unmelodious and unharmonic atonality in the music of the last several years. Thus, in its consequences, the theory of relativity appears to be less a scientific than a political problem.

The flooding of the book market shortly after the war with popular and semi-popular expositions of the theory of relativity naturally could not aim to acquaint the large public interested in natural sciences with the highly difficult logical and mathematical thought-content of the theory. Such a goal cannot be attained in this way. Rather, the effect of these books was to be found mainly on the level of the inner soul and a world view. Some even ventured—and they were not altogether wrong in this assumption—to look upon the theory of relativity as a typical expression of our time. Colin Ross,[2] in his book Die Welt auf der Waage (The World in the Scales), declared that Einstein's theory could have been discovered only in our time,

2 A writer, chiefly famous for his Unser Amerika: Der deutsche Anteil an den Vereinigten Staaten (Our America: The Part Played by the Germans in the United States) (1936), which claimed that the German racial stock in America was superior to the other races in this country.

that the principle of relativity gave our time its keynote and left nothing untouched, no moral law, not even Kant's categorical imperative.

In this manner, assisted by advertising in the newspapers and lectures from the professorial chairs, this purely scientific theory, whose main ingredient was the postulate of relativity, grew into a physical world view. And since it is always impossible for several world views— say, a physical, a philosophical, an astronomical, or a religious world view—to exist simultaneously without affecting and influencing each other, the theory of relativity threatened to become the dominant world view altogether and in every direction. This development became possible only because of the general recognition accorded natural science as a scientific discipline, characterized by the highest objectivity since it supposedly deals exclusively with established facts, whose existence is in no way subject to being conditioned or determined by the cognizing subject. It was deliberately overlooked that all interest in nature in itself presupposes a certain spiritual disposition, and that the perceiving subject has his own manner and content of conception and his own method of inquiry, all of which must depend on himself and his particular endowments. The few who were of different opinions were disregarded. Nevertheless, it remains forever true that the natural scientist in his work remains a son of the people and a representative of their feelings and yearnings, as is also true in the case of the artist and the statesman. This obvious fact could be misunderstood only because nobody took the trouble to delve deeply enough into the wellsprings of natural-scientific inquiry; everyone remained suspended at the point where facts were observed, experiments made, results recorded. To prove the dependence of natural science on racial stock requires less study of results in textbooks and more study of the original works of the great discoverers and their personalities as scientists. Kepler and Newton as Nordic men on one side, Einstein as a typical Jew on the other, are the most illuminating examples—the former because they did not shrink from allowing the reader an insight into their own spiritual life, the latter as a contrast to them.

May the young generation of natural scientists and philosophers recognize, therefore, what is meant by the concept of German natural science! If, however, someone asks: How can we arrive at a German natural science? our answer must be: A new National Socialist science cannot create, as if by sorcery, arbitrary and amateurish world systems and conceptions—only infinite damage could come of this. Rather, it must reverentially immerse itself in nature itself, and in the great

Nordic discoverers and interpreters of nature, to find there the essence of German being in glorious abundance. As for the rest, let us keep as far away as possible anything that comes from the hands of the Jew, and let us be Germans and National Socialists in all our work and thought! Then everything will be all right. I shall close with a variation of a quotation from R. Eichenauer: "Natural science is not a root, but a blossom. Let us take care of the roots. The blossom will appear by itself." [3]

> From *Deutsche Mathematik*, edited by Theodor Vahlen (Leipzig: Kommissionsverlag von S. Hirzel, 1936), pp. 706-711.

Psychotherapy and Political World View
KURT GAUGER

I have chosen as the subject of my address "Psychotherapy and Political World View."

It is clearly indicated that the sense of my talk will be political, since I am standing before you in the uniform of a political soldier, of an SA man.

The connection between psychotherapy and politics may appear strange to many of you, especially those who have come from abroad to participate in this congress, and you may probably look upon the relationship between psychotherapy and politics as a purely tactical matter.

Hence you might, perhaps, be of the opinion that a political address at an international scientific congress, as far as the participants from abroad are concerned, could have only the purpose of winning sympathy for our new state. And our German participants may be of the opinion that such a political report, for them, signifies a directive to the action which we know adequately enough as coordination.[1]

To be sure, it would give me great joy if, through my talk, I were to

[3] Richard Eichenauer, racial theorist, became director of the peasant adult education school (*Bauernhochschule*) in Goslar. Author of works such as *Die Rasse als Lebensgesetz für Geschichte und Gesittung* (1938) (*Race as an Attitude toward Life in History and Morals*).

[1] *Gleichschaltung*: a term used to describe the absorption or control of organizations by the Third Reich.

succeed in giving those of you from abroad a better understanding of what is happening today in Germany. But my utterances, in this sense, are not exclusively directed to our foreign participants. My remarks are made *ad hoc*. I do not want to persuade. . . .

Even the one-sided exponents of the scientific research tendencies in medicine have not dared to assert that such an entity as a human soul does not exist.

They have avoided, however, taking a position on this phenomenon —either by declaring that it was of no interest to them, that it did not fit in with their alembics, levers and screws, or by saying that the psychic life, by its nature, is only apparently different from the physical processes. They meant to say that just as there are definite chemical transformations which can be perceived subjectively as color changes, likewise are there highly complicated chemical physical processes which can be observed with relative convenience as psychic life. It is only because of the temporary inadequacy of our chemico-physical research methods that we cannot yet express a feeling directly as a chemical formula.

For us, on the other hand, it is evident—that is, something not requiring further proof—that this conception of psychic life is not presuppositionless, not extra-scientific, but rather the expression of a philosophical decision along the lines of materialism.

For us it is certain that even perfect chemico-physical research methods, applied to living brains, will always register only chemico-physical processes, and will never show even a trace of a thought or a feeling.

In the same way we reject the twin brother of materialism, namely that "idealism" which, conversely, holds the non-corporeal alone to be essential, but which can just as little find a trace of a corporeal substratum in the most thoroughgoing analysis of thoughts and feelings.

Freud did not look for chemical processes in mental illnesses. In the investigation of mental illnesses he limited himself strictly to psychological methods, but only because he considered that the path of chemistry was not yet traversible. In one passage he expressly states that he regarded all psychological findings so far as provisional, which eventually would be replaced by chemical formulae.

Thus he took an unequivocal position in favor of the materialistic world view and deprived the sphere of the soul of the value peculiarly its own. According to this opinion, even though we have not yet reached the point, one day we shall be able to spare ourselves all spiritual battles and upheavals through the simple medium of a well-mixed intravenous injection.

The philosophical premises of scientific materialism, of which Freud himself obviously was unaware, made it possible for psychotherapy at first to conduct itself exclusively like an exact science. Freudian psychoanalysis is the attempt to apply chemico-physical methods to the investigation of the human psychic life.

We do not dispute the value of physics and chemistry. Nor do we assert that in the future things will depend entirely and only on ideology. . . .

I do not at all oppose the fact that there is and should be a special pathology and therapy in the treatment of neuroses. We do not dispute the value of physics and chemistry. Hence we do not dispute the value of certain theses of Freudian psychoanalysis which were formulated on the basis of such quasi-scientific observation of human psychic life.

Philosophical enmity develops only with the interpretation of the results of such research! To express it differently: We do not fight astronomy, but we will obstruct any astronomer who would want to use astronomical science as a weapon for Communist anti-religious organizations.

Or, let us take a medical example: A genius and a moron could easily at the same time come down with a severe cold. Despite the fact that they have a sickness in common, we would not be apt to mistake the one for the other. Thus we use yardsticks which have nothing directly to do with the common cold. To express it differently: What we miss in Freudian psychoanalysis is a system of values.

To return to the example of the common cold: casuistically, everything relative to the cold which psychoanalysis has etiologically collected may be correct. What is still missing, however, is the sure criterion for the evaluation of the man who has the cold. . . .

The scientific materialism of Freudian psychoanalysis is closely related to the economic materialism of the Marxists.

The specific National Socialist concept of feeling and disposition is alien to both of them, as is the specific National Socialist concept of community.

In turn, materialism is closely connected with individualism.

The political expression of individualism is egoism. Materialism is the world view of egoism. True, even materialism does not teach unbridled egoism. It always calls attention to the fact that other individuals also exist in addition to the single individual. It teaches, rather, a "well-considered egoism," that is, an egoism moderated by a regard for the egoism of others.

The illegitimate political child of Freudian psychoanalysis, namely, Adler's individual psychology, moves in this direction. Adler's individual psychology provided the former German Social Democratic state with a ready-made surrogate for religion, though it must be added that even before 1933 German individual psychology exhibited certain resistances to its establishment on a Marxist basis.

Fidelity, honor, love, comradeship—heroism, Volkdom, homeland —as words with philosophical weight and hence as political factors, have no place in the world view of materialism.

For materialists, for egoistical individualists, a man ready to sacrifice himself for an idea is necessarily a fool, a pathological individual.

If we consider whether the convinced egoist can achieve his philosophical goal, his subjective well-being, the gratification of his egoism, the pitiful fiasco is at once evident. It needs no sharp-sighted speculations, in the manner of Schopenhauer, to know that everything can be satisfied in this world, except egoistic strivings.

Freud speaks of overcoming the pleasure principle. But he cannot name the value system which can be experienced only outside of every egoistic evaluation. Such a system of values is possible only as an expression of a world view that does not have the individual and his well-being as its exclusive goal.

Hitherto, psychotherapy was largely individualistically oriented, and precisely at the point where one spoke of the relationship of the individual to the community. To us, the concept of the individual is at the outset false; it is the expression of an attitude which we call liberalistic.

For us it is not at all the concept of personality but rather the concept of the individual as ens existens per se that from the outset constitutes the negation and falsification of a biological datum, namely, that of a reality that is not merely "metaphysical" but indeed biological, the German people.

As inheritors of the individualistic epoch, we know much about individual conditions of mental illnesses. What we did not hear so much about, however, before Adolf Hitler, are the general conditions of the health of the soul.

If you ask me about the connection between psychotherapy and National Socialism, I must answer that the problem of the health of our people's soul is the basic question with which National Socialism is concerned. Adolf Hitler did not start out from purely economic considerations.

He did not promise his first followers and later the whole German people "more earnings and less work," as had been done earlier by Marxist demagogues. He promised us nothing. He achieved something psychologically unprecedented, in that he made demands rather than promises.

He demanded of every individual the utmost in terms of participation and a disposition prepared for action. And precisely by so doing, he reopened the wellsprings of the healthy soul of our people which had begun to run dry. Since the advent of Adolf Hitler, Volkdom and homeland, discipline, fidelity, and honor, are again words of biological value in Germany! . . .

The term "mental illness" requires, empirically speaking, a more exact explanation. Most people know or think they know what is meant when we speak of mental illness. A mentally ill person is someone who continuously makes senseless and illogical assertions and commits correspondingly irrational and illogical actions, or someone who no doubt thinks and acts logically as it were, but on the basis of emotional and logical presuppositions which nobody but himself considers valid. The layman also usually includes among the mentally ill people who act and think logically but on the level of small children, while in terms of bodily development and age they are adult human beings. It may be questionable whether the traditional designation "mental illness" is actually meaningful in connection with these cases. But under no circumstances can the sick people with whom psychotherapy is concerned be summarily designated as "mentally ill" or as "mentally ill to a lesser degree." The Intelligence Quotient of these patients, if measured against that of healthy people within the same walk of life, is in fact frequently higher than the average.

Soul is a designation that encompasses the whole area of individual human existence, so far as it is not of a corporeal nature. Sickness of soul, therefore, always designates the whole area. The line of demarcation between psychoses (insanity) and psycho-neuroses (soul sickness) becomes perceptible only through a consideration of the total man.

"Health of soul," "sickness of soul," and "insanity" are, therefore, terms indicating the "gradations of the capacity to relate to others."

Hence the concept of illness espoused by German psychotherapy is oriented toward the basic premise that man is a community-building being. At the same time, community building must here be understood in the specific National Socialist or German sense of an essentially psychic process. An association of stockbrokers is in no sense a community according to us.

Hence the German psychotherapeutic concept of illness is "politically" determined, and this means politically in the sense of a definite decision about a world view.

The term "relationship" implies a connection with something extra-personal and supra-personal.

Like every other illness, mental illness can be immediately perceived in the impairment of the vital capacities. As with every other sickness, there are those who come by sickness of soul through heredity and those who come by it through accident, and in both forms there exist degrees of intensity, as in the case of every purely physical sickness. The feeble-minded, the hereditarily insane, and the constitutional psychopath are to be mentioned among those afflicted with hereditary soul sickness.

Heretofore, when dealing with these patients, it was not customary to regard their capacity for forming psychic relationships as a yardstick to measure the degree of their illness. Yet everything depends on just that.

It is entirely analogous with ethnological research: blond or dark-haired, slender or stout, brachycephalic or dolichocephalic, is of "scientific" interest only if these racial features are not evaluated as expression. Only when racial difference also signifies a psychic difference is it of vital importance to us.

And where does the danger of certain racial mixtures lie if not in psychic depravity? Physically, the union of Negroes and whites is entirely possible. Physically, bastards are healthy if their procreators were healthy. Wherein should the incompatibility of such a union lie if not in the realm of the soul?

The situation is similar in the case of those suffering from congenital psychic sickness. For instance, feeble-minded persons frequently —and unfortunately—enjoy the best of physical health. Their health is not animal, but animal-like. The great physical strength of many feeble-minded professional criminals is well known. Equally well known is the animal procreative faculty of feeble-minded persons that is so dangerous in the Volk-biological sense.[2]

[2] See "The Hereditary Health Law," page 90.

But is the term "sickness of soul"—that is, the lack of psychic relationship—at all applicable to these near human beings? The answer is that it is, but only in consideration of their psychic possibilities; only in reference to their "world view" can they be viewed as dangerously sick in a Volk-biological sense. This means that they are not dangerous because they are unable to count and write, but because psychically they cannot relate.

The world view of the feeble-minded embraces his own person, and other persons only to the extent they can serve the gratification of the most primitive instincts. Good-natured feeble-minded persons attach themselves to those who give them food and drink and a bed. Their relationship to other people is therefore essentially of an egoistic nature, hence not a relation in the true sense.

This psychic inability to relate is even more explicit when viewed as a decisive symptom of severe illness in schizophrenics. There are lesser degrees of congenital feeble-mindedness which can be so designated, not because the patient can count up to 20 instead of up to 5, but because some beginnings of true psychic relationship are still at hand, that is, because the patient is still capable of being educated instead of merely drilled. The schizophrenic, on the other hand, is characterized by a total absence of a psychic capacity to relate. The world which he views and perceives is exclusively a dream world. Other persons may enter this dream world in speaking and acting roles, as they may in the normal dream of a healthy individual. But this does not yet constitute a true psychic relationship to real human beings. The schizophrenic, for instance, does not talk to someone who visits him—he talks to an apparition of unknown origin that may perhaps have been stimulated by the visit or that may have been created in his mind purely by accident and entirely independent of the visit. The schizophrenic only seems to talk to his visitor, if he speaks at all. And he may also simultaneously converse with others who are not present, such as someone long dead, or with fabulous beings which he sees.

The diseased state of the constitutional psychopath is of the same kind, if not of the same degree. In contrast to schizophrenics and feeble-minded persons, the psychopath is often entirely capable of truly perceiving the actual world—persons and situations. The psychopath is frequently not lacking in intelligence. Nor is his physical condition decisive. There are both physically strong and physically weak psychopaths.

Again the absence of psychic relationship to others is the decisive

and sociologically important symptom of the sickness. The psychopath is the born egoist. Measured by the degree of his sickness, the
psychopath, despite his intellectual endowment, is more closely related to the schizophrenic than is the good-natured half-wit. Only to a
very inadequate extent is the psychopath capable of a true love relationship of real passion, of true dedication. The talented psychopath,
from a Volk-biological point of view, is infinitely more dangerous than
the obvious severely mentally ill person, or the feeble-minded person,
or the psychotic. The psychopath is incapable of a true bond with a
symbol, with a vital happening. But his talents may enable him to
simulate such a bond.

An untalented psychopath, a liar who believes his own lies, may
also believe that he has a relationship with others but only as long as
he is not called upon to serve such a bond, as long as he can follow his
own egoism, his ambition and desire for power.

This does not mean that ambition and desire for power should fundamentally be designated as psychopathic. They can be thoroughly
manly virtues. It is a question of emphasis; the key word is "only."
"Only" ambition, "only" desire for power, are the distinguishing
marks of the psychopath.

For a normal human being, this distinction, once he has grasped its
importance, is not difficult to make, since it is not an abstract scientific matter, but an emotional, spontaneous expression of his ethical
capacity. At the same time, for the healthy and non-sentimental human being, there can be no doubt that the successes of the pathological egoism which marks the psychopath (just as sit venia verbo the
successes of psychopathological nations) are only apparent. There is
no injustice in the world. The final accounting always balances if one
never loses sight of the realm of the soul. In the life of the individual
as in the life of whole peoples, the final fate is the immediate expression of the attitude of psychic engagement, even if, from a materialistic point of view, the final accounting should not balance. Here again,
men differ along philosophical and political lines, namely, between
those who can experience the defeat of a hero as a victory and those
who are not capable of doing so. Or expressed in another way: There
is a fulfillment of life, but never a gratification of egoism. Happiness is
necessarily unattainable on the level of egoistic gratification, since it is
possible to satisfy everything but egoism itself.

Of necessity, therefore—and as the expression of an implacable in-
ner-worldly justice—the liberalistic-materialistic world view, with its

goal of "the greatest happiness for the greatest possible number," ended in the deepest dissatisfaction, in the inferno of the deepest sickness of our people's soul.

The Third Reich has not inscribed happiness on its banners, but virtue. . . .

Since it is my purpose to discuss, to the best of my ability, some aspects of the fundamentals of German psychotherapy, it is necessary also to say something about the healing process, about the methodology of treating patients with psychic disorders.

In order to treat any sickness and to investigate the path to a cure, it is necessary to know the etiology, the cause of the illness. To a large degree this is identical with a thorough knowledge of the genesis of the development of the illness.

No doubt it is possible to heal many illnesses without an accurate knowledge of the etiology. Pains in the upper stomach frequently disappear if the patient is sent to bed and a special diet and warm bandages are ordered. Such treatment is beneficial under all circumstances, regardless whether the organs of the upper stomach are suffering from a slight inflammation or more serious disorders. But with sicknesses of more severe character it will always be necessary to diagnose not only the affected organ but also the kind of illness.

The same is true with psychic illnesses. A great number of so-called psychic disorders will disappear as the result of suggestive persuasion on the part of the doctor. Frequently the psychotherapist needs only to mention things which the patient has already told himself often enough, but the fact that a qualified physician says them encourages him.

It depends upon the process of perception, which is a necessary ingredient in the healing power.

Perception is a total process and only distantly related to knowledge; just as it defies comparison if a young midwife directs hundreds of births and then should become a mother herself.

Methodologically the road of retrospection is the road of Freud. At the risk of being considered a "Freudian," on this road one must deal with events that have given a name to a whole segment of life in every human being, the age of puberty. Methodologically and taken by themselves, many of Freud's findings are correct, but the interpretation of their meaning and their assigned place in the totality of human affairs appears unbearably wrong to us.

The road of Jung looks forward. Freud asks: Whence? Jung asks:

Whither? Freud is the scientist, only the scientist; Jung is an ethician. One could also call him a seer, in the deepest and most reverent sense of the word. Jung is the poet among psychologists. His subconscious is full of living forms with whom one speaks and consorts like human beings, who can give counsel and warning, with whom one tries to be on a good footing because otherwise they may become "angry." Jung's psychology is a demonology. The essence of a demon is contained in its name. Primordial wisdom has it that one can disarm a demon, even make servant of him, if one knows his name.

This is nothing but the process of perception, which heals like any other form of cognition.

While the true magician knows that his forms are always his forms, even if occasionally they overwhelm him, it can still happen to the sorcerer's apprentice that he seriously believes he can lead German youth to TAO,[3] while we are satisfied with the choral music from the carillon of the Potsdam Garrison Church: "Always practice fidelity and honesty!"

Freudian psychology incorporates all the advantages and dangers of the Jewish spirit, Jungian psychology all those of the Germanic soul.

Freud is atheistic; Jung, not in terms of doctrine but in terms of attitude, is marked by a Catholic piety. . . .

Perception is courageous, active, clear-eyed self-responsibility—an attitude which accepts personal responsibility even for those matters for which the individual human being himself is not responsible. This in the face of the Biblical saying "Man is wicked from youth," or in the face of personal, undeserved calamity.

In such circumstances, the "ego" and the unconscious are not two different entities; they are one, as horse and rider are one when the rider truly knows and understands his horse, can tell him what he wants him to do, and when the horse has understood that it has a good rider.

It is, therefore, not necessary to try to explain that mind and soul do not have to be enemies, or that the destiny of man is his intellectuality, a progressive cerebration. The man who is condemned to die is mistaken if he assumes that the world is coming to an end.

We have described personality as a configuration of actualized possibilities. We can add here that . . . there may be individuals who not only have lived a full, well-rounded life, but also have been gifted

[3] TAO, for Jung, is the unity-giving symbol of Chinese philosophy, an irrational unity of contraries. See *Psychologische Typen* (Zurich, 1930), pp. 303 ff.

with perception: they are the men whom we call the true leaders of the people, the thinkers, poets, and politicians. . . .

A ground plan is an essential part of every architectural design, even if it does not indicate exactly how the rest of the building is to be constructed. The following closing remarks concerning the profession of the psychotherapist should be regarded as a ground plan.

Psychotherapy is closely related to pedagogy. Psychotherapy points up the importance of a correct education by showing that, as a rule, a wrong education, even in the case of healthy material, not only leaves the individual badly educated but frequently leads to the sickness of his soul. (To prevent misunderstanding, let us add here that, from a psychotherapeutic point of view, an especially "good" education frequently turns out to be a particularly "bad" one.)

Psychotherapeutically speaking, the development of specific ethnic virtues must be mentioned as the goal of a healthy education. Our educational ideal is not the education of the personality, but to bring up German boys and girls; young Germans. Personality is the fruit, the organic result, of the ripening of the given ethnic propensities.

At the same time, it must not be forgotten that the term "virtue" does not have an ascetic connotation in Germany. Indeed, the binding National Socialist demand is: "Common interest before self-interest," a demand which, like all the other demands of National Socialism, derives from the biological sphere. Biologically, self-assertion is a necessity of life, and only that self-interest is reprehensible and destructive which harms the common interest. This differentiation is purely psychic and is therefore, for one whose soul is healthy, no more difficult to understand than the equally important distinctions between breeding and training, hardihood and brutality, compassion and weakness, passion and fanaticism, steadfastness and dogmatism, enthusiasm and elation, love and sexual gratification, deep emotion and sentimentality.

Psychotherapy, therefore, can serve as a critic of pedagogy, but it can also have a direct, practical relationship with pedagogy since in many cases the treatment of neuroses is tantamount to overcoming educational mistakes. But in the case of adults, the physician should never be or try to become an educator. Rather, he must undertake only the function of introducing the process of self-education, which is more in keeping with the biological situation of an adult, in contrast to the situation of a child.

Psychotherapy is also related to pastoral work, but only in subject matter. The essential difference between the two is frequently misunderstood. It can best be made clear by the equally customary and equally wrong comparison between the psychotherapeutic session and the Catholic confession. For one thing the confession is based on a fixed moral system and a clear understanding of that system, secondly the concept of sin as a violation of this moral system, and finally a confessor with the power of absolution.

A psychotherapeutic session contains none of this. One may, perhaps, see a certain similarity between a neurotic's feeling of guilt and the religious feeling of transgression. But it would be blasphemy to equate the two. If a sick person with a compulsion to wash his hands, for instance, is in utter despair because on one occasion he shook someone's hand without having had a chance to wash his hands first, it is obvious that the moral system of the compulsion to wash is not of a religious nature, but of a highly private nature. It is also obvious that in such a situation the physician has only an apparent relationship to the confessor. In the beginning the patient may, perhaps, perceive it as such, but great progress in psychotherapeutic treatment will have been achieved when the patient relinquishes the desire for absolution because he begins to understand that it is perception which will set him free. One can perhaps say that basically a deep religious conflict is hidden in each neurosis. But that does not make every neurosis also a religious conflict. The essentially religious conflict can be fought only when, for instance, the patient is no longer concerned with the cleanliness of his hands, but when, with the courage of responsibility, he begins to think about the purity of his heart.

Psychotherapeutical activity can therefore be called pastoral work only in a special sense.

Psychotherapy, as we have described it, has two different tasks—one general, the other particular.

Psychotherapy is first and foremost the philosophical-political foundation of all medical practice and should therefore occupy an essential place in all medical studies.

It is well known that up to now hardly any beginnings have been made in this direction. Lectures on psychology in general and medical psychology in particular that have been introduced here and there are certainly useful, but scientifically they are still based on the concepts of the nineteenth century. A relationship to the problems that have been discussed here is hardly noticeable.

The task of psychotherapy in the narrower sense is to educate physicians with special qualifications for treating soul sickness. In practice, this means that these physicians will have to undergo another course of study in addition to their general medical studies. They must know and should have absorbed the history of thought, especially that of their own people; they must have arrived at a certain judgment with respect to philosophical and metaphysical problems; they must be fully conversant with the social sciences, and especially racial science, to mention only a few "non-medical" disciplines.

The question can also be raised as to whether the opposite way would not be equally possible, namely, to start from the humanistic sciences and then add the necessary medical and biological knowledge. It is known that the leaders of psychotherapeutic schools who are physicians themselves are aware of this possibility and have used it in practice by admitting non-medical students.

> From a lecture given at the Medical Congress for Psychotherapy, Bad Nauheim, 1934, published in *Politische Medizin: Grundriss einer deutschen Psychotherapie* (Hamburg: Hanseatische Verlagsanstalt, 1934), pp. 7, 12-14, 16-17, 23-27, 49, 52-54, 61-63.

The Physician Must Come to Terms with the Irrational
HANNS LÖHR

We National Socialists are of the opinion that the physician, leaving his "ivory tower" work at a university clinic far behind, must first of all, in close contact with the Volk community, come to terms with the "irrational" which forms the bridge between the physician and man if the patient is not to be only a "case" or "material" for study.

Hence the National Socialist state is not interested in stuffing a medical student with a great mass of individual, disconnected facts and imparting anemic bits of knowledge which he usually learns ad hoc—that is, only for his examination—and entirely forgets four weeks later. Rather, it wishes to lead him, through a knowledge of the great biological interconnections to a deep reverence for life. . . .

By no means are we against science. Indeed, we demand from the future physician a great measure of scientific knowledge. However, this can be achieved only by reinvigorating the course of instruction with considerably more emphasis on its relationship to human biology than it has received heretofore through the transmittal of purely abstract and dead subject matter. It is precisely here that a truly rational reform of studies must be inaugurated.

Johannes Stein[1] correctly points out that the medical student comes into contact with the living human being—that is, the patient—much too late. If he has no experience with a sick person until after he has passed his first examination, frequently a profusion of regulations and preconceived notions stands between him and his patient. Let no one misunderstand us. We have no intention of imitating the medical schools of France or even their specific method of instruction, which from the very beginning puts the student in contact with patients, concentrating almost exclusively on medical techniques and methodology and, for the average student, putting no great emphasis on theoretical knowledge.

We believe, however, that it would certainly be useful to require service as a nurse and orderly as a precondition for medical studies. While performing this selfless service for his fellow men, the young student will soon find out whether or not he has chosen the right profession.

On the other hand, this practical nursing service, involving, as it does, sacrifice and self-denial, also presents us with an opportunity for a strict selectivity. A principle of selection which leaves the decision, at the end of the course of instruction, entirely up to the teachers on the basis of purely intellectual abilities must be rejected as altogether wrong. How many highly important men were told by their high-school teachers that they had no ability at all! Nor is the process of selection completed even after the pupil meets all qualifications for medical studies. A year of labor service and an additional half year as a practical nurse allow a much more certain judgment of a young man's character endowments. But even during his academic studies—which will soon undergo a fundamental change, whereby the emphasis will be shifted from the "spectacle" of illnesses in the lecture hall to the sickbed itself—in fact at the end of each semester, instead of receiving the usual probationer's certificate the medical student should be repeatedly subjected to evaluation. In the case of the large institutions this may appear to be a practical impossibility. It is, however, a most important task for every lecturer and every department head in clinics

[1] Johannes Stein was professor of internal medicine (from 1934) and Director of the University Hospital at the University of Heidelberg (from 1936).

Hitler honored Adolf Ziegler's "The Four Elements" by placing it over the mantelpiece of his own room in the "Führer's house" in Munich. This technically accomplished painting, which was also shown in the 1937 Exhibition of German Art, is an example of an artistic realism which leaves nothing to the imagination. Ziegler was president of the Reich Chamber of Art and organized the exhibition of "degenerate art."

I

The ideal Aryan family as represented on the cover of the calendar the "New Volk," issued by the office of racial politics of the NSDAP.

Poster art played an important role in Nazi propaganda. This poster, produced by the German Workers' Front, reminds the workers that the comradeship of the soldiers at the front must be carried over into the "battle for production." The workers were laboring in the shadow of those who had sacrificed all for the Fatherland.

The Honor Cross of the German Mother, modeled after the Iron Cross.

right: Richard Klein's "Awakening," which was shown in the 1937 Exhibition of German Art, combines the realistic with the sentimental. Klein was one of the publishers of the official NSDAP journal of art, *Kunst im dritten Reich*, and director of the Munich Academy of Applied Art

Adolf Ziegler's "The Judgment of Paris," illustrating ideal Aryan types

This painting of the ideal German girl, by Paul Keck, was included in the 1939 Exhibition of German Art.

Reality often failed to correspond to the desired ideal, as this 1936 film advertisement shows.

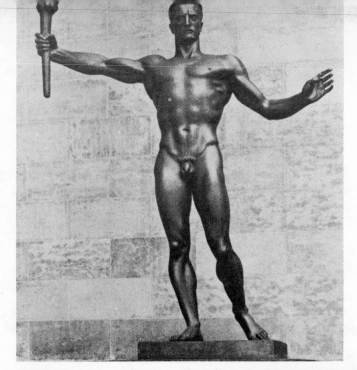

above: Arno Brecker was one of Hitler's favorite sculptors. His "The Party" flanked one of the entrances to the new Reich Chancery. In this sculpture classical realism has been employed to represent the "ideal type" which appears throughout Nazi painting and poster art.

"The Guardian," by Arno Brecker, a good example of the idealized Germanic hero popular in the Third Reich.

A mural by Jürgen Wegener, idealizing active youth.

These two pictures were reproduced side by side in a German art book in order to illustrate the superiority of "true" Nazi art over the "degenerate art" which satirized the front-line soldier. The confrontation pits George Grosz, the Republic's leading left-wing painter, against Elk Eber, an old party member and designer of Nazi propaganda posters.

This "shrine of honor" of the Hitler Youth (in memory of their heroes and martyrs) is a faithful copy of an ancient Germanic hall, complete with the heathen symbols of the "forefathers."

In practice, adhering to the eternal verities often meant copying ancient models. This peasant house would seem to date back to the Middle Ages; it was, in fact, built after 1933 and was praised as "completely modern" while representing a "soil-bound" style.

above: The House of German Art in Munich. Designed by Hitler's favorite architect, Paul Ludwig Troost (1878–1934), it is an example of the imitation of classical forms in monumental public buildings.

One of Hitler's own paintings, in which he has merely copied an historic building. It affords some insight into his artistic tastes.

Hitler as the "friend of children." This photograph accompanied the story reproduced from the children's primer (see page 287).

X

"If all of German youth looked like this, we would have no need to fear for the future."
A class in uniform from the *NSDAP Standarten Kalender 1939.*

The Bund Deutscher Mädel was indoctrinated with "Faith and Beauty," which often involved acting out supposed ancient Germanic customs. These girls are in the dress of the Bronze Age.

Open-air theaters were especially popular because of their romantic and natural settings, mo appropriate for theatrical presentations of the Nazi ideology. This theater was named af Dietrich Eckart, an influential friend of Hitler in the early days.

Above: The famous actor Werner Krauss portraying the typical Jewish stereotype in the Nazi film *Jew Süss* (1940), which dealt with the rise and fall of a Jewish financier in the eighteenth century.

Lothar Müthel in the role of Schlageter, from the first performance of Hanns Johst's drama (1933).

Hermann Otto Hoyer called this mythological painting of Hitler speaking to his early followers "In the Beginning Was the Word." It was included in the 1937 Exhibition of German Art.

Advertisements such as this one were common in the Third Reich. Here the people are exhorted to observe the weekly "one pot" meal, which was supposed to conserve food, especially meat. The legend reads: "the meal of sacrifice for the Reich."

se monumental structures were designed as a setting for mass meetings parades at the Nuremberg Party Days. They are the work of Albert Speer, architect who became Inspector-General of Buildings for Berlin and, later, nister of Armaments and War Production.

Hitler addressing a Party Day meeting in Nuremberg (1935).

and hospitals, and their qualifications as teachers ultimately depend on how well they perform it.

[Wilhelm Frick[2] has said]: "Only he who is his whole being is fully committed to the Volk and seeks nothing for himself and for his own advantage belongs in the university. Whoever is called to study or to teach will not be recognized for his grand words but for his deeds and accomplishments in the service of the Volk community. The National Socialist concept of knowledge and the newly defined task of university studies have by no means lowered the intellectual standards of the university. Rather, it has raised them so that they can be satisfied only by stricter spiritual discipline. If the German student can draw his energies from the deepest dedication to National Socialism, he will do his duty in the way the Volk expects him to do it."

In former years standards of selection sank progressively lower as the number of medical students increased, and more particularly as the medical schools received individuals who neither racially, ethically, nor philosophically were suitable for the medical profession. Consequently, the personal relationship between teacher and student was lost, and with it, naturally, the living model of leadership. The greater the influx of the multitude, the lower the individual accomplishment. In addition, Jewish lecturers occupied the chairs of medicine and despiritualized the art of healing. [According to Reich Physician Leader Gerhard Wagner]: "They have imbued generation after generation of young physicians with their mechanically oriented spirit."   •

A culture ideal prevailed in the liberalistic period, now definitely overcome, that entirely disregarded the character education of the individual.

Hence the building of character and personality, through our teachers, must again be placed in the foreground; next to scientific training, this is the main task of our teachers. Only thus can we return to the ethics and high moral status of an earlier generation of physicians (one has only to read the Hippocratic Oath), which stood on solid philosophical ground and had no peers in terms of its professional knowledge. . . .

Enemies of National Socialism have for years spread the lie that National Socialism by nature stands for an anti-intellectual attitude and has no understanding of the uniqueness of genuine scientific inquiry. Thus the National Socialist movement is considered anti-

[2] Minister of the Interior.

intellectual and alien to the spirit of learning. Allegedly National Socialism would rob science of its inheritance and would restrict all scientific thought in such a way that, in the words of Heinrich Hasse,[3] "the proud mountain ranges of former German culture are leveled into swampy lowlands, fit only to serve as a refuge for intellectual castrates."

Literary émigrés especially tried to make it appear that in Germany today all culture and civilization are endangered—as if a horde of unleashed savages threatened the ideals of all mankind. . . .

The concept of an "unbiased and objective" science, aiming at "absolute truth" based on pure reason, which arose in the liberalist period, has today entirely lost its reason and justification for existing, since we have now come to understand that a realistic science is always based upon a personal contemporary-historical premise. Science can project itself into reality only out of the mainstream of the specific present. Volk community and science are not opposed to each other. The concept of Volk community, heretofore regarded only as a political concept, has now also become a basic scientific principle. . . .

Since the ultimate process of life can never be fully explained through causal-mechanical analyses, the question arises whether the physician, aside from his diagnosis based on the methodology of natural science, may not also have at his disposal some other means of knowledge. At once such concepts as empirical knowledge, consideration of the whole, and intuition spring to mind.

Unquestionably the physician cannot dispense with empirical knowledge, yet, as Hippocrates said, experience is deceptive. Many items of knowledge based solely on experience, no matter for how long they have been considered valid, may one day be discovered to be fundamental errors.

Another question is whether intuition is really a new kind of knowledge, whether or not there is a difference between purely emotional comprehension and the ordinary thought processes. Without a scientific foundation, without a thorough knowledge of biology, there would certainly be no room for intuition in medical science. But what differentiates the truly brilliant, intuitive researcher from his average colleague is that he suddenly receives great, trail-blazing insights

[3] Author of *Schopenhauers Religions Philosophie* (1932) and of works attempting to define the tasks of learning in the Third Reich.

which would never occur to the other. According to Bumke,[4] intuition is an exceedingly great concentration; it is the eye for the "essential which puts not only a great number of single observations and numerous recollections into focus, but at the same time is able to gather the great interconnections into a single thought."

It is self-evident that we cannot train all our students to become geniuses; rather, now as ever, a basic and thorough education in the total biological interconnections is what is required. Anyone who believes he can dispense with scientific knowledge and medical training and depend entirely on intuition in the diagnosis of sickness would soon meet disaster in his diagnostic and therapeutic methods.

We readily admit that from time immemorial there have been "faith healers," people endowed with great medical insight, that is, with intuition. But even these lay practitioners do not always make instantaneous diagnoses; they, too, in the final analysis, make use of a store of experience and empirical knowledge. For, involuntarily, every man, either by inclination or from passion, occupies himself with the field in which he is especially gifted. For example, I have frequently found among the simplest and wholly uneducated strata men with unmatched empirical knowledge of breeding birds, dogs, butterflies, etc., who have never actually studied these subjects. Naturally, these are their favorite hobbies or pursuits. But one will have to admit that here, too, the role of intuition can be seen.

A further cause for the distortion of the concept of the physician in recent times has unquestionably been the progressive Judaicization of our profession. Jewish colleagues soon managed to become the leaders of our professional associations and medical groups. According to Gerhard Wagner: "They debased the concept of professional honor and undermined the ethics and morals intrinsic to our racial stock." Anyone who follows the collection of statistics which show how our profession, especially in the big cities, is dominated by Jews—and they were gathered according to religious and not ethnic or racial principles —will be able to appreciate fully the National Socialist counter-reaction. Reich Physician Leader Gerhard Wagner, in his sweeping report at the Reich Party Convention in 1934 dealing with race and national health, called attention to the fact that in February 1934— that is, a full year after the National Socialist revolution—in Berlin alone 46.8 per cent of the physicians participating in the State Sick

[4] Oswald Bumke was the author of *Das Unterbewusstein* (*The Subconscious*) (1926).

Benefit Fund were Jews. In other big cities the situation is essentially the same. In the light of these facts one can no longer speak of brutal persecution and annihilation of Jews in the medical profession.

But the great influx of Jewish physicians also brought with it a parallel intrusion of Marxist-liberalist thought, which in turn distorted the concept of the physician ever further. The physician became a businessman; moreover, as a servant of the social security and insurance systems, he frequently did shoddy work if he did not want to suffer economically. The art of healing was solely valued in figures and fees!

Simultaneously, the medical practitioner was deprived of what remained of his professional pride by Marxist-oriented insurance administrators and fiduciary physicians.[5] They ordained—and he had to submit—what medicines he could prescribe for his patients.

What was the consequence of all this? The prestige of the medical profession sank lower and lower in the eyes of the people. Because of its dogmatic rejection of all lay medical thought, medical science became alienated from the Volk—simply because it ignored reality. To regain the confidence of the people, it would have been much more correct to submit the ideas and suggestions of Volk medicine to objective study and examination rather than to reject them out of hand. . . .

The social upheaval of the present time will help us to turn from an undue concentration on individual symptoms and organs to the consideration of the "whole" human being, and thus will lead to truly medical-biological thinking. This change in viewpoint has already been reflected of late in numerous contributions to medical publications by leading physicians in all specialized areas of medicine. . . .

The physician has an almost unique opportunity to offer the people real "pastoral care." For the decrease in the birth rate not only is influenced by economic factors but is decisively determined by the inner attitude of the people.

Asking the people to assume moral responsibility is meaningless if at the same time they are not given economic incentives for childbearing. The National Socialist state, however, through its tax legislation[6] and other promulgations, offers economic incentives to those desirous of founding a family and raising children. On the other hand, the appeal to purely economic advantages is completely meaningless if the inner attitude of the individual is not renewed. And here

[5] Those physicians who administered the state medical insurance system.
[6] See page 357.

the purposeful work of the physician must begin. It must not be concerned only with the present generation, but should strive to transcend it and direct its efforts toward the health of the eternal Volk.

In this respect the sterilization law is likewise a pillar of the National Socialist state.[7] If the congenitally healthy person intentionally restricts the number of his children, and the congenitally ill person unrestrictedly and rapidly reproduces himself, after a hundred years, according to the famous calculations of Lenz,[8] the descendants of the healthy people will constitute only 11 per cent of the population whereas the hereditarily defective will represent 88.9 per cent (on the basis of a generation lasting thirty-three years and a uniform rate of reproduction). Thus the quality of the Volk sinks ever lower. Of what use is any attempt to change the spiritual attitude of a people if it consists overwhelmingly of inferior types? We will make no mention here of the enormous costs imposed on our society by congenital defectives, which Dr. Wagner has calculated to be 1.2 billion marks yearly.

The National Socialist physician has the holy obligation to the state not merely to induce patients with congenital diseases to undergo voluntary sterilization but also to report such cases to the authorities. Many a physician may perhaps ask: "But what becomes of the confidence between physician and patient? I for one have no intention of ruining my practice." But the fact is that under the law for the unification of the public health system of July 3, 1934, this crucial problem of medical practice has already been transferred to the public health agencies soon to be established in city and rural districts.

But this does not free the physician from his most important obligation, namely, to do his duty as an alert biological soldier. It is his foremost task to defend the state and his people and their future against asocial elements. I need not emphasize here that the National Socialist physician occupies a basically different position from that taken by the physician of the Marxist-liberalistic period with respect to the problem of artificial interruption of pregnancy. We know of no social need for the destruction of the fruit of the womb.

What tremendous tasks are open to the physician and medical science in the National Socialist state! Our responsibilities and our obligations are greater than ever before. As a Volk physician in the truest

[7] See page 90.
[8] Fritz Lenz was a writer concerned with racial eugenics. Hans F. K. Günther (see page 61) based much of his theory on Lenz's calculations.

sense of the word, the medical practitioner will be able to regain a great deal of his importance as well as the confidence of the people. . . .

Adolf Hitler and his associates have shown the way to the German medical profession.

We university teachers, however, are obliged to teach the student that the health of the Volk stands above the health of the individual as the ultimate aim of the art of medicine, hence to be a doctor to the people is more important than science itself!

We must transmit to the medical student living knowledge taken from the immediate everyday struggles and disputes. We must do this not only by refashioning the curriculum to include such new disciplines as demographic policy and racial eugenics. We are responsible for much more than the growth and advance of science. Rather, those working in Volkish occupations—physicians, judges, and teachers— on whom in the last analysis depends the reconstruction of the Reich, must all be gathered together under the great idea of the National Socialist biological state structure. Hence we also demand for university institutions Volkish teachers, Volkish students, and Volkish physicians. With his biological concept of science and state, the Volkish academician, whether teacher or student, will never run the danger of losing himself in abstract formulations or arid paragraphs.

For him, all work has only one great meaning: the Volk. Here the doctor is restored to the priesthood and the holiness of his calling, which for centuries he possessed in the life of all great nations.

I would like to end my discussion with words from the last important speech by Gerhard Wagner at the Reich Party Congress in 1934:

"Loyal to the will and the instructions of the Führer, we shall fulfill our tasks in the future: to form the new German man, the new German people, which will assert its place in the world in strength, in honor, and in freedom."

From Hanns Löhr, *Über die Stellung und Bedeutung der Heilkunde im nationalsozialistischen Staate* (Berlin: Nornen-Verlag, 1935), pp. 19-23, 26-29, 32-35.

7

Christianity

ɴAZI OPPOSITION to Christianity took the form of elevating its own
world view into a matter of direct religious expression. The prayer for
children on page 241 represents an extreme example of this aim. It
was given to the children by the party welfare organization (NSV) in
a suburb of Cologne—to be recited before and after the free lunch
that was served. But however much the Nazis wanted to substitute
their world view for Christianity, they were careful to keep the traditional forms intact. Even the language they used in their speeches
often employed familiar Christian imagery. Hitler and Goebbels
talked about the "miracle of belief" (now meaning the Nazi faith),
appealed to "Providence," and were not loath to call Mein Kampf the
"sacred book of National Socialism." Indeed, the Führer's closest
companions were called his "apostles," while he himself was often
referred to as the "savior." [1]

The attempt to fill the traditional framework with their own content meant bending Christianity itself into conformity with Nazi ideology and culture. The "German Christians," a group within the
Protestant Church, sought to accomplish this end. Their articles of
faith (1933) stress the figure of Christ and the Scriptures but inte-

[1] Werner Betz, "The National Socialist Vocabulary," The Third Reich (London,
1955), pp. 786-789.

grate them into the community of blood through which they find their sole expression. The German Christians were formed by the Nazi party in 1932 in order to influence the elections to the Prussian State Church which took place in that year. The attempt was a failure and the Nazis learned their lesson.

Hitler now approached the desired transformation of Christianity in a more indirect manner. In its platform the Nazi party had declared its neutrality in religious matters, and Hitler after 1932 repeatedly assured the Churches that he would abide by that principle. In reality the ideas of the German Christians lay in wait, to be applied at the proper time. That the German Christian movement itself suffered many splits after the seizure of power was of scant significance in this regard.

The appointment of Hans Kerrl as Minister of Ecclesiastical Affairs in 1935 should have been a sign for all to read, for he sympathized with German Christianity. His time came in 1938 when the crisis produced by Hitler over the fate of the Germans within Czechoslovakia was at its height. At that point Karl Barth, the famous theologian, who was the spiritual leader of the resistance to a Germanized Christianity, wrote a sympathetic letter to the head of the Czech Protestant Church. The shibboleth of allegiance to the nation could now be invoked against dissidents within the German Protestant Church in order to bring them into line with the desired world view.

The instrument lay at hand. The Thuringian Christians, a splinter group of German Christians, whose membership was not confined to Thuringia, had issued a Manifesto for a new order of the Evangelical Church. This "Godesberg Manifesto" (1937) shrewdly makes use of Hitler's decree of February 15, 1937, which called for a new Church constitution while declaring the Führer's own neutrality as to its form and content: let the communicants themselves choose. This was, after all, in accord with the Nazi party platform. Under the mantle of this decree the Thuringian Christians shrewdly appeal to the separation between Church and politics, a sound Lutheran doctrine. The call for "clear principles" is also in accord with the tradition by which the authorities had always regulated the Lutheran Church. But now this call is turned against the Lutheran concept of "faith alone" and infused with a "God-created Volkdom." When Luther had supported "the Powers that be," for they are "ordained of God" (Romans, xiii, 1), the idea of enforcing a Germanic Christianity in the name of clear principles had not occurred to him—or to his successors. In this manner the Thuringian Christians perverted the Lutheran traditional faith in order to bend it toward the Nazi religion.

Hans Kerrl seized this opportunity and attempted to have the declaration adopted as the official order of the Protestant Church. The bishops balked, and he had to make some changes. But in essence he got his way; the opposition was temporarily disorganized by the accusation of treachery toward the Sudeten Germans. The promised Synod never met; no risks of dissent need be taken when legislation by decree was the order of the day. Hitler could maintain his supposed neutrality, and yet attain many of his true aims.

The real face of the leadership is represented by Martin Bormann in his confidential memorandum sent to all party district leaders (Gauleiters) in 1942. Martin Bormann had been the chief of staff of Deputy Führer Rudolf Hess since 1933, and a year before this memorandum was written had advanced to the position of chief of Hitler's own Chancellory. This, then, represents the thoughts of an official who by 1942 was regarded by many as the second most powerful man in the Reich. This memorandum eventually came into the possession of pastors opposed to the Nazis, who tried to spread it abroad in order to show the party's enmity to Christianity. This, in turn, led to a series of arrests as the secret police attempted to keep Bormann's remarks from receiving wide publicity.

In this revealing document Bormann goes far beyond the German Christians. He opposes what he calls "science" to Christianity, and the very use of this word in connection with his ideology clearly shows a belief in the Nazi world view as the final truth. God is present, but as a world-force which presides over the laws of life which the Nazis alone have understood. This non-Christian theism, tied to Nordic blood, was current in Germany long before Bormann wrote down his own thoughts on the matter. It must now be restored, and the catastrophic mistakes of the past centuries, which had put the power of the state into the hands of the Church, must be avoided. The Gauleiters are advised to conquer the influence of the Christian Churches by keeping them divided, encouraging particularism among them—proceeding in the opposite direction from that taken by the medieval Hohenstaufen emperors, who had restored order in Rome.

This plain speaking revealed the real aims of the Nazis, but in practice they maintained a slow pace: holding out the carrot of institutional freedom and, at the same time, using pressure to eliminate any divergence from their world view. The Protestant Church did react, but in a confused way. Only one consistent group in opposition to official policy emerged. The so-called Emergency Association of Pastors (Pfarrernotbund) was founded by Martin Niemöller in 1933. However, increasing pressure upon dissenting ministers led to the formation of a larger organization, the Confessional Church (Bekennende Kirche). It first met in 1934, and from then on throughout the existence of the Third Reich it managed to hold together. It was not a separate organization, but worked within the German Protestant Church to resist the pressure of the state. These men attempted to expose the tactics by which the Third Reich sought to mold Christianity into its own image. They also protested, with some courage, to the authorities themselves.

The example of such a protest which is reproduced here was addressed, in 1937, to Deputy Führer Hess. This particular pastor was arrested for asserting the Jewish origins of Christianity—the very idea which the German Christians had condemned and which the Thuringian Christians promised to fight "in the name of our unsullied Volkdom."

The education of youth was the key here also: to remove them from religious instruction would, in Bormann's terms, remove the influence of the pastors—and therefore of their "swindle"—from future German generations. Once more the Nazis used an indirect approach in order to accomplish their ends. But it was blatant enough to cause the Ecclesiastical Council (Oberkirchenrat) of Württemberg in 1939 to send a letter to all clergymen under its jurisdiction exposing the Nazi pressure tactics which were being used. In view of the pressures described in this open letter, the pathetic inquiry by some mothers whether Hitler's religious neutrality was still valid is significant. Coming as late as 1939, it can serve to illustrate the success of Hitler's two-faced ecclesiastical policy, the kind of faith in the "justice" of the Führer which many Germans retained to the very end. Ideological instruction never won out over religious instruction before the collapse of the Third Reich, but it certainly made important inroads in the schools.

The Catholic Church faced much the same pressure as the Protestants, and their common concern is acknowledged in the letter of the Württemberg Ecclesiastical Council. Though individual priests and even some bishops resisted this pressure and suffered persecution, no resistance group like the Confessional Church developed. Hitler had made a treaty (Concordat) with the Papacy early in the Third Reich

(1933) and this worked to inhibit opposition to the regime. The Concordat was supposed to guarantee non-interference with Church institutions and organizations, including religious instruction in the schools. But it was constantly eroded through Nazi pressure. To the last, the majority of Catholic bishops clung to the view of the Reich as just another type of government, which in return for political support would give security to the Church and respect its rights. This view of Nazi Germany conflicted with the reality of Nazi aims—and the dilemma which resulted is well illustrated by Cardinal Faulhaber's Advent sermons of 1933.

Cardinal Faulhaber (1869-1952), Archbishop of Munich, was an important and powerful figure in the ecclesiastical hierarchy. His aim in these sermons was to defend both the Old Testament and the Jewish origins of Christianity from the Nazi onslaughts. But this defense had to be made in such a way as to avoid a direct attack on Nazi policies. Faulhaber emphasized the Christian tradition which distinguishes between the Jews before the coming of Christ and those that came after. Modern Jews are cut off from Revelation, their Talmud is merely a human document, and the ceremonial laws of the Old Testament have no validity. These remarks, though they may be well founded from the standpoint of Christian theology, must be read against the accelerating policy of excluding Jews from German life. By the time Cardinal Faulhaber preached his sermon, Jews had already been excluded from the professions and public office and were being forced out of the business world as well. Seven months earlier (April 7, 1933) the term "non-Aryan" had been officially defined to mean any person of Jewish parentage or with at least one Jewish grandparent. To be sure, in view of these circumstances the Cardinal's call to reverence the Jewish religion must have sounded a note of courage. But his distinction between the modern Jews and those who lived before Christ, his denial of the divine inspiration of the holy books of the Jews, introduced a more ambivalent note. When, on November 10, 1938, the synagogues went up in flames there was no open protest by any Catholic bishop, but Cardinal Faulhaber, though he remained silent, was said to have sent a truck to rescue some of the religious objects.[2]

In his sermons Cardinal Faulhaber resolves his ambivalence by making a distinction between the natural order and the order of salva-

[2] Guenter Lewy, The Catholic Church and Nazi Germany (New York, 1964), p. 284.

tion—one being the province of the state and the other belonging to the Church. But this traditional doctrine had already failed in the Middle Ages, and it was to do no better in Nazi Germany. National Socialism was, after all, no mere "political" movement but a total way of life; both the natural order and salvation were contained within its world view. A similar distinction between politics and religion had been used by the Thuringian Christians to press for a Germanic Christianity, and it would not prevent the Nazis from encroaching upon the tasks of the Catholic Church.

The actual inroads made by the Nazis are illustrated by one example: the decline of denominational nurses. Though most of the hospitals were not owned by the Churches, Catholic and Protestant nursing orders played a large part in German hospital care. Their destruction would further extend Nazi influence and at the same time would work to the disadvantage of the Churches. The Nazis formed a nursing order of their own, and these women took the oath of allegiance to Adolf Hitler (1936). The Catholic orders were weakened by the fact that nuns were forbidden to assist in operations performed under the Hereditary Health Law (see page 90). The Church came to realize the handicap of this prohibition and in 1940 the nuns were freed from it. Part of the reason given by the Papacy for this ruling shows what was at stake: if the nuns did not assist in the operations, they would be replaced by others (presumably National Socialist nurses).[3] Here is an example which can be added to the tapestry of actions by which National Socialism attempted to penetrate all institutions that tended to lead a separate life.

Had the Nazis won the war their ecclesiastical policies would have gone beyond those of the German Christians, to the utter destruction of both the Protestant and the Catholic Church. Martin Bormann's religion would have triumphed and the children's prayer become the rule—the liturgical element so strong in Nazi culture would have been the only liturgy available.

G.L.M.

[3] Guenter Lewy, *The Catholic Church and Nazi Germany*, p. 263.

The Führer Bequeathed to Me by the Lord

The new God, in which German youth were to believe, manifests himself in these "invocations" which children in Cologne, local branch Reinau, were instructed to recite at the NSV children's lunch program:

Before Meals:

> Führer, my Führer, bequeathed to me by the Lord,
> Protect and preserve me as long as I live!
> Thou hast rescued Germany from deepest distress,
> I thank thee today for my daily bread.
> Abideth thou long with me, forsaketh me not,
> Führer, my Führer, my faith and my light!
> *Heil, mein Führer!*

After Meals:

> Thank thee for this bountiful meal,
> Protector of youth and friend of the aged!
> I know thou hast cares, but worry not,
> I am with thee by day and by night.
> Lie thy head in my lap,
> Be assured, my Führer, that thou art great.
> *Heil, mein Führer!*

From Johann Neuhäusler, *Kreuz und Hakenkreuz: Der Kampf des Nationalsozialismus gegen die katholische Kirche und der kirchliche Widerstand* (Munich: Verlag Katholische Kirche Bayerns, 1946), p. 251.

Christ in the Community of Blood and Fate

Guidelines for the Movement of German Christians (National Church Movement) in Thuringia (1933)

1. We "German Christians" believe in our Saviour, Jesus Christ, in the power of His cross, and in His resurrection. The life and death of

Jesus teaches us that the way of struggle is also the way of love and
the way of life.

Through God's creation we have been put directly into the community of blood and fate of the German people and as the bearers of
this fate we are responsible for its future. Germany is our task, Christ
our strength!

2. The source and confirmation of our faith are God's Revelation
in the Bible and the witness borne to the faith by the Fathers. The
New Testament is to us the holy attestation of the Saviour, our Lord,
and of His Father's Kingdom.

The Old Testament is an example of divine education of a people.
For our faith, it is of value to the extent to which it permits us to
understand our Saviour's life, cross, and resurrection.

3. As with every people, the eternal God also created a Law for our
people especially suited to its racial character. It acquired form in the
Führer Adolf Hitler and in the National Socialist state which he
formed.

This Law speaks to us in the history of our people, born of our
blood and soil. Loyalty to this Law demands from us the struggle for
honor and freedom.

4. The way to the fulfillment of this German Law is through the
German community of the faithful. In it Christ, the Lord, rules as
grace and forgiveness. Here burns the fire of the holy willingness to
sacrifice. In it alone does the Saviour meet the German people and
bequeath to it the gift of a strong faith. It is from these communities
of German Christians that the "German Christian National Church"
must rise in the National Socialist state of Adolf Hitler, embracing
the whole people.

One People! — One God! — One Reich! — One Church!

From *Kirchliches Jahrbuch für die evangelische Kirche in
Deutschland, 1933-1944*, edited by Joachim Beckmann
(Gütersloh: C. Bertelsmann Verlag, 1948), pp. 32-33.

The Task of Proclaiming Christ among the German People

Principles for a New Order of the Evangelical Church in Keeping with the Needs of the Present Time

Through a decree of the Führer and Reich Chancellor, issued on February 15, 1937, it has been ordained that the Church, in full freedom and according to the decision of the communicants themselves, shall provide itself with a new constitution and thereby with a new order.

Clear principles are required to assure the fruitful preparation and execution of a general synod in the form of an Evangelical Church Congress of Greater Germany.

Such principles are:

1. The Evangelical Church has learned from Martin Luther to distinguish sharply between the realms of reason and faith, politics and religion, state and Church.

The National Socialist world view is the Volkish-political doctrine which determines and forms the German man. And as such it is also binding upon German Christians. The Evangelical Church honors a divinely established order in the state and demands from its members a total service in this order.

2. The Gospel applies to all people and all times. The Evangelical Church, however, has learned from Martin Luther that true Christian faith can powerfully unfold only within a God-created Volkdom. We, therefore, decisively reject the political universalism of Rome and international Protestantism.

3. The National Socialist philosophy fights relentlessly against the political and intellectual influence of the Jewish race on the life of our Volk. In obedience to the divine order of creation, the Evangelical Church affirms its responsibility to preserve the purity of our Volkdom.

Beyond that, in the realm of faith, there is no sharper contrast than that between the message of Christ and the Jewish religion with its sterile legalism and its hope for a political Messiah.

4. The Evangelical Church has the task of proclaiming the message

of the revelation of God in Jesus Christ among the German people in the manner in which the great Reformers, especially Martin Luther, have taught us to understand it.

5. The question whether it is possible to reach a unanimous agreement on this divine message can be solved only if the existing tensions within German Protestantism are borne with a powerful vivifying spirit and if the necessary dialogue is continued in a spirit of truth and conciliation. Therefore, a clear order must be created which assures the preaching of the Gospel and fully provides for the spiritual needs of all members of the Church.

(1937)

From *Kirchliches Jahrbuch für die evangelische Kirche in Deutschland, 1933-1944*, pp. 299-300.

National Socialist and Christian Concepts Are Incompatible
MARTIN BORMANN

National Socialist and Christian concepts are incompatible. The Christian Churches build upon the ignorance of men and strive to keep large portions of the people in ignorance because only in this way can the Christian Churches maintain their power. On the other hand, National Socialism is based on scientific foundations. Christianity's immutable principles, which were laid down almost two thousand years ago, have increasingly stiffened into life-alien dogmas. National Socialism, however, if it wants to fulfill its task further, must always guide itself according to the newest data of scientific researches.

The Christian Churches have long been aware that exact scientific knowledge poses a threat to their existence. Therefore, by means of such pseudo-sciences as theology, they take great pains to suppress or falsify scientific research. Our National Socialist world view stands on a much higher level than the concepts of Christianity, which in their essentials were taken over from Judaism. For this reason, too, we can do without Christianity.

No one would know anything about Christianity if pastors had not crammed it down his throat in his childhood. The so-called loving God by no means reveals the knowledge of His existence to young people, but amazingly enough, and despite His omnipotence, He leaves this to the efforts of a pastor. When in the future our youth no longer hear anything about this Christianity, whose doctrine is far below our own, Christianity will automatically disappear.

It is also astonishing that prior to our own era nothing was known to mankind about this Christian God and even since then the great majority of the inhabitants of our earth have known nothing about Christianity. Because of this, according to the arrogant Christian dogma, they are damned from the outset.

When we National Socialists speak of a belief in God,[1] by God we do not understand, as do naïve Christians and their clerical beneficiaries, a manlike being who is sitting around in some corner of the spheres. Rather, we must open the eyes of mankind to the fact that in addition to our unimportant Earth there exist countless other bodies in the universe, many of them surrounded, like the sun, by planets and these again by smaller bodies, the moons. The force which moves all these bodies in the universe, in accordance with natural law, is what we call the Almighty or God. The assertion that this world-force can worry about the fate of every individual, every bacillus on earth, and that it can be influenced by so-called prayer or other astonishing things, is based either on a suitable dose of naïveté or on outright commercial effrontery.

In contrast, we National Socialists call upon ourselves to live as naturally as possible—that is, in keeping with the laws of life. The more thoroughly we know and attend to the laws of nature and life, the more we adhere to them, the more do we correspond to the will of the Almighty. The deeper our insight into the will of the Almighty, the greater will be our success.

It follows from the incompatibility of National Socialist and Christian concepts that we must oppose any strengthening of existing Christian denominations and must refuse to give them any assistance. We can make no differentiation between the various Christian confessions. That is also why the idea of establishing an Evangelical Reich Church by gathering together the various Evangelical Church bodies has to be finally abandoned. For the Evangelical Church op-

[1] *Gottgläubigkeit*: non-Christian theism.

poses us with the same hostility as the Catholic Church. Any strengthening of the Evangelical Church would merely work against us.

It was a mistake of historical consequence for the German emperors in the Middle Ages to take it upon themselves again and again to establish order at the Vatican in Rome. It is indeed a mistake that we Germans are all too often prone to make, namely, to establish order where our own interests would call for disunity and division. The House of Hohenstaufen should have had the greatest interest in the fragmentation of ecclesiastical power. From the point of view of the German Reich it would have been highly profitable if there had not been only one Pope, but at least two or, better, even more Popes to fight among themselves. Instead, the German emperors and especially those of the House of Hohenstaufen always worked for ecclesiastical order and aided one Pope to gain power over his competitors, with the result that, as soon as the Pope was strong enough, the emperors got it in the neck from their "own" Pope. Yet, to strengthen its own power position the Church has always exploited, and encouraged to the best of its abilities, the particularism of princes and later on that of political parties.

In earlier generations, the leadership of the people lay exclusively in the hands of the Church. The state limited itself to passing laws and regulations and above all to the task of administration. The actual leadership of the people was not vested in the state, but in the Church, which, through the agency of the pastor, exercised the strongest influence over the lives of individuals, families, and the community as a whole. Anything that was not to the liking of the Church was suppressed with unexampled ruthlessness. For centuries the state had to borrow from the influence of the Church through the most varied donations. The Church alone decided whether it would aid the state or range itself against it. The state was fully dependent on the assistance of the Church. The struggles of the German emperors against the Pope, in the Middle Ages and in modern times, were always bound to fail, since it was not the emperor but the Church that exercised leadership over the people.

This ideological dependence of the state on the Church, and the fact that the state had relinquished the leadership of the people, eventually became so obvious that no one dared seriously to question it. Not to take this indisputable fact into consideration was regarded as the acme of political stupidity—up to the time of the [Nazi] seizure of power.

For the first time in German history, the Führer consciously has the leadership of the people entirely in his own hands. With the party, its subordinate apparatus, and the associations connected with it, the Führer wrought for himself and the German Reich leadership an instrument that made him entirely independent of the Church. Any influence that would impair or damage the leadership of the people exercised by the Führer with the aid of the NSDAP has to be eliminated. To an ever increasing degree the people must be wrested from Churches and their agents, the pastors. Obviously, the Churches, from their standpoint, will and must defend themselves against this loss of power. But never again must the Church regain an influence in the leadership of the people. This must absolutely and finally be broken.

Only the Reich leadership, together with the party and the organs and associations connected with it, has a right to lead the people. Just as the harmful influence of astrologists, soothsayers, and other swindlers has been suppressed by the state, so it must be made absolutely impossible for the Church to exercise its old influence. Only after this has been done can the state leadership exert full influence over all racial comrades. Only then will the future of Reich and Volk be secured for all time.

We would be repeating the catastrophic mistakes of past centuries if after our comprehension of the ideological hostility of all Christian denominations we were now in any manner whatever to contribute to the strengthening of the various Churches. The interest of the Reich does not lie in overcoming ecclesiastical particularism but, rather, in maintaining and strengthening it.

M. Bormann
Reich Leader

(1942)

From *Kirchliches Jahrbuch für die evangelische Kirche in Deutschland, 1933-1944*, pp. 470-472.

The Epistle of St. Paul Is in Error

Memorandum from the Confessional Church

In submitting the following facts [of persecution] as they have been reported to us, we would like to address this question to you, Herr Reichminister [Rudolf Hess]: In your opinion, how long will it be possible to maintain domestic peace among our people, among whom doubtless many racial comrades are convinced members of the Christian Church and whose government, on the basis of Article 24 of its party platform, claims to extend protection to positive Christianity, if state officials openly impede and persecute Christianity and the Church? The following will show what we mean.

On Saturday, February 27—that is, on a day which was clearly within the purview of the Führer's decree on choice[1]—Pastor Zedlacher in Hamburg, an Austrian citizen, was interrogated by the Gestapo in connection with a Bible class he had conducted on February 24, 1937. We must call it utterly unworthy of a German official that the material for this interrogation was procured by a professional informer who managed by stealth to gain entrance to the Bible class. We must, furthermore, designate as intolerable and a mockery the fact that, contrary to all assurances that the freedom of preaching would be inviolable, Zedlacher was specifically criticized for using Paul's Epistle to the Romans, Verse 11, as a text for his lesson. It is indisputably asserted in the Epistle to the Romans, Verse 11, that the choice of Israel by God is unalterable. Zedlacher was only acting in accordance with his duties as a Bible teacher when he passed on to his pupils what is written in the Bible. The same applies to the assertions for which the Gestapo criticized Zedlacher—namely, that Jesus was not an Aryan but a Jew, and that despite Reichminister Kerrl's[2] contrary opinion, it cannot be denied that Christ's sonship from God is the fundamental dogma of Christianity from the standpoint of a confessing evangelical Christianity. . . .

More monstrous even than his interrogation was the treatment to which Zedlacher was exposed during the time he spent in protective custody. How can responsible state officials justify the fact that in the

---

[1] This decree made religious instruction in schools a voluntary matter.
[2] Hans Kerrl, Minister of Ecclesiastical Affairs.

concentration camp an official of the Church was called a Jew-lover and a Jew-slave, and was told that the best thing would be to save mankind from the likes of him? How can the protectors of positive Christianity account for the fact that a helpless prisoner was mocked and ridiculed by SS troopers on duty because he still happened to believe in the Bible, and was told that they would soon cure him of his piety? One of these SS men—a guard paid by the state—even had the insolence to ask the prisoner: "Would you like me to give your greetings to your God, Jehova? He's coming to visit us today." When Zedlacher answered that this would not be necessary and that they should not mock the Lord, he was rudely barked at and ordered not to be so impertinent. Seemingly [they said] he did not know where he was, and they warned him that if he said just one more word, he would get a severe beating and be sentenced to five days' solitary confinement on bread and water.

We also see a brutal mockery of Christian belief in the fact that Zedlacher was asked whether he thought the Jew Jesus would help him escape from the concentration camp and from the treatment he was receiving from the guards. We shall spare ourselves the recital of further revolting details, but in this connection we must point out one thing:

To us the deep significance of Zedlacher's reports lies not alone in the fact that they establish how grossly the Christian faith can be mocked and persecuted within the framework of the state, but also in that they force upon our consciousness the renewed awareness that the very existence of concentration camps constitutes a heavy burden for the Christian conscience. Zedlacher's release from the concentration camp, upon the intervention of the Austrian Consul-General, can by no means be considered a reparation for the wrong done, since Zedlacher was expelled from the territories of the Reich and left Hamburg on March 31, 1937, after, by the way, being bid farewell by a large circle of the people among whom he worked.

(1937)

From *Deutsche Kirchendokumente: Die Haltung der Bekennenden Kirche im dritten Reich*, compiled by W. Jannasch (Zollikon-Zurich: Evangelischer Verlag A.G., 1946), pp. 44-47.

To Capture Youth

Stuttgart, June 19, 1939

To: All Deanery Offices
Subject: Ideological Instruction Courses

The attempt by both school authorities and special organizations to induce Evangelical parents in Württemberg to remove their children from classes in religious instruction in school and to register them in so-called classes in ideological instruction, continues even though, according to reports received by us, the actions of parents have clearly indicated how they feel about the question.

In a secondary school for boys, though the parents were openly solicited, only 17 pupils out of 250 registered for the ideological instruction course; in a girls' secondary school, the total was 23 students out of a total of 600. In both cases, the overwhelming majority of parents clung tenaciously to their right to Evangelical or Catholic instruction for their children. It appears necessary to keep our parishes constantly informed of these developments and to provide them with detailed information on the methods by which ideological instruction in the schools of Württemberg is to be furthered.

In one parish in Lower Württemberg, the parents had several months ago declared themselves strongly in favor of regular special children's religious services, and were successful in their demands. Now these same parents with equal decisiveness have rejected the ideological instruction classes. The school principal gave each of the children who had not yet been registered for the ideological instruction classes a mimeographed notice to take home to his parents, dated May 17, 1939, which read as follows:

Your child is to attend a Recreation Camp at —— for the period from —— to ——. According to the latest regulations, this vacation will depend on whether you profess the world view of the Führer and, accordingly, send your child to the government-sponsored National Socialist ideological instruction class. As you have not done so, you are herewith requested to register your child for the ideological instruction. In case you do not wish to do so, please inform us accordingly by a short, written notice.

The Principal

In C., the children of an elementary-school class were told that they had to choose between ideological and religious instruction. They would no longer be graded in religious instruction; instead, only ideological instruction would be entered in their annual progress reports. If any of them planned to attend a higher school later, they would no longer be examined in religion, but only in ideology. Hence they could draw their own conclusions as to what they had to do.

In a municipality in the district of L., the school principal informed the children that their parents would soon be called upon to send them to ideological instruction classes. On May 10, 1939, the parents held a meeting, attended by about 20 men and 150 women, which categorically rejected this demand.

At the same time about 50 fathers were suddenly summoned to the Town Hall without being told why. There they were addressed first by the mayor, then by the local group leader, and finally by the senior master. Then a preprinted form was read to them and they were asked to sign it. All the fathers, with the exception of three or four, did so. It was obvious that the signatures were largely motivated by the senior master's disclosure that ideological instruction was bound to come anyhow and it would therefore be better to sign now.

The event produced tremendous agitation in the community. On the following day, groups of aroused citizens stood in the streets until late at night and discussed the problem of ideological instruction in the schools. Numerous women tearfully implored their husbands to withdraw their children's registration for ideological instruction; again and again one heard the question whether mothers no longer had any rights over their children and whether the Führer's assurance that everyone could seek salvation in his own fashion was still valid. In the morning, before school, some mothers sent their children to their fathers to beg them to withhold or recall their registration for ideological instruction. These requests were all the more justified in view of the fact that the fathers had had to register their decision at the Town Hall within less than half an hour, without being able to form a judgment as to the consequences of their signatures. The distress of consciences and the agitation of the community were markedly great.

In a community near H., recruitment for the ideological instruction was carried out under especially overt pressure and threats. As was reported from the community, a teacher said to a girl in the seventh grade: "If you don't take part in the ideological instruction class, I'll make you read the Bible until you're blue in the face." To another child the teacher said: "What does your father do?" "He's a letter-carrier." "If he doesn't sign, he'll see what will happen; he'll have to become a street-sweeper." The school principal himself flatly told children who arrived without the desired signature: "This stuff in the Bible about the last being the first no longer applies." In this connection, the fathers and mothers, numbering about 100, who had not withdrawn their children from the religious instruction class were invited to a parents' meeting at the schoolhouse on April 28, 1939. The local Evangelical pastor, himself the father of an elementary-school child, was not invited. When he came nevertheless, on the basis of his right as a father, it was most sharply pointed out to him and his wife that he had no right to enter the schoolhouse, that he would be charged with trespass, and that he would only disturb the unanimity of the meeting. Several parishioners witnessed this treatment of their pastor. The evening, therefore, was a very stormy one. It had been planned not to allow any discussion from the floor. The principal's speech, interrupted by many excited catcalls, was followed by sharp and loud protests. The attacks against the clergy were decisively and solidly rejected. The excitement reached new heights when the flying police squad of H. was called to the scene. It could establish only that the parents had vigorously rejected this attempted unprecedented pressure on their consciences. The meeting broke up and the school principal excused himself to a few of those who had remained behind: the hard words that had been exchanged should be forgotten on both sides, since it concerned, in any case, a matter of a voluntary character.

At a meeting on May 4, 47 Evangelical parents and guardians signed and sent the following letter to the Württemberg Minister of Religion:

> For several days the parents of children of school age of this locality have been pressured by teachers to declare their agreement with the introduction of ideological instruction in the classroom. The parents most decisively reject this coercion and demand full freedom of conscience as well as the cessation of the collection of signatures under pressure.
>
> Heil Hitler!

In T., the boys' seventh-grade class had its so-called ideological instruction on April 24, 1939, from 9:30 to 10:30, that is, at a time fully within the regular school schedule. Out of 32 pupils, only 5 attended.

The other 27 were gathered in another room for a spelling lesson and were given such a difficult dictation that the best pupil made seven mistakes, the lowest forty-three. As punishment for this allegedly poor performance, all the pupils were kept in school the next day from 2 to 4 o'clock, and several of them even until 4:30. Complaints were answered by the principal with "This is perfectly in order."

In A., the principal of a secondary school told a father who asked for information on the ideological instruction course: "You know that I myself left the Church and you know my position toward Christianity. I shall introduce ideological instruction along these lines. There are to be no polemics, but the various religious faiths will naturally be dealt with in the upper grades."

When he asked whether it was not true that the Reich Ministry of Education had taken a different position on the problem of ideological instruction and had in fact issued contrary regulations, the father was told: "The regulations of the Reich Ministry of Education are not binding for Württemberg; the official publications of the Reich Ministry are not generally read and only this or that regulation which is important is given any attention here."

Referring to the traditional pre-confirmation instructions, the school principal continued: "Those who attend the ideological instruction could not also attend the confirmation classes." He had told his students in the ideological instruction class that he could not understand why any of them would want to be confirmed anyway. In some places a special celebration was to take place after the fourth grade, but so far there were no general regulations about this.

He denied that any pressure would be exerted to secure registrations for the ideological instruction classes. When told that some teachers had actually used high-pressure tactics, the principal made no answer.

In a community in Franconia, the principal of the two-grade elementary school distributed a form letter to his pupils on Saturday, May 20, at noon, which was to be signed by their parents and returned on the next day, Sunday, May 21, at noon. The form letter contained the well-known text:

The ideological disputations of our time have already led to numerous withdrawals of children from religious instruction and are bound to lead to more. For all pupils who, at the request of their parents, no longer wish to attend religious instruction in school, the Minister of Religion has instituted classes in ideological instruction. A course in ideological instruction has also been initiated at the elementary school in ——. Those desirous of further information are referred to the school principal, who will also accept registrations.

In contrast to similar form letters distributed in other communities, this one carried the notation: "signed Mergenthaler."

This circumstance greatly depressed parents who were economically dependent upon him and caused immeasurable agitation among the independent farmers. On Ascension Day, at a parents' meeting, the school principal propagandized for ideological instruction: From now on, every child simply had to participate in it; if on top of this children were also to take two hours of religious instruction in school and two more hours of denominational instruction from their local pastor, this would be too much for them. Therefore, the parents should take their children out of the religious instruction class at school. The end result was that the school principal had only two registrations for the ideological instruction class—both from his own children.

On Tuesday, May 23, at a meeting of the local school board, the principal tried again to push through the introduction of ideological instruction. He had invited larger numbers of people to the board session. At the first offensive remark about the local pastor, who was present, a storm broke loose against the school principal. He was shouted down. One member of the school board jumped at him, his fists waving, and uttered unmistakable threats. The school principal was told that the form letter with the notation "signed Mergenthaler" was a matter for the courts. The principal from now on should adhere strictly to the legal regulations, which recognized the wishes of the parents as the only criteria for the religious instruction of their children. The principal was told that he was creating chaos in the whole community and was deceiving the people. Ever since he had arrived the whole town had experienced nothing but strife and turmoil; the community had built several schoolhouses at great sacrifice and now he had driven the pastor from the school and declared that he was no longer to be allowed to teach there. This was a grievous offense against the community.

"We would like to see whether we are no longer the masters of the school buildings which we have built with our money!" There were loud shouts of acclaim when it was demanded that the pastor be reinstated as religious instructor in the school. The principal declared that the decision in this matter was not his to make, since it had to be referred to higher authorities. This caused a renewed uproar.

The principal closed his speech with the request that the meeting should arrange a peaceful settlement in the interests of the children. Thereupon the local pastor said that a peaceful settlement could most easily be achieved by permitting him to resume his religious teaching at the school, just as he had done the previous school year. The principal could rest assured that this would restore harmony in the community and that no further difficulties would be raised. All present agreed that this was the only solution which they could advise the principal to take, in his own personal interest. With that the meeting came to an end.

In a number of municipalities, standard-bearers of the Hitler Youth ordered their subordinates to see to it that relatives of Hitler Youth members withdrew from religious instruction classes and applied for ideological instruction within three weeks.

By such procedures a matter that is one of the inalienable rights of parents is withdrawn from the free decision of the parents and propelled toward an anti-Christian solution, despite all official utterances to the contrary.

These matters should, in suitable form, be brought to the attention of all parishes. All rectories are requested, if they have not done so already, to report by July 1 on the methods used and the results attained in all campaigns for ideological instruction classes in the schools. Attention should be given to particular events, for example, to remarks concerning the future education and occupational prospects of children who have not withdrawn from their religious instruction classes; whether there have been threats to withhold child support payments from some families,[1] or whether means of economic pressure have been employed.

WURM[2]

From *Kirchliches Jahrbuch für die evangelische Kirche in Deutschland, 1933-1944,* pp. 343-347.

[1] Child support payments were granted to families with more than three children.
[2] Theophil Wurm (1868-1953), Protestant Bishop of Württemberg, was one of the leaders of the Confessional Church (Bekennende Kirche).

Judaism, Christianity, and Germany
CARDINAL FAULHABER

Already in the year 1899, on the occasion of an anti-Semitic demonstration at Hamburg, and simultaneously in Chamberlain's book *The
Foundations of the Nineteenth Century*,[1] a demand was raised for
the total separation of Judaism from Christianity, and for the complete elimination from Christianity of all Jewish elements. Nearly two
decades later these ideas were once more propagated in such books as
The Sin Against Blood, The Great Fraud, and *The False God*.[2] Judaism and Christianity, it was maintained, were incompatible; the Jewish Bible must be replaced by a German Bible; Martin Luther had
done only half his work, for in his Bible he had included the Scriptures of the Old Testament. Today these single voices have swelled
together into a chorus: Away with the Old Testament! A Christianity
which still clings to the Old Testament is a Jewish religion, irreconcil-
able with the spirit of the German people. Children at school must no
longer be bothered with Bible stories of Joseph the Egyptian or the
ancient Moses. . . . Given the present general attitude of mind, this
outcry is well calculated to shake the foundations of the faith in the
souls of the German people.

Even the Person of Christ is not spared by this religious revolution.
Some have indeed tried to save Him with a forged birth certificate,
and have said that He was not a Jew at all but an Aryan, because there
were Aryans among the inhabitants of Galilee. But so long as historical sources count for more than surmise, there can be no doubt about
the fact. The first chapter of the first gospel gives us the genealogy of
Jesus, with the title: "The book of the generation of Jesus Christ, the
Son of David, the son of Abraham." Similarly, the Epistle to the Romans attests the origin of Jesus from the seed of David (i, 4). Un-
doubtedly the Galileans, a borderland people, were of mixed origin.
But Christ was not born in Galilee; He was born in Bethlehem, the

[1] Houston Stewart Chamberlain's *Die Grundlagen des XIX. Jahrhunderts* (1899)
was one of the most influential books, not only for National Socialism but for
German nationalism in general.
[2] These were anti-Christian tracts, of which the most famous was Artur Dinter's
Die Sünde wider das Blut (1918). This novel praised Aryan purity and saw the
Jews as the incarnation of evil.

city of David, in the land of the tribe of Juda, and officially He was
entered in the register as a descendant of David. And so others now
take up the cry: Then we must renounce Him, if He was a Jew—and
the scene of the Gospel is re-enacted: "They thrust Him out of the
city and brought Him to the brow of the hill whereon their city was
built, that they might cast Him down headlong" (Luke iv, 29).
"Again they took up stones to stone Him" (John x, 31).

When such voices are raised, when such movements are afoot, the
bishop cannot remain silent. When racial research, in itself not a religious matter, makes war upon religion and attacks the foundations of
Christianity; when antagonism to the Jews of the present day is extended to the sacred books of the Old Testament and Christianity is
condemned because it has relations of origin with pre-Christian Judaism; when stones are cast at the Person of our Lord and Saviour, and
this in the very year in which we are celebrating the centenary of His
work of Redemption, then the bishop cannot remain silent. And
therefore I preach these Advent sermons on the Old Testament and
its fulfillment in Christianity.

On this subject I may claim to speak as a specialist, having spent
eleven years of my life lecturing on these questions in the University
of Würzburg, and having held the chair of Old Testament Scripture
in the University of Strassburg. . . .

So that I may be perfectly clear and preclude any possible misunderstanding, let me begin by making three distinctions. We must
first distinguish between the people of Israel before and after the
death of Christ. Before the death of Christ during the period between
the calling of Abraham and the fullness of time, the people of Israel
were the vehicle of Divine Revelation. The Spirit of God raised up
and enlightened men who by the law, the Mosaic Torah, regulated
their religious and civil life, by the Psalms provided them with a
prayer book for family devotion and a hymn book for the public liturgy, by the Sapiential books taught them how to conduct their lives,
and as prophets awakened the conscience of the nation with the living
word. It is only with this Israel of the early biblical period that I shall
deal in my Advent sermons.

After the death of Christ, Israel was dismissed from the service of
Revelation. She had not known the time of her visitation. She had
repudiated and rejected the Lord's Anointed, had driven Him out of
the city and nailed Him to the Cross. Then the veil of the Temple

was rent, and with it the covenant between the Lord and His people. The daughters of Sion received the bill of divorce, and from that time forth Assuerus wanders, forever restless, over the face of the earth. Even after the death of Christ the Jews are still a "mystery," as St. Paul says (Rom. xi, 25); and one day, at the end of time, for them too the hour of grace will strike (Rom. xi, 26). But—I repeat—in these Advent sermons I am speaking only of pre-Christian Judaism.

In the second place we must distinguish between the Scriptures of the Old Testament on the one hand and the Talmudic writings of post-Christian Judaism on the other, whether these be glosses and commentaries on the biblical text or separate religious works; I mean especially the Talmud, the Mischna, and the medieval code of laws, Schulchan Arukh. The Talmudic writings are the work of man; they were not prompted by the Spirit of God. It is only the sacred writings of pre-Christian Judaism, not the Talmud, that the Church of the New Testament has accepted as her inheritance.

Thirdly, we must distinguish in the Old Testament Bible itself between what had only transitory value and what had permanent value. The long genealogies had value in ancient times, but their value was not permanent; similarly the numerous regulations for the ancient sacrifices and ceremonial cleansings. For the purpose of our subject we are concerned only with those religious, ethical, and social values of the Old Testament which remain as values also for Christianity. . . .

Let us venerate the Scriptures of the Old Testament! We do not set the Old Testament and the New on the same level. The Sacred Scriptures of the New Testament, the Gospels, the Acts of the Apostles, the Epistles, and the Apocalypse must hold the place of honor. But the Scriptures of the Old Testament are also inspired, and therefore they are sacred books, precious stones for the building of God's kingdom, priceless values for our religious guidance. And therefore the Church has stretched forth her protecting hand over the Scriptures of the Old Testament; she has gathered together the forty-five books of the Old Testament and the twenty-seven books of the New into one volume, and she has used the text of the Old Testament also in her liturgy. By accepting these books Christianity does not become a Jewish religion. These books were not composed by Jews; they are inspired by the Holy Ghost, and therefore they are the word of God, they are God's books. The writers of them were God's pencils, the Psalm-singers were harps in the hand of God, the prophets

were announcers of God's revelation. It is for this reason that the
Scriptures of the Old Testament are worthy of credence and veneration for all time. Antagonism to the Jews of today must not be extended to the books of pre-Christian Judaism.

In the New Testament, in the Epistle to the Hebrews (ch. 11),
Abel, Enoch, and other figures of Old Testament history are held up
as models of faith to be imitated by Christians. St. Francis of Assisi
once picked up a scrap of paper from the ground. "Let no man tread
this under foot," he said, "for the name of God can be written
thereon." Let no man trample under foot the Sacred Scriptures of the
Old Testament; for the name of God is written there. Cardinal Man-
ning once said to the Jews: "I should not understand my own religion, had I no reverence for yours."

Let us venerate the Scriptures of the Old Testament! And let us
not allow Bible history to be abolished in our schools! These biblical
stories have a great educational value in the school, so long as they are
well selected and told in attractive language, and if the teacher knows
how to make them live.

Side by side with the Bible there is a second source of revelation,
the Tradition of the Church. Side by side with the Book stands the
living teacher, the authority of the Church. Beside the good pasture
stands the good shepherd, beside the precious materials for the building stands the good architect. Therefore the anti-Moses movement
does not affect us Catholics so vitally as our separated brethren, who
regard the Bible as the sole foundation of their faith. To these separated brethren we stretch forth our hand to make common cause with
them in defense of the sacred books of the Old Testament, so that we
may save them for the German nation and preserve this precious
treasury of doctrine for the Christian schools. . . .

From the Church's point of view there is no objection whatever to
racial research and race culture. Nor is there any objection to the
endeavor to keep the national characteristics of a people as far as possible pure and unadulterated, and to foster their national spirit by
emphasis upon the common ties of blood which unite them. From
the Church's point of view we must make only three conditions:
First, love of one's own race must not lead to the hatred of other
nations. Secondly, the individual must never consider himself freed
from the obligation of nourishing his own soul by the persevering use
of the means of grace which the Church provides. The young man

who is always hearing about the blessedness of his own race is apt too easily to conceive that he is no longer bound by duties to God and His Church, duties of humility and chastity. Thirdly, race culture must not assume an attitude of hostility to Christianity. What are we to say of the monstrous contention that Christianity has corrupted the German race, that Christianity—especially because it is burdened with Old Testament ideas—is not adapted to the genius of the nation, and that therefore it is an obstacle in the way of the national consciousness?

What is the relation of Christianity to the German race? Race and Christianity are not mutually opposed, but they do belong to different orders. Race is of the natural order; Christianity is a revealed religion and therefore of the supernatural order. Race means union with the nation; Christianity means primarily union with God. Race is nationally inclusive and exclusive; Christianity is a world-wide message of salvation for all nations. The concepts of revelation and redemption, of supernature and grace must not be watered down. The fourth gospel makes a neat distinction between those who are born of blood and those who are born of God (John i, 13). Christ also clearly distinguished between what flesh and blood had revealed and what was revealed by the Father in Heaven (Matt. xvi, 17 foll.). We are Christians not because we are born of Christian parents; we are Christians because after our birth we were reborn and made a new creature by baptism in Christ (2 Cor. xv, 17).

No nation ever insisted more on race and ties of blood than the Israelites of the Old Testament. But in the fullness of time the dogma of race was eclipsed by the dogma of faith. Around the cradle of Bethlehem there were Jews and pagans, shepherds from the land of Juda and wise men from the East. In the kingdom of this Child, according to the words of His Apostle, "there is no distinction of the Jew and the Greek, for the same is Lord over all" (Rom. x, 12).

What is the relation of Christianity to the German race? The Christian, so long as he observes the above conditions, is not forbidden to stand up for his race and for its rights. It is possible, therefore, without divided allegiance, to be an upright German and at the same time an upright Christian. Hence there is no need to turn our backs upon Christianity and to set up a Nordic or Germanic religion, in order to profess our nationality. But we must never forget: we are not redeemed with German blood. We are redeemed with the Precious Blood of our crucified Lord (1 Pet. i, 9). There is no other name and no other blood under Heaven, in which we can be saved, but the name and the blood of Christ.

> From His Eminence Cardinal Faulhaber, *Judaism, Christianity, and Germany: Advent Sermons Preached in St. Michael's, Munich, in 1933*, translated by Rev. George D. Smith (London: Burns, Oates & Washbourne, Ltd., 1934), pp. 1-6, 13-16, 107-110. (Reprinted by permission of the Macmillan Company, New York. Copyright 1934 by the Macmillan Company; and Burns, Oates & Washbourne, Ltd., British Commonwealth copyright.)

Nurses and Philosophy

For the first time, National Socialist nurses have taken the oath of allegiance to the Führer and Reich Chancellor in the Cologne-Aachen district, according to a report by the National Socialist Party Press Service. District Leader Grohé, who administered the oath in the presence of Reich Women Leader Scholtz-Klink and District Superintendent Hilgenfeldt, explained why the formation of National Socialist Sisterhoods had become necessary.

The number of denominational nurses had fallen off to such an extent that there was no longer any guarantee for efficient nursing service in the future. In addition the future would present tasks which could properly be performed only by men and women fully imbued with the philosophical attitude of National Socialism. The bishops had forbidden nuns working as nurses to assist in the case of certain operations, in consequence of which in the interest of the patients the formation of National Socialist Sisterhoods became an unconditional necessity.

> From the *Frankfurter Zeitung*, Oct. 6, 1936. (Wiener Library Clipping Collection.)

8

The Key: Education of Youth

NAZISM, like any revolutionary movement, attempted to capture the new generation and rally it to the cause. The movement stressed youth, at the expense of the older generation, which might still harbor vestiges of liberalism or even socialism. Education, therefore, can show us the principal application of the cultural impetus within the Third Reich. The Nazis did make changes in the school system, though the federal structure of the Reich made this difficult at first. Until the individual states were abolished, Prussia was the laboratory for much of this change. High schools specializing in natural science and a non-classical curriculum were put on the same footing as the ancient and prestigious humanistic *Gymnasia*. The Nazis attempted to unify the school system, as they "meshed the gears" of all other activities in the Third Reich.

As a matter of fact, changes in curriculum brought all schools closer together. Compulsory training in racial biology (see page 79) and a greater emphasis on German history and literature meant that less time could be spent on other subjects, such as ancient languages and even science. The former were, of course, subjects with a high ideological content. Moreover, at least five hours a day were set aside for physical education, because of its value in building character and discipline as well as for future military usefulness. A valiant attempt was

263

made to give girls quite a different education, in accordance with the Nazi ideal of womanhood (see page 39). They were to be excluded from subjects required for admission to a university, for the woman belonged in the home.

It is difficult to say just how successful the Nazi reshaping of education proved to be in practice. It must have varied greatly from school to school and depended a great deal on individual teachers and principals. For example, until March 1, 1938, the sifting of textbooks for schools was handled in a haphazard way; at times the individual schools did their own censoring. Only after that date did a centralized censorship come into existence, to be exercised by a Nazi party·commission in collaboration with the Ministry of Education. Yet the textbooks were increasingly National Socialist, the teachers were regimented, and, perhaps most important of all, some of the youth responded with great enthusiasm.

Evidence for the enthusiasm of the youth comes to us from all sides. The examples we have chosen should be especially telling, for they were written by opponents of the regime. Inge Scholl tells of herself, her brother and sister, who founded a resistance group among their fellow students at the University of Munich which was called "The White Rose." Sophie and Hans Scholl paid dearly for their convictions—both were executed in 1943. Yet initially the Scholl youngsters were enthusiastic supporters of the Nazi movement and the reasons for their emotional commitment, given in the document, are typical of those held by many of the young people. The description of Hans's early disillusionment is less typical, but it does show how the Nazis attempted to control this youthful enthusiasm.

Paul Oestreich (b. 1878), when writing his memoirs, from which our extract is taken, could look back upon a long career as a progressive educator until the Nazis put an end to it. Oestreich had founded in 1919 his League of Decisive School Reformers (Bund Entschiedener Schulreformer) in order to help to overcome class differences. As a socialist he believed that school children should learn the importance of "production," have some experience with work, and become activists. He blames the parents for the Nazi enthusiasm of the high-school students and gives us a good picture of the social pressures which aided the Nazis in getting rid of the influence of the older generation. Moreover, increasing Nazi discipline did mean an ever greater taming of the original enthusiasm: a condition to which, unlike Hans Scholl, many young men and women submitted gladly on behalf of the cause.

Ilse McKee wrote about her schooldays in Nazi Germany from the perspective of a life lived in England. She sums up what happened in one school during the first years of Nazi rule and what this meant in the life of one schoolgirl. Ilse McKee, now married to an Englishman, is skeptical, but at the very end of her account she also yells "Sieg, Heil!" with all the strength of her lungs.

What sort of children were the "ideal types" of this system of education? The Nazis once more built upon an older tradition. Character building rather than book learning had for a long time been one of the much desired educational ideals. The short statement by the Inspector of National Political Educational Institutions, SS leader Heissmeyer, seems harmless enough; it might have come out of an older Prussian educational tradition or even from that of the English private school. But Heissmeyer was an important party figure (until the war in charge of the central office of the SS), and his ideal boy was to subordinate his qualities completely to the service of the Third Reich. What that service might be, L. Grünberg, the principal of a high school, makes quite clear. "Character" did not mean self-reliance and independence, but a steeling of oneself for service and obedience in the name of the Volk and the Führer. It is small wonder that the hours to be devoted to physical education were increased by order of the Ministry of Education (1933), for physical training was directly related to these goals. In fact, to the Nazis it necessarily went hand in hand with acceptance of the Nazi world view, as the official guidelines for instruction in physical education show well enough. Book learning was always secondary in the educational system of the Third Reich.

Anti-intellectualism is an integral part of every movement built upon irrational premises. Hans Schemm was the leader of the Nazi teachers' union and, after 1933, Minister of Education in Bavaria. What he has to say against "miniature scholars" is certainly authoritative, even though he died in an airplane accident as early as 1934—becoming himself mythologized into the Nazi gallery of heroes.

To inculcate service and obedience, the individualism and the enthusiasm of the schoolboy had to be controlled by instilling within him a sense of community. The liberal ideal of the "cultivated man" had to be replaced with an educational ideal based upon the "fellowship of battle." This is shown in the instructions issued by the Ministry of

Education. The "fellowship" itself was the racial community engaged in "actual battle" against its enemies both without and within. The Ministry of Education ordered this doctrine taught in every school, not only in racial-biology courses but also in the teaching of history. Stories like that by Lucie Alexander, a writer of children's books, drove home the point. She had been active in the party and in 1931-32 founded the first Bund Deutscher Mädel (BDM) in East Prussia. (The BDM, or German Girls' Organization, was the girls' branch of the Hitler Youth.) When writing this book, Lucie Alexander was studying for a doctorate in journalism and literature. She uses the Labor Service, in which all members of the Nazi youth groups performed some manual labor, to illustrate the evil of attempting to withdraw from the Volk.

Boys love a hero, and the Nazis were not slow in providing one for them. Herbert Norkus exemplified the love of battle, the complete devotion to the Volk community for which he sacrificed his life. Norkus was a young boy killed by Communists while on an errand for the party. Rudolf Ramlow, a theater critic, wrote a book for boys which glorified Norkus and went through no less than twenty-five editions in six years. He can show us not only the ideal of fellowship but also, once more, the anti-intellectualism of the Nazi movement. For it is not necessary to understand in order to fight for the party; even a young and uneducated boy can experience the emotions which are those of his blood. Norkus was also the subject of one of the most famous Nazi films, *Hitler Junge Quex*, first shown to Hitler in 1933. This boy became, in a special manner, the hero and martyr of the Hitler Youth: they were charged with his cult. In the passage from his book, reproduced here, Ramlow, without mentioning Norkus himself, points to the general lessons to be learned from the life and death of the Nazi child saint.

We can only sample the schoolbooks used under the Nazis, but our selections are typical of the great many that were produced in this period. The story from the primer merely glorifies Hitler in a way understandable to very small children who have just learned to read, but the other books have a more direct ideological content. The parallel between the oak tree and character building derives from a popular series of readings for the lower grades. The middle and upper grades made much use of books of readings, and our two selections were among the most popular. Baldur von Schirach (b. 1907), the leader of the Hitler Youth, fancied himself a writer and poet. His story has two

themes—the exaltation of the common experience and the enthusiasm in a common cause—and a symbolism in which the sun is linked
with this experience and cause. For the Nazis the sun had a special
meaning, which they took from a wider romantic and Germanic tradition: it was the sign of the heavens, the giver of light to which everything on earth wants to ascend and which links man with the cosmos.
Baldur von Schirach's story for schoolboys exemplifies this kind of
paganism and its fusion with the ideal of the community.

Otto Dietrich (b. 1897) was the press chief of the Reich, and as
Hitler's publicity man had earlier accompanied him on his campaign
trips. Dietrich's "stormy flight" appears in almost every book of readings for use in the schools. The moral needs no explanation, but as
with the other stories, the constant parallel drawn between man and
nature is striking. This was a favorite Nazi device, for it pointed to the
"genuineness" of the emotions and the true rootedness of the ideology through which they were expressed. Here, once more, use was
made of an older romantic tradition. Quite shrewdly, all of these readings appeal to the student's sense of adventure, now channeled into
the Nazi party in the same manner as the activism of their elders.

The list of essay topics assigned to the various grades of a prestigious high school in 1935 was designed to reinforce the desired educational objective. The topics carry their own answers, allowing little
room for original thought. The wars of liberation against Napoleon
are to be seen through the eyes of the nationalist historian Erich
Marcks and then related to the Third Reich. The Nibelungen saga,
treated no doubt as a great national epic, is to be disentangled from
the Christian elements which the nineteenth-century romantic Friedrich Hebbel had added on to it—something which Richard Wagner
had already repudiated. Walther von der Vogelweide was a medieval
minnesinger who at times struck what could be regarded as a patriotic
note. The sacrifice of the farmer's daughter in Hartmann von Aue's
medieval "Poor Henry" could teach a sense of unconditional personal
sacrifice. For this innocent girl had sacrificed herself for her master
and through her act converted him from his vanity and evil ways.
These themes were assigned at a private school near Bonn, but they
could be duplicated elsewhere.

The schools were merely one part of the Nazi effort to direct youth.
Ilse McKee shows us how much of the student's after-school time was
taken up by party and related ideological activity. The Hitler Youth
was central here, and Baldur von Schirach, its leader, explains its or-

ganization and ideals. This all-encompassing youth movement must have dominated the adolescent's life. The idea of service to the community runs through his book *Die Hitler-Jugend* (*The Hitler Youth*) (1934), from which this extract is taken. Moreover, Schirach is quite explicit about the political purpose of those group excursions which he had sentimentalized in his story for the book of readings. Equally important is what he has to say about the relationship of the Hitler Youth to family and school. The family, after all, was a "holy bond" the Nazis wanted to preserve, but Hitler Youth activity did take the student away from home. Schirach attempts a "division of service," but if the parents objected, in practice it was they who lost out and not the organization. We must in this respect remember the ideological differences between children and parents which came from Nazi indoctrination, and the abdication of so many parents which Oestreich describes. The clean division of functions between school and the Hitler Youth did not work out either; indeed, Schirach's book presents a good picture of what the teacher was up against. It also gives us the Third Reich's concept of the "ideal" teacher, while learning is once more subjected to the Nazi definition of character and leadership. Finally, this passage demonstrates the importance of youth to the party, the fear that the older generation might not prove reliable. For all that, the basic aims of the Hitler Youth and the school coincided: to form men and women who were reliable because of their ideal of service and belief in the Nazi world view.

The education of the racial elite, the SS, takes a boy from the Hitler Youth in his eighteenth year. Nothing is said about academic education; indeed his fitness is determined by his work in the Hitler Youth and not in school. Gunter d'Alquen was for a time the publisher of the official SS paper, *Das Schwarze Korps* (*The Black Corps*), and wrote his book on the SS, from which this extract is taken, at Himmler's command.

University students presented a special problem. They were not as easily impressed as their juniors, but they could be aroused by any emotional cause and once this happened they were not easy to deal with. Fortunately for the Nazis, they had made much headway among the students long before coming to power. Gerhard Krüger, the leader of the Nazi students' union, was elected president of the national student organization fully two years before Hitler became Chancellor. From 1933 on, all students were required to belong to this organization, and in its official journal, *Der Deutsche Student*, Krüger calls for a new kind of university community which will liquidate the liberal heritage. On this level also we can see anti-intellectualism at work, spurred on by the fear that students might come to consider themselves a privileged caste in a society in which only leader and Volk mattered. Thus service is stressed and the "socialism" in National Socialism is taken to mean the absence of privileged individuals in a community where only the battle for the Volk has meaning. The value of the individual is determined by how well he serves the Nazi state and such service cannot be based upon excellence of intellect alone (which is, in any case, dangerous, in that it leads to opposition).

This idea of service was made concrete through the students' duty to take part in the Labor Service (*Arbeitsdienst*) side by side with working-class or peasant youths. By performing manual work in the fields or on public-works projects, the university student became the equal of everyone else and himself realized that academic work did not provide the whole content of life. Like Michael, in Goebbels' novel (see page 104), he went out to the people at work. Werner Beumelburg (1899-1963) idealizes these work camps. He was well known as a writer of books dealing with experiences in the war and as a longtime enemy of the "weak" Weimar Republic. The criteria for admission to the University of Berlin show that scholastic attainment was only one of a number of conditions laid down to make sure that the prospective student possessed the proper Nazi character. Thus the student body which Krüger desired was guaranteed in advance. The admissions policy of the University of Berlin was followed throughout the Reich.

The all-encompassing world view was bound to have its effect upon faculty as well as students, for the university community was regarded as an organic whole. All members of faculties were required to join the National Socialist Association of University Lecturers (NSD Dozentenbund). Dr. Walter Schultze, who in 1939 addressed the first meeting of the members of scholarly academies who were also members of the Association, was a doctor of medicine. While he directed the public-health department of the Bavarian Ministry of the Interior, more importantly he was the national leader of the Association from 1935 to 1943. His words in this extract, then, are official doctrine. What matters, in the last resort, is not the devotion to subject matter or the intensity of specialization, but the "binding ideology." Academic freedom is redefined. The Nazis' exploitation of traditional institutions is again prominent: externally, the organization of the university was not changed, the fraternity system was not abolished. But a new spirit was to reign—the new man the Nazis desired to produce was the goal of their effort to transform university life. If the proper character and attitude were created from the elementary school upward, the outward forms of institutions would not matter at all. The victory of the "binding ideology" was primary: Nazi culture would solve all pressing questions, for the liberal age had ended. The reduction of individual ideas to generally held notions is the essence of ideology, and these notions were instilled into youth through the Nazi cultural drive. For Hitler the world view was basic and all other activities, including the Nazi party, were designed merely to activate this ideology (see page 7).

The Jew was the enemy of the new man who was to be formed through education, indeed his very opposite. Boys and girls were taught to recognize his racial characteristics at first glance (see page 80). The continual use of the Jew as an abstraction (Hitler once called him "a principle") robbed him of all individuality; he became the anti-type to the Aryan ideal. The list of alumni of the Kaiser-Friedrich Gymnasium of Frankfurt documents this fact and illustrates vividly the exclusion of Jews not only from the nation but also from the educational system which formed the members of the community. This excellent school faced a problem in the Third Reich, for it counted many Jews among its former students. What was to be done? The answer to this problem, so typical of Nazi Germany, was to transform individuals into abstract numbers. Thus the school could safeguard the purity of an educational system which, in many ways, was the test of whether the thousand-year Reich would be able to fulfill its millennium.

G.L.M.

To Be Part of a Movement!

INGE SCHOLL

One morning, on the school steps, I heard a girl from my class tell another: "Hitler has just taken over the government." And the radio and all the newspapers proclaimed: "Now everything will improve in Germany. Hitler has seized the helm."

For the first time politics entered our lives. Hans at that time was fifteen years old; Sophie was twelve. We heard a great deal of talk about Fatherland, comradeship, community of the Volk, and love of homeland. All this impressed us, and we listened with enthusiasm whenever we heard anyone speak of these things in school or on the street. For we loved our homeland very much—the woods, the great river, and the old gray retaining walls that rose on the steep slopes between groves of fruit trees and vineyards. We were reminded of the smell of moss, of soft earth and spicy apples, when we thought of our homeland. And every square foot of it was well known and very dear to us. Fatherland—what else was it but the greater homeland of all who spoke the same language and belonged to the same people! We loved it, but were hardly able to say why. Until that time we had never lost many words over it. But now it was written large, in blazing letters in the sky. And Hitler, as we heard everywhere, Hitler wanted to bring greatness, happiness, and well-being to this Fatherland; he wanted to see to it that everyone had work and bread; he would not rest or relax until every single German was an independent, free, and happy man in his Fatherland. We found this good, and in whatever might come to pass we were determined to help to the best of our ability. But there was yet one more thing that attracted us with a mysterious force and pulled us along—namely, the compact columns of marching youths with waving flags, eyes looking straight ahead, and the beat of drums and singing. Was it not overwhelming, this fellowship? Thus it was no wonder that all of us—Hans and Sophie and the rest of us—joined the Hitler Youth.

271

We were in it heart and soul, and could not understand why our father did not happily and proudly say "yes" to it all. On the contrary, he was quite opposed to it and on occasions he would say: "Don't believe them; they are wolves and wild beasts, and they are frightfully misusing the German people." And on occasions he compared Hitler with the Pied Piper of Hamelin, who enticed the children with his pipe to follow him into perdition. But Father's words were lost in the wind and his attempts to hold us back came to naught in the face of our youthful enthusiasm.

We went with our comrades of the Hitler Youth on long hikes and rambled in wide sweeps through our homeland, the Swabian Alps.

We marched long and strenuously, but we did not mind; we were much too enthusiastic to admit fatigue. Wasn't it wonderful suddenly to have something in common, a bond with other young people whom otherwise we might never have come to know? In the evenings we met at the den, and someone would read, or we sang, or played games and did craft work. We heard that we should live for a great cause. We were taken seriously, and indeed in a very special way, and that gave us a special buoyancy. We believed ourselves to be members of a great, well-ordered organization which embraced and esteemed everybody from the ten-year-old boy to the adult man. We felt we were part of a process, of a movement that created a people out of a mass. Certain matters that seemed senseless or left us with a bad taste would eventually adjust themselves—or so we believed. One day, after a long bike tour, as we were resting in our tents under an immense starry sky, a fifteen-year-old classmate said to me unexpectedly: "Everything would be fine—but this business about the Jews, I can't swallow that." The girl leader said Hitler must know what he was doing and that for the sake of the greater cause one had to accept what seemed to be difficult and incomprehensible. But the other girl was not entirely satisfied with this answer; others agreed with her and suddenly one could hear in them the voices of their parents. It was a restless night in the tent, but eventually we became too tired to stay awake. And the next day was indescribably beautiful and full of new adventures. For the time being, the talk of the night before was forgotten.

In our groups we held together like close friends. The comradeship was something very beautiful.

Hans had assembled a collection of folk songs, and his young charges loved to listen to him singing, accompanying himself on his guitar. He knew not only the songs of the Hitler Youth but also the folk songs of many peoples and many lands. How magically a Russian or Norwegian song sounded with its dark and dragging melancholy. What did it not tell us of the soul of those people and their home-land!

But some time later a peculiar change took place in Hans; he was no longer the same. Something disturbing had entered his life. It could not be the remonstrances of his father—no, because to them he simply played deaf. It was something else. His songs were forbid-den, the leader had told him. And when he had laughed at this, they threatened him with disciplinary action. Why should he not be per-mitted to sing these beautiful songs? Only because they had been created by other peoples? He could not understand it, and this de-pressed him, and his usual carefree spirit began to wane.

At this particular time he was given a very special assignment. He was to carry the flag of his troop to the party's national rally at Nu-remberg. He was overjoyed. But when he returned we hardly dared trust our eyes. He looked tired, and on his face lay a great disappoint-ment. We did not expect an explanation, but gradually we learned that the youth movement which there had been held up to him as an ideal image was in reality something totally different from what he had imagined the Hitler Youth to be. There drill and uniformity had been extended into every sphere of personal life. But he had always believed that every boy should develop his own special talents. Thus through his imagination, his ingenuity, his unique personality, each member could have enriched the group. But in Nuremberg every-thing had been done according to the same mold. There had been talk, day and night, about loyalty. But what was the keystone of all loyalty if not to be true to oneself? . . . My God! There was a mighty upheaval taking place in Hans.

One day he came home with another prohibition. One of the leaders had taken away a book by his most beloved writer, *Stellar Hours of Mankind* by Stefan Zweig.[1] It was forbidden, he was told. Why? There had been no answer. He heard something similar about another German writer whom he liked very much. This one had been forced to escape from Germany because he had been engaged in spreading pacifist ideas.

Ultimately it came to an open break.

[1] Stefan Zweig (1881-1942), the popular essayist and novelist, was both a liberal and a Jew.

Some time before, Hans had been promoted to standard-bearer. He and his boys had sewn themselves a magnificent flag with a mythical beast in the center. The flag was something very special: it had been dedicated to the Führer himself. The boys had taken an oath on the flag because it was the symbol of their fellowship. But one evening, as they stood with their flag in formation for inspection by a higher leader, something unheard-of happened. The visiting leader suddenly ordered the tiny standard-bearer, a frolicsome twelve-year-old lad, to give up the flag. "You don't need a special flag. Just keep the one that has been prescribed for all." Hans was deeply disturbed. Since when? Didn't the troop leader know what this special flag meant to its standard-bearer? Wasn't it more than just a piece of cloth that could be changed at one's pleasure?

Once more the leader ordered the boy to give up the flag. He stood quiet and motionless. Hans knew what was going on in the little fellow's mind and that he would not obey. When the high leader in a threatening voice ordered the little fellow for the third time, Hans saw the flag waver slightly. He could no longer control himself. He stepped out of line and slapped the visiting leader's face. From then on he was no longer the standard-bearer.

From Inge Scholl, *Die weisse Rose* (Frankfurt: Verlag der Frankfurter Hefte, 1961), pp. 10-15. (Reprinted by permission.)

The Parents Abdicate

PAUL OESTREICH

Youth was—and still is—helpless. Its "leaders" have deceived it and it has been abandoned by its parents. How hopeless, how despairing were all discussions about the education of youth in these ten years! A wornout idealist, the former democratic Minister of Public Education of Saxony, Richard Seyfert, in 1933 accomplished the feat of writing an article about the good fortune of the school in the National Socialist state, where now, freed from all party politics, it could finally devote itself exclusively to its specific educational tasks. A blind man who betrayed himself—and democracy and the people!

And the parents! They had eyes only for the "happiness" of their children—the better ones for the "youth-happiness" of painless growth, the more "normal" ones for their careers. Thus one group kept its thoughts and ideals locked up from their children, so as not to endanger them; the others literally drove their children into complete surrender to the Nazi organizations, since without membership in any of them nobody could hope to acquire education, an apprenticeship, the opportunity for higher studies or a career as an official. A pathological desire for uniforms and insignia infected a youth that formerly had always been idealistic and "revolutionary." These young people now played "old," they assumed military attitudes and arrogance, they advanced in rank and affected an NCO jargon of the oldest vintage—in short, they became "un-young" in every fiber of their being. They were trained for spy work, denunciation, and terror. And the parents (since the teachers had been reduced to mere functionaries, for whom to have conscience was accounted a crime) looked on, shuddering and lamenting only in silence. They neglected the most elementary parental duty of exemplary living and of giving their children true information. In their opinion it was not endurable for their tender children to live painfully in a zone of disagreement between family and state (school). In reality, these parents were too cowardly, too incompetent, too stupid to solve, or even to attack, the problem of education—namely, to put their children squarely in the polar field of life, to develop their ethical understanding through insight into the tragedy of existence and a sense of decision regarding it. Thus they retired into resignation and passivity—and let the children go their own way, barely seeing to it that in the civic and military spheres at least they would grow up unburdened with guilt. The great majority of this youth has grown up abandoned, betrayed, lonesome, and without true parents! No wonder that it permitted "its leaders" to goad it into opposing "old-fashioned" parents and outstripping them. Millions of families experienced deep cleavages, misunderstandings, even open enmity. The Hitler cult subverted the family, while it exalted the clan and presented awards to prolific mothers as if to so many armament workers. Never before had the parental ethos been left to dance so pathetically on the surface of things. After the collapse of military robotry, this youth, with great pain and in deep anger, but also with great joy, will first have to rediscover all the profusion and beauty of a past that has been besmirched by the "mis-leaders." Only then will this youth be able to understand how great was the wrong that was done to us who fought and suffered for the right of youth to enjoy depth and freedom of thought as a total responsibility won in knowledge and struggle. The slaughter of Jews was augmented by the murder of many thousands of old, incurably sick, and mentally disturbed people. As in all other phases of life, so in the sphere of charitable activity, all true love, all reverence, even the awe of death, was ground to dust under the heels of SA and SS boots. A "cleanly" functioning "welfare" apparatus that embraced everyone, was no longer in need of a soul. The youth also now know only institutions, uniforms, ranks, and—as surrogate for true religion—idolatry.

> From Paul Oestreich, *Aus dem Leben eines politischen Pädagogen: Selbstbiographie* (Berlin and Leipzig: Volk und Wissen Verlags Gmbh., 1947), pp. 92-94. (Reprinted by permission.)

Skepticism and Participation
ILSE MCKEE

After Hitler became Chancellor things began to change in Germany. Great provisions were being made for the working classes to ease their lot and improve their standard of living. New houses were being built everywhere and the old slums torn down. There was going to be work for everyone. Fewer and fewer unemployed men were hanging around the cigarette and beer kiosks down by the cinema, shouting, arguing, and drinking. People were wearing better clothes and could afford to buy sufficient food for their families.

Slowly the bait worked. Even those who had been rigidly against Hitler before now became ardent followers. The various youth clubs were closed down and the Hitler Youth organization took their place. Freemasonry was strictly forbidden. Old comrade and student organizations were taken over by the party. There was hardly anything which was not N.S. . . .

As the years went by the pressure on everyone who had not joined the party increased steadily. Those who did not join felt they were outcasts. At last, with a heavy heart and many doubts, Father let me join the Hitler Youth, and he became a member of the NSDAP himself. The fact that his nerves were bad and that he suffered from severe attacks of asthma protected him from any active service.

Things were quite different for me though. I, and all the other girls of my age, had to attend evening classes twice weekly. We had to be present at every public meeting and at youth rallies and sports. The week-ends were crammed full with outings, campings, and marches when we carried heavy packs on our backs. It was all fun in a way and we certainly got plenty of exercise, but it had a bad effect on our school reports. There was hardly ever any time now for homework.

The evening classes were conducted by young girls, usually hardly older than we were ourselves. These young BDM leaders taught us songs and tried desperately to maintain a certain amount of discipline without ever really succeeding. In summer, instead of conducting the class, they would give us a few hours' drill in the yard. We were marched up and down as if we were soldiers on the barrack square, with a girl leader barking orders at us like a regimental sergeant-major.

We were of course lectured a lot on National Socialist ideology, and most of this went right over our heads. In most cases the young girl leader did not know herself what she was talking about. We were told from a very early age to prepare for motherhood, as the mother in the eyes of our beloved leader and the National Socialist Government was the most important person in the nation. We were Germany's hope in the future, and it was our duty to breed and rear the new generation of sons and daughters who would carry on the tradition of the thousand-year-old Reich.

The boys' evening classes were run in exactly the same way and in the same building. Frequently we would all have to go to the auditorium, where some important personage would give a lecture on racial problems and the necessity of raising the birth-rate. He too would remind us of our duties as future fathers and mothers of the nation, and somehow I never managed to suppress a giggle when I looked at those spidery-legged, pimply little cockerels who were supposed to become the fathers of our children.

These lessons soon bore fruit in the shape of quite a few illegitimate small sons and daughters for the Reich, brought forth by teen age members of the BDM and conceived in the grounds of our Hitler Youth Home. The girls felt that they had done their duty and seemed remarkably unconcerned about the scandal. The possible fathers could be heard proudly debating as to who had done it, whenever there was a chance that the girls might be able to overhear.

I soon got tired of it all and frequently found some reason for excusing myself from the evening classes. My education took up more and more of my time now, and doing my homework was a far more satisfying occupation to my inquisitive mind. It also brought my school report up again to a decent level. That this attitude earned me the reputation of a shirker did not worry me much, as there were quite a number of other girls who did exactly the same. . . .

During my third year at the grammar school a great change in the whole educational system took place. The nine years required to obtain the school certificate were reduced to eight. Every subject was now presented from the National Socialist point of view. Most of the old lecture books were replaced by new ones which had been written, compiled, and censored by government officials. Adolf Hitler's *Mein Kampf* became the textbook for our history lessons. We read and discussed it with our master, chapter by chapter, and when we had finished we started again from the beginning. Even though we were supposed to know the contents of the book almost by heart nothing much ever stuck in my mind. I hated politics and distrusted politicians, but I thought, as most people did, that Hitler was far above intrigue and perfidy and would prove to be the saviour that Germany needed. Even so I found his book dull and boring. Rosenberg's *The Mythos of the Twentieth Century*, which the majority of thinking Germans regarded as a bad joke, was the next most important book to *Mein Kampf*. A new subject, the science of the races, was introduced, and religious instruction became optional.

Our school had always been run on very conservative lines and I am sure the situation was difficult for our teachers. Most of them had been doubtful about Hitler, but unless they wanted to lose their jobs they had to make a violent turn in his direction. Even if they sympathized with my attitude towards politics, they could not afford to let me get away with it. Some of the children in each class would not hesitate to act as informers. The Government was probing into the past history of every teacher, exploring his political background. Many were dismissed and it was dangerous to act as anything but a National Socialist.

Once I attended one of the big youth rallies. It was held at Weimar. As I should have to stay away from home for two or three days my father was reluctant to let me go. I was only thirteen, too young in his opinion to go anywhere without the protection of at least one parent, and he had not much faith in our young girl leaders who were to look after us. I promised that I would be very careful in every respect, and he finally gave in.

We were taken to Weimar by coach. Rooms had been booked for us beforehand in private households. I was accommodated by a very nice elderly couple, who seemed delighted to have me and treated me like a daughter. Early the next morning the coach picked me up at my billet to take me, along with all the other girls, to the stadium.

This was such an immense place that most of it was out of our range of view and we could see what was happening only in our own section. Many bands made their ceremonial entry into the great arena and marched round, each one with its own special military appeal. But the one I shall never forget consisted of about twenty-four young boys whose performance was so awe-inspiring that every time they marched past there was a hush. This band was called "The Drums."

The actual drums were very long, reaching from the waist to the knee, and they made an uncanny sound, hollow and threatening, as the boys beat them to the rhythm of the quick march. There was something symbolic about them. The monotony of the low-pitched beat, following the same pattern of rhythm over and over again, made me involuntarily think of doom.

These drum bands were meant to remind us of the drummer boys of hundreds of years ago, who had marched into battle ignoring the wounds they received, drumming until they fell and died. Their unlimited courage was meant to be an example for us throughout our lives. . . .

While the bands played, the gymnasts marched in. The boys, who were dressed in black P.T. kit, formed themselves into the shape of a giant swastika on the arena floor; then the girls, in white P.T. kit, formed a circle around the swastika of boys. Next the gymnasts started to perform, accompanied by appropriate music blaring from the various loudspeakers, and all the while they kept their formation as a gigantic black swastika in a white circle.

Races followed later and, during a sixty-minute break, girls in white dancing dresses performed folk-dances round the maypoles. Then there were more races, followed by a P.T. demonstration given by the younger age group of which I was a member. For this we wore black shorts and white sleeveless vests, and were rather cold. When it came to the prize-giving we were too far away to see anything and too worn out to bother to listen to the results which were announced over the loudspeakers.

To conclude, the boys and girls once more formed the swastika. The area Hitler Youth leader gave a speech and when he had finished we stood at attention at the salute and sang the Hitler Youth song.

Finally the leader stepped forward and shouted: "Adolf Hitler." We replied: "Sieg, Heil! Sieg, Heil! Sieg, Heil!" We yelled these words with all the strength our lungs could muster, and they sounded enormously powerful.

> From Ilse McKee, *Tomorrow the World* (London: J. M. Dent & Sons, 1960), pp. 7-9, 11-15. (Reprinted by permission.)

The Lively Youngster

"What good is a boy," said the Inspector of National Political Educational Institutions, SS Senior Group Leader Heissmeyer, "who is endowed with great intellectual gifts but who for the rest is a weak, hopelessly irresolute, and slack fellow? We have in mind the ideal of the lively youngster who comes from good parents with hereditary virtues, who is physically sound, full of courage, and brings with him spiritual exuberance and alertness."

> From the *Hamburger Fremdenblatt*, Dec. 30, 1941. (Wiener Library Clipping Collection.)

The Test
L. GRÜNBERG

We German educators must rid ourselves altogether of the notion that we are primarily transmitters of knowledge. A coming clash of arms will be the test of whether the German teaching profession has become a useful member of the German people in the Third Reich.

> From L. Grünberg (Principal of the Augusta State School in Berlin), *Wehrgedanke und Schule* (Leipzig: Armanen Verlag, 1934), p. 5.

Physical Education and National Socialism

1. Physical education is a fundamental and inseparable part of National Socialist education.

2. The aim and the content of education follow from the National Socialist world view, which sees the conserving and driving forces of the nation in the Volk community, readiness to bear arms, race-consciousness, and leadership.

National Socialist education is oriented toward the people and the state. It grasps man in his totality in order to make him able and ready to serve the community of the people through the development of all his powers—of the body, the soul, and the mind.

3. In the training of youth in the schools, physical education, within the framework of education as a whole, is of the greatest importance.

Physical education has not been placed on the curriculum merely for the purpose of training the body. Rather, it is a training on the basis of the body, or through the body, that is to say, it reaches out to young people where they are most easily educable: in gymnastics, in play, in sport, in movement.

4. Volk, defense, race, and leadership also serve as guidelines for the structuring of physical education, which accordingly has a fourfold goal:

a) Physical education is education in community. By demanding obedience, coordination, chivalrous conduct, a comradely and manly spirit from the lads in the classroom, in the section, and in the squad without regard to person, it trains them in those virtues which constitute the foundations of the Volk community.

b) Physical education leads the growing man, through the systematic development of his innate instincts for movement, games, and competitive struggle, to the practice of physical accomplishment and to militant engagement of self. Thus it creates the physical and psychic foundations for the ability to defend oneself and for a healthy utilization of leisure time in adulthood.

c) Physical education develops and forms body and soul, as the carriers of the racial heritage, through physical exercises rooted in Volkdom. Through habituation to sports it creates healthy views concerning physical beauty and efficiency. It awakens and demands in the individual and in the community the consciousness of the worth of one's own race and thereby places itself in the service of racial eugenics.

d) Physical education demands from the youngster courage and self-discipline as well as independent and responsible conduct in the community of sport. Thus it creates the possibility of recognizing and fostering talent for leadership in the process of selection. Physical education is education in will and character.

5. Militant accomplishment stands in the center of physical education—not as the end purpose of education but as a means.

It must keep pace with the physical and spiritual development of the young people and their capacity for accomplishment, starting out first from the unconscious and then leading to competition through consciously trained movement.

Good form is the result and the external expression of good accomplishment. The set forms of the drill-like exercises for the purposes of examination and inspection are not compatible with the aims of physical education in the school. Likewise during performances within or outside the school the number of demonstrations should be kept to the necessary minimum.

> From *Richtlinien für die Leibeserziehung in Jungenschulen* (Berlin: Weidmann'sche Verlagsbuchhandlung, 1937), pp. 7-8.

Ten Calories More Character
HANS SCHEMM

The goal of our education is the formation of character.

We don't intend to educate our children into becoming miniature scholars. . . . Until now we have transmitted to them too much knowledge and too little of human nature.

The real values resting in the German child are not awakened by stuffing a great mass of knowledge into him. . . .

Therefore, I say: Let us have, rather, ten pounds less knowledge and ten calories more character!

> From *Hans Schemm spricht: Seine Reden und sein Werk*, edited by G. Kahl-Furthmann (Gauleitung der Bayerischen Ostmark, Hauptamtsleitung des national-sozialistischen Lehrerbundes; Gauverlag Bayerische Ostmark, 1935), pp. 175-178.

The Fellowship of Battle

The National Socialist philosophical revolution has replaced the illusory image of a cultivated personality with the reality of the true German man, whose stature is determined by blood and historical fate. It has substituted for the humanistic conception of culture, which had continued in vogue up to very recently, a system of education which developed out of the fellowship of actual battle.

> From *Erziehung und Unterricht in der höheren Schule* (Amtliche Ausgabe des Reichs- und Preussischen Ministeriums für Wissenschaft, Erziehung und Volksbildung; Berlin: Weidmann'sche Verlagsbuchhandlung, 1938), p. 12.

Racial Instruction and the National Community

Teachers are directed to instruct their pupils in "the nature, causes, and effects of all racial and hereditary problems," to bring home to them the importance of race and heredity for the life and destiny of the German people, and to awaken in them a sense of their responsibility toward "the community of the nation" (their ancestors, the present generation, and posterity), pride in their membership in the German race as a foremost vehicle of hereditary Nordic values, and the will consciously to cooperate in the racial purification of the German stock.

Racial instruction is to begin with the youngest pupils (six years of age) in accordance with the desire of the Führer "that no boy or girl should leave school without complete knowledge of the necessity and meaning of blood purity."

World history is to be portrayed as the history of racially-determined peoples. The racial idea leads to the rejection of democracy or other "equalizing tendencies" (specified as pan-Europa or international civilization) and strengthens understanding for the "leadership idea."

> From an order of the Minister of Education, Dr. Bernhard Rust, for all German schools. *The Times* (London), Jan. 29, 1935. (Wiener Library Clipping Collection.)

Do Not Stand Apart!
LUCIE ALEXANDER

"I want to tell you a story, and I want you all to listen carefully. There is one in our circle who in bitter and lonely hours has begun to understand what Labor Service really means, and who seriously searches herself to determine whether she is capable of this service to her people. She knew from the first that this service would involve sacrifices, as does all service to the community.

"But she was not satisfied with that. Once she had made her decision, she began in her heart to fight the same battle for all her companions. Her only desire was that they, like herself, would become willing to pass through such times with open eyes and clear decisions.

"At first I did not wish to see the necessity of extending responsibility to a whole wide circle of people. Now you have convinced me by your own words: we must all be an indissoluble community! The individual can no longer be left to do or not to do as he or she pleases, unless we want to place obstacles in the path to our common goal.

"It may happen that one has not been received like the rising sun and now finds it comfortable and soothing to withdraw in a sulk to one's own little chamber, to nurse one's holy wounded feelings and say, 'You don't need to count on me any longer. I don't care a hoot and a holler about the whole thing.' Or because one's tender sensitivity has been offended by one thing or another, to spoil the joy of creative achievement for a whole group. Far better would it be to grit one's teeth, to realize that one has taken on duties and obligations, and that one must prove with every act that one is worthy to be a member of our community."

There was a hushed silence among the girls while Elisabeth was speaking. Finally Trude, the factory worker, came to her and said in a loud voice: "You're a terrific girl! It's quite true that most of us never really thought out what all this means: Labor Service and Volk community. I too came here only to escape the numbing loneliness of sitting around the house. What you said about a deeper understanding of our purpose and a sense of duty toward each other, I have never known before."

"But it must be so when Elisabeth says it's so. After all, yesterday she also wanted to help us with her harmonica playing."

"Yes indeed, and today she really put it on the line for us." Marthe was obviously deeply satisfied.

"It's right that one of us should have spoken out," said Kate, who hailed from Rastenburg. "What we need is not heavenly illusions which burst at the first trial like so many soap bubbles, but a solid idealism. . . ."

Now, after the evening meal, Elisabeth, at the insistence of many of the girls, ran upstairs to the dormitory to get her harmonica, so that the group could sing some jolly songs together. In the golden light of the setting sun streaming through the windows, she found Gabriele sitting on the edge of her bed, staring through the window down onto the red-gold waters of the lake. Somewhat surprised, but with her customary graciousness, Elisabeth told her comrade that it was time to come down, for the rest of the girls were already assembled.

Gabriele's eyes began to flash sparks of passionate anger. "I don't want to!" she shouted. "I can't stand so many girls sitting around together!"

For a moment Elisabeth was utterly perplexed. Then she said quietly—but her voice echoed in the large room: "You will just have to force yourself, my dear Gabriele. You must realize that there's no longer a way back for you. You should have thought these things out earlier."

"But I didn't come here of my own free will. I was forced to!"

"That is a serious matter," said Elisabeth quietly, aware that for the moment she could offer no help, since obviously there were matters involved here which she could not understand.

"Whatever it is, it can't be changed now. But you should try.

Come, show a little pep. How shall I make it clear to you? Just make yourself realize that the great circle of which you are afraid, or which you cant' stand, is in actuality composed of many individual members. And believe me, each of them has to face her own fate in her own way. You must know that today each of us will talk about her own life. That should definitely get rid of all feelings of strangeness between us."

"Even that I could never do—lay myself bare to everybody," Gabriele stammered. "Please, understand, I just can't."

"Ah, dear, foolish Gabriele, nobody asks you to," Elisabeth scolded her in a friendly fashion. "Of course, each of us has to keep a little part of herself. We don't need to give up every part of ourselves entirely to the community, but we should strive with all our energies to become rooted in it. But that you deliberately would try to set yourself apart from our community, that I simply can't permit under any circumstances!" And so saying she pulled the still hesitating girl up and took her arm. "In the name of all!" she added forcefully.

Thereupon they went downstairs to the others.

> From Lucie Alexander, *Unser der Weg: Vom Kampf der Jugend unserer Tage* (Berlin: Verlag Hans Wilhelm Rödiger, 1935), pp. 47-51.

Can Youth Be National Socialist?

RUDOLF RAMLOW

The National Socialist movement, whose purpose was to encompass the whole people in order to establish a Reich, could not but sweep the youth along with it. To be National Socialist, there was no need for the youth to know the twenty-five points of the party program by heart, or indeed to know them at all. Because National Socialism is not simply a party slogan but a world view, a life attitude, therefore a little ten-year-old Hitler Youth can be just as much a good exponent of the movement as a high-ranking leader of the SA.

The youngster who out of an innate Volk sensibility loves his homeland and his fatherland, who, through this love and his feeling for our common language, feels an unconscious bond with those who are of the same tribe, with his people—he is no less a national German than the grown man who has consciously used this feeling as a guide to his conduct.

In the lad of the same age marching beside him in the same uniform, each youngster recognizes the comrade, the equal part of the fellowship in which they both march. He knows that it makes no difference how much the fathers of the boys earn, or whether they live in a one-room or an eight-room apartment. He understands that his comrade in the same file is entitled to an equal part of whatever his own thoughtful mother has prepared for him to take along on the hike. He knows that for whatever he does or does not do, not only he himself but the whole community of his comrades is responsible, that the energies of his body and spirit belong to every one of his companions as much as to himself. And if ever he should fall into the temptation to look out for himself rather than for his comrades, his guilty conscience would give him no rest, even if he was formally in the right.

The youngster who feels and acts in this manner, consciously, yet not necessarily from well-thought-out motives—that youngster is a socialist. To maintain comradeship is equivalent to active socialism.

The foremost task of the Hitler Youth is to plant the concept of national comradeship, this national socialism, into the heart of the German youth. Hence its formation was necessary. The movement had to close ranks if it wanted to be victorious. It needed a storm troop of youths, ready to carry on the battle under the same slogans and under the same Führer as the troops of the adults, the SA and SS.

> From Rudolf Ramlow, *Herbert Norkus?—Hier! Opfer und Sieg der Hitler-Jugend* (Berlin: Union Deutsche Verlagsgesellschaft, 1933), pp. 90-91.

A SCHOOLBOOK SAMPLER

The Führer of Elementary-School Children
Adapted from
BALDUR VON SCHIRACH

Far from our homeland, our Führer Adolf Hitler has a beautiful villa. It is located high up in the mountains and is surrounded by an iron fence. Often many people who would like to see and greet the Führer stand in front of it.

One day the Führer came out once again and greeted the people in a very friendly way. They were all full of joy and jubilation and reached out with their hands to him.

In the very first rank stood a little girl with flowers in her hands, and she said in her clear child's voice: "Today is my birthday."

Thereupon the Führer took the little blond girl by the hand and walked slowly with her through the fence and into the villa. Here the little girl was treated to cake and strawberries with thick, sweet cream.

And the little one ate and ate until she could eat no more. Then she said very politely: "I thank you very much!" and "Good-by." Then she made herself as tall as she could, put her little arms around the Führer's neck, and now the little girl gave the great Führer a long, long kiss.

From *Fibel für die Grundschule, im Bezirk Düsseldorf,* edited by Wilhelm Brinkman and Paul Rössing (Gütersloh: Druck und Verlag von C. Bertelsmann, 1935), pp. 67-68.

From the Oak Tree to Certain Victory
WILHELM STECKELINGS

Can you see the oak tree over there atop the bald hill?

Proudly the strong trunk carries the mighty crown. Centuries have passed over it. Legend tells us that the Swedes, as early as the first of the world wars, which they call the Thirty Years' War, used its gnarled branches as gallows. Six men are not able to encompass the mighty trunk with their arms. When, about forty years ago, a terrible hurricane felled hundreds of giant trees in this vicinity like so many matchsticks, the oak tree stood straight and strong through the howling storm and the foul weather.

Where do you think this giant among trees draws its mighty strength?

The mystery is not too difficult to fathom. From its earliest youth this oak tree had to depend on itself. Free and without protection, it stood on its lonely height. It had to defend itself, to hold its own in the battle against wind and water and weather! In summer and winter the storms blew through its crown and bent its trunk until its very roots groaned and moaned.

But that was precisely what made this tree so enormously strong. The wilder the foul weather that fell upon its branches, the stronger did the tree defend itself against the attacker, the deeper the brown roots dug into the soil. The tree had no time for idle rest. Above it stood the law of motion, of survival, of self-defense, of necessity. The tree was a fighter from the beginning.

May this oak tree, German youth, be a picture of yourself. You should be like it! Sound and strong and stately, of tough strength and noble marrow. And it can teach you the secret of its deep strength too. Don't you hear what the leaves up there whisper to you? "Fight! Struggle!" they whisper. "Temper your strength! Then you will become like me. Never back out of a battle! Grow with the obstacles. What does not break you will make you stronger."

And now, German child, come with me into the great forest and hearken to its voices. It too knows the secret of its strength and its powerful life. Listen! Listen to its dialogue with the booming northeast wind that falls crashing into its crowns. There is no asking for mercy. There is only challenge and the joyful certainty of victory:

> "Swing the boys, and swing them strong!"
> Shouts the forest to the storm.
> "Even if they should whimper with fatigue,
> Don't let up on them.
> Only thus can they learn to keep their feet,
> Only thus will marrow fill arm and breast,
> Only thus can they grow to proud heights,
> A joy to my heart to behold.
> For I hate the dwarfish breed
> And the swamp-dweller,
> Huddled against the weather,
> Always in the air of closed rooms.
> Pale and bald in the spring's juice,
> A small breeze will carry them off."

German boy! German maid! This is spoken for you. You also should temper your strength in battle. Rest will make you rusty. Stay-at-homes are pale and bloodless. Their muscles are slack and their minds dim and joyless.

You do not want that! Well, then come with us into the open to the ever-flowing springs of noble joys and true strength. They are called light, air, sun, and water. Come, join us! You will experience wonders. Your tired eye will have a new sparkle. Your pale cheeks will become fresh and red again. Your sluggish blood will flow with fresh movement, your muscles will gain new sap and strength.

From a series of "class reading matter for the New German School": Die Schule im Dritten Reich. No. 59: Deutsche Jugend, gesund und stark! (Berlin: Jugendzeitschriften-Verlag Heinrich Beenken, n.d.), pp. 9-10.

The Sun as a Symbol of Dedicated Youth
BALDUR VON SCHIRACH

One day they marched again. Again the flag waves at the head of the column. Over forest trails, still soft with the rain of the night, they go as far as the main road. There one can see how hard it has rained. There are great puddles. It is not exactly the best road for a marching column. But nobody gives it a thought. The woods, showing the first green of spring, are echoing with songs. Then, during a pause in their own singing, they hear a disembodied sound: "For us the sun never sets." They hearken to it as they march along. The song becomes louder, and they can hear by the voices that the singers are girls. Now they can see them: a long column of the BDM comes marching toward them. Above them too flutters a pennant. It comes ever closer in solid route step. Now, of course, the boys have to show that they can march even better: their boots clang and slap on the road to the rhythm of their marching and the water from the puddles splashes and squirts in every direction. But what of it! . . . Now both columns come to a halt. The girls have been on their march for several days. And they look it too! But their faces beam. For many of the smallest ones this is the first great march. The girls' leader tells how they were surprised yesterday by the cloudburst, but how even the small ones did not lose their spirits, and how even the ten- and eleven-year-olds in the midst of the rain had begun to sing: "For us the sun never sets."

That is what they sing today, in joyful scorn and from an inner impulse: "For us the sun never sets." It is the great German "Nevertheless" that rises up here and represents the overcoming of the Ego. Only common experience can bring something like this into being.

The sun breaks through. The youth leader orders a rest. The boys take out their sandwiches. The girls sit down at the edge of the road. The standards of the boys' and girls' troops are raised side by side. The spring wind blows strongly through the morning. . . . Already the march is about to resume, in different directions, in rank and file, boys as well as girls. Then the leader calls them once more together in a circle:

"Fall in around the standard. . . ."

A pledge to the flag, a holy oath, the song of youth: "Forward, forward, shout the shining fanfares," and then the march into the bright spring morning continues. Soon the girls can no longer be seen. But from the high woods resounds the echo of their song:

"For us the sun never sets."

As if the song itself had brought it fresh strength, the sun has fought its way into the clear sky and now shines radiantly. The steaming woods draw fresh breath. What has just been gray rain now appears in the light of the spring sun as multi-colored dew. The "Nevertheless" was victorious here, as it always is when expressed and lived with full strength.

This strength of the "Nevertheless" the German boy can make his own when he follows the directions of the Führer, who has assigned him the task "to be slim and slender, quick like a greyhound, tough like leather, and hard like Krupp's steel."

From the textbook *Neubau des Deutschunterrichts*, edited by Wilhelm Rathrath. Vol. IV: *Das fünfte und sechste Schuljahr: "Von der Heimat zur Nation"* (Münster: Heinrich Buschmann Verlag, 1936), pp. 238-239.

A Flight Through the Storm and Hitler's Mission
OTTO DIETRICH

On April 8, 1932, a severe storm, beyond all imagining, raged over Germany. Hail rattled down from dark clouds. Flash floods devas-

tated fields and gardens. Muddy foam washed over streets and railroad tracks, and the hurricane uprooted even the oldest and biggest
trees.

We are driving to the Mannheim Airport. Today no one would
dare expose an airplane to the fury of the elements. The German
Lufthansa has suspended all air traffic.

In the teeming rain stands the solid mass of the most undaunted of
our followers. They want to be present, they want to see for themselves when the Führer entrusts himself to an airplane in this raging
storm.

Without a moment's hesitation the Führer orders that we take off
at once. We have an itinerary to keep, for in western Germany hundreds of thousands are waiting.

It is only with the greatest difficulty that the ground crew and the
SA troopers, with long poles in their strong fists, manage to hold on to
the wings of the plane, so that the gale does not hurl it into the air
and wreck it. The giant motors begin to turn over. Impatient with its
fetters, the plane begins to buck and shake, eager for the takeoff on
the open runway.

One more short rearing up and our wild steed sweeps across the
greensward. A few perilous jumps, one last short touch with earth,
and presto we are riding through the air straight into the witches'
broth.

This is no longer flying, this is a whirling dance which today we
remember only as a faraway dream. Now we jump across the aerial
downdrafts, now we whip our way through tattered clouds, again a
whirlpool threatens to drag us down, and then it seems that a giant
catapult hurls us into steep heights.

And yet, what a feeling of security is in us in the face of this fury of
the elements! The Führer's absolute serenity transmits itself to all of
us. In every hour of danger he is ruled by his granite-like faith in his
world-historical mission, the unshakable certainty that Providence will
keep him from danger for the accomplishment of his great task.

Even here he remained the pre-eminent man, who masters danger
because in his innermost being he has risen far above it. In this ruthless contest between man and machine the Führer attentively follows
the heroic battle of our Master Pilot Bauer as he steers straight
through the gale, or quickly jumps across a whole storm field, and
then again narrowly avoids a threatening cloud wall, while the radio

operator on board zealously catches the signals sent by the air-
fields. . . .

> From *Deutsches Lesebuch für Volkschulen. Fünftes und
> sechstes Schuljahr*, Vol. VII (Gemeinschaftsverlag, Braun-
> schweiger Schulbuchverleger, n.d.), pp. 365-366.

Essays with Right Answers

Ninth Grade

Fourth Class: a) The British-Italian conflict over Abyssinia.
                 b) Optimism and Pessimism—a debate.
                 c) Strassburg as a symbol of German-French rela-
                    tions.

Fifth Class: Erich Marcks's speech of 1913: "1813—Ideas and
                 Forces in the German Uprising": structure, con-
                 tent, and orientation, on the basis of the experience
                 of the Third Reich (the speech was read aloud).

Sixth Class: What connects us with the philosophy of the En-
                 lightenment—and what separates us from it?

Seventh Class: External and internal development in the life of
                 Kleist.

Tenth Grade

First Class: a) Why do we need a Reich Army?
                 b) Why do we need automobiles?
                 c) Is money a danger to character?

Second Class: The Führer's speech before the Reichstag in Nu-
                 remberg is to be analyzed and its main points sum-
                 marized.

Third Class: a) My aim in life.
                 b) The national-political importance of learning
                    foreign languages.
                 c) Why I belong to the Hitler Youth.

Fourth Class: Translation of the Song of the Nibelungs into New
                 High German [present-day German].

Fifth Class: Themes according to arrangements agreed upon.

Sixth Class: a) Romanesque and Gothic cathedrals—a com-
                    parison.

b) To what changes did Hebbel subject the material of the Song of the Nibelungs—and why?

c) The task of Aerial Defense.

Seventh Class: a) Walther von der Vogelweide as a political poet.

b) How can the readiness for self-sacrifice of the farmer's daughter in Hartmann von Aue's "Poor Henry" be explained?

c) The significance and importance of national celebrations.

d) Cultural circles of the world.

Eighth Class: The illustrated newspaper as a mirror of the times.

From a report for the school year 1935, Deutsches Kolleg (a private school), Bad Godesberg am Rhein, prepared by the director, Dr. Hans Berendt.

THE PRESSURES OUTSIDE THE SCHOOL

The Hitler Youth

BALDUR VON SCHIRACH

National Socialism recognizes only National Socialist forms of organization, which are structured on the basis of our world view in the same way as are all other institutions of our movement. Organization is not just a haphazard collection of people. Rather, as the term itself implies, it is something that is organic, something fully grown. Organization is the concrete form of our world view.

In the National Socialist organization we must perceive the idea which has given it form. The idea must have the same relation to organization as an artistic concept has to the form in which it is expressed. . . .

The Hitler Youth knows no superiors, only leaders.

The leader is not a private individual who just happens to direct a youth organization from eight to six. His is more than an occupation; it is a calling. He cannot leave his task in the evening like an office worker, for he himself is a part of the task. He is committed far beyond his office hours. National Socialist leadership consists not in insignia, stars, and braids worn on the uniform, but rather in the constant dedication to that accomplishment for which stars and braid are only a token of recognition. The HJ (Hitler-Jugend) leader owes it to his followers to set them an example; he must lead a National Socialist life. He does not need to be physically stronger than the youths he leads, but he should be the strongest of his unit in terms of spiritual and character values. The structure of the HJ is such that the HJ leader cannot simply sit on a throne; he must be a comrade among comrades. His followers should look up to him not because his authority comes from above, but because it is based on the quiet superiority that derives from self-restraint.

A single will leads the Hitler Youth. The HJ leader, from the smallest to the largest unit, enjoys absolute authority. This means that he has the unrestricted right to command because he also has unrestricted responsibility. He knows that greater responsibility takes precedence over the lesser one. Therefore he silently subjects himself to the commands of his leaders, even if they are directed against himself. For him, as well as for the whole of young Germany, the history of the Hitler Youth is proof that even a fellowship of young people can be a success only when it unconditionally recognizes the authority of leadership. The success of National Socialism is the success of discipline; the edifice of the National Socialist youth is likewise erected on the foundation of discipline and obedience. The lesson of the period of the time of persecution likewise applies to the time of our victory and power. Thus the Jungvolk[1] youngster who at the age of ten enters the movement of Adolf Hitler soon learns to subordinate his own petty will to the laws which have built states and made whole nations happy, but the violation of which results in the loss of freedom and the collapse of the Volk. As he grows older, he learns that discipline and subordination are not arbitrary inventions called into being by a few power-hungry men to safeguard their own personal position, but that they are, rather, the premises for his own and his nation's existence.

The great value of organization for a youth rests on this fact. Among those of his own age, and even in play, he acquires knowledge that will serve above all as a setting for adult life. And as he is instructed in discipline in a form in keeping with his mental faculties, he begins to understand that his own blind obedience gives the will of the group the possibility of success. Thus what is learned in early

[1] The Jungvolk was the branch of the Hitler Youth for boys aged ten to fourteen.

years by struggling with small tasks will later benefit the state in the fulfillment of its larger tasks. . . .

Everywhere now new youth hostels of the National Socialist type have come into being. The HJ is aware not only of the great influence of education, but especially of the practical experience of life. If German youth today takes hikes, it does not do so with a false and gushing sentimentality intoxicated with Nature, but even here it subordinates its action to a political purpose. German youth roams the countryside in order to know its fatherland and, above all, comrades in other parts of the Reich. Anyone who has experienced the German Volk community and has learned to appreciate his fatherland in this way, in terms of the National Socialist ideology, will be able, if called upon to do so, to defend this state with his life.

The deeper meaning underlying the idea of hostels is to get the youth of large cities away from the morally corrosive dangers of its environment and to show that there is a form of recreation which is more satisfying than movies and beer joints and which costs less money. Through the youth hostel movement, even the poorest children of our people are given a chance to know the homeland for which they may be called upon to stake their lives. They need no expensive hotel accommodations and for only a few pennies they can be housed in a beautiful and practical building in the most beautiful regions of their homeland. A youth which has learned to know its great fatherland in such a way will in later life have a much wider political horizon than that of the beer hall. . . .

There are above all three forces which, in combination, determine the correct development of youth: the parental home, the school, and the Hitler Youth. The family is the smallest and at the same time the most important unit of our Volk community. It can never be the task of the HJ to interfere with the life of the family and with the work of the parents in bringing up their children. But neither should the parental home interfere with the work of the HJ. The HJ leader, however, should consider it his duty not only to maintain the best relations with the parents of the youngsters entrusted to him, but also to allow them every possible insight into the work of the organization. He must be ready to answer questions put to him by the parents of his young charges and should try to become the confidant of the family. Only that leader knows his young charges who also knows their fathers and mothers, their living conditions, their home, their joys and sorrows.

Every youth movement needs the spiritual cooperation of the parental home. If both parties attempt to undermine each other's authority, then there are wrong leaders at work. The parental home is in an even better position to give unqualified recognition to the service of the Hitler Youth, since this service supports the authority of the parents and does not impair it.

The HJ, especially in the last two years, has suffered from the fact that it did not have sufficient time for the fulfillment of its prescribed tasks. It is impossible for young workers to attend HJ service before eight in the evening. Thus students could not be assembled before this time either, since an earlier and separate assembly of students would have violated the spirit of the whole. But inasmuch as their service could not be continued into the early-morning hours, it was necessary to utilize every weekday evening and every Sunday. Such a situation is intolerable for two reasons: (1) the daily-attendance requirement disrupted family life and was the cause of inferior performances on the part of the youngsters during the day; (2) despite its efforts, the HJ did not have all the time it needed. On Sundays, consideration for the church frequently made it impossible to march out before noon. Further, in line with the agreement with the Evangelical Church, one evening a week and two Sundays each month had to be reserved. A decree of the Ministry of the Interior which stated that all juveniles had to be home by 8 P.M. could not be complied with because most employed youths were unable to do so, especially in localities where it took a young worker an hour or more to reach home after quitting work at 7 P.M. The decree was nullified by reality, coupled with the fact that the HJ in particular did not and could not abandon its principle that in some way time had to be found for the educational work of the state. No police regulations, however well-meaning, could change this situation. This could be done only by a new arrangement —namely, the reservation of a full weekday for the purposes of the HJ. The plan for a State Youth Day provides for five work (or school) days for juveniles; a sixth day will be devoted exclusively to the HJ and its political education; and the seventh day, also exclusively, shall belong to the family. This arrangement, espoused by Reich Minister of Education Bernhard Rust, settled many difficulties which a continuation of the former situation would have created, particularly since the Reich youth leadership on its own decided that with the introduction of the State Youth Day, all weekday evenings, with the exception of Wednesday, should be exempt from service.

Wednesday evening, which is traditionally the den evening of the HJ, will be an educational evening with a unified program prepared by the Reich youth leadership.

Thus the parental home can finally count on a definite division of service. The youth, however, has its own day, the day of the HJ, which it can devote to hiking and sports, a day in which it is led away from the schoolbench and workshop so that it may renew the living experience of its own time, the experience of comradeship.

Thus the relationship between youth organization and family is balanced to some degree. Jointly, both are helping to clarify for German youth its task and mission—the parents by transmitting the lessons of their own lives to their children and by imbuing youthful hearts with the unique experience of German family life; the youth leadership by proclaiming and formulating the demands which National Socialism makes on Young Germany.

The school is education from above; the HJ that from below. In the school it is the teaching staff which educates; in the HJ it is the youth leadership. Obviously, within the school the authority of the teacher must be the highest authority. Equally obvious is the fact that the authority of the HJ leader is the highest authority outside of the school. If both parties scrupulously observe this distinction there can be no friction, particularly if both are also clearly aware that youth education is a unified whole in which both have to integrate themselves meaningfully. Without intending any criticism of the teaching profession, it must be said that a teacher, as such, should not, at the same time, also be an HJ leader. The fact that we also have several hundred teachers in the ranks of the HJ does not contradict this requirement. The HJ leadership comes from all walks of life; hence it also includes members of the teaching profession. But the Reich youth leadership does not as a matter of course recognize in any given teacher a greater aptitude for the office of youth leader than it does in any other Volk comrade. A teacher with special aptitude for youth work has the same possibilities for advancement within the HJ that are open to every other Volk comrade. His profession, however, does not give him a claim to youth leadership. Teaching and leadership are two fundamentally different matters. Even the most experienced and successful schoolmaster may be a complete failure in the leadership of a youth group, just as, on the other hand, an able HJ leader may be incapable of giving regular school instruction. The prerequisites of teaching, in addition to a natural calling, include a definite, planned training routine supervised by the state. The youth leader also is subjected to a certain educational routine, which must, above all, include practical activity within the youth movement. Beyond that, he must possess an ability that no teacher's seminar, no university, and no ministry of public education can give him—namely, the ability to lead, which is inborn. This innate gift of leadership is crucial for the calling of youth leader. Whoever possesses it, whether teacher, peasant, or factory worker, can be employed in youth work. Unfortunately, many a teacher is of the opinion, among other things, that the right to youth leadership was bestowed on him along with his teacher's certificate, as it were. A fateful error! If by some oversight such a teacher should take over the leadership of a youth group, he would unconsciously falsify the meaning of the youth movement, because he would conceive of the youth organization simply as a continuation of scholastic instruction by different means. What for the youngsters is intended as marching and a serious hike then becomes a school outing, etc. All too easily, an office that obligates him to work with youth seduces a teacher into an erroneous self-estimation. He is apt to confound the authority bestowed on him as a teacher by the government with the other, innate authority of the leader. The end result is that the teacher and the youth are both disappointed; the teacher loses faith in himself and the youth loses faith in the idea. Such mistakes are hard to overcome, especially in the field of youth leadership. Hence it is far better to prevent such failures from the outset. Moreover, many a teacher has confirmed to me that a teacher who has a serious conception of the teaching profession would seldom be able to cope simultaneously with the responsibilities of educator and youth leader, since the work load would be much too great.

Moreover, the sociological structure of the Hitler Youth, in which the overwhelming majority are working youths, would confront a teacher who is an HJ leader with a social group altogether different from that which he had imagined from his work at school. The pedagogical qualifications which enable him to deal successfully with his own students within the HJ have no validity as soon as he is surrounded by apprentices from a wide variety of trades who have dropped out of school. And if at first he had presumed that he had to deal only with a school class dressed in uniform, he now becomes fully aware of the fact that the HJ, down to its smallest cell, represents the whole people.

The line of demarcation between school and the HJ cannot be drawn clearly enough. To be sure, the cooperation between youth leaders and teachers must be based on mutual confidence and comradeship. The more frequently that teacher and youth leader discuss the problems of the youths entrusted to their care, the better it will be not only for the school but also for the youth organization. A lazy student (and there are lazy students even in the HJ!) may frequently be more strongly motivated to do better work if his youth leader, after a conference with the teacher, exhorts him to do better, than would be the case if a warning came directly from the teacher. In this connection the following must be given special consideration: with the rise of the National Socialist youth movement, all schools today have classes that include leaders of the JV² and the Hitler Youth as well as of the BDM among its students. The teacher must exercise a great deal of tact in order to find the right tone in dealing with them. Naturally they are pupils just as much as the others in the class. Nevertheless, it is a different thing to reprimand a student who leads a youth group outside of school than to reprimand one who is nothing but a student. Here the teacher must always strive not to reduce unnecessarily the authority of a youth leader in front of his comrades. He should tell him privately what must be said to him in the interest of his education. And if he is unsuccessful, he should get in touch with the superiors of the particular youth leader rather than engage in a disputation with him before the whole class, which frequently will lead only to the psychologically understandable consequence that the Hitler Youth will close ranks against the teacher, because they are unable to distinguish clearly between a reprimand to the pupil and one to their youth-group leader. And if in the excitement of the moment a word should be uttered against the HJ, the confidence of the student body in the teaching staff is destroyed, and it is not easily reestablished. But the more a teacher strives to enter into the spirit and structure of the HJ, the more success will he have. In my opinion, a teacher today must be willing to make the truly small sacrifice of attending this or that affair of the HJ, to show that he takes an interest in what his pupils are doing outside of school. So many teachers in Germany have in this way known how to establish psychological bonds between themselves and their students! But how many have made the mistake of turning their backs on the youth! The latter simply forget that in a higher sense youth is always right because

2 Jungvolk.

youth carries within itself the new life. The inflexible adherence of such teachers to the olden times will only place them outside the new times, and they no longer will have any contact with youth and life.

In these times, the teacher is more necessary than ever. Like the youth leader, he has a great and magnificent task to perform for the sake of the young generation. Less than ever before should he be satisfied to close his books with the final bell and call it a day.

To be sure, youth has no particular respect for knowledge. It respects only the man. Whoever is a real man among the teachers will be able to make an exciting experience even out of the musty classroom. He who is not is beyond help. We can only hope that the breed which looked upon teaching only as a comfortable berth, and saw in the pupil only an unpleasant material that had to be worked, will soon die out. We all know men of this type, called "kettle-drummers" in popular usage. There are fewer of them every day. They can't stand the fresh air of the Third Reich, and as they vanish, the stalwart figures of our young teachers take their places. They, however, stand with both feet in the present, march in rank and file with their comrades in SA and PO,[3] and, like them, are the older comrades of the Hitler Youth.

The liberalistic era invented the horrible title of Head Director of Studies (Oberstudiendirektor). National Socialism will show us what a schoolmaster is.

The HJ is a corporate component of the NSDAP. Its task is to see that new members of the National Socialist movement will grow up in the same spirit through which the Party achieved greatness. Every movement that finds itself in the possession of political power runs the danger of being corrupted by opportunists. Even the National Socialist movement has had its difficulties with these "knights of expediency." In popular usage they are known as the "hundred-and-ten-percenters." These are people who for years have joined whatever political party was dominant, only to leave it at once when the star of political expediency began to wane. They have no interest in a world view nor the slightest spiritual impulse for their political decisions. Their only interest is the possibility of personal profit and advantage.

[3] The Political Organization, or PO, was a subgroup of the Central Party Office (Reichsleitung) and several organizational groups were attached to it, such as the Nazi party cells in factories, the Nazi party women's organization, and the group of artisans and apprentices.

It is obvious that on January 30, 1933, such types also thought they saw opportunities for personal gain in National Socialism. Aware as they are of their own inferiority, these people are always examining the actions of National Socialist leaders to see whether they might not perhaps glimpse a betrayal of the National Socialist idea. Such "followers" of National Socialism are a greater danger to the movement than its real enemies. The NSDAP protects itself from these creatures primarily through its youth organizations. Whoever at the age of ten or twelve joined the JV and until his eighteenth year belonged to the HJ has served such a long probation period that the National Socialist party can be certain of him as an utterly reliable fighter. The party has no other way of safeguarding its inner strength. In the period of struggle, every NSDAP member, by the very fact of belonging to the party, was subjected to sacrifice and persecution; whoever came to us in those years was motivated by his faith. Today membership in the NSDAP carries with it a certain prestige. Rightfully this prestige is even greater the longer the membership has lasted. Today everyone knows that the insignia of the Old Guard of the party are symbols of willing sacrifice and loyal collaboration in the National Socialist movement.

It may well be that our movement, even after January 30, 1933, won hundreds of thousands of loyal and indefatigable members—but none of them, however eager, could any longer subject themselves to the probation of the period of struggle. It would be unjust to doubt whether any of them could prove his mettle if put to the test. The fact remains, however, that the old members, as lonely men, aligned themselves with a lonely Leader, while the new ones, in a chorus of millions, hailed the legal Commander-in-Chief of a nation. And it remains true that there are still men who would like to exploit a great, selfless idea for their personal advantage and to misuse the German freedom movement for their selfish purposes.

Thus, the National Socialist party seeks to increase its ranks from among our youth—from the mass of those who, like the old fighters of National Socialism, have in their early years sworn themselves to follow the flag out of faith and enthusiasm. Membership over a period of years in the HJ provides an opportunity for rightly judging a youngster's inclination and his worth to the community. Not every Hitler Youth necessarily becomes a member of the National Socialist party; membership in the HJ constitutes no title to later membership in the higher "order" of the movement. But whoever in his youth has unfailingly fulfilled his duty to the movement can be sure that on the day of the solemn and ceremonial graduation of youth into the NSDAP, on the ninth of November, the portals of the party will be opened to him.

It is hardly necessary to point out that harmonious cooperation between the NSDAP and the HJ is especially indispensable. The relations between the top leadership of the youth organization and the Reich leadership, as well as those of the regional leadership to the respective provincial National Socialist administration (*Gauleitung*), are imbued by the common will to further and strengthen the movement. Wherever difficulties arise, they will be quickly overcome by joint discussions. The close connection between the HJ and the political organization is clearly expressed in a regulation enacted by Dr. Ley[4] making it compulsory for political leaders to appoint a suitable HJ leader as their aide. Through this measure the PO purposes to acquaint a greater circle of HJ leaders, while they are still active in the HJ, with the scope of duties of political leaders and thereby secure a pool of candidates for political leadership. Thus thousands of HJ members have been ordered to serve as aides to political leaders for a one-year period. Even if they should later on devote themselves exclusively to youth work, the knowledge that they will have acquired in the course of their political activity will be of great and essential value for the relationship between youth and the party. On the whole, the Reich youth leadership strives to bring the individual HJ leader into the closest possible contact with other branches of the movement.

> From Baldur von Schirach, *Die Hitler-Jugend: Idee und Gestalt* (Leipzig: Koehler & Amelang, 1934), pp. 66-69, 150-151, 165-179.

The Development of the SS Man

The development of the SS man is as follows: Once his aptness and suitability for the SS have been determined, the Hitler Youth, at the age of eighteen, becomes an SS applicant. On the occasion of the Reich Party Congress of that year, he will receive his identification as

[4] Robert Ley (1890-1945), since 1933 director of the Nazi Political Organization in the Reich and leader of the German Labor Front (*Deutsche Arbeitsfront*).

an SS candidate and will be enrolled as such in the SS. After a short probation period he will take the oath to the Führer on November 9.

As an SS candidate, during his first year of service he must earn the military sports insignia and the bronze Reich sports insignia. Thereupon, at the age of nineteen or nineteen and a half—depending on when his age group is enrolled—he enters the Labor Service and, following that, the army.

After two additional years, he returns from military service, unless he decides to become an NCO candidate. On his return to the SS, he still remains an applicant for the time being. Before his final acceptance, he will undergo additional specialized ideological training, during which he will be specially instructed in the basic laws of the SS, particularly on compulsory marriage and the honor code of the SS. On November 9, following his return from armed service, and if all other prerequisites have been fulfilled, the applicant will then definitely be admitted into the Elite Guard.

Simultaneously, on November 9, he is given the right to wear the SS dagger and on that occasion he takes an oath that he and all his kin will always obey the basic laws of the SS. From this day on he has not only the right but the duty—according to the law of the Elite Guard—to defend his honor in conformity with the honor code of the Black Corps.

> From Die SS: Geschichte, Aufgabe und Organisation der Schutzstaffeln der NSDAP, edited by Gunter d'Alquen (Berlin: Junker und Dünnhaupt Verlag, 1939), pp. 18-19.

THE UNIVERSITY COMMUNITY

The Renovation of the Academic Community
GERHARD KRÜGER

The aim of the university during the period of classic liberalism was to develop as many all-round educated individuals as possible. The value of a man lay entirely within himself. The more complete and self-contained a personality was, the greater seemed its value for the further development and progress of all mankind. The widely held picture of the old Goethe represents the ideal of that time: to be poet, philosopher, natural scientist, and artist at the same time, to embrace all fields of human culture. In this connection, even his political activity had only one purpose, to lead this one valuable exemplar of man to an ever-increasing perfection and serenity. But it is worthy of notice that the Goethe who was thus idealized in the imagination of great numbers of people increasingly became a master of the joys of living and the pleasures of life.

Later this ideal found an entirely new formulation in the "higher man," the superman of Friedrich Nietzsche—even though this concept in many of its aspects, especially in its deliberate one-sidedness and exaggeration, already constituted the overcoming of the classic ideal of the human personality. Nietzsche also saw the value of mankind exclusively in its most rare and excellent examples, beside whom the rest appeared at best only as garbage or perhaps test material for a nature that was engaged in creating the Superman, and were no more than an abomination and nausea to the "higher man."

During the nineteenth century, the ideal of the harmonious man, as classic liberalism viewed it, gradually degenerated into the one-sidedness of specialists who no longer had any true connection with the community. Specialized education and the overrating of the intellect bred that "spiritualized" human whom nobody has characterized as trenchantly and as ironically as has Nietzsche, who countered him with the demand for a sound, healthy lust for life. The university bred the "brain man," the "instructor." The university itself, and with it its teachers and partly even its students, lost all relationship to the people and the state.

To this bourgeois ideal Marxism counterposed yet another, that of the proletarian, who likewise had no relationship to blood and soil. The class struggle between bourgeoisie and proletariat necessarily had to arise from the confrontation between these two ideals.

The liberal university cannot be absolved of the grievous political guilt of having sown the seed of this struggle through its scientific and educational ideal. And the student of the prewar period cannot be absolved of the guilt of never having instinctively rejected this education.

The student of that period was a privileged being by virtue of his education. He needed to serve only one year in the army. He had his special academic rights and his special attitudes. The feudalistic principles of a few corps[1] spread to all other student fraternities. Accord-

[1] Color-bearing fraternities.

ing to the tradition of those corps the fraternity has only one task, to help its members develop their talents in keeping with classic liberalism. And here, too, as this ideal became all-embracing, the result was one-sidedness and progressive shallowness. Education became ever more external, increasingly and exclusively directed toward empty form and social manners.

It is the fault of the German student fraternities, despite their other merits, not to have perceived in time the danger of these developments for the totality of the life of our people. The result of this development was that German youth no longer found the way to German youth, nor the student to the worker, even though it is normally one of the most striking characteristics of youth to disregard entirely the disputes of the older generation.

Only National Socialism, which grew out of the life at the front during the war, could bring a change. How deep liberalism had impregnated our people, how deep the cleavage it had opened between bourgeois and proletarian, is best illustrated by the fact that National Socialism, despite the shattering experience of the war, needed nearly one and a half decades to prevail. But we must not believe that the enemy has been definitely defeated. If the Volk community is to become a reality, every generation must wrestle anew for the soul of the rest of the people.

To lay the foundation for this is the socialist task of education and of the educators, last but not least at the university level. The liberal university has not yet been entirely overcome; the majority of university teachers intellectually still represent the educational ideal of classic liberalism. The opposition between youth and university cannot be—nor should it be—overcome until the university has recognized its great political and socialist mission and is actively engaged in achieving it.

Our aim is to gather the student body into unified and serried ranks. The student body itself can fulfill its task only if this reconstruction is carried out in its own ranks with all severity and consistency. Even today anyone who in some way has obtained his qualification diploma can attend a university. The intellect is still the only yardstick for admission.

To be able to devote many years exclusively to the training of one's intellect and thereby to attain a higher position in life is a privilege which is granted to an individual by the state and which he must repeatedly strive for by special service to the people as a whole. Intellectual abilities are not the only standard for admission to university studies; rather, above all, the value of an individual for the people as a whole—for the state. In the future we must no longer look upon it as merely a right, but also as a duty, to determine at frequent intervals to what extent the individual student fulfills these requirements. And in time our criteria will have to become ever more strict.

The fraternities and corps, as the educational communities in the universities, must recognize their specific task in this respect. Only in this way can they justify their existence. The prewar fraternity with its feudalistic principles has to be overcome. Belonging to a fraternity or corps must become a testimony to a new form and content of student life that is sharply disciplined and is carried on with the virile austerity of the soldier. The experience of the SA must have a continuous effect here. Only thus can the student fraternities—freed from the stale romanticism of old Heidelberg—become politically valuable and truly Volkish in character.

It is the task of the student body to participate in this renovation of the scholastic community. In some fraternities the first steps toward this development have already been taken. A new type of fraternity house must be created to serve as a center for the new community life. Perhaps the experiment that was tried in Freiberg, where students active in the leadership of the student movement were lodged in the same home with workers, can be carried further. It is an idea that originated in the students' Labor Service.

In the days since the National Socialist revolution, a great deal has been said about a Volk community and socialism, much of it by people who in their innermost being never understood the meaning and spirit of Adolf Hitler's National Socialism. These are mostly the same people who tried to have others believe that the revolution had come to an end with the Day of Potsdam.[2] These are the same men who demanded of us students that we now should return from the political battle to the university and our studies. But the SA student, the political student, can and will never become apolitical, because the battle for the shaping of our people will never end. The SA student can and will never return to classrooms in which are taught subjects

[2] On March 22, 1933, the Reichstag met in the historic town of Potsdam and here Hitler received the blessing of President Hindenburg, himself a symbol of the German past. The former sergeant major had arrived.

that are the product of liberalism, which, through this spirit and its exponents, stand in opposition to the will of the youth.

Socialism has not yet become a reality simply because a socialist-dominated government has been formed. Nor will the demands of socialism be fulfilled when all economic organizations have become "coordinated." True socialism shakes the fundamental concepts of life as it has been lived up to now. It must renew the entire life of our nation down to its last and tiniest units. There can be no limits. There are no autonomous institutions and concepts. Even the universities and learning must in their being be imbued and renovated by the revolution. And here is the great task of the student body—to keep things in a state of restlessness—to be the storm troop.

This is the battle that the student now has to wage for learning and education: not to fall into a negative stance outside the university, not to permit himself to be seduced or to be taken in by a learning that is at bottom liberal, even if it assumes a national costume. But to win learning and the university, in their very being, for National Socialism.

From Gerhard Krüger, "Verpflichtung der Studentenschaft zum Sozialismus," *Der Deutsche Student,* Aug. 1933, pp. 26-30.

Work Is Future

WERNER BEUMELBURG

They speak of German youth, of a sacred will to assume obligations, of sacrifices and skills. The lofty concept of duty comes alive: everyone in his place, even the apprentice. And now the Reich youth leadership and Labor Front call German working youth to a fresh and joyful battle. This will be no boring school hour, no scrambling for high marks, but a struggle as if fought on the battlefield—except that here it will be in the vocational sphere. Everyone should simply show what he can do. He is to become conscious of his shortcomings, and new ways to perfection are to be pointed out to him. Our economy needs good workers and employees. For this reason, the Labor Front also calls upon employers, firms, superiors, parents, and teachers. They should participate spiritually and actively because the way of youth is the way of our people. It should be a matter of honor for

every employer to require every youngster in his charge to participate.

From Werner Beumelburg, *Arbeit ist Zukunft: Ziele des
deutschen Arbeitsdienstes* (Oldenburg i. D.: Gerhard Stalling, 1933), p. 66.

Admission to the Friedrich-Wilhelm University of Berlin

Native Germans (subjects of the German Reich) upon their full
matriculation must present the following:
1. The leaving certificate of an institute of higher learning or an
equivalent attestation.
   Remarks:
   a) Leaving certificates obtained abroad are admissible for the matriculation of native Germans only if they have been recognized
   by the Reich Minister for Science, Education, and Popular Instruction.
   b) Temporary or substitute teachers who intend to study at the
   university must be separated from service in the public school
   system for the duration of their studies.
2. Duty prepared leaving certificates (ex-matrical) of universities already attended. (Simultaneous matriculation at two separate institutions of higher learning is not permissible.)
3. An attestation of the permissibility of the premature separation
   from the original university. Enrollment of students in the second
   or third semester or trimester, respectively, can take place only
   when the student concerned has also been previously matriculated
   at the University of Berlin, or if a certificate of approval from the
   rector of the previous university is available, or if the Reich Students' Leadership had permitted studies abroad. (Regulations concerning the original university and the limitation set on enrollment
   in the second or third semester have been suspended for the time
   being.)
4. Students enrolled from the fourth semester on must submit proof
   of successful participation in basic physical education. (According
   to a decree of the Reich Minister of Education, every German stu-

dent is obliged to participate in basic physical education during his first, second, and third semester. Report to Berlin NW 7, Luisenstrasse 56.)

5. Certification of all academic grades achieved.

6. A police certificate concerning the students' civic behavior. This is not necessary, however, if the student has left another school or university no longer than three months prior to his matriculation.

7. Three unmounted photographs for the student identification card, 4 × 4 cm. in size. (The applicant must not be shown with any party insignia or in uniform in these photographs.)

8. Proof of ancestry: German subjects and ethnic Germans must furnish proof of the type of their ancestry. For this purpose a printed form called "Proof of Ancestry" must be filled out and handed in to the Student Directorate for checking on the basis of documents that must be submitted. Statements in the "Proof of Ancestry" form must be substantiated by the applicant's own birth certificate, the marriage certificate of his parents, and the baptismal certificates of his grandparents. In doubtful cases, documents concerning the great-grandparents likewise may have to be submitted. All submitted documents must be either originals or certified copies. Entries in family Bibles or passports issued to ancestors will be admitted as substantiating evidence. Proof is to be submitted in such a manner that date of birth, name, profession, residence, and religion of the applicant as well as those of his parents and grandparents are clearly discernible.

Married applicants must enter the same proof of ancestry for their marriage partners.

Anyone who presents valid proof of membership in the NSDAP, SA, SS, NSKK,[1] NSFK,[2] Hitler Youth, or BDM, or who by his army identification can prove any promotion (at least to the rank of corporal), is not required to fill out the "Proof of Ancestry" form. In such cases it suffices for the applicant to give written assurance that he knows of no circumstances that would lead to the conclusion that either he or his spouse, if he is married, is of non-Aryan origin.

If the "Proof of Ancestry" form has already been checked against available documents at another university, it must again be presented at the new matriculation at the University of Berlin.

---

[1] National Socialist Motor Corps.
[2] National Socialist Pilots' Association.

9. Proof of completed Labor Service or service with the Students' Social Service, or valid proof of exemption from these services.

Reich Germans of German or related blood species who were born in 1915 or thereafter must serve their time in the Reich Labor Service before admission to studies. Enrollment as a volunteer of the Reich Labor Service must take place in due time at the proper recruitment office of the Labor Service. By regulation of the Reich Labor Leader, candidates for university study may commit themselves to a half-year Labor Service immediately upon leaving school, provided they are at least 16½ years of age and are found physically fit for the Labor Service. They must register in person for the Labor Service prior to their final school examination in December, or January at the latest. Anyone who, despite timely registration, could not be enrolled in the Reich Labor Service upon his matriculation must submit a notice from his local Labor Service office.

Candidates who on the basis of their routine physical examination were found unfit or only partially fit for the Labor Service, must instead serve in the Social Service before they can be admitted to university studies. Applications for enrollment are obtainable at the Reich Students' Leadership Social-Political Office, Division of Labor, Army and Social Services, Berlin W 35, Freidrich-Wilhelm-Strasse 22. Applications must be accompanied by a *curriculum vitae*, two photographs, and a certified excerpt from the army service record.

Those temporarily incapacitated must likewise send their army service record. Or if they have volunteered, the rejection of their application by the Reich Labor Service to the above-mentioned office of the Reich Students' Leadership. On this basis they will receive an acknowledgment of their temporary rejection, which must also be submitted upon their matriculation.

Female candidates who intend to study must likewise have served their time in the Labor Service, or in case of incapacity in the Social Service, before admission to courses. Applications for the Social Service are accepted by the Reich Students' Leadership Social-Political Office, Department for the Care and Fostering of Female Students, Berlin W 35, Friedrich-Wilhelm-Strasse 22. They will be assigned to service in the NSV in the framework of the Mother and Child Welfare Organization.

Remarks: All Reich Germans upon their matriculation must produce either their Labor Service record or the duty book of the German

Students' Organization or their army service record, with a certification of the time served in the Labor Service or proof of service in the Social Service or a certificate from the Reich Students' Leadership stating that they have temporarily been exempt from such service.

From *Personal- und Vorlesungsverzeichnis, Trimester 1941, Friedrich-Wilhelms-Universität zu Berlin* (Berlin: Preussische Druckerei- und Verlags-Aktiengesellschaft, 1941), pp. 10-11.

New Courses for a New Reich

THE VOLK

48 Volk and state (including the army). Monday and Tuesday, 11-12. — Höhn
49 Volk and state. Tuesday and Thursday, 5-6. — Rogge
50 Volk and race (including legislation on racial improvement and eugenics), with slides and field trips. Tuesday and Thursday, 8-10. — Lemmel
51 The family. Thursday and Friday, 11-12. — Siebert
52 Family inheritance and heritage. Monday and Thursday, 11-12. — Titze

SOCIAL ESTATES

53 Workers. Monday, 4-5. — Siebert
54 Economic law (entrepreneurs). Friday, 11-12. — Hedemann

THE STATE

55 Constitution (including the structure of the army). Monday and Tuesday, 9-11. — Höhn
56 Administration. Monday, Tuesday, and Thursday, 12-1. — C. Schmitt[1]
57 Administration. Wednesday and Saturday, 11-1. — Peters

[1] See page 323.

. . . . .

THE SCIENCE OF VOLK AND RACE
1. Racial Science

Selected problems of research in racial psychology (with slides). Monday, 4-5:30.　　Clauss[2]

The role of race in the Volkish character (with slides). Monday, 6-7.　　Clauss

2 See page 65.

2. Volk Science

650　Customs of the German twelvemonth (with slides). Wednesday, Thursday, and Friday, 9-10.　　Spamer

651　Birth, marriage, and death. The life stages in the belief and customs of the Volk (with slides). Monday, 4-6.　　Beitl

Volk Seminar, Dorotheen Str. 3:

652　Main seminar: Usages and customs in Volkish prophesy. Monday, 9-11.　　Spamer

653　Pro-seminar: Practical introduction to Volkish work ways (two hours, to be arranged, with assistant).　　Spamer

654　Work ways and work customs. Introductory exercises on the basis of educational films on Volk science. Monday, 6-8.　　Beitl

655　Study fellowship concerned with the Province Mark (Brandenburg) (time to be arranged).　　Beitl

Institute for Research in Volk Science
Unter den Linden 5:

656　Patterns and themes in German Volk art.　　Hahm

3. Ethnology

657　Primitive thinking, 2nd part. Tuesday, 3-4.　　Thurnwald

658　Changes among the peoples of Africa and the South Seas. Friday, 12-1.　　Thurnwald

659   Retrogressive peoples, primitive races, ancient
         cultures, 1st part (with slides). Friday, 12-1.   Mühlmann
660   Sociology of war. Friday, 2-3. (Open to the
         public.)   Mühlmann

From *Personal-* und *Vorlesungsverzeichnis, Trimester 1941,*
Friedrich-Wilhelms-Universität zu Berlin, pp. 148, 180.

The Nature of Academic Freedom
WALTER SCHULTZE

In our times learning is called to participate in the National Socialist
regeneration of our people's spiritual unity and community. It is in
that sense that National Socialism—represented on the university
level by the NSD Association of University Lecturers—also understands its educational task.

Scientific knowledge must not be carried forward by technical skill
alone—it must be inspired to its very depths by its German mission,
in the sense of a Platonic *universitas* of a purely Nordic character,
which must find its ultimate significance in the state, that is, in the
Volk. This idea does not endanger the German universities themselves, as some people have been impelled to point out. For them the
problem is simply the finding of men capable of leadership, and of
their transformation in accordance with the National Socialist world
view.

The National Socialist movement seized power in Germany on
January 30, 1933. By means of a few highly effective measures, the
movement removed what was useless and created what was necessary
to exercise this power. It would have been easy also to transform the
external and formal elements of the universities. This was not done,
not so much because the external form of the university appeared
inaccessible or even useless, but because the movement discerned that
before anything else the men who lived and worked under these
forms had to undergo a transformation. In fact, neither governmental
or other administrative regulations nor other organizational measures
and decrees can bring forth a National Socialist university. This can
be achieved only by molding the living forces that are the heart of a
university. Hence the reorganization of the entire university system

must not begin with exterior measures; it must begin precisely where the university heretofore has failed: with the human being. The reformation of men, however (or, with respect to our field, perhaps better expressed as the development of a truly National Socialist body of teachers and the creation of a truly German scholar), has been left by the Führer for all time to the party, which must imbue all sectors of public life, including the universities, with its ideology. To make the German universities truly National Socialist—not just to coordinate them here or there, or to "paint them brown"—is therefore the principal task of the NSD Association of University Lecturers.

The Association takes into its ranks all the forces at a university whose character and ideology attest to their unconditional loyalty and readiness to serve, but who beyond that also can point to considerable professional accomplishments. To an increasing extent these forces form a comradeship and a committed community which is in a position to call a halt to the liberalistic philosophy sketched above and to give the mission of the German scholar, researcher, and teacher the prestige that is expected by National Socialism in the Party and in the state and, last but not least, by the people united by National Socialism. The strongest bond connects us not with a vague humanity but above all with our own people, from whom we come, to whom we owe everything, and to whom, therefore, we belong entirely. Today this insight, as was the case in the past, does not stand apart from scholarship: it is not an alien element that enters scholarship from the outside. Rather, it is the origin of our existence and thus the purpose and the point of departure of all our scientific knowledge.

Hence we do not view the *Universitas literarum* as an isolated community of scholarship. Rather, we regard it as an idea living in the totality and community of our people, from whom scholarship flows and to whom it will return. For scholarship, however, the university is the embodiment of this common intellectual task which has meaning and purpose only if all its fields of endeavor are rooted in a common ground, namely, in a world view common to all. Knowledge of this nourishing soil from which every academic discipline must grow, knowledge of a binding ideology, this is the living principle of our German universities. Only the acknowledgment of this principle safeguards the existence of the German university.

Finally, we find that unconditional "academic freedom" is also based on this concept. We proceed here from a notion of freedom that is specifically our own, since we know that freedom must have its limits in the actual existence of the Volk. Freedom is conceivable only as a bond to something that has universal validity, a law of which the whole nation is the bearer. Today, what the great thinkers of German idealism dreamed of, and what was ultimately the kernel of their yearning for liberty, finally comes alive, assumes reality. It fills the gap which in the past repeatedly divided spirit from life, and what is from what ought to be. Never has the German idea of freedom been conceived with greater life and vigor than in our day. This idea of freedom, which at the same time is an idea of personality, in its deepest sense is being lived and thought through today at the university. And we must also understand the freedom of scholarship, the freedom of inquiry and teaching, on this basis. Ultimately freedom is nothing else but responsible service on behalf of the basic values of our being as a Volk.

The task of the National Socialist Association of University Lecturers, acting as a trustee for the party, is to maintain this historically developed academic freedom, the results of whose activity ultimately flow directly to the Volk.

The NSD Association of University Lecturers has taken possession of the great tradition that was founded by the most important men in German intellectual life and will carry it forward in the spirit of our ideology. It is the nucleus of the new "university" and will attract in time the best available forces to shape it in accordance with the demands of our time into a truly Volkish university. Above all else we know one thing, that organization for its own sake is a lifeless structure: only the people within it can make the organization live. This insight came to us after a long struggle for the political freedom of our people. Applied to the universities, it means that the university and the Association of University Lecturers stand or fall with the type of combat-ready political, National Socialist fighter who regards his Volk as the supreme good.

> From *Erste Reichstagung der Wissenschaftlichen Akademien des NSD-Dozentenbundes,* Munich, June 8-10, 1939 (Munich and Berlin: J. F. Lehmanns Verlag, 1939), pp. 16-17.

Jewish Graduates Are Numbers, Not Persons

1915.

387. Ahl, Paul, 2. 11. 1896, Dr. phil., Elektro-Ingenieur, Ffm.
388. Stamm, Georg, 7. 1. 1895, Chemiker, ?.
389. Stiefel, Hermann, 10. 4. 1896, Amtsger.-Rat, Limburg a. L.
390. Weber, Alfred, 7. 3. 1896, ?.
391. Bernhardt, Karl, 13. 9. 1896, Pfarrer, ?.
392. Busch, Fritz, 25. 5. 1897, ?.
393. Cullmann, Fritz, 3. 8. 1896, Kaufmann, Frankfurt a. M.
394. Gabriel, Hans, 7. 5. 1897, gefallen 26. 2. 1916.
395. Giesenregen, Rudolf, 9. 3. 1898, Dr. rer. pol., Dipl.-Kaufmann, Frankfurt a. M.
396. Lummer, Alfred, 9. 5. 1897, Reichsbankrat, Berlin, Reichswirtschaftsministerium.
397. Müller, Wilhelm, 8. 4. 1897, Dr. med., Stabsarzt, Sanatorium Sobernheim/Nahe.
398. Schütz, Heinrich, 22. 8. 1897, Kaufmann, Frankfurt a. M.
399. Vogel, Theodor, 7. 5. 1896, selbst. Wirtschaftsprüfer, Ffm.
400. Zimmerschied, Karl, 13. 5. 1895, Dr. jur., Kaufmann, Berlin, ?.
401.-404. jüd. Abiturienten [Jewish graduates].

1916.

405. Radtke, Adolf, 25. 2. 1898, Kapellmeister, Saarbrücken.

1916. JUNI, KRIEGSREIFEPRÜFUNG
[Wartime Final Examination].

406. Dienstbach, Hermann, 25. 7. 1897, Dr. rer. pol., Syndikus bei der Handelskammer in Solingen.
407. v. Laer, Ernst, 17. 1. 1898, Kaufmann, Aue i. Erzgebirge.
408. Gravenkamp, Erich, 28. 2. 1899, gefallen 10. 3. 1917.
409. Gruber, Karl, 22. 9. 1897, Dr. phil., Stud.-Rat, Kaiser-Wilhelm-Schule, Frankfurt a. M.
410.-411. jüd. Abiturienten [Jewish graduates].

1916. NOVEMBER, KRIEGSREIFEPRÜFUNG
[Wartime Final Examination].

412. Bornemann, Gottfried, 14. 11. 1898, Dr. jur., Landger.-Rat,
     Frankfurt a. M.
413. Jansen, Werner, 15. 11. 1898, Postinspektor, Ffm.-Griesheim.
414. Staat, Bernhard, 27. 11. 1898, Pfarrer, Camberg (Taunus).
415. Rady, Nikolaus, 27. 5. 1898, ?.

1917.

416. Schmidt, Richard, 24. 3. 1899, stud. rer. nat., Grenzschutz
     Ost 23. 6. 1919.
417. Feser, Curt, 6. 3. 1899, Dr. med., prakt. Arzt, Ffm.
418.-419. jüd. Abiturienten [Jewish graduates].

From *Verzeichnis der Abiturienten des staatlichen Kaiser-Friedrich-Gymnasiums zu Frankfurt am Main, zur 50 Jahrfeier der Schule* (1939), pp. 26-27.

9

What Is the State and
Who Are Its Citizens?

THE NAZI REDEFINITION of politics as a "total way of life" also meant a redefinition of the state and citizenship. The state was merely an agent of the race, and thus the Nazi world view, which was based upon race, would determine the actions of the state. Law had one purpose only: to help cement together the community of the people as a Volk. It was the leader who in his person united state and the Volk: he was the living embodiment of the ideology and, through the state, the executor of actions necessary to safeguard the innermost purpose of the race. He was, therefore, both lawmaker and judge. As in all areas of culture, law and justice, state and citizenship, were subjected to a body of thought which desired a total unity.

Carl Schmitt (b. 1888), a legal theoretician, was successively professor of law at the universities of Greifswald (1921), Bonn (1922-1933), and finally Köln and Berlin (1933-1945). During the Republic he had been the most noteworthy opponent of the democratic, parliamentary concept of law, which he repudiated in favor of a dynamic interplay between leadership and people, both united in a common race and Volk. Parliamentary democracy was, for him, an antiquated bourgeois method of government. His ideas found acceptance in the Third Reich, and his book *Staat, Bewegung, Volk* (*State, Movement, Volk*) (1933) gives a good summary of them. Schmitt begins by defining the legal theory of the Nazi seizure of power. To be sure, that seizure took place within the legal framework of the Weimar Constitution, but the context is new. Power now springs from the people, and the Nazi party is the people united in one aim and one world view. The emphasis is on the immediacy of power as against a normative or impartial law: it is a part of politics, of the actions of leadership and people united in the will of the race to realize its aims.

The rejection of government "by laws and not by men" and with it the repudiation of representative government did indeed put the old legal forms into a new context. For Hitler, who prided himself upon having seized power legally, kept most of the old framework intact: the system of courts and judicial officials which he had inherited from the hated Republic. But he changed its spirit by changing the theory of law. Schmitt can serve as an authority on how this was done. The people kept the "external" legal system to which they were accustomed, but in reality they lived under a system of law which was an instrument of power in the hands of the Nazi leadership.

Schmitt's ideas are faithfully reflected in the official Commentary on the Reich Citizenship Law. The authors were ranking officials of the Ministry of the Interior. Wilhelm Stuckart was Secretary of State (the number-two man) and Hans Globke the head of various important divisions. Stuckart was a young man who had risen rapidly by virtue of his party connections. He eventually resigned his position, perhaps because of his dislike of the policy of the "final solution." Hans Globke may have been no more than a nominal party member; it has been claimed that he was a trusted informer for the Catholic Church and supplied information on what went on in his important ministry. Globke fared well in the Federal Republic after 1948, becoming the head of the Federal Chancellery under Konrad Adenauer.

The Reich Citizenship Law was an integral part of the Nuremberg Laws, which excluded the Jews from the German community, going so far as to forbid Jews to have Christian servants in their homes. From the Commentary it is quite plain that the law is directed primarily against Jews, for Danes and Poles living in the Reich are given an opportunity to become Reich citizens. This puzzling edict—the Danes were Nordics, but the Poles were despised Slavs—may be explained by political opportunism: there was a large Polish population in Prussia and the time to deal with it had not yet come. Moreover, the treaty of friendship between Hitler and the Polish dictator, Marshal Pilsudski, played a role in this instance of racial inconsistency.

The distinction between Reich citizens and state citizens gave the leadership power over those people who lived in Germany but had not been admitted to full citizenship. Moreover, by making Reich citizenship an honor that had to be earned, the leadership obtained one more method by which to reward or to punish, and thus to strengthen their hold over the population. In practice state citizenship tended to be a matter of age; after attaining their majority all Aryans became Reich citizens unless they had committed a political crime or a felony. For basic to the law and the Commentary is the concept of the state as the mere instrument of the Volk. Stuckart and Globke expressly reject the Roman-law concept of the state as a separate corporate entity.

Civil rights, by definition, were restricted by the interests of the community of the Volk, and were not ideals protected either by the law or by the state. Both Schmitt and the authors of the Commentary specifically oppose their theories to those of liberalism, an outmoded concept of individual freedom whose day was past. This redefinition of civil liberties pervades all of the Nazi culture, and can be seen in action, for example, where academic freedom was concerned (see pages 314-316).

The view that the Jews were outside the law, implied by Stuckart and Globke, is stated in all its cruelty by Walther Buch, the Supreme Party Judge empowered to deal with intra-party charges of corruption and slander. His remarks were published in the official journal *Deutsche Justiz*. He wrote at a time when "the gloves were off" in connection with the Jews, when the burning of synagogues on November 10, 1938, had symbolized a growing violence which stood midway between the Nuremberg Laws (1935) and the "final solution" of the Jewish question.

A change in legal concepts within older forms is without effect unless the judicial bureaucracy is imbued with the "new spirit." Roland Freisler (1893-1944) calls for just such a change in his preface to the *Kalender* (or Handbook) of the Judicial Civil Service. At that time Freisler was Secretary of State in the Ministry of Justice. In 1940 he became President of the People's Court, which had been created in 1934 to provide speedy justice in cases of treason—a wide jurisdiction at a time when treason had been extended to include not merely concrete acts but opposition in any form to the ideology of the Nazi state. Freisler proved himself an efficient hangman, and it was before him that the leaders of the 1944 revolt against Hitler were tried. Freisler was killed by an Allied bomb in the midst of that trial.

His aim in this preface was to break the resistance of the old-line Prussian civil servant who, much like his English counterpart, regarded himself as being beyond political influence. Here too no man or institution could be allowed to stay beyond the reach of the Volk and its ideology. However, in practice many civil servants were never wholly "reformed," though the Nazis had considerable success with an officialdom which tended to be politically conservative.

The state was merely the "external" instrument of the Volk: the law and judicial administration must be swallowed up by the encompassing world view. The outward forms were kept, for Hitler conceived of his Reich as a "revolution of the spirit." But this kind of revolution did change the German reality, largely through the distinction between form and substance which runs through these documents and many others in this book.

G.L.M.

Public Law in a New Context

CARL SCHMITT

What is the meaning of the Reich Law of March 24, 1933, which in the form of a constitutional revision was adopted by the full two-thirds majority in accordance with Article 76 of the Weimar Constitution? This so-called Enabling Act was decided upon by the Reichstag only in execution of the popular will as it had become perceptible in the Reichstag election of March 5, 1933.[1] In reality the election, even from a legalistic point of view, was nothing but a referendum, a plebiscite through which the German people acknowledged Adolf Hitler, the leader of the National Socialist movement, as the leader of the German nation. The municipal elections of March 12 merely served to reiterate the will of the people. Hence the Reichstag and the Federal Council (Reichsrat) acted merely as the executive organs of the popular will. To the so-called positivistic jurists it seems very natural to see in this law the legal basis for today's state. The expression "Enabling Act" seems even to strengthen the inclination toward such a misconception. It is therefore necessary to recognize the term "Enabling Act" as a juristically inaccurate, even erroneous designation, and it would be more expedient to avoid the term altogether, especially since it is used neither in the title ("Law for the Redress of the Distress of the People and the Reich") nor in the text of the law and has been injected into the law from the outside. In reality, this "Enabling Act" is the temporary constitutional law of the new Germany. . . .

The German revolution was legal—that is, it was formally correct in accordance with the earlier constitution. It stemmed from discipline and the German sense of order. Besides, its legality derives from the Weimar Constitution—that is, it is legal in terms of a discarded

[1] The Reich Law of March 24, 1933, conferred what amounted to absolute powers upon Adolf Hitler. Article 76 stipulated that a two-thirds majority could amend the Constitution. The elections of March 5, 1933, gave the Nazis a bare majority in the Reichstag and 43.9 per cent of the popular vote (almost 90 per cent of the population voted). The Communist party did not take part, for it had already been outlawed, and this election was the last in which the other political parties were allowed to participate. If the Communists had voted, the Nazis would not have received even a bare majority in the Reichstag.

system. It would be juridically wrong and politically an act of sabotage
to regard this kind of legality as being a continuation of the validity of
discarded juristic ideas, institutions, or norms and hence an acceptance of the letter and spirit of the Weimar Constitution. The validity
of the German revolution is not based on the fact that a dozen depu-
ties were ready, by their votes, to make up the 15 per cent difference
between a simple and a two-thirds majority, and the power of today's
German state does not depend on the premises, provisos, or even
mental reservations under which that group gave its acquiescence. It
would be politically, morally, and legally nonsensical to trace power
back to impotence and thus surreptitiously return power to a powerless system. What is alive cannot identify itself with death, and power
cannot legitimize itself in terms of impotence.

When Rudolf Hess, our Führer's deputy, at the party convention
in Nuremberg in 1933, declared that that party convention was in
reality the "Reichstag" of the Third Reich, he was correct. But the
concept "Reichstag" no longer is determined according to the institution of that name as understood by the Weimar Constitution. And
when the Führer's deputy asserts the principle that "all power stems
from the people," that is something entirely different from what the
liberal-democratic Weimar Constitution means when it uses the identical words in its Article 1. Our entire public law, including all regulations still in force taken over from the Weimar Constitution, stands
in an altogether new context. . . . The right of our new state stands
in opposition to all false juristic constructions which would like to
lead the National Socialist state back to the pathways and thought
patterns of the old, superseded theory of state.

In view of the fundamental importance of the idea of leadership, it
is necessary to understand clearly, and on a theoretical basis, the central concept of the National Socialist state law, the concept of leadership, and never to lose sight of its specific uniqueness. In order to
understand the concept in its fullest importance and to defend it
against falsifications and obfuscations, it is first and foremost necessary to confront it with several other, seemingly closely related concepts. For such concepts, though altogether necessary and indispensable in their own spheres, are imbued with a totally different spirit
and are therefore eagerly used to assimilate the idea of leadership,
thereby paralyzing its inherent strength. It is well known that a consistent liberal democracy looks for its ideal in political "leaderless-
ness." It has not yet dawned upon the consciousness of most German

jurists that for more than a century a whole system of specific conceptual formulations has been at work to eliminate the idea of leadership and that the levers of these concepts have been applied precisely at points where they perforce were politically most destructive, and even annihilating.

Under the pretext of building legal concepts, constitutional thinking, dominated by its fundamental principle of security, calculability, and measurability, changed all ideas, concepts, and institutions to abstractions for which norms had been established beforehand. It is maintained, for example, that every duty, if it is to be a lawful obligation and juridically relevant, should have a basis that is normatively measurable and, consequently, its content should be subject to judicial examination. In this simple manner a type of duty inaccessible to individualistic-liberal legal philosophy is eliminated from jurisprudence, and the monopoly of jurisprudence as such creates a definite political world view (which is by no means of specifically legal or scientific character). The vitally necessary duties of allegiance in a leadership state—for example, the duties of obedience on the part of civil servants and racial comrades, which are legal duties in the fullest sense—are thus converted into "merely moral" or "merely political" matters and thereby stripped of their legal core. This line of thought celebrated its triumph in the Leipzig lawsuit brought by the ousted Prussian government of the Weimar system against the German Reich.[2] The allegiance of the various states (*Länder*) to the Reich is obviously a legal duty of political content, yet its essence was destroyed by this separation of law from politics, so that an especially typical representative of the Weimar system could ironically refer to it as "sentimentality." From this point of view, the placing of the National Socialists and the Communists on the same political footing was "law" as differentiated from "politics." On the other hand, to distinguish between the Communist organization (obviously a deadly enemy of the German state) and a German national movement was regarded as an offense against "equality before the law," and as "political" rather than "legal" evaluation. Here the hostility to the state that is at the core of the liberal antithesis of law and politics became manifest. . . .

[2] On July 20, 1932, Chancellor von Papen used his emergency powers in order to depose the Social Democratic government of Prussia. The Prussian government did not resist, but instead brought a lawsuit before the Supreme Court. Hitler's advent to power meant the failure of this action.

Our concept is neither capable of nor does it need any mediating image or representative comparison. It stems neither from baroque allegories and representations nor from a Cartesian *idée générale*. It is a concept of immediate actuality and real presence. For that reason it demands, as a positive requirement, an unconditional similarity of racial stock between leader and followers. The continuous and truthful contact between leader and followers and their reciprocal loyalty rest upon this racial similarity. Only this similarity of racial stock can prevent the leader's power from becoming tyranny and despotism; only this makes it essentially different from the domination of an alien-structured will, no matter how intelligent and well-intentioned it may be.

The racial similarity of the German people in process of unification is, therefore, the indispensable precondition and foundation for the concept of the political leadership of the German people. It was not as a theoretical thought-out postulate that, at the National Socialist German Jurists' Convention in Leipzig in 1933, the idea of race again and again was given the center of attention—as well as in the powerful closing speech by the Führer himself; in the inspiring address by the leader of the German Law Front, Dr. Hans Frank; and in such excellent special reports as that by H. Nicolai. Without the principle of the similarity of kind the National Socialist state could not exist, and its jurisprudence would be unthinkable. It would at once be handed back with all its institutions to its liberal and Marxist enemies, who now either criticize with a show of superiority or offer obsequious assimilation.

It is especially necessary for the scientific jurists of the new German law to become fully conscious of the force with which this concept of similarity of racial stock penetrates all systematic juridical considerations. The idea that a judge is normatively bound to a law has today become theoretically and practically untenable in many fields of practical jurisprudence. No law can any longer provide the calculability and security which, according to constitutional thinking, belongs to the definition of law. Security and calculability do not lie in normativeness but in a situation that is postulated as "normal."

From Carl Schmitt, *Staat, Bewegung, Volk: Die Dreigliederung der politischen Einheit* (Hamburg, 1933), pp. 7-9, 36-37, 42-43.

Civil Rights and the Natural Inequality of Man
WILHELM STUCKART AND HANS GLOBKE

The political science of the past century regarded the state as an entity in itself, as an abstract juristic state-person. On the other hand, the fundamental political value of National Socialism is not the state as such, but the people. Here, perhaps, the deepest differences between the Germanic world of ideas and Romance (Latin) thought are manifest. In Germanic community thinking, the state consists of a system of communities—family, clan, an organized body of a hundred men, Volk community—each of which may encompass a number of more closely knit communities. The entire life of the individual comrade unfolds within these communities. Outside of these communities no human life exists in the legal sense, but only a biological, vegetative existence; thus anyone expelled from the community for a crime is an outlaw. Thus the state is not something "other" in contradistinction to the comrade or even something "above" the comrade. Rather, the comrades of the community in their totality constitute the state.

For Romance thought, however, the state, as an abstract personality with its administrative governmental apparatus, occupies the center. In the individualistic-liberal conception, which was strongly influenced by Romance thought, the primary element was the free and independent individual and the totality of all individuals in society. For this reason alone the state was worthy of protection because, through the "free play of forces," it supposedly achieved the greatest possible happiness for the individual as well as for the sum of individuals. The general public looked upon the state as an apparatus that stood apart from, or even above, the individual, as an independent mechanism which, juristically, was conceived as a political personality floating high above the people. This concept of the state was entirely in keeping with the prevailing mechanistic world view. Exercising a strict control over society, this juristic political personality, entirely cut off from the people, had to promote the free development of the individual and had to see to it that no one's personal liberty was restricted. State and people, the supreme power and the individual subject to it, confronted each other, strictly divided from each other. The lone individual was the opponent of the abstract state personality. Both entered into legal relations with each other, though not as equals. The reality of the Volk and of the state dissolved into a system of legal relations between the state and the isolated individual. The enduring legal nexus between the individual and the state was expressed in the status of citizenship viewed as a legal relationship between the two. The essence of citizenship exhausted itself in its positive-legal relationship within the liberal constitutional state. With painstaking concern for the individual and his rights, the content of citizenship was discussed and precisely determined. Obviously, this concern referred essentially to the rights of the citizen, to his influence on the state and his independence from that state. In accordance with the individualistic mode of thought, the essence of citizenship, save for some obligations of the citizenry, such as service in the armed forces, was regarded as a cluster of rights, the so-called civil rights, which were essentially directed against the state. In every constitution, in particular in the Weimar Constitution, the so-called basic rights played a dominant role. Above all, the principle of equality was most scrupulously guarded. Rights and duties were the same for every citizen. Blood relationship, particularly, was not taken into consideration at all. There was no Volkish foundation for citizenship. The question of the Volkish relationship of the individual citizen was never raised.

The revolution in the conception of the state has perforce changed the concept, essence, and content of nationality and citizenship. National Socialism has put the people directly into the center of thought, faith, and will, of creativity and life. As Reich Minister Frick says, [National Socialism] derives from the mightiest of all traditions on earth: from the eternity of the people which ever renews itself.

"The point of departure of National Socialist doctrine does not lie in the state but in the Volk. That is to say, in order to be able to test, judge, and correct the nullity and hence the appropriateness of external Volkish forms, it is necessary to grasp their purpose above and beyond their suitability as means. Therefore the focal point of all National Socialist thought lies in the living substance which we, according to its historical development, call the German Volk." (From the Führer's final address at the party congress of 1935.) The community of the people, sustained by a community of will and a community consciousness of honor of the racially homogeneous German people, constitutes political unity. This community is not only spiritual but real. The real bond is the common blood. This community of blood creates the Volkish-political unity of the thrust of the will against the surrounding world. The Volkish-political community is the keystone of our entire governmental and Volkish life. Accordingly, we do not look upon the state from the individualistic-liberal point of view—namely, as an abstract state personality with its state apparatus, standing apart from and above the individual. The state is the Volkish-political organization of the living organism—the Volk. The state concept of National Socialism is the idea of the Volkish-political community. The opposition between the state idea and the state purpose, on the one side, and nation and Volkdom on the other, which runs through history—the rupture between Volk and state from which in the past the German people have suffered greatly—has been overcome. Today we understand that the nation is to the state as content is to form, as purpose is to means. The state is the means to the end of safeguarding the people. "Its end is the preservation and promotion of a community of living beings who are physically and psychologically alike. This preservation is first and foremost concerned with the racial stock and thereby permits the free development of all the energies dormant in this race." (The Führer in *Mein Kampf.*)

The Reich is the exterior structure of the law in which the ordered community of the Germans assumes an external appearance. It is the legal concept of German political unity. Consequently, the idea of the Third Reich has a profound constitutional importance. The Third Reich is the German Volk idea become a reality. It should, therefore, not be regarded as a special organism and as an abstract state personality above the people. Rather it is, and will increasingly become, the political-Volkish organization that fully harmonizes with the vital laws of the organism, the people. The Reich is the political and legally constituted Volk community within the German living space. Hence we no longer look upon the Reich as a self-sufficient, abstract state, existing by and for itself. Rather, for us the Reich is the community order of the totality of Volkish life—the highest organizational manifestation of the Volk community, bound by ties of blood, which gathers all the organizations and functions of the people into an active unity, into public power. The Reich organization as such can no longer be considered to have an existence and purpose of its own, as is the case in the individualistic concept of the state. If, however, the state—not its apparatus, but the state in the Volkish-racial sense—derives from the nation, if it is the organization of the living organism, of the people, this, consequently, is also a clear expression of the fact that the state is not an insignificant entity. The people need an organizational structure suitable to their character, and the organizational framework must have its content, if the people are not to be an amorphous mass and the Reich a rigid, dead form. The repudiation of the abstract state personality, however, does not prevent the Reich—as the political-Volkish organization of the people—from being the vehicle of rights and duties; in other words, the Reich has full competence in all legal proceedings. The vehicle of this competence is no longer the abstract legal figure of the state, but the community of the Volk in its politically formed and legally ordered structure.

This conception of Volk and Reich also determines the relationship of the individual to the whole. As we have already emphasized, the liberalistic conception of the state put the individual and society in opposition to the state. It did this by emphasizing the individual's right to the greatest possible degree of unrestricted activity and by assuming that it was its duty to free the citizen from the fetters of an overpowerful state authority and to protect him from state interference. The individual was not looked upon as a member of a community, but as an opponent of the state. The relationship of the individual to the state was determined in terms of the person as such and favored the individual at the expense of society as a whole. According to the National Socialist conception, however, it is not individual human beings, but races, peoples, and nations that constitute the elements of the divinely willed order of this world. The individual is rooted in his Volkdom as a fate. The community of the Volk is the primary value in the life of the whole as well as of the individual. The individual human being can be conceived only as a member of a community of people to whom he is racially similar, from whom he inherits his physical and spiritual endowments (family, Volkdom). National Socialism does not recognize a separate individual sphere which, apart from the community, is to be painstakingly protected from any interference by the state. The moral personality can prove itself only within the community. Every activity of daily life has meaning and value only as a service to the whole. Thus the life of the individual can be developed to the full only in the service of the Volkish community. In the legal order, therefore, the position of the individual is no longer determined in terms of the person as such, but in terms of the community. From the standpoint of the public interest, as against that of a private person, the center of concern is no longer what the individual requires for the free development of his potentialities, or for the attainment of his personal goals, his striving for personal gain and possessions, and how much of this he can forgo for the sake of the community in times of emergency. Rather, on the basis of the highest responsibility to Volk and Reich, National Socialism poses the question: How much scope does the community grant to the rights of the individual? Thus a clear order of rank is created between the needs of the community and the justifiable aspirations of the individual. This does not mean the denial of the individual's civil rights, but his incorporation into a Volkish structure based on social justice and honor. He is evaluated as the smallest unit of the nation and as a part of the whole; he is protected by law for the sake of the whole. Civil rights and duties do not flow from the unrestrained personality of the individual being and from the legal relations between him and the state personality. Instead they derive from his own rank and position in the community. The individual is born as a member of his Volk. This membership creates for him rights and duties toward the Volk as a whole and all its other members. Hence the rights and duties of the individual do not owe their existence to a bilateral legal relationship between the individual person and the state person. Rather, they grow directly out of the individual's membership and position in the community.

Reich citizenship, the totality of all Reich citizens, is the people in its political configuration. Acquirement of citizenship places the racial comrade who belongs to the state in full possession of the rights and duties emanating from his membership in the Volk. The Reich Citizenship Law assigns the German national or citizen of kindred blood his proper place as a full member in the Volkish community. This membership creates full political rights and duties.

The Reich Citizenship Law actualizes the Volkish ordering of the German people on the political level. Thus it has become the safeguarding and supporting foundation of the entire political Volk order of the Third Reich. No other legislation adopted since the National Socialist revolution has so completely rejected the intellectual attitude and the state concept of the past century. In the Reich Citizenship Law, National Socialism sets the doctrine of the equality of man and of the fundamentally restricted freedom of the individual vis-à-vis the state against the hard yet necessary fact of the natural inequality and disparate natures of men. From the dissimilarity of races, peoples, and human beings there follows a necessary differentiation in the rights and duties of the individual. This dissimilarity, based on life and on unalterable natural laws, is reflected in the Reich Citizenship Law in terms of the basic political organization of the German people. Thus, it differentiates between state subjects and Reich citizens. A state subject, according to Paragraph 1 of the Law, is one who is under the protection of the German Reich and who therefore is especially obligated to it. A Reich citizen, on the other hand, is a subject of German or of kindred blood who by his attitude proves that he is willing and able loyally to serve the German people and the Reich. The structure of the Volkish life and Volkish order, and of the leadership state based upon it, requires that state subjects be distinguished from foreigners and stateless persons and that the inner-political Reich right of citizenship be established as the qualification for the exercise of civil rights and duties. It was alien to liberal legal thinking to link the exercise of political rights and duties to the Volkish descent and membership of the individual. It follows from the National Socialist concept of the state that the National Socialist state, as a Volkish state, necessarily makes the exercise of civil rights dependent upon membership in the Volk. What is German, and what either benefits or harms the German people and the Reich, can be sensed, known, and hence determined only by those of German blood. Thus in addition to state citizenship, membership in, or racial kinship with, the German people is a prerequisite for Reich citizenship rights.

Thus the Reich Citizenship Law fulfills a basic demand of the National Socialist party platform:

> Only he who is a racial comrade can be a citizen. Only one who is of German blood, no matter what his religious faith, can be a racial comrade. Therefore no Jew can be a racial comrade. Anyone who is not a citizen can live in Germany only as a guest and is subject to special legislation for foreigners. The right to determine the leadership and legislation of the state may be granted only to citizens. We demand, therefore, that every public office, regardless of its importance, and whether in the Reich, in the Land, or in the municipality, be occupied only by citizens.

The Reich Citizenship Law elevates the bearer of German or racially kindred blood above the rest of the state's subjects by according to him alone the right to assume full Reich citizenship. All persons of alien blood—hence, especially Jews—are automatically excluded from attaining Reich citizenship.

But citizenship is not automatically granted to a subject of German or of racially kindred blood. Rather, the Reich Citizenship Law demands from him the will and ability loyally to serve the German peo-

WHAT IS THE STATE? 333

ple and the Reich. Before assuming the right of citizenship, he must show by his attitude that he has fulfilled this precondition.

In principle, the subjective precondition for Reich citizenship—namely, the will to serve the German people and the Reich—can be assumed as fulfilled unless there is evidence to the contrary. For the Reich Citizenship Law by no means aims to restrict the exercise of political rights to a small fraction of the German people to the exclusion of all other racial comrades. However, it is the sense and purpose of Reich citizenship legislation not to admit indiscriminately every state subject to citizenship upon the attainment of a certain age, but to grant it only after an evaluation of the subject's worthiness and then by an act of sovereign power, namely, the issuance of a patent of citizenship. Consequently, the vast majority of all state subjects will be granted full Reich citizenship upon their attainment of a certain age. On the other hand, by denying or even withdrawing citizenship it is possible to exclude misfits from having a voice in political matters. Crime, offenses against the state, violations of civic obligations, such as refusal or unworthiness to serve in the armed forces, loss of the right to hold public office, professional unworthiness, will exclude the state subject from Reich citizenship. . . .

A member of any minority group demonstrates his ability to serve the German Reich when, without surrendering membership in his own specific Volk group, he loyally carries out his civil duties to the Reich, such as service in the armed forces, etc. Reich citizenship is, therefore, open to racially kindred groups living in Germany, such as Poles, Danes, and others.

It is an altogether different matter with state subjects of alien blood and race. They do not fulfill the blood prerequisites for Reich citizenship. The Jews, who constitute an alien body among all European peoples, are especially characterized by racial foreignness. Jews therefore cannot be regarded as possessing the capability for service to the German people and the Reich. Hence they must remain excluded from Reich citizenship.

According to the law, the Reich citizen alone is the bearer of political rights. Only he can participate in the Reichstag elections or be a candidate in them; only he can take part in plebiscites, occupy honorary offices in state and municipality, or be nominated as a professional or honorary public servant. Hence, in the future no Jew can hold such public office.

In view of its far-reaching consequences and its supreme importance for the nation as well as for the individual, Reich citizenship can be granted only with the greatest prudence and only through the specially empowered offices of the Reich and party leadership. Thus, in accordance with the will of the Führer, the Reich citizenship patent will be the most valuable document that the nation has to bestow and the highest honor that a German citizen can ever earn. Therefore it is obvious that Reich citizenship can be withdrawn if the prerequisites to it, especially conduct worthy of a citizen, no longer hold.

A German state subject does not gain full Reich citizenship simply through his ethnic origin or through activity in behalf of the German people, but only after an investigation of his worthiness and through an act of sovereign power by the grant of the citizenship patent. The necessary continuous examination of the German nation will lead to the exclusion from political life of all elements unfit for the continued development of the German people and the Reich. Thus, for all time, it will put the fate of the German nation into the hands of the bearers of good German heritage and German spirit.

After the Reich citizens, those who alone are authorized racial comrades, the state subjects form a much wider circle. . . . Up to now, the concept of state subject has never been legally established; its interpretation was left to jurisprudence. Now the Reich Citizenship Law provides a legal definition. According to it, the material content of state citizenship is membership in the protective association of the German Reich, that is, the right to the protection of the German Reich. The duties of a state subject to the German Reich are indissolubly linked to this right. State citizenship has importance in internal politics as well as in the sphere of foreign politics. In its relation to international law it distinguishes between the citizen and foreigner, that is, the individual who is either a citizen of another country or stateless. In internal-political terms it is the protective fellowship of all who belong to the same state association. This protective fellowship embraces, in the first place, all Reich citizens, but beyond that all other racial comrades—those who, because of their youth have not yet attained full Reich citizenship, those to whom Reich citizenship has been denied or from whom it has been withdrawn, and finally all subjects of alien ethnic origin. The possession of state citizenship establishes the basis of the legal position of the state subject as a member comrade in the protective state association. This is not a bilateral legal arrangement between the state and the single individual. Rather, the legal position of the state subject within the protective association creates legal relationships extending in diverse directions. The public rights and duties of the state subject emanate from his membership in the state protective association.

Through the separation of state citizenship from the acquisition of state civil rights by virtue of the grant of Reich citizenship, the concept of state citizenship has lost its political content. The political privileges heretofore connected with state citizenship no longer exist. The state citizen as such no longer enjoys any political rights. He can, of course, utilize all public institutions according to prevailing regulations; he can, to the extent that there are no legal restrictions, be gainfully employed; and he enjoys the protection of the state organism. Conversely, he is obligated to help carry all public burdens and in emergencies to come to the defense of the state with everything he possesses. He has, however, no political state rights. The possession of state citizenship does not give him a claim to Reich citizenship.

In contrast to Reich citizenship, state citizenship is not dependent on membership in the blood or ethnic fellowship. Accordingly, even those of alien races may in the future acquire German state citizenship, provided that their total personality fulfills prevailing requirements. To be sure, since the law of May 15, 1935, claims for naturalization are no longer valid. Rather, the grant of German state citizenship depends on the decision of the naturalization authorities, who are duty-bound to conduct a thorough examination and evaluation of the applicant. In the course of time, new regulations pertaining to the acquisition and loss of state citizenship will have to be promulgated, in keeping with the concept already expressed in the law of May 15, 1935, that German state citizenship can no longer be acquired, lost, or changed arbitrarily.

From Wilhelm Stuckart and Hans Globke, *Kommentare zur deutschen Rassengesetzgebung* (Munich and Berlin, 1936), Vol. I, pp. 20-26, 28-30.

The Reich Citizenship Law

The Reichstag has unanimously passed the following law, which is herewith made public:

Para. 1

(1) A state subject is anyone who belongs to the protective association of the German Reich and who therefore is especially obligated to it.
(2) State citizenship is acquired according to the regulations of the Reich and State Citizenship Law.

Para. 2

(1) Only the state citizen of German or of kindred blood who by his conduct proves that he is willing and able loyally to serve the German people and the Reich is a Reich citizen.
(2) The right to Reich citizenship is attained through the conferment of the Reich citizenship patent.
(3) The Reich citizen is the exclusive bearer of full political rights, according to the criteria of the laws.

Para. 3

The Reich Minister of the Interior, in agreement with the deputy of the Führer, shall promulgate the necessary legal and administrative regulations for the execution and supplementation of this law.

Nuremberg, September 15, 1935
At the Reich Party Congress of Freedom
Führer and Reich Chancellor Adolf Hitler
Reich Minister of the Interior Frick

From Wilhelm Stuckart and Hans Globke, *Kommentare zur deutschen Rassengesetzgebung*, Vol. I, p. 31.

The Jew Is Outside the Law
WALTHER BUCH

The Jew is not a human being. He is an appearance of putrescence. Just as the fission-fungus cannot permeate wood until it is rotting, so the Jew was able to creep into the German people, to bring on disas-

ter, only after the German nation, weakened by the loss of blood in
the Thirty Years' War, had begun to rot from within.

> From an article by Supreme Party Judge Walther Buch on
> the idea of German honor, in *Deutsche Justiz*, Oct. 21,
> 1938. (Wiener Library Clipping Collection.)

Anchoring the Civil Service in the Nation
ROLAND FREISLER

Since the 1937 handbook (*Kalender*) for officials in the administration of justice was published, the position of all civil servants in the
new German Reich has undergone a fundamental strengthening. The
German Civil Service Law of January 26, 1937, closed a development
which had been purposely introduced by the National Socialist state
leadership in 1933. It would be wrong to speak injuriously of the body
of civil servants who did their duty during the Weimar interregnum.
However justified the stigma that attached itself to some civil servants
for their corrupt and un-German behavior, it must be acknowledged
that the overwhelming majority of public servants sought to remain
aloof from the immorality of an internally disoriented system, and
succeeded in so doing. It will forever be a claim to fame for the creators of the Prussian civil service that it was able to inject into the
blood of the whole body of German civil servants its own lofty sense
of self-sacrificing duty to people and state, and maintained its essence
even during the ravaging storm of unpatriotic discord that plagued
Germany for fifteen years.

But there was one particular consequence of that storm: the Ger-
man-conscious official could oppose the dangerous, and frequently
forcibly imposed, influence of democratic-Marxist rule only by cling-
ing rigidly to the formalism of bureaucratic procedure. Many examples could be cited how, even in the sphere of the administration of
justice, the enforcement of Marxist ideology foundered on the ardu-
ous utilization and exploitation of legalistic regulations. Thus, in
many cases, the German civil servant was trained in, or forced to
adopt, a purely formalistic mode of thought—a habit of mind that
was out of place the moment the National Socialist revolution swept
away the Marxist phantom.

As a movement born from life itself, and life-creating in turn, National Socialism demands the rejection of formalistic rigidity in thought and action and expects from its officeholders and trustees a living and dynamic attitude. This dynamic must be rooted in the newly awakened soul of the people. It was only a natural consequence of the seizure of power that, by virtue of the Civil Service Law of April 1933, racially and ideologically alien elements were eliminated from the civil service. Beyond and above that, when the unity of party and state had become law, the need arose for a broader and deeper anchoring of the German professional civil service in the service of the Führer and in the totality of the nation.

Thus, even here National Socialism fought its battle in a war against bureaucracy and regulations that, for better or for worse, was bound to become a commonly used slogan—in the better sense because it expressed a sound instinct in opposition to everything that was estranged from life, everything that was dead and moldy, and in the worse sense wherever there were some who seized upon it as a banner to smuggle in the contraband of their own selfish interest and wrongdoing.

Bureaucracy does not exist merely in an office and in the ranks of professional public servants. Bureaucracy can be found in all walks of life. A bureaucrat is not just the man behind a desk who because of a multitude of rules has lost sight of the purpose of his own existence. A bureaucrat, rather, is anyone who goes through life with his eyes fixed on his toes—whether he be a builder who with all his calculations has lost sight of the larger purpose of his enterprise; or a merchant who knows how to deal with figures but not with the goods, the very essence of his business; or the soldier who in a moment of decision clings to service regulations instead of taking responsible action on his own. Bureaucracy, therefore, is a sickness which grows out of the general human condition. However, it finds its most nourishing soil in the air of an office, and it must be fought there as well as everywhere else. Because it grows out of a basic attitude toward life, it must be fought by a renewal of the proper attitude. Thus the struggle against bureaucracy is closely bound up with the demand for a national and socialistic profession of faith from every single civil servant.

Here is the crux of the German Civil Service Law. Thus the law of January 1937, in contrast to all previous civil service legislation, does not begin by setting down the rules and regulations of the civil service. Rather, after a short definition of the conceptual features of public service in general, it puts this principle at the apex: anyone who wants to be or to become a civil servant must be ready to profess unconditional faith in all the obligations which the National Socialist state imposes. The indissoluble bond with the Führer, which the civil servant solemnly affirmed when he took his oath of office on the person of the Führer, can grow only from the deepest permeation with the true spirit of the movement. From this bond stem the roots the civil servant has in the Volk, of which he is a part and member.

From *Kalender für Reichsjustizbeamte* (Berlin: R. v. Decker's Verlag and G. Schenck, 1938), pp. 17-18.

10

Workers and Shopkeepers

THE VOLK was to be an eternal unity and all its members were supposed to be equals in status if not in function. Hierarchy there must be, but the place of individuals within it should be determined by their service to the Volk, and though one member might be an employer and the other a worker who did the employer's bidding, both, theoretically, were equal in status, for they were united by a common ideology and a common purpose. It is clear from the statistics of party membership that this point of view did not greatly appeal to the German working classes; that it attracted instead those who were in fact losing status as their economic position deteriorated. The strong socialist tradition among the German working class made it difficult for the Nazis to win converts among them, though obviously some of the "proletariat" did join the party. Once Hitler was in power the German Labor Front (Deutsche Arbeits-Front) was formed to take the place of the traditional trade unions. Indeed, by the summer of 1934 all salaried employees were required to become members of the Labor Front, which was organized according to the industries in which the workers were employed.

Robert Ley (1890-1945), who became the leader of the German Labor Front, proceeded to build an empire which not only organized and looked after the social well-being of the salaried workers, but also attempted to surround them with the "right" cultural atmosphere. An official publication summed up the nature of the Labor Front: "Above all, the German Labor Front is not an economic organization but a political one. As an organization affiliated with the NSDAP, it is a part of the National Socialist movement." [1] The party and the all-encompassing labor organization were one: the definition of politics as a total culture, which we have had occasion to mention so often in this book, applied in this area as in all others.

The salaried worker could not escape the tentacles of the Labor Front, for it controlled hiring and firing, workmen's compensation and insurance, as well as care for the elderly and disabled workers. The "socialism" in the party title was given concrete expression through a paternalism which was supposed to end class differences on behalf of the unity of the Volk. The essence of this paternalism was represented by the Strength Through Joy (Kraft durch Freude) movement, which had been created as an independent organization in 1933 but had been made a part of the Labor Front a year later.

The idea behind Strength Through Joy was to help the worker improve himself in his leisure time—joining travel groups, going to the theater and the opera, attending lectures, and participating in sports. In 1934 some nine million workers took part in these activities; by 1939 their number had risen to fifty-five million. Through Strength Through Joy the Labor Front owned enterprises of its own, from sea-going ships to the Volkswagen factory—which was attempting to develop a "worker's car." But ideology played a dominant role here too, and one of the most important branches of this movement was that concerned with educating the workers in the Nazi world view. The description of the ideal Nazi spirit in the plant (1938) illustrates how this educational effort operated at the shop level. Here the example is set by the Youth Labor Service, which consisted of those workers (Werkschaaren) singled out as "Nazi fighters" within each plant and who formed an elite cell within each plant organization.

As competition was thought to be essential to efficient industrial management, the Labor Front sponsored contests among the workers. "The Struggle for the Achievement of German Socialism" describes such a competition among elite workers from different crafts and plants—among those who wore the blue blouse, the uniform of the Werkschaaren. Socialism, in Nazi terminology, meant competition in the service of the Volk as opposed to a supposed Marxist proletarian

[1] *Die Deutsche Arbeits-Front: Wesen—Ziel—Weg* (Berlin, 1943), p. 8.

class equality. From 1934 on, the German Labor Front sponsored nation-wide competitions (*Reichsberufwettkampf*)—starting at the local level, where the contestants gave "Testimony of German Workmanship," and leading to finals on the national level, where the rewards were an audience with the Führer and further professional training at state expense.

Militant dedication was desired, and the phraseology of war was taken over by the Labor Front to describe the quest for maximum output; indeed the term "front" as used here is a direct appeal to the mentality of the trenches. Typically enough, this competition was not confined to increased production or better workmanship, but included tests of the workers' knowledge of the Nazi world view. The Labor Front wanted to produce a "new type of worker," far removed from the class-conscious workman of earlier days: thus the picture of the workers sitting on school benches being instructed by the educational branch of the Strength Through Joy movement. But old habits die hard, as the condemnation of loafing and absenteeism by the Reich Trustee of Labor shows (1938). This individual was responsible for the increased production required under the Four-Year Plan, whose main goal was to strengthen Germany's military might. In this context, however, loafing means more than merely slackness on the job; it was the government's fear of strikes which was in large part responsible for this regulation. Striking had been strictly forbidden ever since the abolition of the old trade unions and the arrival of the Labor Front; nevertheless, some (unreported) wildcat strikes did take place during the Third Reich.

How the workers were coerced, what form of "discipline" could be imposed in actual practice, is shown in the official warning to plant managers to respect the rights of the workers. The "border fortifications" mentioned in the document were those of the West Wall, which faced France, and the hundreds of thousands of workers needed to build them were supplied by the Labor Front.

The wage controls set up by the Four-Year Plan affected all salaried employees, not just the stenographers mentioned in our selection (and it must be remembered that at that time there was as much competition for good stenographers as there is in our own day).

Comrade Müller illustrates the "ideal type" of worker, the true German man. Like so many other workers, Müller has been taken in by international Marxism, typified here by Herr Flex. But his true Aryan nature rebels when he finds out that Flex is a traitor to the

Fatherland and, in addition, a tool of the employers. Honesty versus hypocrisy is the theme of this story, as of so much else in Nazi literature—the German Volk is as straight as the trunk of a tree. Walter Dach was a prolific author who more often than not wrote in the service of the Strength Through Joy movement. For that movement he specialized in writing travel books and stories about "true workers," such as the one given here.

The price which had to be paid for the Third Reich involved more than cultural conformity. The wages of salaried workers were frozen and their ability to move from one job to another was rigidly controlled. And there were other financial sacrifices, as the examination of the Nazi taxation system shows. The ideology intrudes into the tax structure. Single persons had to pay significantly higher taxes than people with children; in fact, premiums were paid on an ascending scale for the bearing of children. The "family rich in children," as the Nazi vocabulary has it, not only was a guarantee for the future of the race but also was important for Germany's military strength. Such families had to be Aryan, and the children of women of mixed marriages did not count for tax purposes. Jews themselves had to pay special taxes which were meant to be confiscatory, and which are not mentioned in this account of the Nazi tax structure by a leading democratic Swiss paper.

The rise in the cost of living has to be considered in relation to both the wage freeze for salaried employees and the tax structure. Quite clearly these factors produced a price-wage squeeze for those below the top-income levels. For all the talk of equality in the Volk community, the salaries of the "top brass" in the nation were high enough to provide an escape from the increasingly tight economic situation in which the rest of the Volk found itself.

Small business was affected in a special manner, a fact which is not lacking in irony. For the Nazis in their rise to power had made themselves the champions of small business, and our statistics on party membership show that the merchants were responsive to this Nazi appeal. Throughout the first years of the Third Reich small business fought for leadership in the economy. But it was big business which won the fight in 1936 (increasing economic centralization was one feature of the Four-Year Plan). By 1939 the situation of the retail trade was desperate, as the account of the highly reliable Swiss *Neue Züricher Zeitung* demonstrates. The SS paper, *Das Schwarze Korps*, in its attack on the retail trade a few months before the outbreak of the war, suggested that the merchants adopt another profession. There is no doubt that what it had in mind was the armaments industry—as the *Neue Züricher Zeitung* realized. Price control worked to the same end, though the merchants tried to defeat its purpose. However, punishment for violations of the price-control regulations was instantaneous and severe, as the butchers' guild in Bockum-Höve (a small town near Hamm in Westphalia) discovered. Such united resistance is a measure of the desperation of a whole section of the retail trade, coming as it did at a time when the Third Reich was already six years old and its terror and cultural control in full swing.

The butchers lost their battle; indeed, economically speaking, the middle classes were betrayed. But, for all that, no real resistance movement developed and the manifestations of middle-class restlessness are isolated and minimal. Nor do we have any accounts of significant dissatisfaction among the working classes. To be sure, the risks involved in protest grew greater as the years wore on, and protests eventually led to prison or concentration camps rather than to economic change. But it would not be amiss to see here, once more, the results of a successful cultural drive. Belief in the world view, drummed into the population from all sides, must have helped in overcoming economic dissatisfaction. In addition to the personal security so many people found in the ideology, the workers also enjoyed the security provided by the paternalism of the Labor Front. Not only did the workers benefit from the economic aspects of this organization, but Strength Through Joy opened up cultural vistas hitherto accessible only to the upper classes and made it possible for them to travel to foreign and exotic lands. To a certain extent, at any rate, this chapter demonstrates the Nazi success in "denying primacy to economic considerations in the ordering of the social structure." [2]

[2] *Die Deutsche Arbeits-Front: Wesen—Ziel—Weg*, p. 14.

G.L.M.

THE WORKER: IDEAL AND REALITY

Statistics on Occupational Composition of Members of the Nazi Party

The Social Composition of the NSDAP Compared with That of German Society at Large, 1930 (in per cent)

Occupational Group	NSDAP	Society	Society = 100
Blue-collar workers	28.1	45.9	61.2
White-collar workers	25.6	12.0	213.5
Self-employed	20.7	9.0	230.0
Officials	8.3	5.1	162.7
Civil service employees	6.6	4.2	157.1
Teachers	1.7	0.9	188.9
Farmers	14.0	10.6	132.0
Others	3.3	17.4	18.9
	100.0	100.0	

Social Structure of the NSDAP, 1930 and 1933 (in per cent)

Occupational Group	1930	1933	1930 = 100
Blue-collar workers	26.3	32.5	108.4
White-collar workers	24.4	20.6	85.9
Self-employed	18.9	17.3	91.5
Officials	7.7	6.5	84.4
Farmers	13.2	12.5	94.7
Others	3.4	3.7	108.9
Persons of independent income	1.9	1.6	84.3
Housewives	3.6	4.1	113.6
Students	4.0	1.2	120.0

From Wolfgang Schäfer, NSDAP: Entwicklung und Struktur der Staatspartei des dritten Reiches (Hannover and Frankfurt: Norddeutsche Verlagsanstalt O. Goedel, 1956), pp. 17, 19. (Reprinted by permission.)

The Struggle for the Achievement
of German Socialism

No Need for Cultural Snobbery

In Silesia we watched platoons of hand-picked National Socialist shop and factory workers (*Werkschaaren*) at work, and saw their energetic commitment to the battle for Volkdom and their enormous accomplishments in the "Testimony of German Workmanship." To those for whom this is no more than a mere concept, in the "Testimony of German Workmanship," the work platoons prove not only that they are willing to solve political and cultural problems, but also that they want to set a high standard for their vocational skills. In the "Testimony of German Workmanship," the work platoons prove that they personify the whole varied world of German labor, that everywhere in the Reich where a hammer is swung or a flywheel turns they represent the principle of voluntary maximum output and the most intense spirit of militant dedication. Thus, in the "Testimony of German Workmanship," the work platoons are creating products of superlative quality from their various shops. Electricians demonstrated their skill at splicing telephone cables in the most instructive manner. Woodworkers produced inlay work of the most intricate designs. Glassblowers, using skills of the greatest antiquity, created beautiful vessels out of their shining, diaphanous material.

These are the work platoons in the "Testimony of German Workmanship." We found them as enthusiastic in their participation in festivities as they are in emergencies and in the construction of homes. Wherever men wear the blue blouse,[1] they feel themselves wholly committed to leap into the breach, to tackle any task without reservations; they stake their honor on being the activist storm troop of their workshops and factories.

Now we are among Hannoverian platoons of *Werkschaaren*. Here we find the same display of a sense of duty; here, too, we find the same principle of such platoons at work: Fulfillment of one's daily duties, especially in the life of labor, is the supreme task of every member of the platoon.

To be a helper, to be the best comrade in the shop, is the aim of

[1] The uniform of the elite workers, the *Werkschaaren*.

every Werkschaar man. Where could the National Socialism of the Heart be more honestly exemplified than in the workshop itself, amidst the thousand needs and problems of our everyday working day? There is a greatness about the events of our times, yet there are many among us who are full of doubt and of questions that are of burning and essential importance. The Werkschaar man wants to help his shop comrade, wants to show him the way, wants to give him enlightenment to the best of his will and ability.

But the answers can't be pulled out of one's sleeves, at least not by National Socialists with a sense of responsibility.

"You will find a rare scene here," the District Leader of the work platoon told us when we arrived. And it was indeed a strange scene that confronted us as we entered the red-brick school building and found grown men squeezed together on the low school benches. "Women are not admitted here, nor are civilians," the District Leader explained. "This is a general course of the 'German People's Educational Work' program, and our men come here mainly to get basic answers to any problem that comes up in their shops!"

"German People's Educational Work"? Isn't that a special branch of the NSG [2] Strength Through Joy, which has set up a gigantic education apparatus throughout the Reich? The office whose task it is to make the German worker familiar with the treasures of his national art, to give him the basic foundation of a good general education, and which thus, alongside the vocational training of the "Vocational Education and Shop Management" of the German Labor Front, does the most for popular education? The office which opens up for the German worker one of the many possible ways in which he can achieve social advancement through his own vocational skill and general knowledge?

From SA.—*Geist im Betrieb: Vom Ringen um die Durchsetzung des deutschen Sozialismus* (Munich: Zentralverlag der NSDAP, Frz. Eher Nachf., 1938), pp. 152-153.

The Correct Attitude Toward Work

To assure the success of Reich defense measures and the Four-Year Plan, General Field Marshal Minister-President Göring, as the au-

[2] Nationalsozialistische Gemeinde, or National Socialist Community.

thority responsible for the Four-Year Plan, on June 25, 1938, issued regulations concerning wage structures and transmitted to the Reich Trustee of Labor and the Special Trustee of Labor full power to take all necessary measures for the prevention of any damage to the rearmament program or the Four-Year Plan which might come about through spiraling tendencies in wages and adverse developments in working conditions.

In an important industrial enterprise in the Middle Elbe Economic Region, which had important obligations to fulfill within the framework of the Four-Year Plan, the working discipline was seriously impaired by the fact that part of the labor force frequently absented itself from work—or, as it is called, "loafed"—without any excuse whatever and on the slightest pretexts. As a result of such practices, production was so severely endangered that I was forced to exercise the power vested in me by the regulation of June 25, 1938, to order the strictest adherence to the regular work schedule set for this enterprise, and to declare that any further offenses would be subject to criminal prosecution. Nonetheless, after a short time various members of the work force, who did not yet possess the right attitude toward work and the correct understanding of their duties within the National Socialist state, endangered the productivity of the plant again by repeatedly absenting themselves without cause or permission, giving invalid reasons for their absence. The attitude of these members of the work force evidenced such a lack of responsibility toward the goals of the Four-Year Plan and such deliberate disregard of the idea of the plant community that these offenses could no longer go unpunished. On my request, therefore, the State Prosecutor immediately instituted a criminal court trial against the guilty persons. In accelerated proceedings, three members of the work force of the plant were found guilty of violating Paragraph 2 of the Regulation for Wage Structure of June 25, 1938, and were consequently sentenced to jail for one month, three weeks, and six weeks, respectively.

Several other similar cases are still pending.

Magdeburg, December 2, 1938

The Reich Trustee of Labor
for the Middle Elbe Economic Region

From Official Communications from the Reich Trustee of Labor for the Middle Elbe Economic Region, No. 1, January 5, 1939. (Wiener Library Clipping Collection.)

Plant Managers—This Must Not Be!

. . . And something else: If someone wants to better himself financially in his position, he has a perfect right to do so and nobody can blame him. On the other hand, nobody can blame an industrial enterprise if it tries to stop an inexpedient migration of its skilled workers and attempts to keep those with experience.

But the best way to accomplish this is not by subjecting a worker who could earn more somewhere else to threats and by implying that he will be sent to the "border fortifications." For every German, work on the frontier fortifications is a matter of honor! It would be a shameless degradation of this great work of the Führer if attempts are made to convert it into a form of punishment!

> From *Der Angriff*, Dec. 3, 1938. (Wiener Library Clipping Collection.)

A Wage Freeze for Stenographers

The Reich Trustee of Labor for the Economic Region of Bavaria has now issued a regulation concerning all female clerical employees in industry, trade, workshops, and the professions, especially stenographers, secretaries, and typists. The most important stipulations of this regulation are:

On entering a new employment, female employees may not demand a salary or any other consideration of any sort higher than that received in their previous employment. Business managers may hire such employees only at their previous salary and considerations. If, however, the prevailing salary scale of the new place of employment provides for higher pay, then the higher salary must be paid.

Female employees who have finished their apprenticeship, on entering a new employment or on becoming full-fledged clerks, may not receive pay higher than their salary scale. The same applies to females being employed for the first time.

Increases over the basic salary rates at the time of hiring may not be granted for a period of at least six months from the day the employee entered upon her duties. Any increase—even if granted in individual cases—must be communicated in writing, at least three weeks before becoming effective, to the Reich Trustee of Labor with a full explanation of the reasons for it and with a statement of the previous and proposed salary rates. It is not necessary to report salary increases which fall due within the framework of regular and contractual salary scales. . . . .

Anyone found guilty of violation or evasion of this regulation is subject to a jail sentence and a fine, the latter of undetermined amount, or either one of these penalties. This regulation comes into force July 1.

> From the *Fränkische Tageszeitung* (Nuremberg), July 1, 1939. (Wiener Library Clipping Collection.)

The Conversion of "Comrade" Müller
WALTER DACH

"I must leave again right away," Müller said quickly, after he had swept up his boys, all three of them, in the circle of his mighty arms, the while shouting "Loafers! Vagabonds!" and, in accordance with a long-established custom, carried them out of the kitchen and threw them onto the beds. The youngest, a six-year-old, enjoyed it most, but all three roared and bellowed like lions.

"Must you go out again?" Müller's wife asked with a touch of apprehension. She knew that something was gnawing at him and boiling inside him. He was a regular fanatic in everything he did, and on occasion he easily became thoughtless. The cause of Labor seemed definitely lost; it had been drilled into him for a generation, so that he had to believe it now. But what wholly confused him was that he had no evidence for it. "Hitler is a slave of the bourgeoisie!" they had shouted for many years at political meetings. And now they saw how captains of industry and banker-princes had to ask this Hitler for favors.

"And they will certainly take him in!" Müller had tried to tell himself.

They want to. Could be. But will he permit himself to be taken in? That is the question. Frau Müller had never been particularly inter-

ested in politics. But this much she understood (in fact, she felt it):
Hitler wants the best for the worker; one can trust him. He has himself stood on a scaffold as a simple worker, and he knows what's in the
poor man's heart.

"He will forget, just like all the other big shots we've had before,"
grumbled Müller.

"I don't believe that," said his wife. "The man lives so simply, you
can see that by his clothes. Of course, time will tell. By the way,
there's a letter from the Association of the Saarlanders . . . about
the plebiscite." [1]

Müller mumbled something. Then he shaved, washed up, and
changed his clothes—and in between managed a few bites of food. "I
tell you, this may be my lucky day. This Flex is quite a boy."

"That's just what I don't like," Frau Müller objected. "If somebody is kicked out for swindling . . ."

"I don't like that either," Müller said. "But what's it to do with
me? All that was a long time ago, and none of us knows what really
happened. Perhaps the board of directors may not be quite so clean
either. . . . If you wanted to investigate every individual . . . I tell
you, then . . ."

At the Friedrichstrasse café Müller asked for Herr Flex, because he
was unable to find him right away.

"Herr Director Flex?"

"Damn it all! Is Flex a director? Yes, he always had the devil's own
luck!"

There he was. He was dressed differently now and appeared even
more well-to-do. He approached Müller with mincing steps and
stretched out both hands.

Müller was glad to escape being the center of attention. The ele-
gant manner in which the customers filled their comfortable seats, the
frock-coated waiters, and the music threw Müller into a state of confusion. This was not a beer joint for working stiffs.

Flex escorted Müller through several large rooms, prattling inces-
santly, nimble as a weasel. Finally they came to a smaller, more cozy-

---

[1] At the Treaty of Versailles the coal-rich Saar was given the status of an independent nation (though economically tied to France) pending a plebiscite scheduled for 1935. The population could vote to join either France or Germany or
retain its present status. In January 1935, 90 per cent voted for a return to Germany.

looking room where it was more quiet and just right for a friendly chat. Here Müller became more talkative. . . .

"Yes," said Flex, as he blew a series of smoke rings—he could always do that; sometimes he'd blow ten rings, one right after the other. "The world is large and yet so small. At the chemical plant there was really nothing doing for me. Shall I remain an insignificant clerk all my life and slave for three hundred marks a month or probably even less? While others grow fat and rich? Should I waste my talents in a back-breaking joint like that?"

And how about the swindle at the chemical plant? Müller was thinking.

"No, no, my dear Müller," Flex continued. "I made a big jump from Berlin to Paris. Then I was in Lyons and Strassburg. Not long ago I spent several weeks in Saarbrücken. You can see I'm on top of things now. As director of the agency of a great French-Luxemburger manufacturer. . . . Yes, yes, for the time being I've pitched my tent again in Berlin. But it's different from before, altogether different. . . ."

Müller was saying to himself that you've got to believe him. Flex was wearing a suit of excellent material and workmanship. A golden watch fob dangled from his vest pocket. And he had rings on his fingers that must have cost a fortune. You could say the same of the pearl stickpin in his tie. He must also have a full wallet and a substantial bank account, Müller thought to himself.

"But things like that don't just happen by themselves," Flex continued. "You have to struggle for them. You have to know how to exploit advantages. You have to be alert, Herr Müller. You cannot allow yourself to stumble over obstacles and prejudices."

Müller was thinking: Why does he tell me all this?

"But how about you, my dear Müller? Let's have a good drink. Your health!"

Müller found it difficult keeping up with him. Flex had always been a great wine drinker.

"So you fellows here in Germany have made a little revolution since I've been gone, eh?" Flex looked around carefully and then broke into a boisterous laugh. But he continued in a whisper: "Müller, I must tell you: The Germans . . . they can't even pull off a real revolution . . . something like in France . . ."

"Oh, we've had plenty of changes," Müller broke in. "I can't get over them."

Flex was taken aback for a moment. "But you personally? When they fired Chief Shop Steward Müller, how many hundred marks in pension did they give him?" He laughed again, openly mocking now.

"These are hard times," Müller said, and thought of his old ideals and the many functions and offices he once held.[2]

"In other words, dribblings, real dribblings!" Flex agreed with Müller's complaint. "Abroad we know all about it. I've met enough emigrants." He bent forward. "And will you take it all lying down? I can tell you, there's something cooking in the Saar region. The vote won't go for France, unfortunately. But status quo votes. . . . In the long run it will turn out to be the same thing, I hope. The coal mines will have to go to France. They are vitally important . . . as is the whole Saar . . . in peace as well as in war."

Flex moved his chair closer. "Müller, I have a real big deal—and I need you."

Martin Müller was startled by the green glints in Flex's eyes. "You mean you can offer me another job?"

"Yes. Can you keep silence?"

"Of course, if it's necessary."

"It is, Müller, unconditionally. But you must promise me that you will tell nobody, not a single soul."

That must be a pretty peculiar job if there's so much secrecy involved, Müller thought. But he said: "I promise." Loud and clear. "I brought along my papers and letters of reference from my former positions." He drew them from his inside pocket.

Flex waved him silently away. His hand played with his wineglass. He swallowed another gulp for encouragement and then he began to speak as if he were in a business conference.

"Herr Müller, I have a special commission from the French armaments industry. For many years your chemical factory has been planning the production of a particular gas for industrial purposes. The experiments have now come to a successful end. That much we know. But we are interested in learning about all the details of the technical processes that are involved. My plans are made, but it would not suit my purpose to approach the engineers directly. The whole matter will have to go through three or four different hands. My contact must be a completely unsuspected man, someone who can be led by intermediaries to the secret. I have worked out how that will be done in

[2] In the trade union and the Social Democratic party.

detail. What I still need is the first man in the chain. And that will be you, Müller."

Müller sat motionless. He stared at Flex without blinking. Look how Flex was changing! His nose was growing longer and turning into a beak. His eyes grew craftier and now they were piercing and sharp. His hair seemed to stand on end until it grew into a regular cock's comb. A bird's head, a vulture, a regular carrion kite.

"Here is your chance," Flex continued. "You will receive a sum of money—and nothing to sneeze at either. Besides, you will get your revenge. You will be satisfied, Müller. You don't have any misgivings, do you? You have always been an honest man, my dear Müller. I know. Too honest, in fact. Even as shop steward you could have looked out for yourself a little more. What did it get you? A kick in the behind. But this has nothing to do with honesty or the lack of it. It is merely a business deal, pure and simple. The capitalists of the whole world are related to each other anyway. In another year we would have found that secret in France ourselves. And you can believe me, there are excellent minds in the West, too. But why conduct experiments if there is another, quicker, and more direct way? Let me give you a tip, Müller, just in case you should develop moral scruples. Look at this thing from a political angle. Play a trick on the new regime in Germany. The gas, I can tell you, is a positively horrible thing. It eats its way through tanks and concrete cellars. The next war will be damned funny for Germany. . . ."

Müller still sat motionless and silent before Flex. What things you can see if you select a point on the wall and keep staring at it! Gray, nebulous swaths seem to fill the room. Somewhere, someone was hammering on a piece of iron rail: Gas alarm! Columns of soldiers broke out of their trenches—storming forward, gas masks on their faces. No artillery. A ghostly, silent combat in the field. They drop in ranks, like grass before the blade of the scythe. From the other side a gray fog rolls in. Gas! Gas! There is no defense against it. And three of the thousands who are dying there—are they not Müller's boys?—stretch out their arms toward Müller as they run, drop their rifles helplessly, threatening and cursing—and then they themselves drop, tearing the masks from their faces in the agony of death, still moaning, crying: Father! . . . Father! . . . Traitor! . . . Traitor!

"Müller! What's the matter with you? Wherever I am well off, there is my fatherland! Think of the pile of money! No other worker would hesitate a moment. The world will always go on like this: I come first, what do I care about the others?"

Now Müller stood up, very slowly, his eyes still fixed on the man across the table. He stretched himself to his full height, drew back his right hand—and with the force of a blacksmith's hammer planted his fist in the middle of Flex's face. Blood sprang from his nose like water from a well.

Flex stumbled backward, then took hold of himself, turned the table over, and flung himself at Müller.

"A madman! He's gone crazy!"

Müller moved as if to strike Flex again. Flex backed away. Suddenly Fräulein Wackerhagen, a secretary at the plant, was there, as though she had been lurking in the next room. Waiters and other guests came rushing in.

"Now I'm beginning to see it," Müller said after one glance at the secretary. "You've been spying on me at the plant gate for the longest time, just to see whether I might be willing to do your dirty work for you. But without me, friends. Without me . . ."

There was confusion all around. People were shouting questions and running among the chairs and tables. Everyone was pushing somebody else. Fräulein Wackerhagen was pulling Flex's nose to stop the bleeding.

"I probably will never be a real National Socialist," Müller said, quivering with emotion, "but one thing I do know: The workers don't want another war—and neither does Hitler; he still has his stomach full from the last one. And he has already done several things about it—at least more than any other government before him. That has to be admitted. And the Saar region has nothing to do with war. And a traitor I will not be. My three youngsters . . ."

Suddenly the manager of the café appeared with a policeman, and Flex began to roll his eyes.

"What happened here?" the policeman asked.

"I belted him one," Müller said.

"How could you do such a thing? Are you crazy? A blow of such force . . ."

"It's not too bad," Flex gurgled behind his blood-drenched handkerchief. He sounded so comical that everyone started laughing, including the policeman.

But it also showed that some game was being played which the police must not know anything about, especially since Flex anxiously demanded to pay the bill and to depart with his female associate.

The policeman grabbed him. "All right, off to the precinct station! And then to Alex!" [3]

From Walter Dach, *Volksgenosse Müller II: Erzählungen der Arbeit* (Berlin: Schaffer-Verlag, 1935), pp. 21-31.

THE BILL IS PRESENTED

What the German People Pay in Taxes, 1939

In addition to the armaments race, in terms of numbers of guns, planes, trained soldiers, cadres, etc., there is another "race" among so-called civilized nations that is frequently overlooked—that is, the monstrous growth of taxes with which the citizens are burdened. In this field, too, the Third Reich has registered top accomplishments. It is devoutly to be wished that those in some capitalistic circles in Switzerland and other democracies who are afflicted with admiration for the "order" existing in dictatorial countries, also occasionally give this problem of taxation some attention. In particular, the 1 per cent arms-defense tax over which we are now wrangling in Switzerland must appear as very moderate when compared with what the "racial comrades" in Greater Germany have to pay for their Führer's dreams of glory.

We have before us an official summary of the direct and graduated taxes at present prevailing in Germany. It is a brochure of 120 pages with many statistical tables. The last page holds forth the consolation that "the introduction of changes is always possible." . . . The tax blessings flow constantly further and the nerves grow more tense.

Altogether, there are 21 different taxes in the Reich today—12 property taxes and 9 communication taxes, not counting, of course, the purely local assessments with which municipalities try to cover their own special needs. And beyond those, there are the not inconsiderable "voluntary taxes," such as that of the "Winter Aid." [1]

[3] "Alex" is Berlin slang for police headquarters, in those years located at the Alexander Platz.

[1] A supposedly voluntary collection to help supply the poor with warm clothing and coal.

The twelve property taxes are:

1. Income tax
2. Tax on wages
3. Capital-gains tax
4. Tax on boards of directors
5. Citizen's tax
6. Armaments tax
7. Corporation tax
8. License tax
9. Real-estate tax
10. Economic improvement assessment
11. Reich emigration tax (special tax on those who wish to leave Germany)
12. Inheritance tax

The brochure concludes with a "Tax Dates Calendar," which clearly indicates the days of each month on which part payments on one or another tax are due. There is not a single month in which a part payment on some tax is not due. February and August, for instance, each have eight such Tax Dates—with two different taxes due on the 5th, three more on the 10th, two on the 15th, and one on the 20th. The brochure states: "These payment dates must be strictly observed." Grace periods have been abolished.

The basis of the whole structure is the Reich income tax. Here, from a social point of view, it is worthy of notice that sizable tax reductions are granted to married people in proportion to the number of children they have. The tax burden for single persons is so heavy that they find it next to impossible to put aside sufficient savings for the establishment of homes of their own. Widowed and divorced persons, up to a certain age, are classified as "single."

We give here some of the tax ratings for several categories: single persons (1); married couples without children (2); and married couples with two children (3).

Annual Income (in RM)[2]	Tax Payments (in RM)		
	(1)	(2)	(3)
4,000	640	342	185
6,000	1,024	640	376
10,000	1,984	1,240	910
20,000	5,376	3,360	2,796
50,000	21,568	13,480	12,710
100,000	50,000	33,480	32,600

[2] In 1939 the exchange rate was $1.00 = 2.49 Reichsmarks.

The unmarried "racial comrade" who earns 100,000 Reichsmarks must cough up exactly one half of it. For other high incomes (from 50,000 to 100,000 RM) the tax rate (in percentage figures) remains the same as for a 50,000 RM income. Widowed and divorced men and women who have Jewish children are regarded as single and have to pay the higher tax rate.

The rates for the wage tax, which is deducted in advance from the pay check, are also extremely high. In the middle brackets of wage and salary incomes, the tax amounts to about 15 per cent.

The citizen's tax rises progressively from 2 to 50 RM for incomes of 20,000 RM.

The real-estate and property tax amounts basically to 0.5 per cent.

The inheritance tax is levied on five different levels; it increases from 2 to 15 per cent for small inheritances and amounts to from 7 to 34 per cent for inheritances of 500,000 RM and over.

The license tax is based on the capitalization, revenue, and wage total of the individual enterprise. For the professional middle class, from which a great percentage of Hitler's original followers was recruited, it must be particularly disheartening to find itself now burdened down with this especially oppressive tax.

At any rate, a careful perusal of the brochure conveys the impression that the oft-mentioned "limit of endurance" is a highly variable proposition when it comes to tax assessments. A democracy not only safeguards our civil liberties but also saves us from slaving several months each year exclusively to pay taxes.

England also has a relatively high tax burden, especially for those with large incomes; but since the English and German legislative systems are altogether different, comparisons are extremely difficult to make. The German taxation system demands, in addition, a highly complicated executive and control apparatus, which in turn has to be paid for by the people.

From the National-Zeitung (Basel), Feb. 23, 1939. (Wiener Library Clipping Collection.)

The Cost of Living, 1933-1937

Berlin, May 14—For the first time in a considerable period, the Institute for Market Analysis has analyzed retail prices and the cost of living in Germany. While several weeks ago it was still maintained that the cost of living had advanced by only 3.4 per cent during the four years of National Socialist direction of the economy, the Institute now admits an actual increase of 7.2 per cent. The figures are based on the consumption of the average worker's family, but they can be regarded as only conditionally valid for the whole population, since numerous relief measures and special allowances have been created for certain low-income categories.

For foodstuffs, prices increased by 11.5 per cent since 1933. Compared with prewar prices, costs have gone up 22.3 per cent, but compared with the price levels of 1929, there has been an actual drop of 23.4 per cent. For clothes, the price increase is as much as 17.5 per cent over 1933 and, in comparison with 1914, 24.5 per cent. However, clothing prices are 28 per cent lower than in 1929.

Rents show no great index changes during the past four years. In comparison with 1929, rent is generally 3.7 per cent lower, but in comparison with that of prewar days, 21.3 per cent higher.

Among all categories included in the cost-of-living index, heat and clothing are the only ones whose costs have been reduced—by 1.1 per cent—since 1933. They are 11.3 per cent cheaper than in 1928, but 26.6 per cent more expensive than they were in 1914.

"Miscellaneous" items are 41.9 per cent higher than in 1914 and 0.2 per cent higher than four years ago. In comparison with 1929, there has been a reduction of 17.6 per cent.

The general price rise is even more obvious when present-day retail prices are compared with those of 1933. Butter increased by 35 per cent, margarine by 44 per cent, eggs by 31 per cent, potatoes by 22 per cent, meats generally by 18 per cent. The increase in beef is 18 per cent, in pork 11 per cent. But calf and lamb have risen by 40 and 41 per cent, respectively. Dairy products are generally 15 per cent higher, peas even 52 per cent higher, and beans 31 per cent higher. Oat cereals increased by 5 per cent, rice by 7 per cent, and sugar by 2 per cent. Vegetables are 2 per cent higher; whole milk 7 per cent. Bread is 2 per cent cheaper and other bakery products (pastry, etc.) 1 per cent. Rye bread and mixed breads are 2 per cent cheaper; specialty bread 1 per cent; mill products generally are noted as 2 per cent cheaper.

Under the category of heat and light, coal, gas, and electricity likewise have been reduced—by 1 per cent each. But prices for overcoats, shirts, and shoes advanced 24, 17, and 8 per cent, respectively. For hygiene and care of the body, there has been a cost reduction of 2 per cent, and for transportation of 3 per cent. But the cost of home furnishings has increased 6 per cent, entertainment 1 per cent, newspapers 2 per cent, and cultural activities, 1 per cent.

On the whole, therefore, retail prices have advanced steeply. Price reductions have no relation to price rises. At the same time these figures do not take into consideration a general deterioration in the quality of goods and products. To mention only one example: the quality of bread has been sharply reduced by the complete outmilling of rye and by an admixture of 7 per cent corn meal to wheat flour.

The progressive deterioration in quality, of course, is not easily perceptible in the index figures. But it may be said that it more than counterbalances any modest price reductions, aside from the fact that it forces the consumer to turn to higher-priced products. Thus the price increases for meats are in reality steeper than appears from the index. Since very frequently certain lower-price cuts of meat were not available on the market, there was an enforced changeover to better-grade meat products and in consequence a corresponding increase in the real cost of living. The same can be said in connection with dairy products and certainly also with textile goods, which show a large admixture of artificial silk and wool fibers. Thus it is difficult to understand how the Institute for Market Analysis can present these factors as merely incidental and without real bearing on the actual cost of living.

> From the *Luxemburger Wort* (Luxemburg), May 15-16, 1937. (Wiener Library Clipping Collection.)

They Who Serve Are Well Paid

On the basis of a new Reich salary scale, according to reports from Berlin, the commander of a department of the armed forces, the chief of staff of the supreme command of the armed forces, and the chief of the German Reich police are now receiving a salary of 26,550 Reichsmarks annually. Secretaries of state, presiding judges of the superior courts, general-colonels, general-admirals, generals, and admirals receive 24,000 Reichsmarks per year.

> From *Pester Lloyd* (Budapest), Feb. 23, 1940. (Wiener Library Clipping Collection.)

The Situation of the German Retail Trade

One of the great slogans of the National Socialist economic program during the so-called "Period of Struggle" called for assistance to the small retail stores and handicraft enterprises and for the elimination of the giant department stores. . . .

In the last several years the policy for supplying the population with consumer goods has undergone a complete reversal. . . . The index for retail trade sales has fallen behind the figures for 1928. . . . Even before the outbreak of the war, the scarcity of consumer goods impaired the viability of many small businesses to such an extent that their owners were unable to maintain a minimum standard of living and had to be supported. . . .

The unfavorable position of the retail business gave the National Socialist offices charged with the recruitment of additional labor forces for the undermanned armament industry a welcome opportunity to subject small businesses and workshops to a careful combing over. In Berlin alone, some 10,000 shops and stores were closed under this sorting-out policy. The owners and members of their families lost their independence and were shepherded into the armament and building industries and into the administrative apparatus.

If, because of the scarcity of goods, many small businesses had become unprofitable even before the outbreak of the war, the tendency was definitely strengthened by the ration-card and certificate system which was instituted with the coming of the war. Distribution of goods was further curtailed. . . . As could be expected, many additional business enterprises have now become unprofitable and are already in severe financial difficulties.

> From the *Neue Züricher Zeitung*, Nov. 28, 1939. (Wiener Library Clipping Collection.)

Throttling the Retail Trade

Das Schwarze Korps has repeatedly exposed the fact that there is an excess of manpower in the retail trade and has pointed to the imbalance it creates in the economic system. The recognition of this truth does not find a joyful echo everywhere, but that neither eliminates it nor does it spare our Reich leadership the task of creating a better balance and reducing the bloated apparatus of the distribution trade. . . .

Thus it is evident that today we have more merchants than we can feed and at the same time a shortage of productive forces, which are utterly wasted in the hopeless endeavor to wrest a bare subsistence from superfluous retail-trade establishments. It is likewise understandable that those concerned see a great personal hardship in the proposal that they give up their hopeless profession and adopt another. But they and the German people as a whole have at long last the opportunity to rectify old mistakes and to bring a new order into the distribution of tasks in the community.

We must reduce the number of small distribution businesses to the absolutely necessary minimum and thereby strengthen productivity, safeguard and improve the living of superfluous merchants, and reduce the cost of living for the whole nation.

> From *Das Schwarze Korps*, July 27, 1939. (Wiener Library Clipping Collection.)

The Price Police

Berlin, January 10—Police administrative offices have been advised to pay increased attention to price control and to entrust this important task to specially qualified police officers, who are to be exempted from other duties. . . .

Heretofore, when prices were checked by the police, many retail merchants excused themselves by claiming that they had just begun to mark their wares, or that the goods had just arrived for display. Such excuses are no longer to be accepted. It is of particular importance that imported produce—fruits, vegetables, etc.—should be clearly identified as such on their price tags or on the merchant's bill. The fixed maximum prices are known to be frequently exceeded. Some especially sharp merchants are marking their price tags on both sides. On one side they carry the correct price, and on the other the illegal higher price. When prices are inspected, they simply turn the tags around so that the correct price is showing. . . .

Special care should be taken in the examination of bills and book-keeping methods generally. . . .

> From the *Frankfurter Zeitung*, Jan. 11, 1939. (Wiener Library Clipping Collection.)

A Butcher Resists

The Government Office in Münster reports: At Bockum-Höve I, the members of the butchers' guild refused to abide by the prices for meats as fixed by the county administrator[1] at the behest of the Government Price Control Office. The spokesman for the butchers told the police: "We won't let the county administrator set the prices for us." He was thereupon ordered by the chief administrative officer of the region[2] to be taken into custody and was lodged in the police jail at Recklinghausen.

> From the *Frankfurter Zeitung*, Oct. 15, 1939. (Wiener Library Clipping Collection.)

[1] *Landrat*, the appointed government official who administers a county.
[2] *Regierungspräsident*, the appointed official who administers a whole region for the government.

11

The Assumption of Power

THE EVENTS OF January 30, 1933, when Adolf Hitler became Chancellor of the Reich, affected all Germans, each in his own way. Unfortunately, few descriptions have come down to us of how the Nazi take-over was received by members of the population at large. The elections held in March of that year may be significant in this regard, for though they were conducted under mounting Nazi pressure, they were the last free elections for many years to come. The Nazis did not attain an absolute majority, receiving 43.9 per cent of the vote, but they did increase their strength. The results of these elections served to accelerate the National Socialist effort to absorb all of German political and cultural life.

Just how this was done is illustrated by two excerpts which convey the flavor of what was happening. Otto Knab's account of how the Nazis took over a small Bavarian town near Munich was published in Switzerland in 1934, when the memory of the event must still have been fresh. This was a town in which everyone knew each other, in which the temper of life was placid—and, judging from the composition of the City Council, the prevalent political atmosphere was conservative. The irony which pervades the account of a revolution made by amateurs must not disguise the fact that they were successful, that they did take over the public life of the town, however harmless their actions may have appeared. For the National Socialist revolution did not storm the barricades, but arrived through a legal seizure of power and threw the might of the government of the Reich behind the aims of the party.

In Herne, an industrial city in the Ruhr Valley (in 1931 it had 98,400 inhabitants), the Nazis did not fare very well, even two months after Hitler's seizure of power. In the municipal elections of March 12, 1933, the NSDAP emerged as the largest single party, but only on the basis of a third of the total vote cast. The Catholic Center party came next—only to be expected in a Catholic region—and the Communists ran third: apparently a self-conscious working class still existed in this highly industrialized part of Germany. Their relatively bad showing need not have worried the Nazis, for the Reich government came to their aid; by the end of the year all rival political parties had been dissolved. Moreover, a new law on local government (1934) gave the party the decisive voice in appointing or firing mayors and aldermen.

Meanwhile the party proceeded to change the tempo of life in the city. Not only were street names changed and voluntary organizations taken over, but the Nazis employed methods which had served them well during their rise to power. A constant round of mass meetings, parades, and the flying of flags kept the population in a permanent state of excitement. A host of party-sponsored activities sooner or later involved every citizen with the Nazis whether he liked it or not. The city historian of Herne graphically describes the methods used to take over his town and the changed tempo of life which resulted. Though he writes much after the event (1963), he has only to list what actually took place for us to visualize what life must have been like during those stormy days of 1933.

The take-over on the local level was as bloodless as the take-over in the Reich as a whole. The proceedings of the City Council of Cologne at its first meeting after Hitler became Chancellor give little evidence of an opposition still physically present in the chamber. Konrad Adenauer and the Catholic Center party had ruled Cologne for sixteen years. Both vanished in the wave of enthusiasm for the Nazis. For until this meeting the Nazis had been a tiny minority on the City Council. The Nazi speaker, Joseph Grohé (b. 1902), was Gauleiter of the Köln-Aachen district of the NSDAP and "leader" of the Nazi aldermen. He was also a member of the Prussian State Diet. Indeed, Grohé had joined the party as early as 1921, and this speech was reprinted in a book published to celebrate his twentieth anniversary as a party member (1941). By that time he had served as Gauleiter for ten years, and he was to continue in that office until the collapse of the Third Reich. No doubt, this speech, indeed this council session, represents the highlight of his career.

For the average citizen it may well have been little things rather than the bigger political events that impressed the change upon his mind. Hermann Stresau, novelist and opponent of the regime, looks back upon a few such incidents.

All of these descriptions of what happened at the assumption of power are far from complete, but they should serve to give an impression of the take-over on the local level, where it affected each citizen most immediately and deeply. As far as the average citizen was concerned, the changes were instituted peacefully; nevertheless, they were ruthlessly complete. It was possible simply to go along, to swim with the current, and to slide into the Nazi pattern of life. Indeed, this was the path of least resistance, even if one had not voted for the Nazis in March 1933. Once a beginning had been made, everything else followed—the Nazi cultural drive began to get hold of and to mold the population. What this meant we have seen in this book.

The working classes of Herne had voted Communist in considerable numbers as late as March 1933. But with their unions destroyed and their party proscribed, there was little left to stiffen any resistance they might have offered. Above all, unemployment had been done away with by the end of 1933, and this achievement spoke louder than the sentiments of bygone times. The old ruling classes of the Empire, a nobility which had successfully survived throughout the Republic, offered scattered resistance. A mass movement frightened their aristocratic sensibilities, and the Christianity to which they had a deep allegiance seemed menaced by the Nazi ideology. However, many of this class, led by the Princes of Prussia, who hoped that Hitler would restore the monarchy, joined the Nazi movement. Most took the view of the high-born lady, Baroness Richthofen, which is recalled by Erich Ebermayer in his memoirs. That lady had to defend her acquiescence in the Nazi regime to Ebermayer's mother, the wife of the one-time Chief Public Prosecutor of the Republic and, like her son, an opponent of all the Nazis stood for.

The attitude of Baroness Richthofen was by no means confined to members of her class; it provided a powerful rationale for the acceptance of evil, and not just in Germany. If there had been barricades instead of legality in 1933, men and women would have been forced to make more reasoned decisions. The legal assumption of power, however, allowed them to drift into the open arms of the Third Reich, finding themselves in an embrace from which there was no escape, except prison or exile. Conformity took precedence over personal friendships, however old and valued. Yet we must always remember that there were many who were enthusiastic for the new order, to whom the Nazi ideology seemed to give a new meaning to life.

Fellow traveler or adept, both found themselves partners in the most far-reaching attempt to impose a monolithic cultural pattern upon a modern nation which the Western world had yet seen. Throughout this book we have been concerned with the way in which this pattern was made to penetrate into the population, and with it the world view for which it stood. We can now see the Nazi assumption of power in its proper dimensions—as opening the gate through which this Nazi culture poured down upon the people. That it struck so many responsive chords is perhaps the greatest tragedy of all. Men will rationalize, will allow themselves to drift into situations, but that millions should have identified themselves wholly and unconditionally with Nazi culture gives a seriousness to these documents which cannot be brushed aside as merely the creation of clever or successful propaganda.

G.L.M.

Our Town under the Swastika

OTTO MICHAEL KNAB

If somewhere a situation arises which causes people to say: "There's something in the air," one talks strikingly little about this situation and about this air which brings forebodings of some ominous occurrence. Such was the case between March 5 and 6, 1933, in our little town on the lake. The mood was one of slight weariness, like the early-March cloudy sky. The elections, carried out amid the enthusiasm of January 30, were over. Some of those who never grow weary even dreamed about the possibility of a coalition. Nobody joined them in their fantasies. Something like a hangover (though no one would admit it) stuck to the remembrances of these election results of March 5.[1] Those who before had declared that one must give Hitler a chance—maybe he will still make it, they would say, because otherwise we will have Bolshevism—seemed to have become somewhat unsure of what was in the offing. On the side of the victors, on the Brown one that is, such a suspicious stillness prevailed that no one could see clearly what was to come.

Then, with the first announcements, the bombs exploded! There were rumors, quickly denied, spread anew, again denied, and eventually repeated as facts: there was a revolution in Munich. Now it was a matter of indifference whether Held had resigned or had been arrested, or whether Stützel defended himself or not, or whether Epp had been appointed State Commissioner, whether he was already in Munich or only on the plane.[2]

The only important thing was that the Brown revolution had begun. What would happen now?

Timid persons recalled 1918.[3] Utterances like "arrest of hostages," "put them against the wall," "surrender arms," were heard. Threats which had been uttered during the election campaigns a hundred

[1] See note, page 323.
[2] On March 9, 1933, Hitler carried out a coup d'état in Bavaria, deposing the government of Heinrich Held (1924-1933) and installing General Franz Ritter von Epp as commissioner with absolute power. Karl Stützel was the Bavarian Minister of the Interior.
[3] In 1918 a left-wing socialist revolution took place in Munich.

times now took on the shape of reality. What was in the making?

In the meanwhile, the National Socialist leaders of the town clung feverishly to the telephone. What they heard from the party offices was no more certain than the rumors that ran through the streets. Confirmation, denial, alarm, denial. Confirmation, denial, but finally a sure, hard fact: Alarm! The order was sent out all over the country.

"The swastika is to be raised above all public buildings. Resistance is to be crushed!" The public did not know about this order, but they saw the results of its execution. The twilight had not yet been wholly tinged with darkness, when the SA was already under arms.

"The SA under arms" represented not one but two conceptions. First, "the SA"! The "old fighters" were long known in the town; some were looked upon with pity, with understanding, some with tolerance, others with repulsion and disgust. The townsfolk did not know the others who had joined since January 30 and who now marched in the brown uniform. There were many young people especially. Now they were standing alongside the veterans, who had many fights behind them, palpitant with a lust for action.

"Under arms"! This was the second conception. In the cities where the SA was old enough to have been trained in the handling of guns, it must have been quite a military spectacle to see the Brown army equipped with all the accouterments of war. Here in the town the spectacle was of a military character only in the first ranks of the battalion; the other ranks looked more romantic than military. The marching went well, at least as far as one could judge in the darkness. The sudden wheeling to the right or left and the about-faces were reminiscent of recruits on the parade ground. At the order "Halt!" there was a picturesque potpourri, as in some movie scenes in which masses of Bedouins gesticulate wildly with rifles. Anyone who was not afraid to keep step with the marching executive committee of the revolution could hear the battle-scarred veterans giving all sorts of coarse admonitions to the young revolutionaries, such as: "Hold your rifle up, dummox!"

The only dangerous aspect about these goings-on was that the rifles were loaded with live ammunition. All that was needed was an unfortunate accident to set off this mostly untrained horde on a wild shooting spree. But who wanted to prevent a revolution in a little town? Therefore the SA marched under arms to carry out their first deed.

The District Office peacefully submitted to the violence and capitulated before the rifles; it hung a red banner with a black swastika from the skylight. An armed guard stayed behind for the security of the fluttering revolution. The mayor was not in the City Hall, but this too was of no importance. Whether he agreed or not, the banner would have been hoisted anyway. Again two guards stepped forward and placed themselves under the raised banner. By now several hundred people had arrived on the scene. They looked around here and there, like inspectors, and they asked one another what the name of the song was which the armed men were singing in celebration of their victory. Hardly anyone knew the song. It was the "Horst Wessel" song. One of the initiated explained: "They've just sung 'Lift high the banner' ('Die Fahne hoch')."

So much had the will of the people been fulfilled in this revolution.

But now there were not enough banners. That is, there were enough banners to fit in windows, but no big ones such as were proper for public buildings. But an order is an order! So they took the largest of the small banners—it measured about one meter on each side— and marched off with it toward the flagpole at the railroad station.

Again: "Attention!" Again: "Lift high the banner!" And the little red cloth hastily climbed up, ten times higher than its own length. It must have been quite lonesome up there for the little emblem of the great revolution. Thus the first victory had been achieved without bloodshed. The inn near the railroad station had become supreme political headquarters. Here the fighters met to drink toasts to their victory, while the older ones had some private scores to settle. They marched to the dwellings of the Red officials and took their first prisoners without encountering resistance. But it was only on the following day that people learned who had been beaten up, who had been delivered to Munich, whose houses had been searched. Outwardly everything looked peaceful, just as everything looks peaceful today. The burghers went to their regular tables in the pubs that night, even if they were not in their usual gay mood. A club meeting was held, but its members were somewhat distracted. Housewives were late in placing dinner on the table, and workers stayed home.

But armed guards stood at attention in front of three buildings in the town. But did they really stand, so to speak? At about ten o'clock that night two lads were leaning against an apartment building next to the City Hall, the collars of their civilian coats turned up, for the olive-green uniform coats of the SA had not yet been designed at that time. On their heads they wore the SA caps, signs of their revolutionary dignity, and on their left arms was the red band bearing the

swastika. They were flirting excitedly with two well-stacked young
women. It was a rather cold night. A cigarette might warm them up.
So each of the lads stuck a cigarette in his mouth and the girls lit the
matches, holding them under the noses of their heroes.

At this moment a man passed by. He was a member of the Stahlhelm,[4] hence not especially a friend—indeed, the very opposite. He
walked up to the guards, who were comfortably leaning against the
wall, and stood there, his legs spread, and yelled: "You louts! Don't
you know that you're not supposed to smoke and flirt while you're on
guard duty?" As if a superior had reprimanded them, the heroes of
the day dropped their cigarettes and went to fetch their rifles, which
were leaning peacefully against the wall. And they went back to the
City Hall, marching like soldiers.

The Stahlhelmer had long since disappeared. So had the ladies.
The banner of the revolution waved above its guards, who were silent
and tight-lipped—until a gust of wind ripped the proud banner on
the roof gutter, tearing it from top to bottom. It was wounded on the
first day! . . .

Earlier, our little town had had a Town Council. Today this institution is called the "Council of the Town." Not only clothes make the
man, but also words. But before things had gone that far, two stages
had to be passed through. First of all, the Town Council had to be
formed legally in accordance with the results of the March elections.
Thus it was not racially pure, not yet all Brown. There were two Black-
white-reds, two Reds, and four Blacks, opposing eleven Browns.[5]

During the first session there were clashes between Black-white-reds
and Blacks, attacks by the Browns, and declarations of loyalty by those
who were not Brown. Finally, in order to get rid of the former mayor
in a nice way, he was appointed honorary mayor. But this is a story in
itself and not without charm.

The example of the big cities was followed during the second session: the Reds were kicked out. This is how it happened: The two
little men of the color, one of whom by the way had several weeks of
concentration camp behind him, had so much character that they did

[4] The largest German veterans' organization, a competitor at first to the Nazis for
the allegiance of the German right.
[5] The Black-white-reds were the members of the German National party (DNVP),
who used the old colors of imperial Germany. The Blacks were the members of the
Catholic Bavarian People's party. The Browns, or Brownshirts, were the Nazis.

not utter the greeting "Heil Hitler" and lift their hand in a salute as had become the custom during the opening ceremonies of the sessions. Had they done so, they would have been reviled for their hypocrisy. Since they did not do so, the new mayor poured a flood of invective on them and ordered them to leave the session once and for all in their own interest. They took their hats and left. Councillor Elert, a member of the German National party, . . . had the courage to ask for the legal basis of such procedures. In very energetic terms he was told that National Socialist procedures, as revolutionary acts, did not require any legal justification. Besides, this was going to be done everywhere now and the laws justifying these steps would come later: he must realize that a revolution was going on, which certain persons obviously had forgotten.

At the third session the Blacks also disappeared. In accordance with an order issued by the Bavarian Minister of the Interior, Herr Wagner, they had been arrested all over the *Land* and had been released only after signing written declarations in which they agreed to quit the Bavarian People's party and give up their elective offices (in town, municipal, and *Land* governments). Thus a specific means was found for expelling each specific group. But the effects were deadly for all.

In the subsequent period the German Nationals were gradually coordinated with the Nazis and squeezed against the wall until they had become completely meaningless. Then they were accepted as guests in the Nazi groups and placed the Brown uniform over their Black-white-red souls as a cover. In our town there was only one left. Thus did the day come on April 24, 1933, when the "Council of the Town" became racially pure along National Socialist lines. . . .

It was high time that something was done about culture in our little town. During the years of struggle the movement had had no time to waste on such a luxury item as culture. Now, however, overnight, a man had been appointed whose job was to foster and promote culture. He was a kind of obscure character and his name was Rücke. Up to now nobody had ever heard of him, so he had to make people talk about him. There were about 120 clubs and associations in the town, about one third of which concerned themselves with cultural matters, not only those of the body but also those of the soul. There were music and choral societies, theater groups, and modest quartets, and folklore and literary circles.

Some of them were quite active. Since the city was near, hardly a week went by without the announcement of a concert or a lecture by some famous person. In addition, a large artists' colony was being established on the shores of the lake. Thus anyone who wanted to partake of the joys of culture could help himself freely. But even a cultural guardian of a town wants to do something on occasion. So he convened sessions for the purpose of discussing how another dozen performances could be added to the already existing fifty monthly performances, and how all the clubs and societies and their work could be united in one hand (centralization was now the last word)—in a Brown hand, of course. For this purpose a new association was called into being, the National Socialist Cultural Community.

The first thing it did was to make an ass of itself.

The cultural guardian called for a public meeting and delivered a long speech. At the end of it everybody wondered: What exactly did he want?

Strangely enough, he allowed free discussion. So he was asked what his speech had been all about and just what new plans he had in mind. The cultural guardian, no lazy man he, freely admitted that this was exactly what he would like to find out from the people assembled there. He would like to get his plan, and an idea on how to launch something novel, from the discussions. The people in the audience were vastly amused by this, but they were shy with suggestions after seeing one of the local physicians being treated quite rudely. The meeting had one result at least. A sheet of paper was passed around and all those who wanted to apply for membership and were prepared to contribute fifty pfennigs monthly were invited to sign it.

Then the cultural guardian himself had some ideas. Since it seemed to him that German culture had been neglected in recent years, he started the first cultural evening with a talk on the topic: "Five Years in Rumania." His daughter sang and read Rumanian poems, which, of course, nobody understood, but everyone applauded vigorously. Later she performed a Rumanian national dance with some other girls —I don't know whether it really was Rumanian. Finally he gave a two-hour lecture, during which he projected on the wall all the postcards he had received during his five-year stay in Rumania.

When the lights in the hall were switched on again the entire assemblage woke up with a fright, rubbing the sleep out of their eyes.

On Herr Rücke's second cultural evening, someone who had been in the Far East and Java told some fantastic stories which would have made Karl May[6] turn green with envy.

After this double debut of German culture the cultural guardian disappeared ingloriously and into his place stepped a certain Doctor Zweihäuser. His first project was the elimination of the National Socialist Cultural Community, whose function was taken over by the Combat Groups for German Culture. The members reaped several advantages from this new arrangement. First, instead of paying fifty pfennigs monthly, they were now privileged to pay one mark every month. The real advantage was that the new society did not bother them with any kind of performances, save for the collection of the dues. Instead something new was being founded, the Group for German Performances, which was to bring true National Socialist theater to the people. One had merely to become a member of this organization and pay for a seat in the theater each month and everything else was in perfect order.

> From Otto Michael Knab, *Kleinstadt unterm Hakenkreuz: Groteske Erinnerungen aus Bayern* (Lucerne: Verlag Räber & Cie., 1934), pp. 11-16, 23-25, 76-79.

The Changed Tempo of Life: The City of Herne

The life of the citizens had changed. Even old familiar streets now had other names. Thus Rathausplatz was now called Adolf-Hitler-Platz, Bebelstrasse became Hermann-Göring-Strasse, Otto-Hue-Strasse became Schlageterstrasse,[1] Neustrasse became Franz-Seldte-Strasse,[2] Rathenau-Platz became Josef-Wagner-Platz (when Gauleiter Wagner fell into disgrace it was renamed Hans-Schemm-Platz[3]).

Later the first part of Behrenstrasse was named Strasse der SA, Rosenstrasse became Willi-Woide-Strasse, and the first part of the

---

[6] Karl May (1842-1912) was a writer of adventure stories, the most famous of which dealt with the American Indians. Most Germans had read these "Wild West" stories in their youth.

[1] See page 94.

[2] Franz Seldte was the Nazi Minister of Labor, formerly the leader of the Stahlhelm veterans' organization.

[3] See page 265.

old Shamrockstrasse became Gustloffstrasse.[4] The citizens got used to
the new names as they got used to everything else. It was a bad time
for individualists, because the party and the state reached out their
hands for all people. Anyone who was looking for a job or needed a
passport, or even merely wanted to join a club, had to present his
genealogical chart. Thus marriage-license bureaus and the parish rectories were kept quite busy. If two people wanted to get married they
had to present a letter from the public health authorities stating that
they were suitable for marriage. If there were certain illnesses in the
family, this created enormous difficulties and led to investigations in
accordance with the Law of July 14, 1933, for the prevention of hereditary diseases among the rising generation. New courts were set up,
such as the Hereditary Health Court (for Herne-Bochum)[5] and the
Entailed Estates Court at Herne, where the twenty-one entailed
farmers who were still left over in Herne ultimately had to file appeals in cases dealing with their farms. The work book was an essential personal document in many professions. New authorities were
called into being, such as the Draft Board and the District Army
Command in the Masonic Lodge building on Hermann-Löns-Strasse,
as a result of the establishment of the Wehrmacht, and the Reich
Labor Service. On October 1, 1935, the first age groups of young
people eligible for labor service were called up and the first age group
eligible for military service moved out on November 1, 1935. At the
same time, those born in 1913 and 1916 were mustered for labor and
military service respectively on November 13.

The party itself displayed great inventiveness in interfering in all
spheres of life. It simply controlled everything through its secondary
organizations: no welfare activity could be conducted without the interference of the National Socialist Public Welfare Organization, no
cultural event could take place without the Strength Through Joy.[6]
New notions and slogans were always being coined in order to organize and to levy financial contributions, for such purposes as thanks
offerings to the nation, National Labor Days, tributes to the prolific
German families, thanks offerings to the workers of Germany, excursions for old party members, the banner of the DAF [7] National Socialist Model Factory . . .

[4] Wilhelm Gustloff was the Nazi leader in Switzerland. He was assassinated in
1936.
[5] See page 90.
[6] See page 342.
[7] The German Workers' Front.

There were always new organizations and institutions, such as the Country School for Mothers, the Mother and Child Welfare Organization, Childrensland Camps, the Food-Supply Welfare Organization. Further: Winter Aid, the one-dish meal on Sunday, National Solidarity Day . . .

And orders constantly rang out: "Display the flag!" and only the swastika banner was allowed to be displayed; the old Reich colors—black, white, and red, much used at first—were soon prohibited. There was always a reason for celebration, marches, and demonstrations. The course of the year took on a new rhythm. A cycle of festivities was arranged which was always being repeated. And the racial experts of the party already spoke reverently about renewing the myth. The traditional festivals had to take a back seat. Christmas developed into a feast of the winter solstice. The Hitler Youth no longer sang Christian Christmas carols, but "High Night of Clear Skies." All the while the propaganda machines went on working briskly, and the great hubbub and eternal thundering, the constant repetition of slogans (the one-dish meal on Sunday required at least six impressive admonitions in the newspaper) which accompanied this must not be forgotten. And in fact the events did unfold obtrusively and noisily and a plain sober description of them cannot give a proper idea of the fuss and fanfare that accompanied them.

From *Herne 1933-1945: Die Zeit des Nationalsozialismus,* edited by Hermann Meyerhoff (Herne, 1963), pp. 94, 96.

The Nazis Take Over Cologne

First City Council Meeting after the Assumption of Power
March 30, 1933

GROHÉ:[1] German men and women! Today, for the first time, the City Council of Cologne is meeting under the auspices and at the bidding of the national uprising of the German people. All of Cologne stands under the spell of our gathering. Tens of thousands are assembled in streets and squares so that they may experience this

[1] See page 366.

event with us over the loudspeakers. And additional hundreds of thousands are anxiously awaiting the press dispatches that will announce that the decisions of this meeting will be in harmony with the will of the overwhelming majority of the people of Cologne.

First we must thank the city administration of Cologne for the festive adornment of the hall in which we are meeting, so much in keeping with the importance of this day. We greet the coat of arms of our city of Cologne. We bow our heads to those black, white, and red flags which once proclaimed Germany's greatness and glory to the world, and we look with pride and satisfaction at yonder Swastika banner which Adolf Hitler bequeathed to us and under which Germany's resurrection out of the abyss was prepared and was enabled to achieve the greatness of this day. (Loud applause.)

We see in this hall the portraits of our venerable General Field Marshal and Reich President von Hindenburg, and the German People's Chancellor and Führer, who will lead us to national freedom and social justice: Adolf Hitler. (Shouts of "Bravo!" and "Heil!") With veneration for their personal greatness and for the greatness of their deeds, and with a pledge of unconditional obedience, we implore them both this day to accept honorary citizenship of our metropolis on the Rhine. (Loud applause.) It is a great hour that we celebrate today. The proudest, most heroic, and most industrious people in the world were torn apart and plunged into a gruesome abyss by the revolt of November 1918. The most exemplary people on earth became a conglomeration of selfish interest groups and a chaotic tangle of class hatred and obscurantist caste prejudice. A people of power and outstanding honor became the plaything of other nations and a victim of international capitalistic exploiters.

For us, the representatives of the people of Cologne, this fall from the greatest heights to the lower depths was even more painful and shameful, for the spirit of treason and fratricidal warfare of 1918 raised its head in our city. And as if that were not enough, the torch of separatism, lighted by our enemies, was first raised in our city and destroyed great values of national prestige and the feeling of Volkish togetherness.

Now the day has dawned for the re-establishment of German existence in Cologne. What the history of our city has so far never been able to record (without doubt, the result of the oppression and endeavors of our enemies) has now become reality: the people of Cologne have overwhelmingly avowed their faith in German Volkdom and in the national unity of a great German Reich. (Loud shouts of "Bravo!") And this, German men and women, we owe to the German *Volksmann* Adolf Hitler, who, from nothing and as an unknown among the millions of our people, began the battle against degradation and stupidity and who, in the face of countless difficulties, awakened in the German people the national revolution which we have celebrated with unbounded jubilation in these last weeks and days. We owe this revolution also to the many Germans, known and unknown, who in years of devoted labor left nothing untried in their efforts to help the idea of national honor and social justice to break through to victory. In this hour we also think of the thousands, and thousands of thousands, of National Socialist SA and SS men and other party comrades who, in constant disregard of their own personal interest, fought as soldiers of Adolf Hitler, and thus as soldiers in the rehabilitation of Germany, and who by their tenacity, courage, and fidelity ushered in the day of national renaissance. (Bravos and applause.)

We know that not all of our opponents acted against their better knowledge. In everything pertaining to their sense of honor, we esteem the German people too much to assume that most of them opposed the National Socialist movement out of malice. Rather, we are of the opinion that only a small fraction of our people—and mainly those so-called German "citizens" who have nothing in common with the German racial community because of their alien blood values— tried to thwart the rebirth of the German nation. We want, therefore, to take no revenge on those who heretofore have opposed us. We fully open our arms and the gates of our movement to receive and to include in our Volk community all who still have a feeling for the glory and heroism of the German past and for the necessity to re-establish the German Volk community. (Loud applause.) In deep veneration, therefore, we bow our heads before our brothers who fell on the battlefield in the Great World War. To honor them let us rise from our seats and remember, with equal veneration and gratitude, those racial comrades who lost their lives as heroes of the national revolution in their unselfish battle for a new Germany and for a new greatness of our people. (Loud "Pfuis!" from the left. Shouts: "Stand Up!" "Outside with you scoundrels!" "Scoundrels!" The chairman rings his bell.)

I notice, German men and women, that you have risen from your seats in honor of our heroes, and I thank you.

German men and women! We are experiencing the most enthusiastic renaissance of the German people under the sign of the Swastika. The national revolution has been accomplished with a discipline and order unprecedented in German history. Let us draw the conclusion from the needs of our times and from the form in which the revolution was carried through. Just as the spirit of discord and self-interest has been overcome, so the period of the party state and party coalitions has likewise come to an end. (Loud applause.)

If the unity of the German people in its overwhelming majority was possible only in the spirit of Adolf Hitler and National Socialism, then the new Reich can be built only in the same spirit and according to the same principles.

Everybody has to come to terms with the fact that this has been the last multi-party election.[2] (Applause.) The new election scheduled four years from now will deal, as far as it is humanly possible to foresee, with the plan of a new constitution (Loud applause), which will eliminate the selfishness of classes and programmatic party faiths and instead will ensure a new Volkish state structure. (Applause.)

With the assumption of power, Adolf Hitler and his fellow warriors have once and for all overcome the system of coalitions and barter. (Stormy applause.)

Thus despair and wretchedness have been uprooted in accordance with the will of the majority of the German people.

In addition, we have established the basis for unleashing the constructive forces of the nation—personal incorruptibility, strength of character, and competence for action and accomplishment—and for gathering all, without regard to their previous political allegiance, into one force for honest and cooperative labor in the interest of the whole people. (Applause.) It is your task, German men and women, to accept the new way of life ushered in by us—to obey our justified and proven will to create and to help us to realize our basic demands. Your previous efforts and your legitimate demands in the economic and cultural spheres, you will now find easier to maintain in the new Reich of Adolf Hitler and the Swastika than was possible in the multi-party state.

But we want to make it absolutely clear that we are determined to eradicate ruthlessly all those who endanger the people, and that we shall not under any circumstances permit corruption and the propaga-

[2] The reference is to the election of March 1933. See page 323.

tion of any special interests that are inimical to the common welfare. (Applause.)

As a matter of principle, we deny Marxists the right to any activity within Germany. (Loud and lasting applause.) Therefore the question can never arise whether Marxist parties should be admitted to the councils of the city parliament. ("True, true!" Applause.) Anyone who believes in the class struggle and is internationally oriented cannot at the same time claim that he is willing to serve the interest of our city and our people. ("True!")

Only the interests of our city and our people will be represented and realized in this Chamber. We confess that we have succumbed to the sentimentality that clings to the German people when today we merely exclude from politics those who are responsible for the misery of our people and who betrayed our country—without at the same time calling them humanly and personally to account. ("Hear! Hear!")

Let us remember how thousands of our comrades who strove for nothing else but to save Germany were thrown out of work to starve, were tossed into jail, were beaten and murdered by the hundreds, how the National Socialist newspapers were suppressed, and how the refusal to make public halls available and the curtailment of the right of assembly were invoked to make the work of building a new and better Germany more difficult and even impossible. (Shouts of "Pfui!") Representatives of Social Democracy are still sitting here in this representative assembly, even though most of their leading comrades not only are accomplices in Germany's former shame but even today spread the basest slander against the new Germany abroad. (Stormy shouts of "Pfui!") These Social Democrats have good reason to lift their eyes in thankfulness that they have not received the treatment which they could rightfully expect in the light of their past deeds.

Just recall what Ebel had to suffer in this Chamber when he was our one and only council member. ("Hear! Hear!") Recall also how we were treated before the last election, when only three National Socialists sat in this Chamber, and how you curtailed our right to free speech and did not even allow us to present motions. (Shouts of "Pfui!")

Think of the malicious and mocking manner with which for years you tried to degrade us in the eyes of the people, and then measure, by our present magnanimity, the energy and human greatness which motivates us National Socialists.

We removed Herr Adenauer[3] from office, not because he was a member of the Center party, but because we recognized him as a man whose concepts of morality and character we fail to understand ("Hear! Hear!") and because his actions were absolutely detrimental to Cologne and the whole of Germany. (Applause.)

We cannot, therefore, acknowledge that any group of this Chamber which values honor, decency, and moral cleanliness seriously believes that it could rally to the defense of this man and his deeds. Identification with the person of the discarded Lord Mayor is an identification with the attitude and deeds of this man and consequently deserves the same judgment and militant hostility. ("Hear! Hear!" Applause.)

In this hour, we reavow the promises we made to the national-minded, Germany-conscious population to fulfill to the last letter everything we represented and asserted in the years of battle and opposition. (Loud applause.)

We stretch out our hand to all racial comrades of good will and bid them welcome as fellow workers in the accomplishment of our great German task. Together we will rebuild our Rhenish cathedral city into an ornament of German Volkish life and will make its administration a model of cleanliness and frugality. (Applause.)

Finally, we thank the new head of the city of Cologne for his ready and responsible work and for his great skill in the choice of his co-workers.

(The National Socialist members rise and break into spirited shouts of "Heil!" to the incoming Lord Mayor.)

We shall work closely with the new leader of our city and his administration and shall endeavor to create a cleaner Cologne and thus eventually add to the prestige and greatness of Germany. Long live Cologne! Long live Germany!

(Enthusiastic shouts of "Heil!" The assembly rises and sings the national anthem.)

> From Peter Schmidt, *Zwanzig Jahre Soldat Adolf Hitlers, Zehn Jahre Gauleiter: Ein Buch von Kampf und Treue* (Cologne: Verlag Westdeutscher Beobachter, 1941), pp. 198-204.

[3] Konrad Adenauer was Lord Mayor of Cologne from 1917 to 1933.

Little Things Create Pressures
HERMANN STRESAU

The German way or, rather, that which is German sits closer than ever on the body, it constricts one, and at times takes one's breath away. Hitler's rule is no longer the rule of Hitler alone. One could almost think he had become a secondary figure or, even, an advertising poster. But this does not change anything of that pressure.

It is hard to explain what this pressure consists of. Nothing happens to us personally. We hardly notice the party out here as long as we do not leave our forest. But on the way to Berlin one hears and sees many things. These are not always special events, but small, unimportant experiences which keep the feeling of pressure alive. For example, the following little event on a bus: It is evening, just before departure time. A short man sits in front of me. By profession he is a gardener and he has a part-time job as a night watchman in the settlement. I know him because Jackie once replaced him. He is a timid, rather simple-minded, talkative but completely harmless person. A tall, broad-shouldered chap wearing a black melon-shaped hat entered the bus. He had an unpleasant appearance and looked something like the way a policeman in civilian clothes looks in the movies. He sat down next to the short fellow and greeted him after he had called out a "Heil Hitler!" in a baritone voice to everyone in the bus. They talked about the weather, the frost, and the little gardener observed quite harmlessly: "Strict rulers don't rule for long." This is a popular saying that one can hear in almost every conversation touching on that kind of frosty weather. What did the fat fellow do? He bent forward, cleared his throat, and said with noticeable emphasis: "I don't quite understand what you mean by that, Mr. ——." The little fellow obviously did not know how close he came to being thrown into a concentration camp.

Another time a young mother was sitting in the bus with her little girl, who was about four or five. She was standing on the seat and was looking at the world outside her window with great interest. A young SA man was walking up and down in front of the waiting bus. Suddenly the little girl said: "Look, Mommy! That man won't come in here, will he?" Horrified, the mother placed her hand on the child's mouth and warned her to be quiet.

This is called the Volk community. . . .

To this must be added the turnover in generations: there are more and more people growing up who have had no experience of the war. They are oblivious of the experiences of the older generation and are apt to look upon war as a refreshing adventure or even as an opportunity to develop great virtues. I cannot so easily forget one morning in the library when a colleague and I, working on a catalog, got to talking about the war novels, most of them anti-war, which were at that time being published in great numbers. Without being dramatic, the two of us shared the opinion that war was a "swinish business," since we had taken part in the war and had had a belly full of war once and for all. At this point a little girl employee, who was still on probation, interrupted us and rather insolently asserted that there was something elevating about war. "How's that?" I asked her. The little girl who was not yet twenty, a beautiful, delicately built thing, and on top of this slightly deformed, baffled us. Why? Well, after all, war brings out the best qualities: a sense of sacrifice, comradeship, and courage. What was one supposed to say to this? My colleague grouchily advised her first to live through the whole "swinish business" herself. But one cannot refute the argument of an idealistic young girl this way. She will usually answer with a contemptuous, disparaging facial expression, perhaps even rightly so. I tried to explain to her: in ancient times there were epidemics, such as plagues and cholera, which also provided plenty of opportunities to develop human virtues —readiness to help others, a sense of sacrifice, etc. I asked her whether because of these virtues we ought to regret that we have successfully exterminated these epidemics? The girl had no comment to make on this, but she did not seem to be overly convinced. At least she didn't offer the most stupid of all arguments, which some people have come up with: there have always been wars, therefore we will always have wars. The stupidity of this logic becomes apparent only when millions of people have paid for it with their lives.

From Hermann Stresau, Von Jahr zu Jahr (Berlin: Minerva-Verlag, 1948), pp. 94-95, 168.

Vanishing Friends
ERICH EBERMAYER

Leipzig, May 9, 1933

One becomes ever more lonely.

Everywhere friends declare their faith in Adolf Hitler. It is as if an airless stratum surrounds us few who remain unable to make such avowals.

Of my young friends it is the best who now radically proclaim their allegiance to National Socialism. This is not to be denied. The two sons of the Leipzig art historian Wilhelm Pinder, two excellent young men of the first-class breed—the younger one had closely attached himself to me for a long time—are downright possessed Nazis. One can't even discuss things with them, because they believe. And there are no rational arguments against faith. They run around in the plain Hitler Youth uniform, radiant with happiness and pride. When today in the Schreber pool, our reopened Thomaner[1] meeting place, I made an attempt to have a talk with Eberhard Pinder, daring to express— how weak and powerless one already is vis-à-vis this triumphant youth!—the idea that perhaps our whole ancient culture, the patrimony of the intellectual and artistic values of the last four hundred years, would go under in the vortex of our time. And the triumphant little gentleman, naïvely and a little bit shamelessly, said: "And what if it does, my dear friend! This culture is really not so important! According to the word of the Führer, the Thousand-Year Reich is already arising. And it will create a new culture for itself!"

My mother experienced something similar. She already had a radical falling out over politics with Baroness Richthofen, one of her closest friends. It was over the new flag. Frau von Richthofen demanded that she should now at last get a swastika flag made for herself. Mother indignantly rejected the idea, saying she would never think of such a thing, and if anybody forced her she would hang out "this rag from the toilet window." A beautiful, clear, and German language . . . otherwise not customary among the ladies of high society. . . . The Baroness then took offense with an audible noise, and

---

[1] Thomaner were alumni of a famous Gymnasium in Leipzig.

the old friendship broke up. Mother suffers from it more than she admits.

From Erich Ebermayer, *Denn heute gehört uns Deutschland* . . . : *Persönliches und politisches Tagebuch, von der Machtergreifung bis zum 31 Dezember 1935* (Hamburg and Vienna: Paul Zsolnay Verlag, 1959), pp. 75-76. (Reprinted by permission of Paul Zsolnay Verlag and Erich Ebermayer.)